KU-661-391

This Day in Irish History

Padraic Coffey was born in Sligo and grew up in Tubbercurry. He attended University College Dublin, where he received a BA in 2008 and an MA in 2010. After graduating from college, he worked in a freelance capacity for the *Sunday Independent*, as well as some other publications. This is his first book, which was inspired by his social media account of the same name. He currently resides in Vancouver, Canada, with his wife.

This Day in Irish History

From the social media sensation @ThisDayIrish

Padraic Coffey

Foreword by Joe Duffy

THE O'BRIEN PRESS
DUBLIN

First published 2021 by The O'Brien Press Ltd.
12 Terenure Road East, Rathgar, Dublin 6, D06 HD27, Ireland.
Tel: +353 1 4923333 Fax: +353 1 4922777
Email: books@obrien.ie
Website: www.obrien.ie
The O'Brien Press is a member of Publishing Ireland.

ISBN 978-1-78849-257-7

Design and layout by Emma Byrne

Photos on PP33, 37, 223 courtesy of the National Library of Ireland; P61 (and back cover) courtesy of the National Museum of Ireland; P32 (and back cover) courtesy of ESB Archives; and PP19 (and cover), 25, 26, 38, 57, 66, 92 (and cover), 100, 105 (and cover), 114, 129, 137, 138, 140, 142 (and cover), 145 (and cover), 160 (and cover), 161 (and cover), 164, 178, 188 (and cover), 213, 248, 264 and 280 courtesy of Shutterstock.

10 9 8 7 6 5 4 3 2 1
25 24 23 22 21

Printed and bound in Great Britain by Clays Ltd, Elcograf S.p.A.

The paper in this book is produced using pulp from managed forests.

Published in:

To my mother and father,
Anne and Martin Coffey

Acknowledgements

I would like to thank my agent Paul Feldstein of the Feldstein Agency for helping me to find the right publisher for *This Day in Irish History*, and all at The O'Brien Press, including Ivan O'Brien, the managing director; Nicola Reddy, the project manager for this book; designer Emma Byrne; Brendan O'Brien, who was the editor; Ruth Heneghan and Triona Marshall of the publicity and marketing team; and Michael O'Brien, founder of The O'Brien Press. I would also like to thank Joe Duffy for his very generous foreword to the book. Thank you to all who have engaged with my social media account since 2018. Finally, I would like to thank my wife Nicola for her love and support during the writing of this book.

Contents

Foreword by Joe Duffy 17

1 January 1892	Annie Moore passes through Ellis Island	19
2 January 1904	Arthur Griffith publishes 'The Resurrection of Hungary'	20
3 January 1602	The Battle of Kinsale	21
4 January 1909	The Irish Transport and General Workers' Union is founded	21
5 January 1871	The Franco-Irish Ambulance Brigade is released from duty	22
6 January 1839	The Night of the Big Wind	23
7 January 1922	Dáil Éireann ratifies the Anglo-Irish Treaty	24
8 January 1979	The Whiddy Island disaster	25
9 January 1980	Charles Haughey: 'living away beyond our means'	26
10 January 1877	Eliza Walker Dunbar becomes first woman doctor	27
11 January 1970	Sinn Féin splits over abstentionism	28
12 January 1870	Pope Pius condemns Fenianism	29
13 January 1847	Queen Victoria appeals for famine relief	29
14 January 1965	Seán Lemass and Terence O'Neill meet	30
15 January 1947	Electricity is introduced to rural Ireland	31
16 January 1922	Dublin Castle is handed over to Michael Collins	32
17 January 1992	Peter Brooke sings 'Oh My Darling, Clementine'	34
18 January 1978	Judgement is reached in 'Ireland v. the United Kingdom'	34
19 January 1947	The Big Freeze begins	35
20 January 1961	John F. Kennedy is inaugurated	36
21 January 1919	The first sitting of Dáil Éireann	37
22 January 1972	Ireland signs Treaty of Accession to the European Communities	38
23 January 1834	St Vincent's is founded: first hospital staffed by women	39
24 January 1824	Daniel O'Connell introduces Catholic Rent	40
25 January 1917	Sinking of the *Laurentic*	41
26 January 1942	First American troops arrive in Belfast	41
27 January 1982	Dáil is dissolved over VAT on children's shoes	43
28 January 1842	Address from the People of Ireland is read in Boston	43
29 January 1967	Northern Ireland Civil Rights Association is formed	44
30 January 1972	Bloody Sunday (Derry)	45
31 January 1984	Death of Ann Lovett	46

1 February 1815	Daniel O'Connell duels with John Norcott D'Esterre	47
2 February 1880	Parnell addresses House of Representatives	47
3 February 1919	Éamon de Valera escapes from Lincoln Prison	48
4 February 1880	The 'Black' Donnellys are murdered	49
5 February 1917	George Plunkett is elected abstentionist MP	50
6 February 1800	Irish parliament approves the Act of Union	51
7 February 1991	Provisional IRA attempts to assassinate John Major	52
8 February 1983	Shergar is kidnapped	53
9 February 1846	Robert Mallet presents paper on earthquakes	54
10 February 1932	Army Comrades Association is formed	54
11 February 1926	W. B. Yeats: 'You have disgraced yourselves again'	55
12 February 1997	Last killing of a British soldier in the Troubles	56
13 February 1966	'Bishop and nightie' incident on *The Late Late Show*	57
14 February 1981	Stardust fire	58
15 February 1995	Lansdowne Road football riot	59
16 February 1932	Fianna Fáil becomes largest party in Irish state	60
17 February 1980	Derrynaflan Chalice is found	60
18 February 1366	The Statutes of Kilkenny	61
19 February 1901	Irish is spoken in the House of Commons	62
20 February 1985	Desmond O'Malley abstains on Family Planning bill	63
21 February 1941	First flight over the Donegal Corridor	64
22 February 1832	First interment in Glasnevin Cemetery	64
23 February 1943	Fire in St Joseph's Orphanage	65
24 February 2007	'God Save the Queen' is sung in Croke Park	66
25 February 1915	Execution of the Iron 12	67
26 February 1962	IRA border campaign ends	68
27 February 1983	Eamonn Coghlan sets world record for indoor mile	69
28 February 1979	Charles Haughey: 'An Irish solution to an Irish problem'	70
29 February 1924	Last killing of a Dublin Metropolitan Police officer	70

1 March 1981	Bobby Sands begins hunger strike	71
2 March 1978	U2 make television debut	72
3 March 1831	First clash of Tithe War	73
4 March 1804	Castle Hill rebellion	74
5 March 1867	Fenian Rising	74
6 March 1988	Gibraltar killings	75

7 March 1964	Arkle wins Cheltenham	76
8 March 1973	Northern Ireland border poll	77
9 March 1942	Tom McGrath escapes German POW camp	78
10 March 2009	Martin McGuinness deems dissident republicans 'traitors'	78
11 March 1597	Explosion destroys Dublin quays	79
12 March 1974	Senator Billy Fox is shot dead	80
13 March 1846	Ballinlass evictions	81
14 March 1984	Assassination attempt on Gerry Adams	82
15 March 1745	First maternity hospital in the British Empire is founded	82
16 March 1988	Milltown Cemetery attack	83
17 March 1943	Éamon de Valera's 'happy maidens' St Patrick's Day address	84
18 March 1977	Disappearance of Mary Boyle	85
19 March 1642	Adventurers' Act is passed	86
20 March 1914	The Curragh incident	87
21 March 1879	First successful test of Brennan torpedo	87
22 March 1895	Discovery of Bridget Cleary's body	88
23 March 1847	Choctaw Nation raises money for famine relief	89
24 March 1968	Tuskar Rock air disaster	90
25 March 1920	Black and Tans arrive in Ireland	91
26 March 1990	*My Left Foot* wins two Oscars	92
27 March 1650	Kilkenny surrenders to Cromwell	93
28 March 1646	The first Ormond Peace	94
29 March 2004	Smoking ban is introduced	95
30 March 1849	The Doolough Tragedy	95
31 March 1912	Home Rule monster meeting in Dublin	96
1 April 1234	The Battle of the Curragh	97
2 April 1993	Annie Murphy is interviewed on *The Late Late Show*	98
3 April 1970	First killing of a Garda in the Troubles	98
4 April 2007	Ian Paisley shakes hands with Bertie Ahern	99
5 April 1895	Oscar Wilde is arrested	100
6 April 2005	Gerry Adams tells IRA: 'Now there is an alternative'	101
7 April 1776	John Barry leads capture of HMS *Edward*	102
8 April 1886	Gladstone introduces First Home Rule Bill	103
9 April 1912	Balmoral anti-Home Rule demonstration	104
10 April 1998	The Good Friday Agreement is signed	105

11 April 1951	Dr Noël Browne resigns over Mother and Child Scheme	106
12 April 1928	First transatlantic flight from east to west	107
13 April 1742	Handel's *Messiah* makes world debut in Dublin	108
14 April 1848	Irish tricolour is unveiled for the first time	108
15 April 1941	The Belfast Blitz	109
16 April 1782	Henry Grattan: 'Ireland is now a nation'	110
17 April 1876	The *Catalpa* rescue	111
18 April 1949	Republic of Ireland is declared	112
19 April 1916	'Castle Document' is read at Dublin Corporation meeting	112
20 April 1954	Last execution in the Irish state	113
21 April 1916	Roger Casement is arrested	114
22 April 1969	Bernadette Devlin gives maiden speech	115
23 April 1014	The Battle of Clontarf	116
24 April 1916	Easter Rising begins	117
25 April 1938	Anglo-Irish Trade Agreement is signed	118
26 April 1916	Killing of Francis Sheehy-Skeffington	119
27 April 1916	Hulluch gas attacks	120
28 April 1916	The Battle of Ashbourne	120
29 April 1916	Easter Rising ends	121
30 April 1994	Riverdance debuts at Eurovision	122
1 May 1169	Norman invasion of Wexford	123
2 May 1945	De Valera offers condolences to German minister	124
3 May 1921	Partition of Ireland	125
4 May 1925	Oonah Keogh becomes world's first woman stockbroker	125
5 May 1981	Death of Bobby Sands	126
6 May 1882	Phoenix Park murders	127
7 May 1915	Sinking of the *Lusitania*	128
8 May 2007	Ian Paisley and Martin McGuinness are sworn in	129
9 May 1671	Thomas Blood steals the Crown Jewels of England	130
10 May 1318	The Battle of Dysert O'Dea	131
11 May 1745	The Battle of Fontenoy	132
12 May 1957	The *Rose Tattoo* scandal	132
13 May 1937	Statue of George II is blown up	133
14 May 1974	Ulster Workers' Council strike announced	134
15 May 2007	Bertie Ahern addresses British parliament	135

16 May 1945	De Valera responds to Winston Churchill	136
17 May 1974	Dublin and Monaghan bombings	136
18 May 2011	Queen Elizabeth speaks in Dublin Castle	138
19 May 1998	John Hume and David Trimble share stage with Bono	139
20 May 2009	Ryan Report is published	140
21 May 1932	Amelia Earhart lands in Co. Derry	141
22 May 2015	Same-sex marriage referendum	142
23 May 2002	The Saipan incident	143
24 May 1923	The Civil War ends	144
25 May 2018	Referendum on repeal of the Eighth Amendment	145
26 May 1315	Edward Bruce arrives in Ireland	146
27 May 1936	First Aer Lingus flight	147
28 May 1970	Charles Haughey and Neil Blaney are arrested	148
29 May 1972	Official IRA ceasefire	149
30 May 1986	Knock Airport is opened	150
31 May 1941	The North Strand bombing	150
1 June 1997	Tony Blair issues statement on the Famine	151
2 June 1866	The Battle of Ridgeway	152
3 June 1844	Hypodermic needle is used for first time	153
4 June 1984	Ronald Reagan addresses the Oireachtas	154
5 June 1798	The Battle of New Ross	155
6 June 1944	Redmond Cunningham earns Military Cross on D-Day	155
7 June 1996	Detective Garda Jerry McCabe is shot dead	156
8 June 1917	Butte mining disaster	157
9 June 597	Death of St Colmcille	158
10 June 1904	James Joyce meets Nora Barnacle	159
11 June 1925	W. B. Yeats: 'We are no petty people'	160
12 June 1988	Ireland beat England in Stuttgart	161
13 June 1912	Members of Irish Women's Franchise League are arrested	162
14 June 1690	William of Orange lands at Carrickfergus	163
15 June 1919	Alcock and Brown land in Galway	164
16 June 1954	The first Bloomsday	165
17 June 1959	Irish voters reject first-past-the-post	166
18 June 1264	Earliest recorded meeting of an Irish parliament	167
19 June 1920	The Listowel Mutiny	167

20 June 1631	The Sack of Baltimore	168
21 June 1877	Molly Maguires are executed	169
22 June 1921	George V opens Northern Ireland parliament	170
23 June 1985	Air India Flight 182 bombing	171
24 June 1993	Homosexuality is decriminalised	172
25 June 1938	Douglas Hyde becomes first President of Ireland	173
26 June 1996	Veronica Guerin is shot dead	173
27 June 1963	John F. Kennedy visits Dunganstown, Co. Wexford	174
28 June 1922	The Civil War begins	175
29 June 1948	Mike Flanagan steals tanks for Haganah	176
30 June 1922	Public Record Office is destroyed	177
1 July 1690	The Battle of the Boyne	178
2 July 1990	Nelson Mandela addresses Dáil Éireann	179
3 July 1863	The 69th Pennsylvania repels Pickett's charge	180
4 July 1957	De Valera condemns Fethard boycott	181
5 July 1828	Daniel O'Connell is elected in Clare	181
6 July 1907	Theft of the Irish Crown Jewels	182
7 July 1903	Mother Jones leads the March of the Mill Children	183
8 July 1985	Ryanair begins operations	184
9 July 1921	Truce in War of Independence	185
10 July 1927	Kevin O'Higgins is shot dead	186
11 July 1792	Meeting of the Harpers in Belfast	186
12 July 1691	The Battle of Aughrim	187
13 July 1985	Live Aid	188
14 July 1789	James F. X. Whyte is 'liberated' from the Bastille	189
15 July 1942	'Paddy' Finucane is shot down over the English Channel	190
16 July 1936	Assassination attempt on Edward VIII	191
17 July 1904	Camogie is first played in public	191
18 July 1912	Suffragettes protest Asquith's Dublin visit	192
19 July 1997	Provisional IRA ceasefire	193
20 July 1974	Women 'invade' Forty Foot	194
21 July 1976	Assassination of Christopher Ewart-Biggs	195
22 July 1822	'Martin's Law' is introduced by Galway MP	196
23 July 1803	Robert Emmet's rebellion	196
24 July 1907	Police strike in Belfast	197

25 July 1917	First meeting of the Irish Convention	198
26 July 1914	Bachelors Walk killings	199
27 July 1866	First successful transatlantic telegraph cable	200
28 July 2005	Provisional IRA announces end of campaign	201
29 July 1848	Young Ireland rebellion	201
30 July 1928	Pat O'Callaghan wins gold for Ireland at the Olympics	202
31 July 1893	The Gaelic League is founded	203
1 August 1915	Graveside oration for O'Donovan Rossa	204
2 August 1924	First modern Tailteann Games	205
3 August 1955	Premiere of *Waiting for Godot*	206
4 August 1918	Gaelic Sunday	206
5 August 1901	Peter O'Connor sets world record for long jump	207
6 August 1998	Michelle Smith de Bruin receives swimming ban	208
7 August 1986	Peter Robinson is arrested in Clontibret	209
8 August 1914	Arthur Griffith opposes Irish involvement in First World War	210
9 August 1971	Internment is introduced in Northern Ireland	211
10 August 1976	Death of the Maguire children	211
11 August 1927	Éamon de Valera signs the oath of allegiance	212
12 August 1969	The Battle of the Bogside	213
13 August 1969	Jack Lynch reacts to riots in Derry	214
14 August 1903	Wyndham Land Act is passed	215
15 August 1998	The Omagh bombing	216
16 August 1982	Patrick Connolly resigns ('GUBU')	217
17 August 1882	The Maamtrasna murders	218
18 August 1994	Martin Cahill is shot dead	218
19 August 1504	The Battle of Knockdoe	219
20 August 1775	Tucson, Arizona is founded by Hugh O'Conor	220
21 August 1879	Apparition in Knock	221
22 August 1922	Michael Collins is shot dead	222
23 August 1170	Strongbow lands in Waterford	222
24 August 1990	Brian Keenan is released	224
25 August 1803	Robert Emmet is arrested	224
26 August 1913	Dublin Lockout begins	225
27 August 1979	Killing of Lord Mountbatten	226
28 August 1676	Irish donation to Massachusetts	227

29 August 1975	Death of Éamon de Valera	228
30 August 1977	Jimmy Carter makes statement on Northern Ireland	229
31 August 1910	Lilian Bland pilots her own plane	230
1 September 1870	Inaugural meeting of Home Government Organisation	230
2 September 1939	The Emergency is declared	231
3 September 1939	Sinking of the SS *Athenia*	232
4 September 1828	Annaghdown boating tragedy	233
5 September 1926	Dromcollogher fire	234
6 September 1593	Grace O'Malley meets Elizabeth I	234
7 September 1948	Repeal of External Relations Act is announced	236
8 September 1798	The Battle of Ballinamuck	236
9 September 1982	Killing of Declan Flynn	237
10 September 1966	Donogh O'Malley announces free secondary education	238
11 September 1649	Siege of Drogheda ends	239
12 September 1969	Cameron Report is published	240
13 September 1961	The Siege of Jadotville	241
14 September 1607	The Flight of the Earls	242
15 September 1916	Walter Gordon Wilson's tanks are first used	242
16 September 1937	Kirkintilloch disaster	243
17 September 1948	W. B. Yeats is reinterred in Sligo	244
18 September 1914	Government of Ireland Act is signed into law	245
19 September 1880	Parnell introduces 'boycotting'	246
20 September 1920	The Sack of Balbriggan	246
21 September 1949	Ireland defeat England on English soil	247
22 September 1970	Beginning of the Arms Trial	248
23 September 1911	Edward Carson first addresses Belfast supporters	249
24 September 1914	Irish Volunteers split	250
25 September 1917	Thomas Ashe dies on hunger strike	251
26 September 1791	The *Queen* convict ship arrives in Sydney	252
27 September 1913	SS *Hare* relieves Dublin strikers	252
28 September 1912	The Ulster Covenant is signed	253
29 September 1979	Pope John Paul II visits Ireland	254
30 September 1994	Boris Yeltsin incident at Shannon	255

1 October 1843	O'Connell's last 'monster meeting', Mullaghmast	256
2 October 1996	Death of Brigid McCole	257
3 October 1992	Sinéad O'Connor tears up a photo of the Pope	257
4 October 1940	First Brian O'Nolan column in the *Irish Times*	258
5 October 1968	Duke Street march in Derry	259
6 October 1175	Treaty of Windsor is signed	260
7 October 1843	Daniel O'Connell cancels rally in Clontarf	261
8 October 1871	Catherine O'Leary is blamed for Great Chicago Fire	261
9 October 1979	Josie Airey wins free legal aid case	262
10 October 1918	Sinking of RMS *Leinster*	*263*
11 October 1988	Ian Paisley interrupts Pope John Paul II	264
12 October 1975	Oliver Plunkett is declared a saint	265
13 October 1792	James Hoban oversees White House construction	266
14 October 1906	Laurence Ginnell launches Ranch War	267
15 October 1842	First issue of *The Nation* is published	267
16 October 1843	William Rowan Hamilton discovers quaternions	268
17 October 1907	Wireless message is sent from Clifden to Nova Scotia	269
18 October 1791	Inaugural meeting of United Irishmen	270
19 October 1989	Guildford Four are released	271
20 October 1881	Land League is proscribed	272
21 October 1975	Siege to rescue Tiede Herrema begins	273
22 October 1884	Nine Graces are awarded degrees	274
23 October 1986	Disappearance of Philip Cairns	274
24 October 1641	Phelim O'Neill issues Proclamation of Dungannon	275
25 October 1996	Last Magdalene Laundry closes	276
26 October 1988	Case of Norris v. Ireland is decided	277
27 October 1904	New York City Subway opens	278
28 October 1927	The Cleggan Bay disaster	278
29 October 1816	Burning of Wildgoose Lodge	279
30 October 1997	Mary McAleese is elected President	280
31 October 1981	The 'Armalite and ballot box' strategy	281
1 November 1884	Gaelic Athletic Association is founded	282
2 November 1847	Killing of Denis Mahon	283
3 November 1324	Petronilla de Meath is burned at the stake	284
4 November 1908	Irish Women's Franchise League is formed	284

5 November 1913 William Mulholland turns on Los Angeles Aqueduct 285
6 November 1887 Celtic football club is founded 286
7 November 1990 Mary Robinson becomes first female President of Ireland 287
8 November 1960 Niemba ambush 288
9 November 1888 Last Jack the Ripper victim is killed 289
10 November 1798 Wolfe Tone's speech from the dock 290
11 November 1919 First Armistice Day in Ireland 290
12 November 1216 Magna Carta Hiberniae 291
13 November 1887 Bloody Sunday (London) 292
14 November 1926 IRA raids Garda stations 293
15 November 1985 Anglo-Irish Agreement is signed 294
16 November 1688 Ann Glover is hanged in Boston 295
17 November 1890 Parnell is named in O'Shea divorce case 296
18 November 1916 The Battle of the Somme ends 296
19 November 1984 Margaret Thatcher dismisses New Ireland Forum findings 297
20 November 1807 Sinking of *Rochdale* and *Prince of Wales* 298
21 November 1920 Bloody Sunday (Dublin) 299
22 November 1963 Assassination of John F. Kennedy 300
23 November 1867 Manchester Martyrs are hanged 301
24 November 1995 Divorce referendum 302
25 November 1892 'The Necessity for De-Anglicising Ireland' 303
26 November 1998 Tony Blair addresses the Oireachtas 304
27 November 1985 Anglo-Irish Agreement is passed in House of Commons 304
28 November 1920 Kilmichael Ambush 305
29 November 1996 Michael Lowry revelations 306
30 November 1909 'People's budget' sparks Constitutional crisis 307

1 December 1494 Poynings' parliament is summoned 308
2 December 1999 Articles 2 and 3 are changed 309
3 December 1925 Boundary Commission agreement 309
4 December 1971 McGurk's Bar bombing 310
5 December 1640 John Atherton is hanged 311
6 December 1922 Irish Free State is established 312
7 December 1995 Seamus Heaney accepts the Nobel Prize 313
8 December 1980 First Anglo-Irish summit in Dublin Castle 313
9 December 1973 Sunningdale Agreement is signed 314

10 December 1998	John Hume and David Trimble receive Nobel Peace Prize	315
11 December 1920	The Burning of Cork	316
12 December 1936	External Relations Act is signed into law	317
13 December 1999	First meeting of North/South Ministerial Council	317
14 December 1918	Sinn Féin wins a majority of Irish seats	318
15 December 1993	Downing Street Declaration is issued	319
16 December 1983	Rescue of Don Tidey	320
17 December 1834	First dedicated commuter railway line opens	321
18 December 1834	Rathcormac massacre	321
19 December 1973	Contraceptive laws are ruled unconstitutional	322
20 December 1909	James Joyce opens Ireland's first cinema	323
21 December 1967	Solar alignment is observed at Newgrange	324
22 December 1691	The Flight of the Wild Geese	325
23 December 1920	Government of Ireland Act is given royal assent	326
24 December 1895	Kingstown lifeboat disaster	326
25 December 1351	William Buí O'Kelly hosts Christmas feast	327
26 December 1883	Harbour Grace Affray	328
27 December 1904	Abbey Theatre opens	329
28 December 1969	IRA splits into Official and Provisional factions	330
29 December 1937	Constitution of Ireland comes into force	331
30 December 999	The Battle of Glenn Máma	331
31 December 1759	Brewery is leased to Arthur Guinness	332

Bibliography 334

Chronology 356

Foreword

by Joe Duffy

This is a monumental book. It is not only a collection of entries for the 366 days of the year (yes, Padraic with his attention to detail includes 29 February!) but also a fascinating social, political and economic history of Ireland and beyond.

Where else could you read in detail about John Fitzgerald Kennedy, Veronica Guerin, Sinéad O'Connor, Brigid McCole, Charlie Haughey, Ronald Reagan and Michelle Smith de Bruin in a single volume?

Places echo through these pages: the Statutes of Kilkenny, Glasnevin Cemetery, the Phoenix Park and Maamtrasna murders, Ellis Island and the Bachelors Walk killings are all to be found. I can think of no other book where Handel's *Messiah*, James Joyce's *Ulysses*, Shergar, U2, *Riverdance* and Seamus Heaney are written about in such engaging and accurate detail.

Battles – of Glenn Máma, Clontarf, the Curragh, Dysert O'Dea, Knockdoe, Kinsale, the Boyne, Aughrim, New Ross, Ballinamuck, Ashbourne and the Bogside – are retold in terms of their historical context and human cost. Given our tortured history, it's no surprise that Bloody Sundays (London, Dublin and Derry), the IRA murder of Detective Garda Jerry McCabe, the Dublin, Monaghan and Omagh bombings, the Gibraltar killings and the false imprisonment of the Guildford Four feature among other horrific events etched into our memories.

It is a mark of the importance of each entry that when writing about the IRA murder of Lord Mountbatten, Padraic Coffey – unlike some politicians and writers – gives equal prominence to the three other people murdered in the attack: Doreen Bradbourne and two children, Nicholas Knatchbull and Paul Maxwell. He also notes that the man convicted of the murders, Thomas McMahon, was released early under the Good Friday Agreement and went on to work on Martin McGuinness' failed presidential campaign.

We are reminded of avoidable tragedies, from Doolough to the Kingstown lifeboat disaster and fatal fires in Dromcollogher, St Joseph's Orphanage in Cavan, Whiddy Island and the Stardust nightclub in Dublin. Often forgotten events that impacted our lives are of course included: an axe attack by suffragettes on the British Prime

Minister on Dublin's O'Connell Bridge, the first Bloomsday, the Fethard boycott, the 'Bishop and the Nightie' affair on Gay Byrne's *Late Late Show*, Josie Airey's successful campaign for free legal aid, women invading the Forty Foot. The smoking ban, the Ryan Report on child abuse in institutions run by the Catholic Church and the same-sex marriage referendum are brought vividly to life.

Names that mean so much to us simply by their mention – St Colmcille, Roger Casement, Bernadette Devlin, the Maguire children, Mary Boyle, Philip Cairns, Ann Lovett, Bobby Sands and many more – are given due respect and importance. The opening of the Guinness brewery, the first transatlantic telegraph cable, rural electrification, Myles na gCopaleen's first newspaper column, the Arkle story, the 1979 papal visit, the Derrynaflan Chalice find and Ireland's first Oscar winners feature in their glorious Technicolor and eccentricity.

Of course, the urge will be for you to go immediately to your birthday. Once you do, you'll be hooked, because one of the joys of this book is that you can read it any way you choose: forwards, backwards or lucky dip! Whichever way you read it, you will find it unputdownable, educational, thoroughly enjoyable and historically accurate.

And I can fairly say it will appeal to all ages and interests: even to those who sometimes find books daunting! With an extensive bibliography and a chronology of events giving even more ballast, I guarantee that not only will you learn something new about our history and our lives, but you will be encouraged to read even more.

This Day in Irish History is a magisterial work of research, brilliantly written and beautifully presented.

Joe Duffy, broadcaster and author

1 January 1892

Annie Moore passes through Ellis Island

When Annie Moore stepped off the SS *Nevada* on 1 January 1892, little could she have known that she would be recorded as the first immigrant ever to pass through Ellis Island. Annie had departed from Cobh (known as Queenstown at the time), Co. Cork, with her brothers Anthony and Philip, aged 12 and 15 respectively. She was the eldest, at 17, and all three were travelling 3,000 miles to meet their parents, who had emigrated four years earlier and landed at the first US immigration station, Castle Garden.

Annie was the first of 12 million immigrants to pass through Ellis Island between 1892 and 1954, whose descendants comprise an estimated third of the people living in the United States. When she first saw the Statue of Liberty it had been in New York Harbour less than six years, having been dedicated on 28 October 1886.

The day after Annie's arrival, the *New York Times* wrote: 'The honor [of being the first to pass through] was reserved for a little rosy-cheeked Irish girl. She was Annie Moore, fifteen [*sic*] years of age, lately a resident of County Cork.' It would not be the last time that Annie's age would be incorrectly recorded. When songwriter Brendan

Graham penned his own tribute to Annie, 'Isle of Hope, Isle of Tears', he did the same.

In 2008, she was honoured at a ceremony in Calvary Cemetery, Queens, where a letter by then Democratic presidential nominee Barack Obama was read out, which said: 'The idea of honoring those who came before you by sacrificing on behalf of those who follow is at the heart of the American experience. Irish Americans like your ancestors, and mine from Co. Offaly, understood this well.'

2 January 1904

Arthur Griffith publishes 'The Resurrection of Hungary'

On this day, the first in a series of articles by Arthur Griffith known as 'The Resurrection of Hungary' was published in the *United Irishman*, the newspaper co-founded by Griffith in 1899. The articles would continue to appear until 2 July of that year. All 27 were collectively published under the same title, with the subtitle 'A Parallel for Ireland', in a pamphlet in November 1904.

Griffith had previously alluded to 'the Hungarian Policy' in a speech at the third Cumann na nGaedheal convention on 26 October 1902, saying that members of the then dominant Irish Parliamentary Party should replace their policy of attending Westminster with 'the policy of the Hungarian deputies ... refusing to attend the British Parliament or to recognise its right to legislate for Ireland'. Hungary, once dominated by its neighbour Austria, had reached the Compromise of 1867, which established a dual monarchy for the two countries and ended 18 years of animosity.

Griffith was not as hostile to Britain as some may assume – he advocated separate governments for Britain and Ireland, but suggested a common monarch be retained. His policy of abstentionism from the House of Commons would become a linchpin of Sinn Féin, the party Griffith founded in 1905. However, the proposal of a common monarch was dropped.

When Sinn Féin won 73 of the 105 Irish seats in the 1918 United Kingdom general election, Griffith's policy was put into practice, and the first Dáil Éireann was established. Griffith is perhaps best known today, outside of his role as founder of Sinn Féin, as one of the signatories of the Anglo-Irish Treaty of 1921, a compromise hated by anti-Treaty republicans, including modern-day Sinn Féin. Nonetheless, the Treaty was arguably consistent with the compromise he had been proposing in print since 2 January 1904.

3 January 1602
The Battle of Kinsale

On 3 January 1602, the Battle of Kinsale was fought: a decisive moment in the Nine Years' War, which had begun with Hugh O'Neill, the second Earl of Tyrone, resisting attempts by William FitzWilliam, Lord Deputy of Ireland, to install an English Sheriff in the province of Ulster. Though the war had been primarily about territory, O'Neill had explicitly invoked the Catholic religion, particularly through 22 articles in November 1599 that began by insisting that 'the Catholic, Apostolic and Roman religion be openly preached and taught throughout all Ireland, as well cities as borough towns, by Bishops, seminary priests, Jesuits and other religious men'.

Because of this religious connection, O'Neill sought help from Catholic Spain, led by Philip II, with whom he had been communicating since 1591. Spanish troops numbering around 3,300, led by commander Juan del Águila, finally landed in Ireland in 1601: in Kinsale, Co. Cork, far away from O'Neill's stronghold in Ulster. Upon learning of their arrival, Lord Mountjoy, the Lord Deputy of Ireland, sent approximately 7,000 troops to besiege the Spanish. O'Neill and his ally Hugh Roe O'Donnell marched south to meet their allies. When they finally joined, on 3 January 1602 (or, using the Julian calendar, Christmas Eve 1601), the battle lasted only two hours. O'Neill's army was broken up by the English cavalry, with the majority forced to retreat to Ulster. The Spanish, realising they could not win, were permitted to return to Spain without admitting defeat.

The Battle of Kinsale did not end the Nine Years' War, but it solidified the eventual Tudor victory, the Treaty of Mellifont in 1603, and the Flight of the Earls in 1607, when O'Neill and Rory O'Donnell, the first Earl of Tyrconnell, left Ireland never to return, thus paving the way for the Plantation of Ulster.

4 January 1909
The Irish Transport and General Workers' Union is founded

On 4 January 1909, William X. O'Brien wrote in his diary: 'the Irish Transport and General Workers Union founded officially from this date'. O'Brien was one of the co-founders, along with James Larkin. Larkin was born in Liverpool in 1876 to parents from Co. Armagh, and had come to Belfast in 1907 to organise the city's dock workers on behalf of the National Union of Dock Labourers (NUDL).

However, tension between Larkin and William Sexton, General Secretary of NUDL, resulted in Larkin's expulsion in 1908. As a result, the ITGWU was founded. In May 1909, the ITGWU posed a rhetorical question in the preamble to its rules: 'Are we going to continue the policy of grafting ourselves on the English Trades Union movement, losing our own identity as a nation in the great world of organised labour? We say emphatically, No!'

The pivotal moment for the ITGWU was the Dublin Lockout of 1913. William Martin Murphy, chairman of the Dublin United Tramways Company (DUTC), dismissed 340 workers he suspected of being ITGWU members. Murphy wanted his employees to sign a pledge stating that they would not be members of Larkin's union. This led to a strike by the tramway workers in August 1913. Other employers – eventually 404 – tried to force their workers to sign a similar pledge; these workers went on strike in solidarity with the tram workers, leading to several months of industrial action which brought Dublin to a standstill.

In January 1914, the ITGWU advised workers to end the ultimately unsuccessful strike. Nonetheless, the Lockout, along with the Easter Rising of 1916, has come to define the city of Dublin in the early part of the twentieth century.

5 January 1871

The Franco-Irish Ambulance Brigade is released from duty

On 5 January 1871, the Franco-Irish Ambulance Brigade – a volunteer medical corps comprising surgeons, medical students and ambulance drivers – was released from its duties by the French authorities. Also known as the Ambulance Irlandais, it had been established in Dublin the previous year to assist France in its war with Prussia, which ostensibly started over the infamous Ems telegram. Soon after, the Committee for the Relief of the Sick and Wounded of the French Army and Navy was established, headed by Fr Tom Burke.

In October 1870, a notice in the *Irish Times* stated that 'Volunteers for the Irish Ambulance Corps who have passed the final examination as to eligibility, are required to present themselves at the office.' The 250 or so volunteers left that month, arriving at Le Havre on a ship called *La Fontaine*. France was already losing the war quite badly.

One novel feature of the Brigade was that it managed to circumvent the Foreign Enlistment Act of 1870, which forbade anyone in Ireland or Great Britain from accepting 'any commission or engagement in the military or naval service of any foreign state at war with any foreign state at peace with Her Majesty'.

Though its purpose was to aid sick and wounded soldiers, several members of the Brigade joined the French Foreign Legion upon arrival. This led to the arrest of one 'John McDonald' (real name Joseph Patrick McDonnell, a former Fenian) in London, who was thought to have been the principal recruiter for the Brigade.

Shortly before the Armistice of Versailles, the Ambulance Irlandais returned to Ireland. It had earned a good reputation on the battlefields of continental Europe, having come to the aid of several wounded French soldiers.

6 January 1839

The Night of the Big Wind

When the Old Age Pensions Act became law on 1 January 1909, it entitled men and women over the age of 70 in the United Kingdom – of which Ireland was still a part – to an annual payment of £13, on a means-tested basis. Within three months, 261,668 applications had been made in Ireland: proportionally, far more than in England, Scotland or Wales. Since the compulsory registration of births had not come into force in Ireland until 1863, it was difficult to prove that those saying they were old enough to receive a pension were telling the truth.

As a result, a novel way of establishing someone's age came about: applicants were asked whether they remembered the Night of the Big Wind, a storm that began in Ireland on 6 January 1839 and was the most devastating in the recorded history of the country. It is estimated that between 300 and 800 people died.

In all, 4,846 chimneys were said to have been knocked off their perches during the storm, and more people were left homeless than in all the evictions over subsequent decades in Ireland. The event was immortalised in 'Oíche na Gaoithe Móire, nó Deireadh An tSaoil' (The Night of the Big Wind, or the End of the World) by Galway poet Michael Burke.

The *Dublin Evening Post*, writing at the time, said: 'it remains not only without a parallel, but leaves far away in the distance all that ever occurred in Ireland before … Ireland has been the chief victim of the hurricane – every part of Ireland – every field, every town, every village in Ireland have felt its dire effects, from Galway to Dublin – from the Giant's Causeway to Valentia.'

7 January 1922
Dáil Éireann ratifies the Anglo-Irish Treaty

On 7 January 1922, a vote was taken in Dáil Éireann on whether to ratify the Anglo-Irish Treaty that had been signed the previous month by, among others, Michael Collins and Arthur Griffith. Debates on the treaty had begun on 14 December 1921. Éamon de Valera made no secret of his disdain for it, introducing the debate by saying, 'It would be ridiculous to think that we could send five men to complete a treaty without the right of ratification by this assembly.'

The treaty was narrowly ratified, by 64 votes to 57. After the vote was taken, a disappointed de Valera said, 'It will, of course, be my duty to resign my office as Chief Executive … There is one thing I want to say – I want it to go to the country and to the world, and it is this: the Irish people established a Republic … The Republic can only be disestablished by the Irish people.'

Collins was cautious in welcoming the result, perhaps aware of the impending Civil War, which would ultimately claim his life. Replying to de Valera, he said, 'I do not regard the passing of this thing as being any kind of triumph over the other side. I will do my best in the future, as I have done in the past, for the nation … we will all do our best to preserve the public safety', to which de Valera replied, 'hear, hear'.

Less forgiving was Mary MacSwiney, TD (Teachta Dála) for Cork Borough, who, shortly after Collins and de Valera had finished their exchanges, called the ratification of the Treaty 'the grossest act of betrayal that Ireland ever endured'. She and many others took the Anti-Treaty side during the Irish Civil War.

8 January 1979

The Whiddy Island disaster

On 8 January 1979, an oil tanker exploded in Bantry Bay, Co. Cork, claiming the lives of 50 people – 42 French, seven Irish and one British. In its coverage, the *Irish Independent* led with the headline 'The holocaust that claimed 50 lives – what went wrong'. In later years, Michael Kingston, whose father, Tim, was one of the dead, compared the incident and its treatment by successive Irish governments to the Hillsborough disaster in Sheffield in 1989.

Construction by the Gulf Oil Corporation of the oil terminal on Whiddy Island, Bantry Bay, started in 1967 and finished in 1969. The company was struggling to maintain its viability by the late 1970s. The ill-fated oil tanker – the *Betelgeuse* – arrived at the terminal with a full cargo of crude oil, having left the Saudi port of Ras Tanura on 24 November 1978. While it was discharging 114,000 tonnes of crude oil – expected to take 36 hours – a cracking noise was heard, followed by the explosion in the hull, at around 1:00 a.m. on 8 January.

The Irish government appointed a tribunal to investigate the disaster, chaired by Mr Justice Declan Costello. Its 480-page report found three main causes: firstly, the poor condition of the 11-year-old vessel, owned by the French company Total SA; secondly, incorrectly unloading procedures, also the responsibility of Total SA; thirdly, the poorly maintained emergency services at Whiddy Island.

On the 40th anniversary of the incident, Michael Kingston, now a lawyer based in London, spoke at a commemoration, saying, 'Our relatives were left to die by a company and management who made a decision to reduce safety and were clearly guilty of death by gross negligence.' Tragically, only 27 bodies were ever recovered.

9 January 1980

Charles Haughey: 'living away beyond our means'

Charles Haughey became Taoiseach on 11 December 1979, a year after Ireland recorded a budget deficit of 17.6 per cent of GDP: a record for developed countries, according to the International Monetary Fund. Haughey's ascent to head of government occurred at a time of steadily rising unemployment, which would increase from 7 per cent in 1979 to 17 per cent in 1986.

It was against this backdrop that Haughey took to RTÉ to deliver a live public address, only the third time in the history of the state that a Taoiseach had done so. His tone was sombre from the beginning: 'I wish to talk to you this evening about

the state of the nation's affairs, and the picture I have to paint is not, unfortunately, a very cheerful one.' He then uttered a sentence that would become infamous, given subsequent revelations about his personal expenditure: 'As a community we are living away beyond our means.'

The Taoiseach continued, clarifying that the rate of borrowing to keep the country afloat was unsustainable. Haughey also accused industrial actions as having contributed to the negative state of the country's economy: 'Strikes, go-slows, work-to-rules, stoppages in key industries and essential services were too often a feature of life in 1979.' He also stated that 'apportioning blame, however, is not going to get us anywhere'.

When the Moriarty Tribunal was established in 1997 to inquire into the finances of Haughey and former Fine Gael TD Michael Lowry, it emerged that, at the time of Haughey's 1980 address, his personal debts with Allied Irish Banks (AIB) totalled £1.143 million. These revelations permanently tainted Haughey's reputation, and his 1980 speech is now seen by many as staggeringly hypocritical.

10 January 1877

Eliza Walker Dunbar becomes first woman doctor

On 10 January 1877, Eliza Walker Dunbar became the first woman to qualify with a medical licence from an institution in either Ireland or Great Britain, having taken her clinical and written examinations the previous day at the King and Queen's College of Physicians in Ireland (subsequently renamed the Royal College of Physicians). Walker was not Irish – she had been born in India to a Scottish father, and educated in Cheltenham. Indeed, being based in Great Britain was to her advantage; the Council of the King and Queen's College of Physicians would not have viewed her as a competitor to medical practitioners in Ireland.

The decision to allow women to receive their medical licences in Ireland had its roots in opposition to the 1858 Medical Act, which established the General Medical Council (GMC) to regulate doctors. Though not barring women explicitly, the 1858 Act made it practically impossible for them to qualify as doctors in the United Kingdom, as they were prohibited from studying medicine at Royal Colleges, universities and medical institutions. However, loopholes allowed women who had obtained their medical degrees outside the United Kingdom before 1858, like Elizabeth Blackwell, to have their names added to the GMC register.

Walker Dunbar's medical licence came about as a result of the so-called Enabling Act of 1876, introduced to Parliament by Russell Gurney MP, whose support had been won by campaigners like Sophia Jex-Blake. It allowed all 19 examining boards in the UK to admit women to their examinations if they chose. The following year, the King and Queen's College of Physicians in Ireland became the first institution to take advantage of the new legislation, a moment that Sophia Jex-Blake called 'the turning point in the whole struggle'.

11 January 1970

Sinn Féin splits over abstentionism

The birth of 'Provisional' Sinn Féin on 11 January 1970 was both an ending and a beginning. It was an ending of tensions that had existed within the self-styled Republican Movement over the policy of abstentionism, and the perceived failure to protect Catholic communities in Northern Ireland from pogroms and other attacks. It was also the beginning of a new movement within Irish republicanism, more ruthless than any previous incarnation, which had the stamina to sustain its campaign for far longer than the periods of the War of Independence and subsequent Civil War combined.

The split in Sinn Féin came during an Ard Fheis (party conference) in the Intercontinental Hotel in Dublin. There had been a split in the IRA weeks earlier, with Chief of Staff Cathal Goulding calling for abstentionism to be dropped. Abstentionism meant that Sinn Féin would not take up seats in Dáil Éireann – indeed, members of Sinn Féin did not even use the term 'Dáil Éireann' when referring to the Irish parliament; among hard-line Republicans it was exclusively referred to as 'Leinster House'.

Abstentionism was not a matter for the IRA per se, but for Sinn Féin, the political wing of the movement, and so the matter was put to a vote on 11 January 1970. According to Ruairí Ó Brádaigh, who was opposed to dropping abstentionism, a two-thirds majority was needed to change the party's policy. This was not achieved, but there was enough support for taking seats in Dáil Éireann that Ó Brádaigh led 80 delegates out of the Intercontinental Hotel, setting up 'Provisional' Sinn Féin, the political wing of the Provisional IRA for the next three decades (as distinct from 'Official' Sinn Féin, led by Tomás Mac Giolla).

In 1986, another split over abstentionism would see Ó Brádaigh further ostracised.

12 January 1870

Pope Pius condemns Fenianism

On 12 January 1870, Pope Pius IX stated that he had 'decreed and declared that the American or Irish society called Fenian is comprised among the societies forbidden and condemned in the Constitutions of the Supreme Pontiff'. This was a clarification of a bull that the Pope had issued on 29 October 1868, which excommunicated 'those who become members of the Masonic sect, of the Carbonari, or of other similar sects that plot either openly or secretly against the Church or legitimate authorities'.

This was not the first or last time that a high-ranking Catholic leader would clash with the ideology espoused by physical-force Irish republicans. On 17 February 1867, the Bishop of Kerry, David Moriarty, denounced a recent rebellion attempt by the Irish Republican Brotherhood (whose American counterpart was the Fenian Brotherhood, though 'Fenians' and 'IRB' were and are often used interchangeably). Moriarty said of the rebels: 'they are not our people, or, if they ever were, they have lost the Irish character in the cities of America ... eternity is not long enough nor hell hot enough to punish such miscreants.'

Pius IX's statement was largely the result of a request from Ireland's first ever cardinal, Paul Cullen. However, condemnation of the Fenians was not universal among the clergy. Fr Patrick Lavelle was a supporter, as was his superior, Dr John MacHale, the Archbishop of Tuam. MacHale was the one Irish bishop who did not welcome a public ban on large demonstrations sympathetic to the Fenians in the wake of public hangings of the so-called Manchester Martyrs in November 1867. It was in the context of such events that the Irish bishops in Rome for the First Vatican Council decided to ask for the condemnation.

13 January 1847

Queen Victoria appeals for famine relief

Queen Victoria was 26 years old when the blight that ravaged Ireland's potato crops first appeared in 1845. Though stories are often told of how she turned her back on the Irish during that period – with figures as low as £50 or even £5 cited as what she donated for famine aid, and the nickname 'the Famine Queen' bestowed upon her in some circles – the truth is more complex. Victoria was, in fact, the largest individual contributor to famine relief.

On 13 January 1847, a letter written by the Queen was published in *The Times*, asking for an appeal to be read in churches across England and for ministers to 'excite their parishioners to a liberal contribution', which would be used 'for the relief of a large portion of the population in Ireland and in some districts of Scotland'. Five-sixths of the money raised went to Ireland.

Victoria was asked to be the first benefactor of the British Association for the Relief of Distress in Ireland and in the Highlands and Islands of Scotland. The first donation to this group was £2,000, from Victoria, with a separate grant of £500 to 'the Ladies Clothing Association'. Eight other members of the royal family made donations that came to a total of £3,700, and employees in the Queen's household made a private collection of £247.

Wednesday, 24 March 1847, was designated a national day of 'fast and humiliation' throughout the United Kingdom. It raised £171,533, which was given to the British Relief Association. Another letter from the Queen, published in October of that year, resulted in a far smaller figure being raised – £30,167 – and was referred to in *The Times* as 'ill-advised'.

14 January 1965

Seán Lemass and Terence O'Neill meet

On 14 January 1965, Seán Lemass travelled to Belfast to meet Terence O'Neill. It was the first time that the leaders of both states on the island of Ireland had officially met since the enactment of the Anglo-Irish Treaty of 1921 – a treaty that Lemass, in his youth, had fought against.

Although a momentous occasion, subsequently commemorated in a stamp issued by An Post for its 50th anniversary, the meeting was low-key. O'Neill had not alerted his cabinet members to Lemass's impending arrival until the previous day, and one of them – Harry West – refused to show up. A press statement from the Northern

Ireland government was later released: 'An historic meeting took place in Belfast today, when for the first time since the partition of Ireland over 40 years ago, the Prime Ministers of Northern Ireland and Republic met.'

Lemass had hinted at a thawing of relations during an Oxford Union debate in 1959, rhetorically asking 'is it not common sense that the two existing communities in our small island should seek every opportunity of working together in practical matters for their mutual and common good?'

One person who, perhaps unexpectedly, echoed this pragmatism was George Clark, Grand Master of the Orange Order, who said, 'One country lives beside another, and it is surely common sense that the two leaders meet to discuss ways of expanding their economies.' Not all in Northern Ireland shared Clark's view. One of the most critical of the meeting was Ian Paisley, who would go on to found the Democratic Unionist Party. O'Neill dismissed Paisley and his fellow travellers as 'self-appointed and self-styled loyalists who see moderation as treason and decency as weakness'. Nevertheless, Paisley would be an enormously influential figure in Northern Ireland over the coming decades.

15 January 1947

Electricity is introduced to rural Ireland

On 15 January 1947, Oldtown, Co. Dublin became the first village in Ireland where electricity was switched on as part of the Rural Electrification Scheme, introduced the previous year by the Electricity Supply Board (ESB). At the time there were 250,000 electrical consumers in urban parts of Ireland, but rural Ireland had been making do with 19th-century methods of farming, as well as lamps and candles for light.

As a result of the Rural Electrification Scheme, which was referred to as the 'Quiet Revolution', 420,000 homes in rural Ireland were electrified between 1946 and 1979, by which time an estimated 98 per cent of homes in the country had electricity. It has been described as the greatest social revolution in Ireland since the Land Reforms of the 1880s and 1890s.

The first new consumer of electricity was McCullough's pub in Oldtown. On the night in question, the Engineer-in-Charge, W. F. Roe, was to give a speech in Oldtown Hall at 8 o'clock, the time for the 'switch on', to be accompanied by a gramophone

turntable playing 'Cockles and Mussels' (perhaps better known as 'Molly Malone'), the unofficial anthem of Dublin. However, at 8 o'clock, Roe noticed that no electricity was forthcoming, as did the crowd assembled. Anxiety filled the room but was soon assuaged when the gramophone came to life, playing 'Cockles and Mussels' as planned. The delay had been caused by the severe winter weather that the country had recently experienced.

The Rural Electrification Scheme was costly, involving 75,000 miles of new line and up to a million ESB poles. The first of these poles was erected in Kilsallaghan, Co. Dublin on 5 November 1946. The moment electricity was switched on in Oldtown signalled the start of modern Ireland.

16 January 1922

Dublin Castle is handed over to Michael Collins

In accordance with Article 17 of the Anglo-Irish Treaty, a 'provisional Government' was needed to govern what was at that time called Southern Ireland, until the Irish Free State was formally established in 1922. Michael Collins (pictured on facing page leaving Dublin Castle with Kevin O'Higgins and W. T. Cosgrave. Collins is marked with an X) was appointed Chairman; on 16 January he and seven other ministers went to Dublin Castle, which Collins would refer to as 'that dread Bastille of Ireland',

for the official handover from Lord Edmund FitzAlan-Howard, the last ever Lord Lieutenant of Ireland, to the Provisional Government.

There are many unverified accounts of what was said between Collins and those ceding power to the new government. James Macmahon, the Belfast-born Under Secretary for Ireland, is said to have greeted the Chairman by saying, 'We're glad to see you, Mr Collins', to which Collins allegedly replied, 'Ye are like hell, boy.' The most famous exchange – almost certainly apocryphal – is that FitzAlan-Howard said to Collins, 'You are seven minutes late', to which Collins responded, 'We've been waiting 700 years. You can have the seven minutes.'

Dublin Castle released an official account of the handover that afternoon, stating that 'his Excellency the Lord Lieutenant received Mr. Michael Collins as the head of the Provisional Government ... The existence and authority of the Provisional Government were then formally and officially acknowledged ... The Lord-Lieutenant congratulated Mr. Collins and ... expressed the earnest hope that under their auspices the ideal of a happy, free, and prosperous Ireland would be attained.'

The Provisional Government released its own official statement, which was more triumphalist in its language: 'Members of Rialtas Sealadach na hÉireann [Provisional Government of Ireland] received the surrender of Dublin Castle at 1.45 p.m. today. It is now in the hands of the Irish nation.'

17 January 1992

Peter Brooke sings 'Oh My Darling, Clementine'

Peter Brooke became Secretary of State for Northern Ireland in July 1989. He was not overtly combative in his attitude to Irish republicans, stating in November of that year that the British government 'would need to be imaginative' in its response if the paramilitary groups were to 'withdraw from their activities'. Famously, he announced that 'the British Government has no selfish, strategic or economic interest in Northern Ireland' in November 1990, a statement often credited with opening the door for Sinn Féin to enter negotiations.

However, Brooke's tenure as Secretary of State ended abruptly in 1992, after an appearance on RTÉ's *The Late Late Show* on 17 January of that year. Brooke was in Dublin to meet with Gerry Collins, the Minister for Foreign Affairs, and scheduled for an interview with *Late Late Show* host Gay Byrne that evening. On the same day, a Provisional IRA bomb exploded at Teebane Crossroads, Co. Tyrone, killing eight construction workers and injuring another six. The Provisional IRA later released a statement describing those killed as 'collaborators engaged in rebuilding Lisanelly Barracks'.

Brooke was asked about the incident on *The Late Late Show*. He replied: 'The first thing you say is profound sympathy to the families of those who were involved.' The interview continued, and the subjects of Brooke's faith and his recent marriage were brought up. Byrne went on to ask the Secretary of State if he ever sang, and finally coaxed him into joining pianist Frank McNamara in a rendition of 'Oh My Darling, Clementine', which he was clearly reluctant to do.

Afterwards, Byrne told Brooke, 'I imagine that singing that song will give a fair amount of ammunition to a lot of people.' He wasn't wrong. The incident caused outrage among unionist politicians in Northern Ireland, and Brooke offered his resignation soon after.

18 January 1978

Judgement is reached in 'Ireland v. the United Kingdom'

On 18 January 1978, a verdict was reached by the European Court of Human Rights in a case that the Irish government had brought against the British government, regarding what came to be known as the 'five techniques', interrogation methods used in Northern Ireland.

The origin of this case was the introduction of internment in Northern Ireland in August 1971. Fourteen men – all Roman Catholics – were taken from their homes to Ballykelly Airfield. There, they were subjected to the five techniques – hooded for an extended period, blasted with continuous loud noise, deprived of sleep, deprived of food and drink, and made to stand against a wall for extended periods. When allegations of the techniques reached the media, they were not universally condemned. Even the left-leaning *Guardian* wrote, 'Discomfort ... cannot be weighed against the number of human lives which will be lost if the security forces do not get a continuing flow of intelligence.'

In November 1971, the Irish government brought its case against the British government, and the European Commission on Human Rights issued its verdict in January 1976, finding the United Kingdom guilty of torture. However, this was appealed, and on 18 January 197 8, the European Court of Human Rights, by 13 votes to four, concluded that the techniques did not constitute torture. However, it did find that the UK had treated the so-called 'hooded men' in an 'inhuman and degrading' way, and thus was still in breach of Article 3 of the European Convention on Human Rights.

19 January 1947
The Big Freeze begins

On 19 January 1947, Ireland began to experience a cold spell that would last for two months, bring transport to a halt, lead to rationing, and see the death rate in Dublin more than double. It became known as the Big Freeze. The origin of the event was 'a persistent anti-cyclone centred over Norway and Sweden ... attracting freezing winds from North Russia', as reported in New Zealand newspaper the *Evening Star*.

Ireland was already in a weak position, along with the rest of Europe, as a result of the Second World War – or 'Emergency' as it had been designated. Predicting the upcoming crisis, an editorial in the *Irish Press* on 14 January stated that, in terms of supplies, the country's position was as 'bad as it was in the worst war years'. Future Taoiseach Seán Lemass, who was then Minister for Industry and Commerce, had begun rationing flour and bread earlier in the month.

The cold spell got much worse on 24 January, with temperatures falling to between -2 and -6°C. On 30 January the temperature was -13°C, colder than that recorded in Antarctica that day. Wicklow was one of the worst-hit counties. In March, it was planned that Royal Air Force jets would drop parcels of food on villages in Wicklow, but by the time the plane arrived at Baldonnel's airbase, many homes in those villages had been reached and so the plan was abandoned.

An exact death toll of the Big Freeze was not recorded, though historian Kevin C. Kearns believes it to have been in the hundreds. One of the most tragic events occurred when six children playing hockey fell into a hole in a quarry that had frozen over in Kimmage, Co. Dublin. Three of them died, the youngest of whom was eight years old.

20 January 1961

John F. Kennedy is inaugurated

On 20 January 1961, John Fitzgerald Kennedy was sworn in as the 35th President of the United States, using the bible that his great-grandfather Thomas Fitzgerald had brought from the village of Bruff, Co. Limerick when he emigrated in the mid-19th century. Kennedy wasn't the first US President of Irish descent – several could trace their roots back to Ireland, notably Andrew Jackson, the seventh President, who was a son of Presbyterians from Co. Antrim.

However, Kennedy's ascent to the White House was of particular importance to most people in Ireland because he was the first to share their Catholic faith – publicly, at least. He would also become the first sitting US President to visit Ireland, in June 1963, a few months before his death.

The place in Ireland most closely associated with Kennedy is New Ross, Co. Wexford, near Dunganstown, where his great-grandfather Patrick Kennedy had lived before emigrating to America. Andrew Minihan, chairman of New Ross Urban District Council, would later recall, 'We had celebrations at exactly the same hour as the president was being inaugurated.' Kennedy recorded a message to the people of New Ross, pledging to visit his great-grandfather's hometown.

He was as good as his word, and spoke there on 27 June 1963: 'I am glad to be here. It took 115 years to make this trip, and 6,000 miles, and three generations. But

I am proud to be here ... When my great grandfather left here to become a cooper in East Boston, he carried nothing with him except two things: a strong religious faith and a strong desire for liberty. I am glad to say that all of his great-grandchildren have valued that inheritance.'

21 January 1919

The first sitting of Dáil Éireann

On 21 January 1919, 27 Sinn Féin Teachtaí Dála (TDs) assembled in the Mansion House, Dublin, for the first sitting of Dáil Éireann. Most of the 69 TDs who had been elected the previous month could not attend, many because they were in prison.

Up to 3,000 members of the public attended the session, almost half of whom were women. Also present were 70–100 journalists. The *New York Times* was prompted to write, 'Today's proceedings seemed tame ... due to the fact that they were conducted in the dead language of the Irish tongue.' This description of the language may have irked many, though, as Sinn Féin TD Piaras Béaslaí, who organised the session, noted: 'I was determined to leave nothing to chance ... Every speaker must know when he was to be called up and must be word perfect in his speech. This was particularly important when all the speeches were in Irish and some of our proposed speakers were not very much at ease in that language.'

On the same day as the first sitting of Dáil Éireann, the Soloheadbeg Ambush took place in Co. Tipperary. Nine Irish Volunteers – led by Séumas Robinson, Dan Breen and Seán Treacy – ambushed and killed two Royal Irish Constabulary (RIC)

policemen – Patrick O'Connell and James McDonnell. This event is often seen as the start of the Irish War of Independence, though it was not officially sanctioned.

Richard Mulcahy, who was Chief of Staff of the Irish Republican Army from March 1919, would later write: 'This episode has … been outrageously propagandised … it took place on the day that the Dáil was being assembled for the first time … bloodshed should have been unnecessary in the light of the type of episode it was; it completely disturbed the general public situation in the area.'

22 January 1972

Ireland signs Treaty of Accession to the European Communities

On 22 January 1972, Jack Lynch and Dr Patrick Hillery, the Taoiseach and Minister for Foreign Affairs respectively, signed the Treaty of Accession for Ireland to join the European Communities in Brussels (pictured below. Lynch is on the right). This was the beginning of Ireland's place within what would come to be known as the European Union.

Though a necessary step, the signing of the Treaty was not a sufficient one – it was subject to a public vote. When Irish voters cast their ballots on 10 May 1972, 83.1 per cent supported the third amendment to the Irish constitution, allowing the state to join. Lynch described the result as 'a great tribute to our people's innately sound judgement'.

Representatives of the UK, Denmark and Norway signed the Treaty on the same

day as Lynch and Hillery. Denmark and Norway would hold their own referenda on joining the European Communities, but the outcomes would differ – 63.1 per cent of Danish voters supported entering, but 53.5 per cent of Norwegian voters opposed it. Members of the British House of Commons voted in favour of the European Communities Act, 301 to 284, though the British public at large would not get a say on the UK's place within the EC until 5 June 1975. Of those who turned out, 67.23 per cent supported continued membership.

Membership of the European Union greatly improved the economic condition of Ireland – when it joined it had, according to the Irish Council of the European Movement, 'the lowest living standards and poorest social services in Western Europe'. By the late 1990s it had become one of the wealthiest countries; *The Economist* asked if Ireland's Celtic Tiger was 'Europe's shining light.' It also made the border between Northern Ireland and the Republic virtually frictionless, facilitating peace on the island.

23 January 1834

St Vincent's is founded: first hospital staffed by women

On 23 January 1834, possession was taken of the former townhouse of the Earl of Meath at 56 St Stephen's Green, Dublin. It was here that St Vincent's Hospital was founded, by Mother Mary Aikenhead, the first hospital in either Ireland or Great Britain staffed and managed by women. In the following years it would expand, incorporating a nursing home in 1910.

Though most of the sick poor in Dublin at the time were Catholic, the hospital was founded to treat all in need equally. Its prospectus read: 'The institution would be such in which every friend of humanity would feel an interest and … would present to individuals of every sect, and every creed equal advantages and equal attention.' This reflected Aikenhead's ecumenical background.

She was the daughter of David Aikenhead, who was of Scottish Protestant descent, and Mary Stackpole, an aristocratic Catholic. Though baptised a Protestant, Mary Aikenhead mixed with poor Catholics when she was fostered by Mary and John Rorke on Eason's Hill in Co. Cork, before returning to her parents aged six. She was received into the Catholic Church at age 15, largely as a result of the influence of her aunt, Rebecca Gorman, who had stayed in a convent in Bruges.

By the time St Vincent's Hospital opened, Mary was ill, having been confined to a wheelchair from the age of 44 due to spinal problems, dropsy and paralysis. Nonetheless, she continued to work hard, sending 4,000 letters from her sickbed, appealing for donations to start the hospital. Her attitude to the founding of a hospital run by women was that 'just because it has never been done before, there is no reason why it should not be done now.'

24 January 1824

Daniel O'Connell introduces Catholic Rent

On 24 January 1824, at a meeting of the Catholic Association, Daniel O'Connell introduced a scheme that would have a dramatic effect on the organisation and its desire to secure Catholic Emancipation – that is, a campaign for the right of Catholics not only to vote (which Catholics who held freeholds worth 40 shillings or more could do) but to sit in parliament. This scheme became known as the Catholic Rent. O'Connell told those assembled that 'every Catholic in Ireland should be called upon to contribute a monthly sum from one penny up to two shillings, the utmost to which any person should be expected to subscribe; and by a general effort of that kind, the people of England would see that Catholic millions felt a deep interest in the cause, and not confined, as is supposed, to those styled "agitators".'

This was not the first time that a Catholic Rent was suggested. Thomas Browne, Lord Kenmare – one of the few remaining Catholic landowners in Ireland at the end of the 18th century – had put a similar idea in a letter to Francis Moylan, Bishop of Cork, in 1785. In 1811, William Parnell – whose grandson, Charles Stewart Parnell, would one day lead the Irish Parliamentary Party – suggested calling 'every nerve and sinew of the Catholic body into action by quarterly meetings of all Parishes throughout Ireland'.

In order to collect this rent, association branches were formed throughout Ireland. In 1826, pro-Catholic Emancipation candidates were elected in Louth and Waterford, and O'Connell himself was elected in Clare in 1829. This led to the Roman Catholic Relief Act of the same year – which, though a milestone, raised the franchise eligibility from land ownership worth 40 shillings to £10.

25 January 1917

Sinking of the *Laurentic*

On 25 January 1917, the SS *Laurentic* made a stop at a naval port in Buncrana, Co. Donegal, having left Liverpool two days earlier. It was carrying 479 passengers and crew, mostly Royal Navy personnel, as well as 43 tons of gold bullion valued at £5,000,000. It stopped in Buncrana to allow four ratings, suspected of having yellow fever, to be dropped off, then continued its scheduled journey towards Halifax, Nova Scotia with the remaining passengers and crew. Two hours later, the *Laurentic* struck two mines that had been left by a German U-boat off Lough Swilly, and sank within an hour. Of the 475 on board, 354 perished.

A hunt for the gold bullion, which was to be used to buy munitions for the ongoing war from Canada and the United States, was led by Commander Guybon Damant, a diving expert. Petty Officer Augustus Dent, who had survived the sinking of the *Laurentic*, was one of the divers chosen for the mission. It all had to be done in secret, lest the Germans learn of the sunken gold. Another reason for secrecy was that the United States was still officially neutral at this time.

The salvage operations went on for seven years, and 3,186 of 3,211 gold ingots were eventually retrieved. The cost was £128,000: significantly less than the value of the gold recovered.

Submitting his report on 21 September 1924, Damant said: 'This satisfactory result is due above all things to the loyal and dogged work of naval divers, inspired by no selfish motive of reward … It is with profound gratitude to those who have helped me to foresee and guard against danger that I record the fact that there has been no loss of life or serious accident in the whole course of the work.'

26 January 1942

First American troops arrive in Belfast

On 26 January 1942, the first American troops officially entered the European Theatre of Operations for the Second World War, landing at Dufferin Quay in Belfast. The man credited with being the first American GI to land on European soil was Private First Class Milburn H. Henke of Minnesota. This, however, was a publicity

stunt, as by the time Henke was presented to cameras, approximately 500 men had already disembarked from HMTS *Strathaird*, a passenger liner that had been converted to a troop ship.

The Irish state would remain neutral throughout the Second World War, a decision that remains controversial. Éamon de Valera was Taoiseach, and wasted no time in expressing his displeasure at not being consulted on the decision to land troops on the island of Ireland. The Constitution of Ireland, effective since December 1937, stated in Article 2 that 'the national territory consists of the whole island of Ireland', a claim that outraged unionists north of the border.

De Valera sent a statement to Washington, DC: 'The people of Ireland have no feeling of hostility towards and no desire to be brought in any way into conflict with the United States ... but it is our duty to make it clearly understood that, no matter what troops occupy the six counties, the Irish people's claim for the union of the whole of the national territory and for supreme jurisdiction over it will remain unabated.'

The reply, authorised by Roosevelt, made it clear that the American government did not regard Northern Ireland as Irish territory: 'The decision to dispatch troops to the British Isles was reached in close consultation with the British Government as part of our strategic plan to defeat the Axis aggressors. There was not, and is not now, the slightest thought or intention of invading Irish territory or of threatening Irish security.'

27 January 1982

Dáil is dissolved over VAT on children's shoes

On 27 January 1982, the 22nd Dáil came to an end after only 252 days, following a controversial budget introduced by Minister for Finance and future Taoiseach John Bruton. Bruton announced 18 per cent value-added tax (VAT) on clothing and footwear. The issue of children's footwear not being exempt became a focal point, thanks to what Taoiseach Garret FitzGerald would insist was a throwaway remark – FitzGerald told the media that some women with small feet could take advantage were the tax children's shoes not included.

The government, led by Fine Gael in coalition with Labour, relied on the support of independent TDs like Jim Kemmy. However, Kemmy voted against the budget, along with Joe Sherlock of Sinn Féin the Workers Party and another independent, Sean Loftus. Noël Browne of the Socialist Labour Party was the only TD to vote with Fine Gael and Labour on the budget, but it was not enough for it to pass. It was defeated by 82 to 81 votes, making an election imminent.

FitzGerald would later write in the *Irish Times* that the issue of VAT on children's footwear was a 'myth'. Nevertheless, it became synonymous with the fall of his government. After the defeat of his budget, FitzGerald went to Áras an Uachtaráin, home of President Patrick Hillery, to seek a dissolution of the 22nd Dáil.

These events would have repercussions for Irish politics during the 1990 Presidential election, when it was alleged that Presidential candidate and former Fianna Fáil TD Brian Lenihan had phoned Hillery on 27 January 1982, asking him not to grant a dissolution of the Dáil. Had Hillery heeded Lenihan's supposed request, Fianna Fáil could have formed a government without the need for an election. Lenihan denied this, but it led to his being dismissed from government in 1990.

28 January 1842

Address from the People of Ireland is read in Boston

On 28 January 1842, an Address from the People of Ireland to their Countrymen and Countrywomen in America, signed by approximately 60,000 people, was first presented to an audience in Faneuil Hall, Boston. This was an important moment in the history of Ireland–US relations, in the anti-slavery movement, and in the career of Daniel O'Connell, one of the last people to add his name, and arguably the most famous signatory, along with Father Theobald Mathew.

The address was relatively short. It made its purpose clear early: 'The object of this address is to call your attention to the subject of slavery in America ... Irishmen and Irishwomen! Treat the colored people as your equals, as brethren. By all your memories of Ireland, continue to love liberty – hate slavery – cling by the abolitionists – and in America you will do honor to the name of Ireland.'

The authors of the text were Richard Davis Webb and James Haughton, two of the founders of the Hibernian Anti-Slavery Society; it was brought to America by Charles Lenox Remond after a tour of the United Kingdom. Haughton had raised the subject with O'Connell in January 1840, speaking of the Irish in America and saying, '[Y]our influence over their minds is very great, would you think it wise to address them on this subject one of your powerful appeals?'

Reaction to the address was mixed, however. Bishop John J. Hughes of New York cast doubt on its authenticity, and said it was 'the duty of every naturalized Irishman to resist and repudiate the Address with indignation ... I am no friend of slavery, but I am still less friendly to any attempt of foreign origin to abolish.'

29 January 1967

Northern Ireland Civil Rights Association is formed

On 29 January 1967, a meeting was held in Belfast's International Hotel, organised by the Belfast Wolfe Tone Society: specifically, members Fred Heatley and Jack Bennett. Its purpose was to unify various groups in Northern Ireland under the common cause of democratic reform and civil rights for all. Over 100 people turned up, and it was here that the Northern Ireland Civil Rights Association (NICRA) was formed, with a 13-person committee, though its constitution would not be ratified until 9 April that year.

The committee was a broad church, representing several parties. Though the issue of civil rights was often seen as one primarily for Catholics, NICRA was not an exclusively Catholic or nationalist organisation. It did include open republicans, such as Heatley and Bennett, Billy McMillen – who would be killed as a member of the

Official IRA in a feud in 1975 – and Paddy Devlin of the Northern Ireland Labour Party, who had been interned as a member of the IRA during the Second World War.

However, a letter was read out at the meeting from James Chichester-Clark, who was then Chief Whip of the Ulster Unionist Party, and a few days later, it was unanimously agreed to co-opt Robin Cole, a former Chairman of the Young Unionists at Queen's University, to the committee.

NICRA's influence petered out in the early 1970s. Nevertheless, its importance in bringing international attention what it saw as injustices and the need for democratic reform in Northern Ireland should not be underestimated. It is likely, for example, that without the influence of NICRA elections in Northern Ireland would not have switched from the first-past-the-post system, which had given the Ulster Unionists a clear advantage in every election between 1929 and 1973, to proportional representation and the single transferable vote.

30 January 1972

Bloody Sunday (Derry)

On 30 January 1972, a march was held in Derry, organised by the Northern Ireland Civil Rights Association (NICRA), protesting against the policy of internment without trial that had been introduced in August 1971. It began at approximately 2:50 p.m. and was routed to start in the Creggan area of the city and end at Guildhall, where the Derry and Strabane District Council met. Approximately 15,000 to 20,000 people were in attendance, and when the march reached the junction of William Street and Rossville Street, several people diverged. According to the Bloody Sunday inquiry chaired by Lord Saville and published in 2010, these included 'those who were eager for a confrontation with the security forces'.

Shortly after, Colonel Derek Wilford, commander of the 1st battalion of the British Army's Parachute Regiment, failed to comply with the orders of Brigadier Pat MacLellan, to whom he was answerable. MacLellan had authorised Wilford to send one company of soldiers to mount an arrest operation, but Wilford sent a second one. The soldiers soon opened fire, shooting 28 people. Thirteen of those hit died on the day; another died four months later. All were male, aged between 17 and 59.

Bloody Sunday was a pivotal moment in the Northern Ireland Troubles. Other events saw more people die in a single day, but none saw as many die openly at the hands of those acting on behalf of the state. Derry native and future Nobel Peace Prize recipient John Hume urged the 'strongest possible action, including the immediate withdrawal of the uniformed murderers from our streets'. Prime Minister David Cameron would formally apologise upon the publication of the Saville Inquiry report in 2010: 'You do not defend the British Army by defending the indefensible ... The events of Bloody Sunday were in no way justified ... On behalf of our country, I am deeply sorry.'

31 January 1984

Death of Ann Lovett

On 31 January 1984, Ann Lovett, a 15-year-old schoolgirl, gave birth to a stillborn baby boy beside a grotto of the Virgin Mary in Granard, Co. Longford. A few hours later, Ann herself died in Mullingar hospital, 42 kilometres away. The death shocked not only the village of Granard (population 1,285) but the whole country. Ann's baby boy was posthumously baptised Pat, and the two were buried in the same coffin three days later.

Among those who attended the funeral was Fianna Fáil TD John Wilson, who would later serve as Tánaiste. The news of Ann's death reached most of the country when reporter Emily O'Reilly covered the story for the *Sunday Tribune* of 5 February, two days after the funeral.

Fine Gael TD Nuala Fennell, Minister of State for Women's Affairs and Family Law at the time, said Ann's death was a 'national tragedy' and called for an inquiry, 'regardless of whose sensibilities are hurt'. However, no inquiry ever took place. Gay Byrne would broach the subject on his radio show, *The Gay Byrne Hour*. After a report from Kevin O'Connor about Ann's death, the show received, according to Byrne, hundreds of letters from 'all over the country ... who were saying to us, "We know exactly what happened here, and let us tell you our story."'

On 23 February, several of these letters were read out. One said: 'The reaction to the tragic death of young Ann Lovett has been typically Irish – looking for an inquiry, looking for someone to blame. We are all to blame. Those who say they cannot see how such a thing could happen in Irish society today are blind. The biggest tragedy is that it has taken the death of a young girl to highlight the repressive attitude to young mothers.'

1 February 1815

Daniel O'Connell duels with John Norcott D'Esterre

On 1 February 1815, Daniel O'Connell faced John Norcott D'Esterre, a member of Dublin Corporation, in a duel. Both men are said to have been skilled with a pistol, and the outcome was not a foregone conclusion. It originated in D'Esterre's taking umbrage with O'Connell over his description of Dublin Corporation as 'beggarly' in a speech given less than a fortnight earlier. Writing to O'Connell on 26 January, D'Esterre said that 'such language was not warranted or provoked by anything on the part of the corporation', and asked O'Connell to confirm whether he had said it.

O'Connell sent a reply in which he neither confirmed nor denied it, but made clear his feelings: 'from the calumnious manner in which the religion and character of the Catholics of Ireland are treated in that body, no terms attributed to me, however reproachful, can exceed the contemptuous feelings I entertain for that body in its corporate capacity.' Soon afterwards, O'Connell was challenged to a duel, as D'Esterre was heavily in debt as a merchant and contractor, and, according to *Irish Magazine*, 'saw fortune beckoning to him through the perforated corpse of O'Connell'.

At approximately 4:00 p.m. on 1 February, D'Esterre – arriving an hour late – disembarked from his carriage at Bishopscourt, Naas, Co. Kildare, where the duel was to take place. D'Esterre fired first, but missed, and when O'Connell returned the shot, he hit his opponent in his abdomen. D'Esterre died two days later.

O'Connell later repudiated violence, in stark contrast to many figures in Irish nationalism, describing his decision to participate in the duel as 'the vanity of a criminal obedience to a more than criminal custom'. He famously said that 'no political change whatsoever is worth the shedding of a single drop of human blood.'

2 February 1880

Parnell addresses House of Representatives

On 2 February 1880, Charles Stewart Parnell became the fourth foreign leader to address the United States House of Representatives. At the time, Ireland was being hit by famine, though not as severely as in 1845–1852. Parnell used his opportunity to address this issue and others to the members of the House.

Just a few months previously, in October 1879, Parnell had been elected President of the Irish National Land League, an organisation that sought to abolish landlordism in Ireland and enable poor tenants to own the land on which they worked. He and fellow Land League member John Dillon had gone to North America on a three-month fundraising tour, eventually raising $300,000, and visiting 62 cities, including Montreal. It was after his appearance there that journalist and future Member of Parliament (MP) Tim Healy described Parnell as the 'uncrowned king' of Ireland.

Before his address to the House of Representatives, Parnell was introduced by Speaker Samuel J. Randall of Pennsylvania, who said he 'comes among us to speak of the distresses of his country'. Parnell began by referencing the then current famine, saying, '[T]his catastrophe was clearly foreseen and predicted six months ago in Ireland ... But the British government not only refused to do anything, but with extraordinary perversity persisted in denying that there was any danger of famine ... The present famine, as all other famines in Ireland, has been the direct result of the system of land tenure which is maintained there.'

Parnell's address, which lasted 32 minutes, was deemed 'tame and spiritless' by the *Chicago Tribune*. Nevertheless, that Parnell would secure such an opportunity spoke to his strengths as a leader, and the money raised on the tour, as well as the founding of the Irish National Land League of America, had major repercussions for Ireland.

3 February 1919

Éamon de Valera escapes from Lincoln Prison

On 3 February 1919, Éamon de Valera, leader of Sinn Féin, along with Sean Milroy and Sean McGarry, escaped from Lincoln Prison, England. Shortly afterwards, the three men were met by Michael Collins and Harry Boland, before being whisked off to Worksop in Nottinghamshire and finally to a safe house in Manchester.

The escape had been rather ingeniously, if not entirely successfully, conceived. Noticing a locked door in the exercise yard, de Valera – who had been arrested in May 1918 for allegedly engaging in 'treasonable communication' – hatched a plan to make an impression of the chaplain's key in a piece of candle wax. Milroy was tasked with drawing a life-size image of the key on a postcard, disguised as part of a cartoon. The prison authorities were none the wiser when it was sent out at Christmas in 1918. A

replica of the key depicted on the postcard was made, and smuggled into the prison inside a cake. Unluckily, it was too small, the wax having shrunk.

After another failed attempt, a blank key was smuggled in, along with a set of files. Prisoner Peter de Loughry was able to fashion a master key after dismantling one of the locks. It was this that de Valera used to escape. In his haste to leave, he did not close the door behind him. Years later, he would recall 'Had I locked that door, nobody would ever have known how we had escaped.'

When he returned to Dublin, de Valera (pictured above (right) with Harry Boland (left) and Michael Collins) stayed in the home of Dr Robert Farnan. Though his whereabouts were kept secret, he managed to get a statement read out at a meeting of the Sinn Féin ard chomhairle (executive) later that month: 'My message to the Irish people is that I have escaped from Lincoln to do the country's work, and I am doing it.'

4 February 1880

The 'Black' Donnellys are murdered

On 4 February 1880, the 'Black' Donnellys, an Irish family who had settled in Lucan, Ontario, were killed in their home by a vigilante mob that included police constable James Carroll, himself of Irish parentage. This was the end of more than 30 years of squatting, destruction of property and murder in the area. The matriarch and patriarch were James and Johannah Donnelly (née Magee). Both had left Tipperary for Ontario in 1842 with their son, James Jr.

In 1845, a year after their second son, William, was born, the family built a home on 100 acres belonging to an absentee landlord named John Grace, who didn't realise the family was there until years later. In 1855, Grace sold the entire plot to one Michael Maher for $200, and attempted to have the Donnellys ejected. However, he relented and sold them 50 acres of it for far less than Maher had paid ($50).

In 1857, James Sr killed Patrick Farrell, a fellow Catholic who, it is alleged, disliked the Donnellys' fraternising with Protestants. James turned himself in in 1858, and was sentenced to seven years' imprisonment. In the 1870s, William decided to set up a stagecoach business, but was met with fierce competition from a local called Patrick Flanagan, leading to a vicious feud that involved attacks on animals, arson, and damage to property. When James Carroll was made constable, he vowed to rid the township of the family.

And so, on 4 February 1880, he and the so-called Vigilance Society arrived at the Donnellys' homestead. James and Johannah were killed, as were sons John and Thomas and James's niece Bridget. Though Carroll was arrested, he was found not guilty of the murders, and the rest of the prisoners were granted bail. None of them were ever tried again for the death of the Donnellys.

5 February 1917

George Plunkett is elected abstentionist MP

On 5 February 1917, it was announced that Count George Noble Plunkett had won a by-election in North Roscommon held two days earlier. Plunkett's son, Joseph, was one of the seven signatories of the 1916 Proclamation, who had been executed for taking part in the Easter Rising seven months earlier.

Count Plunkett had vowed not to take his seat in Westminster, telling a crowd in the town of Boyle shortly afterwards: 'I recognise no parliament in existence as having the right over the people of Ireland.' This policy of abstentionism, popularised by Arthur Griffith in his 'Resurrection of Hungary' articles in 1904, would become a cornerstone of Sinn Féin policy in the 1918 election, in which it won 73 of the 105 seats contested for Ireland.

Plunkett's victory was also the beginning of the end of the Irish Parliamentary Party (IPP), which until that time had comfortably been the largest party in Ireland. The by-election came about when IPP MP James Joseph O'Kelly, who had held the North Roscommon seat unopposed since 1895, died. The IPP selected Thomas Devine to replace him in the seat. However, Plunkett received 3,022 votes, while Devine received 1,708. In the 1918 election, the number of seats held by the IPP would shrink to six.

Although Plunkett's victory paved the way for Sinn Féin's success in the 1918 election, he was not, contrary to popular belief, the first Sinn Féin MP to be elected. Plunkett's daughter Geraldine would write, 'He was not a member of Sinn Féin, but a separatist supported by a combination of separatists and almost all advanced Nationalist opinion.' Nonetheless, in the era immediately after the Easter Rising, which had not had popular support while it was happening, the election of the father of one of the leaders on an abstentionist ticket showed the way forward for Irish nationalism.

6 February 1800

Irish parliament approves the Act of Union

On 6 February 1800, the Irish House of Commons effectively voted itself out of existence: a proposal to form a Union with the Kingdom of Great Britain was carried by 158 votes to 115. This was not the first time that the proposal had been put before the parliament in Dublin. On 24 January 1799, a similar one had been defeated by 111 votes to 106. This time, a majority of representatives were persuaded to accept what William Pitt, the British Prime Minister, had put forward, which included compensating members of the Irish parliament.

It is said that £32,336 was used secretly to buy votes, when a £5,000 cap on the secret-service budget was in place. Pitt had been rattled by the United Irishmen rebellion of 1798. He later supported the Union in the British parliament, saying that 'Ireland is subject to great and deplorable evils' and that the remedy was a 'legislature standing aloof from local party connection, sufficiently removed from the influence of contending factions to be the advocate or champion of neither'.

Following the vote in Dublin, the Act of Union was passed on 2 July, and on 1 January 1801, the United Kingdom of Great Britain and Ireland was born. The following day, the *Belfast News Letter* hailed the event, telling its readers 'it is now become an interest as well as the duty of the whole to bury, if possible, all political differences – all religious animosities – all local prejudices; to consider the Empire, not as composed of distinct political bodies, each having views incompatible with the happiness and prosperity of the rest – but as containing only one people, united in interest as in dominion.'

Disappointingly for many, Pitt was later forced to abandon plans for Catholic Emancipation, a promise that had led to many Catholics in Ireland supporting the act.

7 February 1991

Provisional IRA attempts to assassinate John Major

On 7 February 1991, the Provisional IRA launched three mortar shells from an abandoned van approximately 200 yards from 10 Downing Street, where British Prime Minister John Major was meeting with his War Cabinet to discuss the conflict in the Persian Gulf, which had begun on 17 January. One of the shells exploded in the back garden.

Though the Provisional IRA had sometimes given warnings before launching attacks in the past, no warning was given in this case. It was the first time the group had used mortars outside Northern Ireland, and at least the second time it had attempted to assassinate a sitting British Prime Minister (after the Brighton hotel bombing of 1984, which killed five people).

Major was unhurt but startled, telling those assembled: 'I think we'd better start again somewhere else.' Later, the Provisional IRA released a statement: 'The operation had been planned over a number of months. Its inception predates both John Major's coming to power and the beginning of British involvement in the gulf war … while nationalist people in the six counties are forced to live under British rule, then the British Cabinet will be forced to meet in bunkers.'

Major was resolute in the House of Commons that day, stating: 'I think it is clear that it was a deliberate attempt this morning both to kill the Cabinet and to do damage to our democratic system of government … The IRA's record is one of failure in every respect, and that failure was demonstrated yet again today. It's about time they learned that democracies cannot be intimidated by terrorism, and we treat them with contempt.' The reaction from Neil Kinnock, the leader of the Labour Party, was equally condemnatory: 'The attack in Whitehall today was both vicious and futile.'

8 February 1983

Shergar is kidnapped

On 8 February 1983, Shergar, the most valuable racehorse in the world, was kidnapped from Ballymany Stud in Co. Kildare. He was never seen again. The abduction shocked both Ireland and Great Britain, where Shergar had won the 1981 Epsom Derby by a record 10 lengths. He was valued at $10 million at the time.

The stable groom at Ballymany, Jim Fitzgerald, along with his wife and seven children, was held at gunpoint when a group of men entered at approximately 8:30 p.m. He was forced to take the gunmen to the stable, where Shergar was put into a horsebox. Fitzgerald was then driven away in a van, and let out 40 kilometres from Ballymany Stud.

The kidnapping coincided – probably deliberately – with the year's biggest horse auction at Goffs nearby. As a result, there were horseboxes all over the area, making it even more difficult to locate Shergar. Though no one has ever admitted responsibility for kidnapping the horse, at least two former members of the Provisional IRA claimed that the paramilitary organisation carried it out. Sean O'Callaghan, who worked as an intelligence agent for the Irish government within the Garda Síochána's Special Branch, said that he was told Shergar had to be killed because he could not be kept under control, and that he was buried in Ballinamore, Co. Leitrim.

Kieran Conway, another former member of the Provisional IRA, said in 2018 that 'clearly' the IRA was behind the kidnapping. 'He was an extremely valuable horse, the Aga Khan [Shergar's owner] was known to be an extremely rich man. He would not be concerned about the political implications of giving the IRA money unlike perhaps a southern businessman. I had no difficulty with that operation at all.'

9 February 1846

Robert Mallet presents paper on earthquakes

On 9 February 1846, Irish geophysicist Robert Mallet presented his paper 'On the Dynamics of Earthquakes' to the Royal Irish Academy. It began: 'The present Paper constitutes, so far as I am aware, the first attempt to bring the phenomena of the earthquake within the range of exact science, by reducing to system the enormous mass of disconnected and often discordant and ill-observed facts which the multiplied narratives of earthquakes present.'

Mallet would spend the next 30 years researching the science of seismology (indeed, he is credited with coining the word 'seismology'), compiling a list of every recorded earthquake in history. In 1849, he detonated 11 kg of gunpowder on Killiney Beach, Dublin, to measure the speed of shock waves travelling through different types of rocks. He went on to experiment with explosions in Dalkey Quarry.

In December 1857, the Basilicata region of Italy was hit with what was at the time the third largest earthquake in recorded history. Mallet travelled there on a grant to conduct the first detailed scientific study of an earthquake, deducing that the cause was shock waves from a deep focus or 'epicentre' (another term he coined).

Mallet was born in Dublin in 1801, to a family who owned an ironmongery. He studied at Trinity College Dublin, where he later applied to be chair of engineering, a position he did not get.

The year that he published his groundbreaking paper, Mallet became President of the Royal Geological Society of Ireland. Sadly, for the last seven years of his life he had no eyesight; he died in 1881. His unofficial status as the 'father of seismology' marks him out as one of the most important scientists in Irish history.

10 February 1932

Army Comrades Association is formed

On 10 February 1932, a meeting was held in Wynn's Hotel in Dublin, six days before a general election in which Fianna Fáil was poised to emerge as the largest party for the first time since the foundation of the state. It is generally accepted that the meeting was presided over by Thomas F. O'Higgins, whose brother Kevin O'Higgins had been shot dead by anti-Treaty IRA men while serving as Minister for Justice in 1927, and whose father had also died at the hands of the IRA, in 1923.

Given that Fianna Fáil had been founded by those on the losing side in the Civil War, tensions were high. There were rumours that a Fianna Fáil government might cut the pensions of members of the National Army of 1922–1924. Also, some still viewed Cumann na nGaedheal (the government party up to this point) as having sold out the ideals of the Irish Republic. As IRA man Frank Ryan would say, 'while we have fists, hands and boots to use, and guns, if necessary, there shall be no free speech for traitors.'

Thus, it was decided that an organisation should be formed to counter the IRA, and the Army Comrades Association (ACA) was born. In time, it would come to be better known by the unofficial nickname, the Blueshirts. Having been rebranded as the National Guard by leader Eoin O'Duffy in July 1933, the Blueshirts would be absorbed into Fine Gael in September 1933. Many decades on, the term 'Blueshirts' is still used pejoratively towards Fine Gael.

Though it is often claimed the Blueshirts were a fascist organisation on a par with Mussolini's Blackshirts or Hitler's Brownshirts, it is worth remembering that little actual violence is attributed to the organisation. Even Eoin O'Duffy, who left Fine Gael in 1934, repudiated anti-Semitism, telling a fascist conference in Montreux that he 'could not subscribe to the principle of the persecution of any race'.

11 February 1926

W. B. Yeats: 'You have disgraced yourselves again'

On 11 February 1926, during a performance of Sean O'Casey's *The Plough and the Stars*, a riot broke out. At its premiere in the Abbey Theatre in Dublin on 8 February, the play, which was set during the Easter Rising, had been attended mainly by government officials – including Ernest Blythe, Minister for Finance, and Kevin O'Higgins, Minister for Justice – and was well received.

On the second night, Sighle Humphreys, vice-president of women's republican group Cumann na mBan, began to hiss from the back row. Her uncle, Michael Joseph O'Rahilly, had been killed in the Easter Rising, so she had a personal connection to the events being depicted. The play's third performance, on 11 February, was attended not only by Humphreys but by Kathleen Clarke (whose husband and brother were executed after the Rising), Maud Gonne and several other women with republican connections. When the first act began, showing prostitute Rosie Redmond, played by Ria Mooney, the women demanded she be taken off the stage. At the beginning of the second act, attempts were made to calm the situation, to little avail. One woman shouted: 'Ask O'Casey to remove that scene and we will willingly look at the play. It is a disgrace in a Catholic country.'

Individuals rushed the stage, and several audience members left. Uniformed Gardaí also arrived, as well as playwright and senator W. B. Yeats, who addressed the audience: 'You have disgraced yourselves again. Is this to be an ever-recurring celebration of the arrival of Irish genius?' This was a reference to the riots that had occurred in 1907 during a performance of John Millington Synge's *The Playboy of the Western World*. Yeats could scarcely be heard over the noise, but his remarks would be widely remembered.

12 February 1997

Last killing of a British soldier in the Troubles

On 12 February 1997, Stephen Restorick, a 23-year-old lance bombardier in the British Army, was shot through the neck by a Provisional IRA sniper. He died shortly afterwards, the last of over 700 military personnel to be killed in Northern Ireland since the outbreak of the Troubles.

At the time he was shot, Restorick had just handed back a driving licence to Lorraine McElroy, who was returning to her children with ice cream. The bullet grazed McElroy on the forehead, but she was otherwise uninjured: 'The soldier checked my licence, handed it back to me and smiled, and thanked me. And just straightaway there was what I would describe as a crack and a flash ... There was blood pouring from my head. I actually thought that I had been shot, and my husband who was with me thought the same. I then heard the soldier groaning; he was on the ground beside my car ... I wanted to help him, you know. There was nothing I could do.'

Restorick's killing came at a febrile time in Northern Ireland. The Provisional IRA had announced a ceasefire in 1994, but it had collapsed in 1996 with the bombing of London's Docklands. Within the Provisional IRA – and its political counterpart, Sinn Féin – there were tensions over the path being followed by the leadership.

Bernard McGinn, the Provisional IRA member who was charged with the killing of Restorick, was sentenced to 490 years but released in 2000 under the terms of the Good Friday Agreement, having served 16 months. In 2006, Peter Rowe noted that more British soldiers had been killed on duty in Northern Ireland than in all the subsequent international armed conflicts in which they had been involved since the outbreak of the Troubles, including the Falklands, the Gulf War, Kosovo, Afghanistan and Iraq.

13 February 1966

'Bishop and nightie' incident on *The Late Late Show*

On 13 February 1966, the Bishop of Clonfert, Thomas Ryan, gave a sermon in which he condemned an episode of *The Late Late Show* that had been broadcast on Teilifís Éireann the night before. He had also sent a telegram to the host of the show, Gay Byrne, simply saying, 'Disgusted with disgraceful performance.' The bishop, addressing his parishioners in St Brendan's Cathedral, Loughrea, told them that parts of show were 'unworthy of Irish television, unworthy of Irish producers, unworthy of the Irish audiences for whom the programme was destined, unworthy of a public service which is being maintained by public monies contributed in taxes by Irish people'.

The source of the Bishop's ire was a segment in which a married couple, Richard and Eileen Fox from Terenure in Dublin, were asked various questions, separately, to see how closely their answers corresponded. One of the questions Byrne asked the woman was the colour of her 'honeymoon nightie', to which she replied that she hadn't worn anything at all. Byrne feigned incredulity, the audience erupted in laughter, and the quiz continued. Nonetheless, after the Bishop's sermon, audiences were divided over how to react.

Gay Byrne, often credited with bringing Ireland into the modern age, was forced to issue an apology shortly afterwards. He said: 'In my five years' association with *The Late Late Show* it has never been our intention that viewers should be embarrassed by the programme. It has always been our hope to make it as enjoyable as possible for as many people as possible, bearing in mind that it is an "ad lib" late night show for adult viewing. We now realise that part of last Saturday's show was embarrassing to a section of viewers and we would like to say that we are sorry for this.'

14 February 1981

Stardust fire

In the early hours of 14 February, Valentine's Day, 1981, a fire broke out in the Stardust nightclub in Artane, Dublin. Forty-eight people died and 128 were seriously injured, with minor injury to 86 others. The average age of those killed was 19. Some of the bodies were so badly burned that it would take until April 2007 for them to be correctly identified using DNA techniques, as in the case of Richard Bennett, Michael French, Murt Kavanagh, Eamon Loughman and Paul Wade.

There was an immediate public outcry, and a Tribunal of Inquiry was established, headed by High Court judge Ronan Keane. In November of that year it concluded that arson was the probable cause of the fire. The families of the victims rejected this verdict, and pushed for a new inquiry.

In 2008, Paul Coffey SC was appointed to conduct a review, and ruled out arson as a possibility, though the actual cause was not found. On 23 January 2009, the government said in a statement: 'None of the victims of the Stardust disaster or the persons present at the Stardust on the night of the fire can be held responsible for the fire.' However, it resisted calls for a fresh inquiry, saying that the lack of new evidence would mean that 'any such further inquiry would only at best produce a hypothetical finding of no forensic value.'

Family members of the victims welcomed the fact that arson had been ruled out. Antoinette Keegan, who lost two sisters, Martina and Mary, in the fire, said: 'We never believed it was arson and it is now recognised.' However, they disagreed with the conclusion that there was insufficient new evidence for another inquiry. In September 2019, the Attorney General, Séamus Woulfe, announced that new inquests would be held for the victims of the fire.

15 February 1995

Lansdowne Road football riot

On 15 February 1995, an international football match between the Republic of Ireland and England being played in Lansdowne Road, Dublin, had to be abandoned after 27 minutes when riots broke out in the stadium. This was shortly after David Kelly scored the only goal of the match, 22 minutes in. A goal from England's David Platt in the 26th minute was ruled offside, a decision that prompted England fans to begin hurling down missiles from the West Upper Stand, including bottles and pieces of wood broken off from seats. Underneath them, fans in the lower stands poured onto the pitch to avoid being hit.

The manager of the Ireland team at the time was England's own Jack Charlton. Fearing a backlash for the England team, as well as the possibility that England would no longer be allowed to host the 1996 UEFA European Football Championship, Charlton said, 'The whole nation is going to suffer because of 2,000 lunatics. It's crazy!' He consulted with England manager Terry Venables, saying, 'Get your lads together and we'll try to get away on the one bus.' Brendan O'Byrne, security officer for the Football Association of Ireland (FAI), would later say, 'It was like Beirut up there, a war zone.' Riot police were called in, dozens were injured, and 40 arrests were made.

It transpired that the England fans had been infiltrated by members of neo-Nazi group Combat 18, who had been planning the riot for three months. Peter Bain, MP for Neath, in a letter to *The Guardian*, said that 'Wednesday night's events were not mindless thuggery but organised political violence. Leaflets were circulated at football matches in London last Saturday which advertised the Ireland match and actively encouraged violence.'

16 February 1932

Fianna Fáil becomes largest party in Irish state

On 16 February 1932, an election took place that *Irish Times* journalist Ronan McGreevy has described as 'the most important in the history of the State'. For the first time, Fianna Fáil, the party founded by Éamon de Valera, overtook Cumann na nGaedheal, securing 72 seats on 44.5 per cent of the popular vote, and becoming the largest party in the country. It would remain the largest at every subsequent election until 2011, holding office for longer than any other party in any European country.

Debate leading up to the election was heated. The Irish Civil War had ended less than 10 years earlier, with approximately 1,150 killed on both sides. Cumann na nGaedheal, which would merge with smaller parties to form Fine Gael in 1933, took out a full-page advertisement on the cover of the *Irish Times*, which stated that 'The gunmen and communists are voting for Fianna Fail [*sic*] to-day – The party of "peace, plenty and piety" – How are *you* voting? – Vote for the government party.'

The ad also featured quotes from figures in Fianna Fáil – Dan Breen, Seán T. O'Kelly and Séamus Moore – as well as Peadar O'Donnell, the leader of the far-left political party Saor Éire. The attempt to draw parallels between the IRA and Fianna Fáil was obvious. Fianna Fáil's election material had described the Cumann na nGaedheal government as 'Government by the Rich and for the Rich'.

In any case, Fianna Fáil's strategy was the more successful. Though it fell short of an overall majority, its 72 seats were enough to form a government, with the help of the Labour Party, which had won seven seats and offered its support. De Valera become President of the Executive Council (a role later changed to Taoiseach) on 7 March 1932.

17 February 1980

Derrynaflan Chalice is found

On 17 February 1980, Michael Webb and his 16-year-old son found five eucharistic vessels at an ancient church near Killenaule, Co. Tipperary. The most famous of these was what came to be known as the Derrynaflan Chalice. Derrynaflan is an island surrounded by bogland, on which an abbey was sited. It is thought that the

hoard was buried in the ninth or tenth century to hide it from Viking raiders.

Reporting on the discovery on RTÉ, Don McManus said it had been described as 'the archaeological find of the century'. Michael was using a metal detector in the area, and initially got a weak signal. His son (also Michael), who was on half-term break from school, used his own detector to confirm the presence of something in the ground. In all, the discovery happened in about 20 minutes.

In March, the Derrynaflan Chalice was unveiled to the public in the National Museum of Ireland on Kildare Street, Dublin. An estimated 5,000 people showed up to see it – 600 in the first hour. Staff at the museum said it was the busiest day they had had since 1941, when an exhibition commemorated the 25th anniversary of the Easter Rising.

Accompanying the chalice were a paten, a liturgical strainer, and a bronze basin. The Webbs sought compensation to the full value of the hoard, refusing the £10,000 reward fee. In 1986, the High Court ruled in their favour, estimating the value at £5.5 million, which the government were instructed to pay to the Webbs. However, the Supreme Court ruled that the chalice belonged to the state. The National Monuments (Amendment) Act of 1987 later made it illegal to use a metal detector without express permission or a licence.

18 February 1366

The Statutes of Kilkenny

On 18 February 1366, Lionel of Antwerp, the son of King Edward III of England, summoned a parliament in Kilkenny. Lionel, who had been appointed Governor of Ireland in 1361, sought to put an end to the integration of Anglo-Norman landowners and the native Gaelic Irish, who had been intermarrying since Richard de Clare (Strongbow) married Aoife Ní Diarmait in 1171. These marriages, and the general absorption of Anglo-Normans into Irish society, would later be referred to in the phrase *Hiberniores Hibernis ipsis* or, in English, 'More Irish than the Irish themselves'.

The assimilation of the so-called 'old English' was a source of consternation to

Lionel. Thus, he enacted, on that day in February 1366, the Statutes of Kilkenny. These 35 clauses began with a preamble admonishing the English in Ireland for 'forsaking the English language, manners, mode of riding, laws and usages' and choosing to 'live and govern themselves according to the manners, fashion, and language of the Irish enemies'.

Marriages between the English and the Irish were now forbidden, as was the speaking of any language other than English by both the English and the Irish. Even hurling, described as a game 'with great sticks and a ball upon the ground', was prohibited. Men were instructed to accustom themselves to more 'gentlemanlike games' such as archery.

The Statutes of Kilkenny were ultimately impossible to enforce. Lionel left Ireland in 1367 and died the following year. The Hiberno-Norman Lordship of Ireland, which had begun in approximately 1171, came to an end in 1542 when Henry VIII was declared King of Ireland.

19 February 1901

Irish is spoken in the House of Commons

On 19 February 1901, Thomas O'Donnell, a recently elected MP for West Kerry and member of the Irish Parliamentary Party (IPP), was preparing to give his maiden speech in the House of Commons. Shortly after he began, he was interrupted by the Speaker, William Gully, who said, 'Order, order! The honourable member is proposing to address the House in a language with which I am not familiar, but which I presume is Irish, and he will not be in order in doing so.'

The rough translation of what O'Donnell said was: 'As an Irishman from an Irish-speaking constituency, a member of a nation which still preserves a language of its own and is still striving bravely for freedom ...' He continued, even after he had been told to stop, to which Gully said, 'The honourable member is disregarding my ruling, and I cannot allow him to address the House in any other language but English.' John Redmond, leader of the IPP, intervened, in English, saying to Gully: 'I wish to ask if there is any rule, written or unwritten, to prevent an honourable member speaking in the language which is most familiar to him ... in my own experience I have heard in one of the legislatures of the Empire – that of New Zealand – Maori members speaking in their own language, although the language used by the general body of the members was the English tongue.'

Edmund Leamy, IPP MP for North Kildare, brought up the 'fact that when the Irish Chieftains came over to England representing the Irish Parliament – which was being absorbed by this Parliament at the time of the Union – they were allowed to speak in the Irish language.' The commotion continued, until Redmond told O'Donnell not to address the house in Irish, but not to do so in English either.

20 February 1985

Desmond O'Malley abstains on Family Planning bill

On 20 February 1985, the Health (Family Planning) (Amendment) Act was being debated in Dáil Eireann. This amendment to the 1979 Act meant that, rather than needing a prescription to access contraceptives, people over the age of 18 could buy them from designated places, such as pharmaceutical chemists. It was introduced by the Minister for Health, Barry Desmond, a member of the Labour Party which, with Fine Gael, had formed a coalition in November 1982.

The party in opposition was Fianna Fáil, led by Charles Haughey, who opposed the amendment. However, Desmond O'Malley, a prominent Fianna Fáil TD, decided not to vote with his party. O'Malley gave a speech in which he referenced not only the issue of contraceptives, but the role played by the Roman Catholic Church in the Irish state, one of the reasons unionists in Northern Ireland were so opposed to a united Ireland: 'I am certain of one thing in relation to partition: we will never see a 32-county republic on this island until first of all we have here a 26-county republic … practising real republican traditions. Otherwise, we can forget about the possibility of ever succeeding in persuading our fellow Irishmen in the North to join us … In a democratic republic people should not think in terms of having laws other than those that allow citizens to make their own free choice in so far as these private matters are concerned … I stand by the Republic and accordingly I will not oppose this Bill.' O'Malley did not vote in favour of the Fine Gael–Labour bill, but he did not oppose it either, and it passed by 83 votes to 80.

Six days later, on 26 February 1985, O'Malley was expelled from Fianna Fáil for 'conduct unbecoming'. He went on to form his own party, the Progressive Democrats.

21 February 1941

First flight over the Donegal Corridor

On 21 February 1941, the first flight took place over the so-called 'Donegal Corridor', a thin strip of airspace between Northern Ireland and the Atlantic Ocean located in the Irish state. The approximately four-mile-long strip allowed Royal Air Force planes to travel from Belleek in Co. Fermanagh to Ballyshannon in Co. Donegal.

Ireland's neutrality throughout the period known as 'the Emergency' was a source of contention not only for the British but also for the United States, which put pressure on the government in Dublin to allow the airspace to be used, although the USA would not enter the war until after the attack on Pearl Harbor in December 1941.

In the lead-up to the first flight, Éamon de Valera met Sir John Maffey, the United Kingdom Representative to Éire, in London on 21 January, where an agreement was made. It was kept secret, with instructions for planes to keep at a 'good height' and not to fly over the Irish military installation Finner Camp near Ballyshannon. Indeed, on many occasions, members of the Irish Defence Forces helped recover men who had crashed in the Corridor and bring them to Belleek to be handed across the border. According to local Fermanagh historian Joe O'Loughlin, on one occasion a senior RAF man thanked the officer in charge of the Irish Army for the honour that had been paid to his dead comrades. 'Ours may be the honour, but yours is the glory', replied the Irish captain.

The corridor reduced the unprotected gap in the mid-Atlantic by at least 100 miles. The first flight over it was by a Stranraer flying boat, escorting the damaged SS *Jessmore* back to port.

22 February 1832

First interment in Glasnevin Cemetery

On 22 February 1832, Michael Carey, an 11-year-old from Francis Street in Dublin, became the first person to be buried in Glasnevin Cemetery. The boy had died the day before from tuberculosis, or consumption, as it was known at the time. Since then, more than a million people have been laid to rest there, including high-profile figures in Irish history such as Charles Stewart Parnell, Michael Collins, Éamon de Valera,

Constance Markiewicz, Maud Gonne, and Brendan Behan.

Another of the well-known figures buried in Glasnevin is Daniel O'Connell, who played a significant role in the cemetery being established. From the time of the Reformation onwards, Roman Catholics were forbidden from reciting funeral prayers in graveyards. In September 1823, the funeral of Arthur D'Arcy was taking place in St Kevin's Churchyard. When Dr Michael Blake, Catholic archdeacon of the Dublin diocese, was about to offer graveside prayers, he was stopped by a Protestant sexton.

The incident caused quite a bit of controversy, and O'Connell, who had founded the Catholic Association, became determined to establish a cemetery that was open to all religions. In 1828, a site at Goldenbridge in Inchicore was secured for the first Catholic cemetery in Dublin since the Reformation, for £600. Glasnevin Cemetery – initially known as Prospect Cemetery – was the sister cemetery of the one at Goldenbridge.

In 2007, shortly before he stood down as Taoiseach, Bertie Ahern announced plans, in conjunction with the Office of Public Works, to spend €25 million restoring Glasnevin Cemetery in time for the anniversary of the 1916 Rising, to put it, in the words of Glasnevin Trust CEO George McCullough, 'on a par with the likes of Arlington National Cemetery in Washington, DC and Père Lachaise in Paris'.

23 February 1943

Fire in St Joseph's Orphanage

On 23 February 1943, a fire broke out in St Joseph's Orphanage, an industrial school in Co. Cavan. Thirty-five girls, aged from four to 18, perished, as well as 80-year-old Maggie Smith, who was employed as a cook. As well as Cavan, the girls came from Dublin, Belfast and Enniskillen. The orphanage was run by the Poor Clares, an order of Roman Catholic nuns, and had officially opened in 1869.

The fire broke out in the basement of the building, where laundry was done, but not noticed until the very early hours of 24 February. When the alarm was raised, the 80 girls in the orphanage were gathered into an upstairs dormitory rather than evacuated from the building. As the fire spread, it became impossible for them to be evacuated through the main entrance.

Cavan did not have its own fire service, so Dundalk Fire Brigade, over 50 miles away, was the first to be contacted. When it arrived, its ladders could not reach the upstairs room. Some of the girls jumped, but many were too frightened to do so.

A public inquiry followed the tragedy, chaired by Judge Joseph McCarthy. It found that an electrical fault had started the fire. Secretary to the inquiry was Brian O'Nolan – better known by the pseudonym Flann O'Brien, under which he wrote novels such as *An Béal Bocht* and *At Swim-Two-Birds*. O'Nolan would compose a bitter limerick, with future Fine Gael TD Tom Francis O'Higgins, which stated that McCarthy had decided 'it had to be caused by a wire' to avoid blaming the nuns. This reflected the belief that the Poor Clares had not done all they could have to save the girls.

24 February 2007

'God Save the Queen' is sung in Croke Park

On 24 February 2007, Ireland and England faced off in a rugby match played in Croke Park, the headquarters of the Gaelic Athletic Association (GAA). (The usual international rugby venue at Lansdowne Road had been demolished for redevelopment.) As was customary, the British national anthem 'God Save the Queen' was to be sung before the game. This was quite controversial, not least because Croke Park had been the site of one of the most notorious mass shootings during the War of Independence, in which the Royal Irish Constabulary, accompanied by Auxiliary

forces, killed or fatally wounded 14 people in retaliation for attacks carried out by the IRA on the same day.

This would not be the first time that 'God Save the Queen' was heard in the stadium – it had been played in 2003 when Dublin hosted the Special Olympics – but in a game in which England and Ireland were directly in opposition, the symbolism was not lost. Another reason why the game was contentious was that Rule 42 of the GAA had only recently been amended, allowing so-called 'foreign games' such as rugby to be played in GAA-owned stadiums. Since its inception in 1884, the GAA had sought to work for 'the preservation and cultivation of our national pastimes', meaning mainly Gaelic football, hurling and camogie.

In the end, 'God Save the Queen' was sung with no disruption. There had been protestors outside the stadium from Republican Sinn Féin – a minor group that opposed the peace process and the Good Friday Agreement of 1998 – but they had little effect on what took place inside. When the time came for the Irish national anthem, 'Amhrán na bhFiann', to be sung, John Hayes, known also as 'the Bull' (pictured on facing page with team captain Brian O'Driscoll (left)), was in tears. The image of the burly rugby player caught up in the emotion of the occasion was seen throughout Ireland and Great Britain.

Ireland defeated England 43–13.

25 February 1915

Execution of the Iron 12

On 25 February 1915, 11 soldiers, a majority of whom were Irish, and a civilian were shot dead by German forces in Guise, northern France: the largest execution of its kind on the Western Front during the First World War. The killings took place in the courtyard of a château in the French town, where the soldiers had been hiding.

At the time, French and British soldiers had withdrawn to the River Marne after losing the Battle of Mons on 23 August 1914. The soldiers in question – six Irish, five English – were hiding in the woods nears Iron in the Aisne region of France. Locals brought them food and, with weather conditions worsening, they were taken in by the Chalandre and Logez families.

The executions resulted from a betrayal. Louis Bachelet, a Franco-Prussian war veteran in his 60s, informed the German authorities about the whereabouts of the men, because Vincent Chalandre's 16-year-old son Clovis was having an affair with the same woman as Bachelet. The woman in question was Blanche Griselin, a 22-year-old mother whose husband was away at the front.

When the men were found, they were badly beaten and forced to dig their own graves. Vincent was the 12th person shot. Tragically, his wife Olympe spent almost the rest of her life in a German prison, and died shortly after being released, having contracted tuberculosis meningitis. Clovis only lived to be 50, drinking himself to death on Armistice Day in 1948.

Despite being only 10 per cent of the British Expeditionary Force at the time, Irishmen amounted to 40 per cent of those executed (10 out of 24). After the 1916 Rising, German forces hoped to win sympathy from Irish prisoners of war and have them swap sides, a strategy that was ultimately unsuccessful.

26 February 1962

IRA border campaign ends

On 26 February 1962, the IRA's border campaign, codenamed Operation Harvest, officially came to an end, five years after it had begun. Launched on 12 December 1956, it was not a success. The IRA had promised that a 'new Ireland' would 'emerge, upright and free'. Instead, six members of the Royal Ulster Constabulary were killed, as well as eight IRA men, and four civilians with republican sympathies. Measures taken by the governments north and south of the border had led to internment for IRA suspects and harsh prison sentences for those convicted of IRA membership.

Drafted by IRA Chief of Staff Ruairí Ó Brádaigh, the 1962 statement began by saying that the 'leadership of the Resistance Movement has ordered the termination of the Campaign of Resistance to British occupation.' It acknowledged the lack of support for the IRA's campaign. A united Ireland, though still referenced in Articles 2 and 3 of the Irish Constitution, was not a pressing concern for most people: 'Foremost among the factors motivating this course of action has been the attitude of the general public whose minds have been deliberately distracted from the supreme issue facing the Irish people – the unity and freedom of Ireland.'

Charles Haughey, who was Minister for Justice at the time, welcomed the statement: 'It is good news that the campaign of violence in the vicinity of the border has been called off. It was a policy which Irish public opinion had rejected decisively.'

The failure of the campaign led to Ó Brádaigh standing down, to be replaced by the more Marxist Cathal Goulding. Goulding wanted the IRA to engage in parliamentary politics and for Sinn Féin to drop its abstentionist policy towards Dáil Eireann, something that was anathema to the more militant wing of the movement. Tensions at the end of the 1960s led to a split, and the birth of the Provisional IRA.

27 February 1983

Eamonn Coghlan sets world record for indoor mile

On 27 February 1983, Eamonn Coghlan, representing Ireland, set a new world record for running the indoor mile, becoming the first athlete to do so in less than 3 minutes 50 seconds. Coghlan was born in Drimnagh, Dublin, and educated in Glasnevin. He had set a world record for the indoor mile twice before, in 1979 and again in 1981 (both in San Diego). In 1983, he did it in the Brendan Byrne Arena in East Rutherford, named for the New Jersey Governor who was himself the grandson of Irish immigrants.

It had been a difficult month for Coghlan, whose father, Bill, died of a heart attack while visiting his son to see him run in the Wanamaker Millrose Games at Madison Square Garden. Coghlan's coach, Gerry Farnam, had died the year before. Speaking after the new record was set, the Dubliner said he had thought to himself, 'This is for you guys.'

Coghlan's nickname was 'the Chairman of the Boards', because of his mastery of the indoor mile. The record he set in New Jersey in 1983 remains the best time for any European athlete. In 1994, he came out of retirement to become the first athlete over the age of 40 to run an indoor mile in under four minutes, at Harvard Arena, Boston. Later in life, he was appointed to the Seanad (Irish Senate) by Taoiseach Enda Kenny.

Looking back on his time as an athlete, Coghlan commended those who supported him: 'Irish athletes were performing at the highest level and whether it was New York, Toronto, Dallas, Los Angeles or London, the Irish, more so than any other nationality, came out to cheer us guys on. It was great to be competing at the highest level on a consistent basis.'

28 February 1979

Charles Haughey: 'An Irish solution to an Irish problem'

On 28 February 1979, Charles Haughey, the Minister for Health, introduced a bill that allowed for the selling of contraceptives in chemist shops, with a doctor's prescription. Far from being a liberal breakthrough, it meant that Ireland was the only country in Western Europe where a prescription was required to buy condoms. Nevertheless, it was a step away from the Criminal Law Amendment Act of 1935, which had made it illegal for anyone to import or sell any contraceptive.

Haughey used a phrase when describing the act that would become synonymous with how people in Ireland addressed issues in ways that would not work elsewhere: 'This Bill seeks to provide an Irish solution to an Irish problem. I have not regarded it as necessary that we should conform to the position obtaining in any other country.'

Though the bill later passed, not all in the Dáil were pleased about its content. Dr Noël Browne, who had resigned from government in 1951 when his fellow cabinet members withdrew their support for his Mother and Child Scheme, slammed Haughey's bill, alluding to the 'Irish solution' line: 'That was one of the unwisest statements of all made about the Bill ... it was introduced only under duress following the Supreme Court ruling in the case brought by that unfortunate and courageous lady, Mrs McGee, in order to establish her rights to have family planning if she so wished.'

Mary McGee, a mother of four, had been told by her doctor that her life would be in danger if she had another child. She had attempted to import spermicidal jelly to use as birth control, but it was confiscated by the state, leading to a case in the Irish Supreme Court, which found in her favour in 1973.

29 February 1924

Last killing of a Dublin Metropolitan Police officer

Established in 1836, the Dublin Metropolitan Police (DMP) was one of two police forces in Ireland up to the birth of the Irish Free State, the other being the Royal Irish Constabulary. In 1925, it was amalgamated with the recently formed An Garda Síochána.

In the three-year period between establishment of Saorstát Éireann and the disbandment of the DMP, only one officer in Dublin was killed on duty – Arthur Nolan, on 29 February 1924. Nolan had joined the IRA in 1914 and taken the pro-Treaty side in 1922. He went on to become an Assistant Inspector in the Criminal Investigation Department (CID), a plain-clothes police force formed to tackle the anti-Treaty IRA during the Civil War. When the CID was disbanded, Nolan began working for the DMP. He was married and a father of eight.

On the evening of 29 February 1924, he was stationed in the barracks on Great Brunswick Street (since renamed Pearse Street), when a 55-year-old homeless man named George Lane entered the building. One of the policemen, Sergeant William Gibney, was familiar with Lane, who had made complaints against the DMP in the past. Lane was dismissed by Gibney as being 'not all there', and he left, only to return a few minutes later with a hatchet. Nolan was sitting at his desk, and did not have time to react before he was assaulted by Lane. Lane continued to swing the weapon at other men in the barracks, before several DMP men overpowered him.

Nolan succumbed to his injuries on 11 March. His funeral was held on 13 March in St Joseph's Church, Terenure, and his coffin, draped in the Irish tricolour, was brought to Glasnevin Cemetery, where he was buried. Lane was found to be suffering from 'persistent delusions of persecution' by Dr Hackett of Mountjoy Prison; he was sent to an asylum.

1 March 1981

Bobby Sands begins hunger strike

On 1 March 1981, Bobby Sands, a Provisional IRA member serving a 14-year prison sentence for firearms possession, began refusing food. This was the start of the 1981 hunger strike, an event that would see 10 men starve to death, and, crucially, popular support for the Provisional IRA expressed at the ballot box for the first time in Northern Ireland.

The 1981 hunger strike lasted 217 days in total. Its origins lay in the ending of so-called 'special category status' (SCS) for those convicted of terrorism offences in Northern Ireland, which had meant that such prisoners would not have to wear uniforms, could receive food parcels and were not required to work, among other privileges. These measures were withdrawn by Secretary of State for Northern

Ireland Merlyn Rees in 1976.

Five years on from that decision, Sands began his protest. A statement was issued by Richard O'Rawe, press officer for the Provisional IRA, and Danny Morrison, a spokesman for Sands: 'a number of our comrades, beginning today with Bobby Sands, will hunger-strike to the death unless the British Government abandons its criminalisation policy and meets our demands.'

The British Prime Minister, Margaret Thatcher, was uncompromising in her stance. Thatcher's close friend and colleague Airey Neave had been killed by an INLA bomb in 1979, prompting her to say, 'Some devils got him, and they must never, never, never be allowed to triumph. They must never prevail.' Shortly after the beginning of Sands' hunger strike, Thatcher remained steadfast. Speaking in Belfast, she said, 'There is no such thing as political murder, political bombing or political violence. There is only criminal murder, criminal bombing and criminal violence … There will be no political status.'

2 March 1978

U2 make television debut

On 2 March 1978, a band from Dublin called the Hype made their first ever television appearance, performing the song 'Street Mission' on the RTÉ show *Youngline*. A couple of weeks later, the Hype changed their name to U2; within a decade they were one of the most successful bands on the planet, their fifth album, *The Joshua Tree*, becoming the fastest-selling record in UK history to that point.

At the time of their TV debut, the members were still in their teens. Lead singer Bono (Paul Hewson) was 17, as was guitarist The Edge (David Evans). Bassist Adam Clayton was the oldest member at 18, and drummer Larry Mullen Jr was a mere 16 years of age. Mullen had started the group after posting a sign on a noticeboard in Mount Temple Comprehensive School in Dublin two years earlier looking for fellow musicians.

The spot on *Youngline* was secured through slightly deceptive means. Having heard that an RTÉ producer was visiting Mount Temple, Bono asked music teacher Albert Bradshaw if the band could audition for him. Bradshaw obliged, and brought the producer along. The Hype performed two songs – both covers of the Ramones – which the producer was told were original. Impressed, he invited them on the show.

As RTÉ was the state broadcaster, and many viewers were not old enough to see the Hype live, appearing on television opened them up to a much wider audience. Shortly afterwards, U2 won the top prize at the Limerick Civic Week Pop '78 contest, receiving £500 and a demo session with CBS Ireland. Accepting the award, Bono told reporters, 'This means we can solve our money problems in a big way, particularly with regard to equipment. Now we hope to be able to buy a van.'

3 March 1831

First clash of Tithe War

On 3 March 1831, 120 members of the Irish Constabulary, accompanied by a Major Brown, entered the village of Graiguenamanagh, Co. Kilkenny (referred to in Brown's statement as 'Graigue') with the purpose of seizing cattle in lieu of payment of the tithe, a tax of one-tenth of produce, and later cash, to be paid to the Church of Ireland. The police were, according to Brown, 'indefatigable in their exertions, out every day, and frequently twice a day'. This was corroborated by a letter from Sir John Harvey, dated 27 March 1831, in which he wrote 'This county continues in a very unpleasant state of determined hostility to the payment of tithes.'

The tithe was strongly disliked by Roman Catholics, who made up the majority of the people of Ireland, as well as Presbyterians. Though it had existed in Ireland since the sixteenth century, resistance came to a head when a local priest in Graigue, Fr Martin Doyle, told his parishioners not to pay it, nor to bid on any animals at auction that had been taken as compensation. This resistance spread throughout most of Leinster and eastern Munster.

It turned violent on occasion, as when at least 12 people were shot dead in Newtownbarry (now Bunclody), Co. Wexford, after throwing stones at police and yeomen. A process server named Edmund Butler was killed in Kilkenny in December 1831, along with a dozen men who had been hired to protect him.

The tithe war spread throughout Ireland, except for the predominantly Protestant counties of northeast Ulster. It was effectively ended by the Irish Tithe Act of 1838, which made landowners – most of whom were members of the established religion – liable for payment, rather than the Catholic renters.

4 March 1804
Castle Hill rebellion

On 4 March 1804, approximately 200 convicts working on the government farm at Castle Hill, New South Wales, rebelled, seizing weapons and starting fires, before following instructions from their leader, Philip Cunningham. Cunningham was a native of Clonmel, Co. Tipperary, and a veteran of the 1798 United Irishmen rebellion, whose death sentence for sedition had been commuted to life at Botany Bay upon his conviction in 1799. A skilled stonemason, Cunningham ended up in New South Wales working at Castle Hill. He tried to escape on a French vessel in 1802, for which he received 100 lashes.

Cunningham laid out plans to the rebels on 4 March, to attack the nearby towns of Parramatta and Sydney. However, the alarm was raised in Parramatta, and a 60-strong garrison prepared to defend it, aided by civilian volunteers. Learning of this, the rebels opted not to attack, but headed for the settlement of Toongabbie, apparently to induce other convicts to join them.

News of the rebellion reached Sydney, and a detachment of 56 men was sent to Parramatta under Major George Johnston. When Johnston met the rebels, he tried to coax a surrender, using Irish priest Fr James Dixon, who himself had been sent to Australia after being convicted on suspicion of involvement in the 1798 rebellion. Cunningham is said to have replied 'Liberty or Death' before being captured.

Soldiers opened fire on the rebels, numbering 260, who scattered. Fifteen were killed, six wounded, and 26 captured. Nine convicts, including Cunningham, would be hanged for their involvement in the failed rebellion, with nine others badly flogged. The site became known as Vinegar Hill, after the site of the battle outside Enniscorthy, Co. Wexford in 1798.

5 March 1867
Fenian Rising

On 5 March 1867, rebellions were staged throughout Ireland by the Irish Republican Brotherhood. This event would be, according to the 1916 Proclamation, the last of six times that the right to an independent Ireland had previously been 'asserted … in arms'. The 1867 rebels also issued a Proclamation, which began, 'The Irish People of the World: We have suffered centuries of outrage, enforced poverty, and bitter misery. Our rights and liberties have been trampled on by an alien aristocracy, who treating us as foes, usurped our lands, and drew away from our unfortunate country all material riches.'

The reference to 'Irish People of the World' may have been influenced by the fact that many of those involved in the rebellion had fought in the American Civil War, on both sides. One such veteran, General John McCafferty, had been a Confederate officer during that war but was arrested before the 1867 rebellion began.

The uprising was centred in Tallaght, a village located 20 km from Dublin; nearby hills made it easy for the rebels to escape. The plan was to lure troops from Dublin city, at which time the Fenians would take over military barracks there.

Barracks were captured in Dundrum, Stepaside and Glencullen, but the uprising was a failure, partly because of informants such as John Joseph Corydon, the Brotherhood's chief transatlantic courier, but also because of the efforts of Sub-Inspector Dominic Burke, who led the 14 armed constables that helped disperse several hundred Fenians in Tallaght after an exchange of shots that killed two of the rebels. Uprisings also took place Limerick, Tipperary, Cork, Monaghan and Louth, but were minor by comparison. The total death toll was 12.

The success of the Irish Constabulary in suppressing the rising led to the prefix 'Royal' being added to its name.

6 March 1988

Gibraltar killings

On 6 March 1988, three members of the Provisional IRA – Seán Savage, Daniel McCann and Mairéad Farrell – were shot dead by the Special Air Service (SAS) in Gibraltar. Though details of the event are hazy, with conflicting eyewitness testimony, it was confirmed by British Foreign Secretary Sir Geoffrey Howe the following day that all three were unarmed at the time of the shooting, and that the car parked by Savage near the residence of the Governor of Gibraltar did not contain any explosives, as had been reported. However, a set of car keys found on Farrell led to the discovery of a Ford Fiesta in Marbella that did contain a large quantity of Semtex, 200 rounds of ammunition, four detonators and two timers.

The killings were, unsurprisingly, a source of great controversy. Labour MP Eric Heffer sponsored a motion, signed by 60 fellow Labour MPs, that said the shootings were 'tantamount to capital punishment without trial' and 'an act of terrorism'. Taoiseach Charles Haughey said, 'We are greatly perturbed at the shooting dead of three unarmed Irish people in circumstances where it appears from reports that they could have been arrested by the security forces.'

The three IRA members became martyrs to the Republican cause, particularly Farrell, who had been released from HM Armagh prison in October 1986, having been sentenced to 14 years in 1976 for possessions of explosives and IRA membership. Farrell, aged 31 at the time of her death, has frequently been quoted as saying, 'I am oppressed as a woman, and I'm also oppressed as an Irish person.'

The Gibraltar killings took on greater significance on 16 March, when the funeral of the three IRA members in Milltown Cemetery was attacked by loyalist gunman Michael Stone.

7 March 1964
Arkle wins Cheltenham

On 7 March 1964, Arkle, a thoroughbred racehorse born at Ballymacoll Stud, Co. Meath, beat his rival, Mill House, in the Cheltenham Gold Cup. This was described by the *Irish Independent* as 'an extraordinary victory for an Irish horse' that sparked 'a huge outpouring of national pride'. Arkle would go on to win a total of three Cheltenham Gold Cups. He was owned by Anne Grosnevor, the Duchess of Westminster, trained by Tom Dreaper, and ridden by Pat Taaffe.

Mill House and Arkle had met before at the Hennessy Gold Cup in Newbury, where Mill House beat the Irish horse, and, indeed, Mill House won the Cheltenham Gold Cup in 1963. Though an English horse, Mill House had been purchased from Ireland by retired businessman Bill Gollings. On the Saturday in question, audiences tuned in to hear commentator Peter O'Sullevan describe the closing moments of the race: 'Here they come into the last. Arkle over first. Mill House over second on the run-in with 150 yards to go. It's Arkle for Ireland!'

Dominic Behan, the man behind such ballads as 'The Patriot Game' and 'McAlpine's Fusiliers', penned a song for the occasion, named after the racehorse. It depicted Dreaper as the object of ridicule by his English counterparts, told, 'If you think your horse can beat us you're runnin' short on brains', before Arkle's eventual victory. In 1966, *TV Times* magazine asked readers to vote for the most popular personality of the year. The Beatles came third, England captain Bobby Moore was runner-up, and Arkle was first.

Sadly, after an injury in December of that year, Arkle never ran again. His skeleton is on display at the Irish National Study in Tully, Co. Kildare.

8 March 1973

Northern Ireland border poll

On 8 March 1973, a 'border poll' was held in Northern Ireland. Voters were given the chance to express at the ballot box whether they wanted 'Northern Ireland to remain part of the United Kingdom' or 'to be joined with the Republic of Ireland outside the United Kingdom'. It was clear, unambiguous wording, though the details of how such a new constitutional arrangement as a united Ireland could be brought about were left unaddressed.

The reason was obvious – there was no hope whatsoever of a majority in Northern Ireland voting to leave the United Kingdom. Nationalists held that the Northern Ireland state had, since its creation in 1920, guaranteed a unionist majority in perpetuity, and that any attempt at a lasting peace would need to factor in the island as a whole.

Leading members of both the SDLP and Sinn Féin rejected the border poll. SDLP leader Gerry Fitt told the party's supporters in January of that year to 'ignore completely the referendum and reject this extremely irresponsible decision by the British Government'.

It would seem that Fitt's advice was heeded. Turnout was not high – 58.7 per cent – though, of those who did show up, an overwhelming 98.9 per cent (591,820 voters) said they wanted to retain the status quo, while 1.1 per cent (6,463 voters) supported unity with the Republic.

Shortly afterwards, Dáithí Ó Conaill, Vice-President of Sinn Féin, addressed supporters in Donegal: 'The Border poll will be viewed as one of the most stupid acts of the British Government. It is an insult to all Irish people that a foreign government should usurp the inalienable right of the people of this country to determine their own future ... British plebiscites retard the emergence of the New Ireland.'

9 March 1942

Tom McGrath escapes German POW camp

On 9 March 1942, Tom McGrath, a native of Co. Waterford and a corporal in the British Army, escaped from Stalag XXA, a German prisoner-of-war camp in northern Poland, where he was one of 20–30 Irish-born captives. For this, he received three medals, including the Military Medal for bravery, as reported in the *London Gazette* in May 1943. However, it was only in 2018, long after his death, that the medals would be collected by his son, also Tom, in a ceremony at the British Embassy in Dublin.

McGrath moved to Britain shortly after the Second World War began, and was serving in the 51st Highland Division when he was captured at Dunkirk in 1940. He was sent to Stalag XXA, which housed approximately 40,000 prisoners of war. Two years later, McGrath spotted a gap in the wire that surrounded the camp, and escaped with 200 Reichsmarks, a bar of soap and some chocolate.

Initially sheltered by locals, he was brought by train to Berlin on a fake ID, then on to occupied Paris. After crossing into Spain via the Pyrenees, he was captured by Spanish authorities and interned until 14 April 1943, before being sent back to Britain through Gibraltar. McGrath never returned to duty, opting to return to his home town of Portlaw, Co. Waterford, where he worked as a mechanic and set up a café. He died in 1968, when his son Tom was 16.

Speaking of his father years after the incident, Tom Jr said, 'That was a time in Ireland when you would not broadcast the fact that you were in the British army.' Though initially told that his father had forfeited the medals by not returning to service, Tom Jr appealed, and collected the medals in 2018.

10 March 2009

Martin McGuinness deems dissident republicans 'traitors'

On 10 March 2009, Martin McGuinness stood outside Stormont Castle with Peter Robinson, First Minister and leader of the DUP, and Hugh Orde, Chief Constable of the Police Service of Northern Ireland (PSNI). The three were giving a press conference in response to killings that had been carried out that week by so-called dissident republicans – IRA splinter groups opposed to the Good Friday Agreement.

Two off-duty British soldiers had been shot dead outside Massereene Barracks in Antrim town on 7 March, and PSNI officer Stephen Carroll had died at the hands of dissidents who fired into his car in Craigavon, Co. Armagh, the morning that the press conference took place.

McGuinness was now Deputy First Minister of Northern Ireland, a far cry from the days when he told attendees at a Sinn Féin Ard Fheis that he could 'give a commitment on behalf of the leadership that we have absolutely no intention' of taking up seats at Stormont. Though he claimed to have left the Provisional IRA in 1974, McGuinness never wavered in his support for IRA actions throughout the 1980s and 1990s.

Referring to the killings, McGuinness said, 'I have to appeal to my community and to everybody within the community to assist the police services, North and South, to defeat these people … they are traitors to the island of Ireland.'

It was an extraordinary moment. Hugh Orde would later say, '[H]ad I not been so tired, I think I would have fallen over.' Peter Robinson said, 'I didn't know he was going to use those words, nor do I think did his colleagues – it showed just how angry he was by what happened.' It also showed that McGuinness, despite his past, was firmly committed to maintaining peace in Northern Ireland at that time: a commitment that even his most fervent critics on the unionist side shared.

In response to the comments, Frankie Gallagher of the loyalist Ulster Political Research Group said that McGuinness and Sinn Féin had 'stepped up to the line and beyond it … They have demonstrated to the people in unionist communities that they are now committed and wedded to peace and non-violence.'

11 March 1597

Explosion destroys Dublin quays

On 11 March 1597, an accidental explosion ripped through the quays of Dublin, destroying between 20 and 40 houses and killing 126 people – 76 of them locals, 50 'strangers'. The population of Dublin at the time was approximately 10,000, meaning that more than one per cent of the city died in the blast. The equivalent number today would be in the thousands.

The backdrop of the explosion was the so-called Nine Years' War being waged against Hugh O'Neill, the second Earl of Tyrone. A consignment of gunpowder barrels had been shipped from the Tower of London and was being unloaded; 140 of the barrels, stacked near Wood Quay, were ignited. The cause has never been determined.

The effect of the explosion was made worse by the fact that a strike was taking place that very day: porters and carters were protesting the poor wages paid by one John Allen, a Royal officer who had left the quays shortly before the explosion to 'drink a pot of ale'. This led to a pile-up of barrels. William Russell, the Lord Deputy of Ireland, wrote in a letter shortly afterwards that a horse's hoof had most likely struck the cobbles and lit the spark. That did not stop Allen from being suspected of colluding with O'Neill, although, as historian Dr Colm Lennon noted, it 'is inconceivable that a citizen would deliberately be an agent of such an outrage given the closely-knit nature of the small urban community.'

This event, tragic as it was, led to a great expansion of the city eastwards in the mid-sixteenth century, and the use of brick in the construction of buildings, as opposed to timber.

12 March 1974

Senator Billy Fox is shot dead

On 12 March 1974, Billy Fox, a member of Seanad Éireann and former Fine Gael TD for the border constituency of Monaghan, was shot dead at the home of his partner, Marjorie Coulson. Both Fox and Coulson were members of the Church of Ireland, part of the minority Protestant population of the Irish state.

On the night in question, Coulson's home was raided by a dozen or so gunmen. Rumours had been circulating that the family were using their home to store weapons for loyalists. As Fox drove up to the house, he was approached by the intruders. Fleeing the scene, he was shot and left for dead in a nearby field. The Coulson home was set on fire.

Fox would be the only member of the Oireachtas – the Irish legislature – to be killed by paramilitaries during the Troubles, and the first since Patrick Reynolds of Cumann na nGaedheal in 1932. North of the border, political assassinations were more frequent – John Barnhill of the Ulster Unionist Party, killed in 1971 by the Official IRA; William Johnston of the UUP, killed in 1972 by the Provisional IRA; Paddy Wilson of the SDLP, killed in 1973 by the Ulster Freedom Fighters.

Fox's killing shocked the country. Future Taoiseach John Bruton said in 2004: 'If I am still angry, I can only imagine the feelings of those much closer to him than I.' George Coulson, father of Marjorie, would tell RTÉ, 'It left a lot of the community afraid at the time. Some of them thought they were next. The reason I think was to put a bit of fear into the Protestant community in the area.'

Five members of the Provisional IRA were found guilty of the murder, and sentenced to life imprisonment.

13 March 1846
Ballinlass evictions

On 13 March 1846, Mrs Marcella Gerrard evicted 300 tenants from her 7,000-acre estate in Ballinlass, east Galway. The tenants did not owe Mrs Gerrard any money; rather, they were forcibly removed, with the assistance of police and a large force of the 49th Regiment, so that the land could be used to graze livestock. Sixty houses were destroyed; one remained, that of a man and woman sick with fever.

Lord Londonderry, Charles Vane – a staunch Tory and Ulster landlord – investigated the incident, and, in the House of Lords on 30 March, said that he was 'deeply grieved' by it: '76 families, comprising 300 individuals, had not only been turned out of their houses but had even – the unfortunate wretches – been mercilessly driven from the ditches to which they had betaken themselves for shelter and where they were attempting to get up a covering of some kind by means of sticks and mud … these unfortunate people had their rents actually ready … If scenes like this occurred, was it to be wondered at … that deeds of outrage and violence should occasionally be attempted.'

Sympathy for the tenants was not universally shared in the House of Lords. Speaking days after the incident, Lord Brougham said, 'Undoubtedly it was the landlord's right to do as he pleased, and if he abstained he conferred a favour and was doing an act of kindness. If on the other hand he chose to stand on his right, the tenants must be taught by the strong arm of the law that they had no power to oppose or resist. Such was the law of the land, and property would be valueless and capital would no longer be invested in cultivation of land if it were not acknowledged that it was the landlord's undoubted, indefeasible and most sacred right to deal with his property as he wished.'

14 March 1984

Assassination attempt on Gerry Adams

On 14 March 1984, loyalist gunmen from the Ulster Freedom Fighters (a cover name for the Ulster Defence Association) opened fire on Gerry Adams while he was travelling in a car through the streets of Belfast. Adams was struck in the neck and shoulder, and rushed to the Royal Victoria Hospital. Despite the severity of his injuries, he survived.

Three men were arrested shortly afterwards, one of whom had accidentally shot himself in the leg. John Gregg and Gerard Welsh were sentenced to 18 years' imprisonment in March 1985, while driver Colin Gray was sentenced to 12 years. Had the men succeeded in killing Adams, it would have been one of the most high-profile political assassinations in Northern Ireland. Adams had taken over as leader of Sinn Féin in November 1983, a role he would retain for more than 34 years. He had also been elected as an abstentionist MP for West Belfast the previous year.

The UFF released a statement, acknowledging responsibility for the attempted killing of Adams and identifying him as 'Chief of Staff of the Provisional IRA ... responsible for the continuing murder campaign being waged against Ulster Protestants and ... therefore regarded as a legitimate target of war.' The statement continued: 'in the absence of any effective security measures taken to protect the lives of Ulster Protestants we are determined to seek out and destroy any or all key personnel within the republican terror organizations as they become amenable.'

Ian Paisley, leader of the DUP, who would share power with Sinn Féin after the signing of the St Andrew's Agreement in 2006, had little good to say about Adams on the day of his shooting: 'I have followed too many coffins in Northern Ireland over which Gerry Adams has rejoiced to feel any pain or sorrow over what took place today.'

15 March 1745

First maternity hospital in the British Empire is founded

On 15 March 1745, Bartholomew Mosse, a surgeon from Portlaoise (then Maryborough), opened the first maternity hospital not only in Ireland but in all of what was known as the British Empire. Mosse had travelled through England, France and Holland, committing himself to obstetrics.

At the time, expectant mothers in Dublin were forced to give birth in horrendous conditions. Mosse purchased a three-storey building in George's Lane, once a theatre where famed actress Peg Woffington used to perform. This new makeshift hospital opened with 10 beds and very basic equipment. The first patient was Judith Rochford, who gave birth on 20 March; within a year, 208 women had been admitted, and all their babies delivered, although only 109 survived, reflecting the tragic infant mortality rate in Dublin at the time. Demand for entry to the new premises was high, and Mosse continued to raise money through lotteries, concerts and other entertainments in the hope of expanding the hospital.

By the time a new hospital opened in what is now Parnell Square on 8 December 1757, 4,000 babies had been born in the George's Lane building. It was known as the Lying-In Hospital, but became better known as the Rotunda Hospital, designed by Richard Cassels, the same architect who had worked on Leinster House.

The Rotunda would be the site of many firsts. In 1947, its 200th anniversary was marked two years after the fact. The British Congress of Obstetrics and Gynaecology was divided between the Rotunda and the Royal College of Surgeons and Physicians, marking the first major international conference in the field of obstetrics since the outbreak of the Second World War. To this day, the Rotunda remains the oldest continuously operated maternity hospital in the world.

16 March 1988

Milltown Cemetery attack

On 16 March 1988, funerals were taking place for members of the Provisional IRA who had been shot dead in Gibraltar 10 days earlier – Daniel McCann, Seán Savage and Mairéad Farrell. The three were to be buried in Milltown Cemetery in Belfast, with an estimated 10,000 mourners attending, including the leaders of Sinn Féin, Gerry Adams and Martin McGuinness. As the third coffin was being lowered into the ground, an explosion was heard. Loyalist Michael Stone, a member of the Ulster Defence Association, had entered the cemetery and thrown grenades in the direction of those gathered around the plot. He also fired a Browning 9 mm pistol into the crowd.

People sought shelter behind headstones, and in the confusion and panic, 60 of those present were injured by shrapnel, bullets and splinters of marble. As Stone fled the scene, several people gave pursuit. He shot three men dead – Thomas McErlean, John Murray and IRA member Kevin Brady (also known as Caoimhín Mac Brádaigh). The crowd eventually caught up with Stone before the RUC intervened, saving his life. He was sentenced to a minimum of 30 years for the attacks, but released under the terms of the Good Friday Agreement in 2000. However, another attack on Adams and McGuinness in 2006, this time at Stormont, led to his being sentenced to 18 years in 2008.

The fallout from the Milltown Cemetery attacks was perhaps even more shocking. While Brady's funeral was being held three days later, two British corporals – Tony Wood and David Robert Howes – drove into the cortège. It is unclear whether this was an attempt to mount an attack or to provoke the mourners, or simply the result of carelessness on the men's part. In any case, the men were taken, stripped, beaten, and finally shot dead. Amnesty International described the killings as a 'gross breach of minimum humanitarian standards'.

17 March 1943

Éamon de Valera's 'happy maidens' St Patrick's Day address

On 17 March 1943, in the midst of the Second World War, Éamon de Valera took to Radio Éireann to give his St Patrick's Day address, an annual tradition since 1933. De Valera acknowledged what was happening outside the country's borders, but was focused on delivering a vision of a humble, self-sufficient Ireland, a mere two decades after the end of the Civil War.

After a preamble in Irish, he began by saying: 'Before the present war began, I was accustomed on St Patrick's Day to speak to our kinsfolk in foreign lands, particularly those in the United States, and to tell them year by year of the progress being made towards building up the Ireland of their dreams and ours … the home of a people who valued material wealth only as a basis of right living, of a people who were satisfied with frugal comfort and devoted their leisure to the things of the spirit – a land whose countryside would be bright with cosy homesteads, whose fields and villages would be joyous with the sounds of industry, with the romping of sturdy children, the contests of athletic youths and the laughter of happy maidens, whose firesides would be forums for the wisdom of serene old age.'

De Valera marked the religious holiday by mentioning St Patrick, who, he said, 'came to our ancestors 1,500 years ago' and helped make the 'country worthy to be called the Island of Saints and Scholars'. He also commemorated the fiftieth anniversary of the founding of the Gaelic League by Douglas Hyde, and stated that 'The Irish language spoken in Ireland today is the direct descendant without break of the language our ancestors spoke in those far-off days. As a vehicle of 3,000 years of our history, the language is for us precious beyond measure.'

18 March 1977

Disappearance of Mary Boyle

On 18 March 1977, Mary Boyle, a six-year-old girl from Co. Donegal, was last seen in Cashelard, Ballyshannon, where she and her family had been visiting her grandparents. Hers would become the longest-running missing persons case in the history of the Irish state.

Having stayed overnight in Cashelard for St Patrick's Day, Mary was playing outside with her twin sister Ann and brother Paddy, as well as two cousins. When uncle Gerry Gallagher was returning a ladder to a neighbour's home 400 yards away, Mary followed, but turned back when the two came to a water-filled patch. This was at approximately 3:45 p.m. At 4:30 p.m., Gerry returned, and it was discovered that Mary was missing.

Her mother would recall, 'I remember in desperation asking my mother to light a candle. I shook holy water all over the place. I felt so panicky and I remember I ran out to the rocks shouting and crying. I hoped and prayed that God would protect her … I got into the car and drove along the road in different directions. It was a nightmare.' Although the lake at Upper Cashelard was drained and a trench dug by a mechanical digger, no body was ever found.

Years later, Ann married, though not before pushing back the date repeatedly, hoping her sister would return and act as bridesmaid. Over the years, she would visit Stormont, Westminster, Brussels and Washington DC, raising awareness of Mary's disappearance, in the hope that help would be forthcoming. She was accompanied by controversial Irish journalist Gemma O'Doherty, whose 2016 documentary *Mary Boyle: The Untold Story* helped reignite interest in the case, though it led to O'Doherty being sued for defamation by Fianna Fáil politician and Donegal businessman Sean McEniff. In 2018, Gardaí made a renewed appeal for information relating to the case.

19 March 1642

Adventurers' Act is passed

On 19 March 1642, an act was passed in the Parliament of England with the rather cumbersome title 'An Act for the speedy and effectual reducing of the rebels in His Majesty's Kingdom of Ireland', though it became known more commonly as the Adventurer's Act. This piece of legislation sought to raise money to help England suppress the uprisings that had broken out in Ireland the previous year, in exchange for land confiscated from the rebels.

The Confederation of Kilkenny had been formed after the Irish rebellion of 1641, and would govern two-thirds of the island until the end of the decade. It posed a direct threat to the authority of Charles I, and necessitated action. The cost of land that the general public could purchase varied from province to province: in Leinster, 1,000 acres of lands, estates and manors were to be given in exchange for £600; in Munster £450; in Connacht £300; and in Ulster £200. In total, 2,500,000 acres of land in Ireland was set aside to satisfy the public debt, about 18 per cent of the total profitable land there.

By 1652, Ireland was declared subdued, largely because of the conquest by Oliver Cromwell and his New Model Army. Though many of those who had invested in Ireland sold their land, the need to compensate investors led to the Act for the Settling of Ireland on 12 August 1652, under which, it is said, 80,000 people were liable for the death penalty. Those who could not prove they had assisted the Parliamentary Army throughout the rebellion were to remove themselves west of the River Shannon, to Connacht or Clare, by 1 May 1654.

20 March 1914

The Curragh incident

In March 1914, tension was rising in Ireland over the issue of Home Rule. The Government of Ireland Act was likely to be passed on its third reading, and with Ulster Volunteers determined not to come under the jurisdiction of any devolved parliament in Dublin, civil war on the island looked a distinct possibility.

Sir Arthur Paget, commander-in-chief of Ireland, was summoned to London and told by War Secretary Arthur Seely that 800 men were to be sent to Ulster to reinforce depots and arms stores there. The Curragh Camp in Co. Kildare was the main military base of the British Army in Ireland at that point.

Returning to Ireland on 20 March, Paget relayed what he understood to be his orders to his staff officers, telling them that 'Active operations were to be begun in Ulster.' Outraged, 57 of the 70 officers in the Curragh opted to resign. This became known as the Curragh Mutiny, though 'mutiny' is perhaps not the right word to use, given that resignation was optional.

News of the resignations forced Asquith to publicly claim that the incident arose from an 'honest misunderstanding'. Hubert Gough, one of the officers who stood down, met with Seely shortly afterwards, and was given, in his own words, 'a signed guarantee that in no circumstances shall we be used to force Home Rule on the Ulster people'. The *Morning Post* triumphantly proclaimed that 'the Army has killed the Home Rule Bill'.

Meanwhile, nationalists in Ireland were furious at how Home Rule was being scuppered by what they saw as armed defiance. Roger Casement wrote a letter to the *Irish Independent* describing it as the 'Curragh coup d'état', and saying, 'We all know in our hearts that the "Union" means the military occupation of Ireland ... the cat is out of the Irish bag.'

21 March 1879

First successful test of Brennan torpedo

Born in Castlebar in 1852, Louis Brennan has been described as 'surely Ireland's most remarkable inventor', though he lived most of his life elsewhere. Shortly after his ninth birthday, Brennan moved with his family to Melbourne, Australia during the Victorian gold rush. At least five of his 10 siblings are said to have died during the Famine. Growing up, Brennan was a keen student, particularly curious about mechanical toys. It was this curiosity that led to the invention for which he would be most often remembered – the Brennan torpedo, the world's first practical guided missile.

The torpedo was successfully tested for the first time on 21 March 1879 in Hobsons Bay, Melbourne, where it 'excited wonder and approbation' among journalists, politicians and military officers. The missile travelled 400 yards for just over a minute at a speed of 11 knots, hitting its target, a boat that was offshore. Brennan had been granted a patent for his invention on 1 February 1878, with the title 'Improvements in machinery for propelling and guiding vessels on land and through air and water'. Rear Admiral J. Wilson RN, Commodore of the Royal Navy's Australian Squadron, sent a favourable report to the Admiralty shortly thereafter.

Though the test had demonstrated the workability of the Brennan torpedo, it would be years before it could be put into wide-scale use. Brennan and his partner, Melbourne businessman John Temperley, continued to work on the invention until, in 1887, the British parliament agreed the payment of £110,000 to the War Office for exclusive use of the torpedo: an enormous figure at the time. It would become a standard harbour defence throughout the British Empire, used everywhere from Malta to Hong Kong, until production was discontinued in 1906.

22 March 1895

Discovery of Bridget Cleary's body

On 22 March 1895, the body of Bridget Cleary, a 26-year-old dressmaker from Ballyvadlea, Co. Tipperary, was found in a shallow grave a quarter of a mile from where she lived. When details of the events that led to this discovery emerged, Justice William O'Brien said it 'spread a tale of horror and pity throughout the civilised world'. Bridget had been ill since at least 11 March; local doctor William Crean diagnosed her with bronchitis on 13 March. On the same day, she was visited by her priest, Fr Cornelius Ryan, who administered the last rites.

The following day, William Simpson and his wife, neighbours of the Clearys, visited the homestead and found Bridget being held down by three of her cousins and doused with a 'noxious liquid' (urine) by her husband, Michael, who had become convinced that the woman in his home was not his wife, but a fairy that had taken her place. Michael had been told by local *seanchaí* (traditional storyteller) Jack Dunne that, when a loved one was replaced by a 'changeling', there were nine days to reverse the act.

On 15 March, still unconvinced that the person in question was his wife, Michael set fire to Bridget using hot paraffin. After her body was found, he and several other people were arrested. Michael was convicted of manslaughter, while those who witnessed the crime or participated were found guilty of 'wounding' Bridget; they received sentences from six months to five years of penal servitude.

The killing had wider repercussions for Ireland, which, at that time, was seeking a form of self-government within the United Kingdom, known as Home Rule. The London correspondent of the *New York Times* wrote on 31 March 1895 that the episode was being 'cited by the anti-Irish papers here as evidence of the mental degradation and savagery of the Irish peasant population'.

23 March 1847

Choctaw Nation raises money for famine relief

On 23 March 1847, a meeting was chaired by William Armstrong at the Choctaw Agency in Scullyville, Oklahoma, for 'the relief of the starving poor of Ireland'. Armstrong, the son of a man from Co. Fermanagh, read to those assembled details of the blight that had infected the potato crops on which most of the people of Ireland subsisted, and the poor conditions in which those affected were living as a result. At the conclusion of the meeting, $170 was collected, though the larger figure of $710 has also been cited. In any case, it was an enormous amount of money for the Choctaw Nation to have contributed, having themselves been uprooted from their lands east of the Mississippi River 16 years previously.

Their generosity towards the Irish people at that time is remembered with great affection and gratitude. In 1995, President Mary Robinson visited the Choctaw Nation in Oklahoma to thank them personally, describing how Ireland was 'thousands of miles away, in no way linked to the Choctaw Nation until then, the only link being a common humanity, a common sense of another people suffering as the Choctaw Nation had suffered'.

In 2017, Chief Gary Dale Batton, the 47th Chief of the Choctaw Nation, travelled to Ireland with a delegation of approximately 20 members of the nation. They made their way to Bailick Park, Midleton, Co. Cork for the unveiling of *Kindred Spirits*, a sculpture dedicated to the Choctaw for their contribution. Speaking at the event, Batton said: 'It is hard for me to express what a great honour this is, this tribute to our Choctaw ancestors ... We know the story of the tragedy of all our people that we endured and overcame ... We have endured — the Choctaw people and the people of Ireland.'

24 March 1968

Tuskar Rock air disaster

On Sunday 24 March 1968, Ireland's worst air disaster took place. Aer Lingus Flight 712 left Cork on its way to London Heathrow at approximately 10:30 a.m., but lost control just before 12 noon and crashed near Tuskar Rock, Co. Wexford. The last message sent out by co-pilot Paul Heffernan was '12,000 ft descending, spinning rapidly.' All on board – 57 passengers and four crew members – died. More than half on board (36) were from the Cork area, with passengers from Great Britain, Switzerland, Belgium and the United States also among the dead. Only 14 bodies were recovered.

The exact cause has never been conclusively determined. In 2002, a report was compiled at the request of Minister for Public Enterprise Mary O'Rourke 'to shed further light, if possible, on the cause or causes of the accident'. The report found that the crash may have been the result of 'metal fatigue, corrosion, flutter or a bird strike'. However, it concluded that the related files should be closed.

One theory floated was that the flight was hit by a test missile launched from the British Ministry for Defence establishment at Aberporth in Wales. This was ruled out by the report, which stated: 'The International Team have carefully examined all aspects of the tests conducted in the UK ranges and of the sea and air activities performed on that Sunday. It is their opinion that all theories involving the presence of another aircraft can be rejected.' In response, a British Embassy spokesman said that the report 'puts to rest once and for all misleading suggestions that the disaster was caused by a UK aircraft or missile … Our thoughts are with the relatives and friends of those who were lost in the tragedy.'

25 March 1920

Black and Tans arrive in Ireland

On 25 March 1920, the first English recruits to the Royal Irish Constabulary disembarked at North Wall dock in Dublin. Because of a shortage of RIC uniforms, the men wore a mixture of dark green trousers and khaki tunics, a distinctive look that earned them the nickname 'Black and Tans'.

Paid 10 shillings a day, many of the Black and Tans were veterans of the First World War, and had little training as policemen. The guerrilla war launched by the IRA in January 1919 was ongoing, making Ireland increasingly difficult to govern. Field-Marshal Sir Henry Wilson wrote in his diary in January 1920: 'The state of Ireland is terrible. No one's life is safe, spies and murderers everywhere, the Cabinet absolutely apathetic. I urge with all my force the necessity for doubling the police and not employing the military.'

The Black and Tans would come to be notorious for their part in reprisals against civilians in Ireland, such as the sack of Balbriggan in September 1920 and the burning of Cork in December 1920 – despite the fact that an estimated one-fifth of them were

Irish-born. They were also on the receiving end of quite a lot of violence as part of the RIC. According to historian D. M. Leeson, 890 policemen were killed or wounded between July 1920 and July 1921, and of those attacked by the IRA, only a third escaped unharmed: 42 per cent were injured, and 24 per cent died.

Winston Churchill would later write: 'It has become customary to lavish abuse upon the Black and Tans and to treat them as a mob of bravos and terrorists suddenly let loose upon the fair pastures of Ireland. In fact, however, they were selected from a great press of applicants on account of their intelligence, their characters and their records in the war. Originally they were intended to supplement the hard-pressed Royal Irish Constabulary; but in grappling with murder they developed within themselves a very strong counter-terrorist activity.'

26 March 1990

My Left Foot wins two Oscars

On 26 March 1990, Jim Sheridan's film *My Left Foot* won two Academy Awards, having been nominated for five. Accepting his Oscar for Best Actor in a Leading Role, Daniel Day-Lewis began by saying, 'You've just provided me with the makings of one hell of a weekend in Dublin.' Day-Lewis's co-star Brenda Fricker also took home an Oscar, for Best Supporting Actress. More than 40 million viewers in the United States alone heard Fricker thank the Academy for 'giving me this, which I will take very proudly with me back to Ireland'. She was the first Irish-born actor to receive one since Barry Fitzgerald in 1945.

Inspired by the true story of artist Christy Brown, who was born in Crumlin in 1932 and soon after diagnosed with severe cerebral palsy, *My Left Foot* came at a time when Irish cinema was all but dead. Bord Scannán na hÉireann, the Irish Film Board, had been tentatively established in 1980 but abolished in

1987. None of the features it produced during that period were particularly successful.

My Left Foot changed that. Director Jim Sheridan's next film, *The Field*, also secured an Oscar nomination for its lead actor, Richard Harris. Neil Jordan, whose debut *Angel* had been the first film funded by the Irish Film Board, won an Oscar for Best Original Screenplay for *The Crying Game*.

In 1993, the Minister for Arts, Culture and the Gaeltacht, Michael D. Higgins, decided that funding should be reinstated. Years later, he would namecheck *My Left Foot* and the films that came after, saying 'The success of these projects coupled with intensive local lobbying by members of the film community led to my being able to convince the Cabinet of the day of the case for the re-establishment of the Irish Film Board.'

27 March 1650

Kilkenny surrenders to Cromwell

On 27 March 1650, Kilkenny, the capital of Confederate Ireland, surrendered to Oliver Cromwell. This was a decisive moment in ending the Irish Catholic Confederacy established in 1642, which had aligned itself with Charles I in the English Civil War. Charles had been executed on 30 January 1649, and Cromwell set out to regain control of Ireland, landing on 15 August 1649. He also sought vengeance for the massacre of Protestants in the 1641 rebellion.

In a declaration as Lord Lieutenant, on 14 January 1649, Cromwell said: 'Remember, ye hypocrites, Ireland was once united to England ... Englishmen had good inheritances which many of them purchased with their money; they and their ancestors, from you and your ancestors ... They lived peaceably and honestly amongst you ... You broke this "union"! You, unprovoked, put the English to the most unheard-of and most barbarous Massacre (without respect of sex or age) that ever the Sun beheld.'

By the time Cromwell reached Kilkenny in 1650, towns such as Fethard and Callan had already been taken. Cromwell hoped to bribe a Captain Tickell (Tickle) to allow him entry to the town, but this plot was discovered and Tickell hanged.

Kilkenny was controlled by Sir Walter Butler, whom Cromwell summoned to surrender on 22 March. Though Butler initially refused, Cromwell's Parliamentary forces overthrew Irish Town, and opened a breach in the wall of Kilkenny on 25 March.

Butler, knowing that resistance was futile, surrendered two days later. Unlike comparable skirmishes in Wexford and Drogheda, no civilians were killed at Kilkenny, and Cromwell even complimented Butler's Royalist garrison on its defence.

28 March 1646

The first Ormond Peace

In 1645, England was in the throes of a civil war. Charles I and his Royalists, at loggerheads with Parliamentarians, sought the military assistance of Confederate Ireland. Charles sent Edward Somerset, the Earl of Glamorgan, to negotiate on his behalf. Glamorgan, being a Welsh Catholic, seemed well suited to reach an agreement that allowed greater concessions to Irish Catholics regarding the practice of their faith.

Shortly before terms were agreed, Giovanni Battista Rinuccini, the Papal Nuncio to Ireland, caught wind of the negotiations, and expressed scepticism at the fact that they were taking place in secret. Before the terms could be finalised, a copy of the treaty was leaked and published by the English parliament, forcing Charles I to deny any knowledge and declare Glamorgan a traitor.

Glamorgan was then arrested by James Butler, the Marquess of Ormond, who was Lord Lieutenant of Ireland. Ormond was less forthcoming with allowances to the Catholics of Ireland, but, with Glamorgan out of the picture, he was unrivalled when it came to bargaining on behalf of Charles I. Thus, on 28 March 1646, the so-called Ormond Peace was signed. In exchange for greater freedom of religion, the Irish Catholics would send troops to reinforce Chester in England, which had been under siege since February 1645. However, this was unhelpful, as Chester had already fallen.

The Ormond Peace divided the Confederation. Rinuccini felt the concessions were not generous enough. He denounced all who supported the treaty, ordering their excommunication, and in September 1646, he joined with Irish clergy to create the 'New Supreme Council' in Kilkenny. The peace deal soon collapsed, with Confederate armies of Leinster and Ulster besieging Dublin later that year. It wasn't until the second Ormond Peace in 1649 that an alliance between the Royalists and the Confederates was secured.

29 March 2004

Smoking ban is introduced

On 29 March 2004, Ireland became the first country in the world to introduce a ban on smoking in all workplaces. Professor Luke Clancy, chairman of Action on Smoking and Health (ASH), described it as 'the health initiative of the century'. In 2003, Minister for Health Micheál Martin had announced his intention to have smoking prohibited in all workplaces by 1 January the following year. Though arriving a little later than expected, it was a success, which led to other countries following suit.

It was not without hitches, however. Prior to the ban, Martin's fellow Corkman Vincent Keaney, owner of a *Titanic*-themed bar and restaurant in Cobh, called for the minister to be dismissed by Taoiseach Bertie Ahern 'for acting like an idiot and … for being a zealot'. Keaney's sentiment was shared by many publicans throughout the country, where 10,000 bars, restaurants and nightclubs would no longer be able to allow indoor smoking without risking a €3,000 fine. The Irish Cigarette Machine Operators Association (ICMOA), which had 450 members, said they faced 'their darkest day'. According to spokesman Gerry Lawlor, 'All of our members are small business people and this ban … will have a devastating effect on our lives.'

The ban did not get off to the smoothest of starts. Fine Gael spokesperson for Justice, Equality and Law Reform John Deasy was sacked a mere two days after its introduction, when he lit up in the Dáil bar. In July, Fibber Magees on Eyre Square in Galway flouted the ban, inviting its patrons to smoke on its premises, for which it was fined €9,400. Nonetheless, within 12 months a reported 7,000 people had given up smoking, and cigarette sales in bars fell by 60 per cent.

30 March 1849

The Doolough Tragedy

On 30 March 1849, hundreds of Irish paupers were forced to walk overnight from the town of Louisburgh, Co. Mayo, to Delphi Lodge, roughly 10 miles south. An estimated 16 men, women and children died en route, on the road overlooking Doolough Lake. The event became known as the Doolough Tragedy. The people in question were in receipt of outdoor famine relief, and two commissioners had arrived in

Louisburgh to determine whether allowances of grain should be continued. The men departed Louisburgh for Delphi Lodge without the inspection having taken place.

The people were ordered to follow the commissioners to the lodge, and so, overnight, according to a letter printed shortly afterwards in the *Mayo Constitution*, 'hundreds of these unfortunate living skeletons, men, women and children, might have been seen struggling through the mountain passes and roads for the appointed place.' The letter was unsparing in its detail of the gruesome fate of those who died: a local woman named Dalton was said to have perished with her son and daughter, and two unnamed men were found a mile from Louisburgh, where they 'lay exposed on the road side for three or four days and nights, for the dogs and ravens to feed upon'.

From 1988 onwards, an annual commemorative walk was held by AfrI (Action from Ireland) between Louisburgh and Doolough. People such as Archbishop Desmond Tutu and Waylon Gary White Deer of the Choctaw Nation took part over the years. In 2013, Delphi Lodge allowed the walk to finish within its 1,000-acre estate: 'By opening our gates to the Afri Famine Walk, Delphi Lodge is acknowledging our part in what happened in 1849, instead of ignoring it, while showing to the world what we are today: an Irish country house which offers a welcome to all.'

31 March 1912

Home Rule monster meeting in Dublin

On 31 March 1912, an enormous rally was held in Dublin in favour of the imminent Government of Ireland Act, better known as the Home Rule Bill. More than 100,000 people gathered for the event, with 64 special trains bringing them from all over the country. On Sackville Street (later O'Connell Street), four platforms were erected, and on the one nearest to the Parnell Monument John Redmond took the stage.

In a speech that lasted just under 20 minutes, Redmond waxed lyrical about the crowd that had shown up: 'Every class is represented here, landlords and tenants, labourers and artisans ... In fact it is no exaggeration to say that this meeting is Ireland.'

Of course, at least one class was not represented: Ulster unionists, whose Dublin-born leader Edward Carson had described Home Rule as a 'nefarious conspiracy'. Redmond did try to reach out to unionists: 'I say to these fellow countrymen of ours, they may repudiate Ireland. Ireland will never repudiate them, and we today look forward with absolute confidence, in the certainty of the near approach of that day when they will form a powerful and respected portion of a self-governed Irish nation.'

On the third platform, Patrick Pearse, who would come to prominence four years later as one of the leaders of the Easter Rising, spoke with reluctance of his support for the Home Rule Bill: 'I should think myself a traitor to my country if I did not answer the summons to this gathering, for it is clear to me that the Bill which we support today will be for the good of Ireland and that we shall be stronger with it than without it ... Let the Gall [English] understand that if we are cheated once more there will be red war in Ireland.'

1 April 1234

The Battle of the Curragh

Richard de Clare, better known as Strongbow, arrived in Waterford in 1170, ushering in what is commonly referred to as the Norman conquest of Ireland. On 1 April 1234, his grandson Richard Marshal, the Earl of Pembroke, was wounded in the Battle of the Curragh in Co. Kildare; he died just over two weeks later.

At the time, Henry III was torn between two factions – baronial and Poitevin. Marshal had been a leader of the baronial party in England, and was unhappy with 'foreign' influence over the king from figures such as Peter des Roches, Bishop of Winchester and Peter de Rivaux, both Poitevins. In 1233, Richard refused to visit Henry at Gloucester for fear of an ambush, though the two reached a truce the following year on condition that Peter de Rivaux be removed from court.

However, in Ireland, conflict had broken out between Marshal's brothers and supporters of Henry III. Richard formed an alliance with Welsh prince Llywelyn the Great and crossed the water to Ireland, where he was met by Maurice FitzGerald, justiciar of Ireland, Walter de Lacy, Lord of Meath, and Hugh de Lacy, Earl of Ulster. Marshal was greatly outnumbered, with only 15 knights against a force of 140, though he is said to have done 'terrible execution. With one blow he lopped off the two hands of a gigantic Irishman who had stretched out his arms to seize him.'

It was rumoured that Peter des Roches had instigated the battle, which lasted for six hours. After being knocked off his horse, Richard was taken to Kilkenny Castle, where he died on 16 April.

2 April 1993

Annie Murphy is interviewed on *The Late Late Show*

On 2 April 1993, Gay Byrne interviewed Annie Murphy on *The Late Late Show*. The previous year, Bishop of Galway Eamon Casey had resigned following revelations that he had fathered a child, Peter, with Murphy in the 1970s, and had taken £70,000 from diocesan funds in Galway, which he had given to her. Prior to the interview, Murphy had written a book, *Forbidden Fruit: The True Story of My Secret Love for the Bishop of Galway*, a title that many saw as salacious in what was still one of the most devout nations on the planet.

Byrne was careful to present his questions in such a way as not to demonise Casey. At one point it was claimed that Murphy had introduced an audience member to a man – not Casey – whom she described as 'the father of my child'. 'That is a lie', Murphy flatly responded. Byrne at one point suggested that the book 'presumably ... will become a movie in due course', a comment that seemed to imply a financial motive to Murphy's actions.

Murphy brought up the fact that Casey had tried to persuade her to give Peter up for adoption. Byrne countered, 'He would say he was doing that, Annie, because he didn't have faith in your capacity to look after the child. That's what he would say.' 'And how do you know that?' Murphy replied.

Perhaps the most infamous exchange came towards the end of the interview, when Byrne said, 'If your son is half as good a man as his father, he won't be doing too badly.' 'I'm not so bad either, Mr Byrne', Murphy shot back, as the audience broke into applause.

3 April 1970

First killing of a Garda in the Troubles

On 3 April 1970, Garda Richard Fallon was shot dead by the Irish republican group Saor Éire while they were robbing a Bank of Ireland branch on Arran Quay in Dublin. He was the first member of An Garda Síochána to be killed since the Troubles in Northern Ireland broke out the previous year – indeed, the first to die at the hands of gunmen in more than two decades. Though a £5,000 reward was offered for information that would lead to the arrest of his killers, no one was ever convicted of the crime.

Fallon was 42 years old and a father of five. He became the first Garda to receive the Scott Medal for bravery posthumously, one of 92 medals given between 1923 and 1972. However, his son, also Richard, later noted with regard to the treatment of Fallon's wife, Deirdre: 'My mother paid for my father's funeral herself ... It was a complete circus around the funeral and then nothing, no backup, absolutely nothing.'

Journalist Stephen Collins spoke of members of the Irish cabinet who were rumoured to have ties to paramilitary groups such as Saor Éire: 'In the days following Garda Fallon's funeral there was outrage among the Gardaí when stories of indiscriminate ministerial contacts with subversives, including Saor Éire, gained wide currency.'

Saor Éire issued a statement in which it was unapologetic about Fallon's death: 'The Saor Eire Action Group wishes to draw attention to the fascist tactics employed by [Minister for Justice] Michael O'Morain and his political police in connection with the death of Garda Fallon ... We deny that Garda Fallon was killed, as the Government and the anti-socialist press suggest, in the course of protecting the public. He died protecting the property of the ruling class, who are too cowardly and clever to do their own dirty work.'

4 April 2007

Ian Paisley shakes hands with Bertie Ahern

On 4 April 2007, Ian Paisley, leader of the Democratic Unionist Party, publicly shook hands with an Irish head of government for the first time. Before meeting Bertie Ahern in Farmleigh House, Phoenix Park, Paisley said, almost inaudibly, to the press assembled: 'I have to shake hands with this man. Give him a grip!' The DUP and Sinn Féin, once bitter foes, would now be working together in a new Northern Ireland Executive.

For years, Paisley was the face of unionist intransigence. He was fiercely critical of former Northern Ireland Prime Minister and Ulster Unionist Terence O'Neill when O'Neill met Ahern's predecessor Seán Lemass in 1965. He had referred to the Irish government as 'our traditional enemy' in Brussels in 1979. He famously said that

'never, never, never' should the Irish state be given a say in Northern Ireland, in light of the Anglo-Irish Treaty of 1985. When the Good Friday Agreement was endorsed by 71.1 per cent of voters in Northern Ireland in 1998, he described it as 'the saddest day that Ulster has ever had since the founding of the province'.

Now, with the DUP the largest party in Northern Ireland and Paisley (pictured above with Bertie Ahern (right)) poised to take up the most powerful role there, his tune had changed. He expressed gratitude to Ahern for extending a welcome to him in the Irish capital: 'I would like to thank the Prime Minister for his invitation to meet with him today … I am proud to be an Ulsterman, but I am also proud of my Irish roots. My father's birth certificate was lodged here in the courts after he was born. Like many of his generation he fought to see, as a member of Carson's army, Ireland remain within the Union. But that, of course, was not as history planned it.'

5 April 1895

Oscar Wilde is arrested

On 5 April 1895, Oscar Wilde was arrested in room 120 (later suite 118) of the Cadogan Hotel in London. He had that very day withdrawn his libel suit against the

Marquess of Queensbury, with whose son Wilde was engaged in a sexual relationship.

The arrest could scarcely have come at a worse time for Wilde. Perhaps his most celebrated play, *The Importance of Being Earnest*, had opened at St James's Theatre in London on 14 February, on a night when Queensbury had to be prevented from entering the venue.

Queensbury, furious at the affair between his son and Wilde, later left a calling card at Wilde's West End club, describing him, in near illegible writing, as a 'posing somdomite [*sic*]'. Under the 1885 Criminal Law Amendment Act and the 1861 Offences Against the Person Act, sodomy was a criminal offence, and so Wilde decided to prosecute Queensbury for libel: a decision seen by many both at the time and in retrospect as a grave mistake. Queensbury's counsel was none other than Edward Carson, future leader of the Irish Unionist Party. When Carson asked Wilde if he had kissed a young male servant named Walter Grainger, Wilde foolishly replied 'Oh, no, he was a peculiarly plain boy … [and] unfortunately … very ugly.'

Under advice from his lawyer, Sir Edward Clarke, Wilde withdrew from his prosecution, and the trial collapsed on 5 April at 11:15 a.m. An arrest warrant for Wilde was issued at 4:55 p.m., and he was apprehended at 6:20 p.m., an event later immortalised in John Betjeman's poem 'The Arrest of Oscar Wilde at the Cadogan Hotel'. He was later convicted of gross indecency and sentenced to two years' hard labour, after which he fled to France, never to return to either Great Britain or his native Ireland again.

6 April 2005

Gerry Adams tells IRA: 'Now there is an alternative'

On 6 April 2005, Gerry Adams gave a statement in Belfast in which he called on the Provisional IRA to 'take courageous initiatives which will achieve your aims by purely political and democratic activity'. The previous December, £26.5 million had been stolen from the Belfast headquarters of Northern Bank. Hugh Orde, Chief Constable of the Police Service of Northern Ireland (PSNI), publicly accused the Provisional IRA of being behind the robbery.

In February of that year, Irish Minister for Justice Michael McDowell claimed that Sinn Féin and the Provisional IRA were 'directed by the same leadership'. Though

Adams denied being a member of the Provisional IRA, and said in relation to the Northern Bank robbery that 'No republican worthy of the name can be involved in criminality of any kind', his claims seemed to be falling on deaf ears. Even Senator Edward Kennedy, once one of Adams' closest allies in the United States, declined to meet him on St Patrick's Day, 'given the IRA's ongoing criminal activity and contempt for the rule of law'.

It was in this context that Adams called on the Provisional IRA to 'fully embrace and accept' democratic measures to bring about its aim of a united Ireland. Adams was unapologetic about his public support for the Provisionals, maintaining that 'there was no alternative' for nationalists in Northern Ireland: a claim somewhat undermined by the greater support for the SDLP throughout the Troubles.

He also laid out his vision for the future: 'In the past I have defended the right of the IRA to engage in armed struggle ... Now there is an alternative. I have clearly set out my view of what that alternative is. The way forward is by building political support for republican and democratic objectives across Ireland and by winning support for these goals internationally.'

7 April 1776

John Barry leads capture of HMS *Edward*

On 7 April 1776, Captain John Barry led the first capture of a British warship by an American cruiser. It was a far cry from Barry's roots in Tacumshane, Co. Wexford, where he and his family had once been evicted from their tenant farm.

Growing up, Barry expressed an interest in sailing, and under the tutelage of his uncle, Nicholas, who was captain of a fishing skiff at Rosslare, the young boy went from being a ship's cabin boy to a seaman. He later emigrated to what was then the Thirteen Colonies at the age of 16.

In his first contest at sea, Barry – who had been given a Captain's commission in the Continental Navy, signed by President of Congress John Hancock – led the USS *Lexington* in a one-hour battle with its British counterpart, the HMS *Edward*, at the end of which the British surrendered. Barry wrote to Congress detailing the escapade: 'Gentlemen: I have the pleasure to acquaint you, that at 1:00 p.m. this day, I fell in with the sloop, Edward belonging to the Liverpool frigate ... We shattered her in a terrible manner as you will see … I have the pleasure to acquaint you that all our people behaved with much courage.'

Residents of Philadelphia were delighted to see the *Edward* taken into the harbour. British Captain Andrew Snape Hammond would say, 'The North Side of Delaware Bay is encompassed with shoals and shallow water and this passage Mr. Barry is at present master of. I have chased him several times but can never draw him into the sea.'

Years later, Barry – often called 'the father of the American Navy' – would be honoured with a statue in Wexford. In 1963, visiting US President John F. Kennedy laid a wreath there.

8 April 1886

Gladstone introduces First Home Rule Bill

On 8 April 1886, the First Home Rule Bill – officially known as the Government of Ireland Bill – was introduced in the House of Commons. Prime Minister William Ewart Gladstone gave a speech extolling the virtues of Irish self-government, while acknowledging the resistance to it from 'a certain portion of Ulster'.

Gladstone had opposed Home Rule for Ireland earlier in his career, but said he was convinced of its necessity now, because 'five-sixths of its lawfully-chosen representatives are of one mind in this matter … I cannot allow it to be said that a Protestant minority in Ulster, or elsewhere, is to rule the question at large for Ireland.' The fact that Gladstone relied on support from Irish Parliamentary Party MPs to remain in power solidified his support for Home Rule.

However, though he may have wished for the bill to pass, resistance to it in Ulster was fierce, backed by Lord Randolph Churchill, father of the future Prime Minister, who had proclaimed in Larne that 'Ulster will fight, and Ulster will be right!'

Gladstone acknowledged that Anglo-Irish relations had been fraught: 'Go into the length and breadth of the world … find, if you can, a single voice, a single book … a single newspaper article … in which the conduct of England towards Ireland is anywhere treated except with profound and bitter condemnation … Think, I beseech you, think well, think wisely, think, not for the moment, but for the years that are to come, before you reject this Bill.'

However, the Bill *was* rejected, by 343 votes to 313. Ninety-three members of Gladstone's own party, the Liberals, were among those who voted against it. The defeat was celebrated in Ulster with rioting in Belfast, Derry and Ballymena, resulting in the deaths of seven people. Gladstone called a general election, and the Conservatives came to power, relying on the support of the new Liberal Unionist Party.

9 April 1912

Balmoral anti-Home Rule demonstration

On 9 April 1912, two days before Herbert Asquith was to introduce the Third Home Rule Bill, an enormous rally was held in Belfast, the largest demonstration yet against a Government of Ireland Act. At the Balmoral Agricultural Showgrounds, Edward Carson addressed a crowd of unionists, the exact number of whom is unknown, though it was said to surpass the 100,000 seen in Dublin the previous month in support of Asquith's bill.

In all, 70 Conservative MPs had come to Belfast for the meeting, and, as in Dublin, scores of trains had taken people to the showgrounds. Leader of the Opposition Bonar Law, whose roots were in Ulster, addressed the crowd: 'Once more you hold the pass, the pass for the Empire. You are a besieged city. The timid have left you: your Lundys have betrayed you; but you have closed the gates. The Government have erected by their Parliament Act a boom against you to shut you off from the help of the British people. You will burst that boom.'

That very day, the *Morning Post* published a poem by Rudyard Kipling – titled 'Ulster' – that laid out his sympathy for those opposed to Home Rule.

When Carson took the stage in Balmoral, he acknowledged that it was not just Ulstermen assembled, but also 'my own fellow citizens from Dublin, from Wicklow, from Clare, yes, from Cork, rebel Cork, who are now holding the hands of Ulster.' He continued: 'I tell you that when they are trying to force this Home Rule policy upon us by methods of this kind, it gives us the right to say: "Your bill has no moral force. We will not accept it, and as you have treated us with force, if necessary we will treat you with force."'

10 April 1998

The Good Friday Agreement is signed

On 10 April 1998, the Good Friday Agreement was signed. Alternatively known as the Belfast Agreement, it came after two years of talks between the British and Irish governments, as well as most of the major parties in Northern Ireland, and set out its stall with the first point of its six-point Declaration of Support, which described it as 'a truly historic opportunity for a new beginning'.

The agreement recognised the 'birthright of all the people of Northern Ireland to identify themselves and be accepted as Irish or British, or both', but also that 'the present wish of a majority of the people of Northern Ireland, freely exercised and legitimate, is to maintain the Union.' It would see the release of those convicted of terrorism offences after an 'accelerated' period of two years, provided that the organisations of which they were members were on ceasefire. It would also see the establishment of a new police service with 'support from the community as a whole', and North–South co-operation in agriculture, education, tourism, health and other areas.

Tony Blair and Bertie Ahern – British and Irish heads of government (pictured below on right and left respectively, with US Senator George Mitchell) – were

co-signatories, and clearly proud of the outcome. Ulster Unionist leader David Trimble said, 'I have risen from this table with the Union stronger than when I sat down.' Sinn Féin's Gerry Adams was less effusive, but nonetheless described the agreement as 'part of our collective journey from the failures of the past and towards a future of equals'.

The agreement would have to be put to a vote in Northern Ireland, as well as in the Republic, where Articles 2 and 3 of the Constitution needed to be changed as part of the process. Referendums were held concurrently on 22 May 1998, with 71.1 per cent of voters approving the Agreement in Northern Ireland and 94.39 per cent south of the border. The people had spoken.

11 April 1951

Dr Noël Browne resigns over Mother and Child Scheme

On 11 April 1951, Dr Noël Browne, then Minister for Health, resigned from government amid controversy over his plan to introduce the 'Mother and Child Scheme', which would offer free healthcare to expectant mothers and their children up to the age of 16. It was a shocking blow not only to Browne, but to the coalition government comprising Fine Gael, the Labour Party, Clann na Poblachta (of which Browne was a member), Clann na Talmhan and the National Labour Party. The government collapsed two months later.

The Taoiseach, John A. Costello, had privately warned Browne that he would not be supporting the bill on 14 March, but it was a letter to the Taoiseach from the Catholic hierarchy, signed by Archbishop John Charles McQuaid, that put the nail in the coffin for the Mother and Child Scheme: it outlined, in seven points, why the scheme was 'opposed to Catholic social teaching'. All the members of the cabinet withdrew their support, and Clann na Poblachta leader Seán MacBride requested Browne's resignation.

The day after he stood down, Browne spoke in the Dáil, saying that he accepted 'unequivocally and unreservedly the views of the hierarchy' but could not accept 'the manner in which this matter has been dealt with by my former colleagues in the government'. An *Irish Times* editorial the same day chillingly noted that 'the Roman Catholic Church would seem to be the effective government of this country.'

In the midst of the incident, Costello made a remark that, in retrospect, reaffirmed unionist fears from decades earlier that Home Rule meant Rome Rule: 'I am an Irishman second; I am a Catholic first. If the Hierarchy give me direction with regard to Catholic social teaching or Catholic moral teaching, I accept without qualification in all respects the teaching of the Hierarchy and the church to which I belong.'

12 April 1928

First transatlantic flight from east to west

On 12 April 1928, Captain James Fitzmaurice took off from Baldonnel Aerodrome in south Co. Dublin as co-pilot of the *Bremen*, a low-wing Junkers monoplane. Fitzmaurice, who was raised in Co. Laois, was accompanied by Captain Hermann Köhl and Baron Ehrenfried Günther Freiherr von Hünefeld, owner of the *Bremen*. This would be a historic event in aviation – the first transatlantic flight from east to west. Nine years earlier, Britain's John Alcock and Arthur Brown had left St John's, Newfoundland and arrived in Clifden, Connemara: the first non-stop transatlantic flight. What Fitzmaurice and co. were about to undertake was even more challenging – their course was set against prevailing westerly winds.

Fitzmaurice had been interested in aviation from a young age, joining in when neighbours the Aldritts, a family firm of motor engineers, built their own ultimately unsuccessful aircraft, modelled on the Wright brothers'. Fitzmaurice fought in his teens in the First World War, when he also trained as a bomber pilot, though the conflict was coming to an end by the time he could fly.

The 1928 flight lasted 36 hours and ended with the *Bremen* landing on a frozen reservoir on Greenly Island, Quebec, on 13 April. Though their planned destination of New York had not been reached, it was a momentous achievement. The three were honoured with a ticker-tape parade in New York later that month, and became the first foreigners to be awarded the Distinguished Flying Cross, by US President Calvin Coolidge. They also received the Freedom of the City of Dublin in June 1928.

Seventy-five years after the *Bremen* left Baldonnel, the flight was recreated by Brigadier General Ralph James, the Chief of the Irish Air Corps, in a 21st-century twin-propeller plane.

13 April 1742

Handel's *Messiah* makes world debut in Dublin

On 13 April 1742, George Frideric Handel's *Messiah* was performed for the first time anywhere in the world, in Neal's Musick Hall on Fishamble Street in Dublin. The hall had been opened in October 1741, just as Ireland was coming to the end of a two-year famine that surpassed that of the mid-19th century in terms of the proportion affected (between 13 and 20 per cent of the 2.4 million people who lived on the island died). Two hospitals in Dublin – the Charitable Infirmary on Inns Quay and Mercer's Hospital in Stephen's Street – were full to capacity due to the outbreak of diseases that accompanied the famine. Thus, the Charitable Musical Society hit on the idea of inviting Handel, a German composer based in London, to perform a concert in order to raise money to help the poor.

Handel himself was in financial difficulty, and was more than happy to debut the oratorio, based on passages from the scriptures selected by his friend Charles Jennens. He arrived on 17 November 1741, and wrote to Jennens on 23 December: 'I cannot sufficiently express the kind treatment I receive here; but the Politeness of this generous Nation cannot be unknown to you.'

Rehearsals got under way in February 1742, with Handel personally asking for permission from Jonathan Swift – Dean of St Patrick's Cathedral – for its choir to take part. An early preview of the show was reviewed in *Faulkner's Dublin Journal*, describing it as 'the Finest Composition of Musik that ever was heard'. Over 700 people attended the premiere on 13 April, with another review in the *Journal* gushing, 'Words are wanting to express the exquisite delight it afforded to the admiring and crowded Audience.' The concert raised £400 to be divided among three charities; Handel did not take a fee.

14 April 1848

Irish tricolour is unveiled for the first time

On 14 April 1848, Thomas Francis Meagher unveiled the Irish tricolour – later to be designated the national flag of Ireland – to an audience of 2,000 in Dublin's Music Hall. Meagher, a founding member of pro-independence movement the

Irish Confederation, had just returned from Paris, accompanied by William Smith O'Brien and Edward Hollywood. All three had visited the French capital to mark the recent revolution there; indeed, the iconic French national flag of three vertical panels inspired its Irish counterpart. Meagher ostensibly received it from some French women sympathetic to the Young Ireland movement.

Addressing those assembled, Meagher said: 'From Paris, the city of the tricolour and the barricade, this flag has been proudly borne. I present it to my native land … I need not explain its meaning … The white in the centre signifies a lasting truce between the "orange" and the "green" – and I trust that beneath its folds the hands of Irish Protestants and Irish Catholics may be clasped in generous and heroic brotherhood.' Meagher's fellow Young Irelander John Mitchel is alleged to have looked upon the tricolour and said 'I hope to see that flag one day waving, as our national banner.'

Though neither Meagher nor Mitchel would live to see the tricolour become the national flag of Ireland, their words were prophetic, to a point. After 1922, it flew over government buildings in the newly established Irish state, but remained – and remains – a contentious symbol north of the border, where it most certainly is not seen by a majority of Protestants or unionists as symbolic of 'heroic brotherhood'. In 1964, there were riots in Belfast when a young firebrand named Ian Paisley insisted the tricolour be removed from Republican Party headquarters on Divis Street in Belfast.

15 April 1941

The Belfast Blitz

On 15 April 1941, approximately 180 Luftwaffe bombers flew over Belfast, dropping 203 tonnes of bombs and 800 firebomb cannisters. More than 900 people were killed in the attack, and 1,500 were injured. With the exception of London, no other city in the United Kingdom suffered as much in a single night. A Luftwaffe pilot would later say: 'Wherever Churchill is hiding his war material we will go … Belfast is as worthy a target as Coventry, Birmingham, Bristol or Glasgow.'

The Belfast Blitz of 15 April mostly hit residential areas in the north of the city. Phone lines to Great Britain were severed, and a railway telegraph was sent to Dublin asking for assistance. Éamon de Valera sent 71 firemen with 13 tenders from Dublin,

Dún Laoghaire, Drogheda and Dundalk to help extinguish the fire. A few days later, de Valera said in a speech in Castlebar, Co. Mayo: 'In the past, and probably in the present, too, a number of them did not see eye to eye with us politically, but they are our people – we are one and the same people – and their sorrows in the present instance are also our sorrows.'

One American living in the city later wrote a letter to his parents expressing his dismay as what he thought of as the cowardice of Belfast's fire brigade: 'You have heard about how tough the Irish are – well all I can say is that the tough Irish must come from [Southern] Ireland, because the boys up in [Northern] Ireland are a bunch of chicken-shit yellow bastards – 90 per cent of them left everything and ran like hell.'

Another attack came on 4 May, killing 191 people – a smaller number than before, partly because so many had fled the city.

16 April 1782

Henry Grattan: 'Ireland is now a nation'

On 16 April 1782, Henry Grattan spoke in the Irish Parliament, welcoming the news that legislative independence from the House of Commons had been granted (to an extent). A lawyer who represented the constituency of Charlemont in Co. Armagh, Grattan was so influential in securing this new-found control that the legislature in College Green where men would sit for the next 18 years became known as 'Grattan's Parliament'.

'I am now to address a free people,' Grattan began on 16 April. 'Spirit of Swift! Spirit of Molyneux! Your genius has prevailed. Ireland is now a nation.' Some believe the references to Jonathan Swift and William Molyneux were retroactively added to printed versions of the speech and not actually said by Grattan on the day. Nevertheless, they have become inseparable from the event.

Of course, freedom in this case was an exclusively male and Protestant privilege: the vast majority of the people of Ireland were not included. Grattan was, however, a supporter of Catholic Emancipation: 'The question is now, whether we shall grant Roman Catholics a power of enjoying estates, or whether we shall be a Protestant settlement or an Irish nation … So long as the penal code remains, we never can be a great nation; the penal code is the shell in which the Protestant power has been hatched, and now it is become a bird, it must burst the shell asunder, or perish in it.'

The Irish Parliament was abolished in 1800, after the failed United Irishmen rebellion of 1798. Grattan's son, also Henry, was a Member of Parliament for Dublin City from 1826 to 1830, and represented Meath for Daniel O'Connell's Repeal Association, which secured the Catholic Emancipation of which his father was a supporter. Grattan's great-grandson Sir Thomas Grattan Esmonde later became a Senator in the independent Irish Free State.

17 April 1876

The *Catalpa* rescue

On 17 April 1876, six Fenian prisoners escaped from Fremantle, Western Australia. Two years earlier, one of the prisoners smuggled out a letter to John Boyle O'Reilly, himself an escapee from the colony in 1869. Together with John Devoy, O'Reilly hatched a plan to spring their fellow Irish republicans from captivity. They arranged for a whaling ship called the *Catalpa*, captained by George Anthony, to set sail from New Bedford, Massachusetts on a round trip to Australia.

Devoy and O'Reilly also had IRB member John J. Breslin set out for Fremantle from San Francisco, posing as a British agent named James Collins, who would tell the Fremantle prison superintendent he was undertaking a surprise inspection. While this 'inspection' was taking place, notes were passed around by the six prisoners, detailing how the escape would be carried out. On 17 April, Easter Monday, the prisoners left the prison unguarded, on the understanding that they would report for work in the town. An escape by land seemed impossible to their supervisors.

They met with the rescue party, comprising Breslin and Thomas Desmond, and rowed for seven hours to reach the *Catalpa*, anchored far from the shore, only to be met by a British frigate, the *Georgette*. The Water Police in Fremantle had learned of the escape, and sent their fastest steamer to intercept the prisoners.

The prisoners made it on board, and the *Catalpa* was able to depart after it raised its colours and Captain Anthony declared, 'That's the American flag; I am on the high seas; my flag protects me; if you fire on this ship you fire on the American flag.' Anthony was happy to discharge his passengers in New York on 19 August, from where news of the escape of the 'Fenian Six' soon made its way around the world.

18 April 1949

Republic of Ireland is declared

On Easter Monday, 18 April 1949 – 33 years after the Easter Rising – the Republic of Ireland Act came into force, having been signed into law the previous December. This meant that the Irish state, comprising 26 of the 32 counties on the island, could be described as 'the Republic of Ireland'. There were those who insisted that Ireland had already achieved this status, including Éamon de Valera, who told independent TD James Dillon 'we are' a republic in the Dáil in 1945.

Now, however, Ireland would be officially leaving the Commonwealth, its last constitutional link to Britain. To mark the occasion, ceremonies were held in Dublin, Dún Laoghaire and Cork. On O'Connell Bridge, a 21-gun salute was fired by men of the 19th Field Battery. A detachment of 150 men from the FCA (Fórsa Cosanta Áitiúil, the local defence force) then fired a *feu de joie*, and buglers of the Army No 1 Band sounded the Reveille.

In Dún Laoghaire, a 21-gun salute was fired from the pier a minute after midnight, and in Cork, thousands gathered in Parnell Place and the South Mall, where Tom Barry, a veteran of the War of Independence and Civil War, read the 1916 Proclamation from the steps of City Hall. A minute after midnight, Radio Éireann broadcast the following message: 'These are the first moments of Easter Monday, April 18th, 1949. Since midnight, for the first time in history, international recognition has been accorded to the Republic of Ireland. Our listeners will join us in asking God's blessing on the Republic, and in praying that it will not be long until the sovereignty of the Republic extends over the whole of our national territory.'

19 April 1916

'Castle Document' is read at Dublin Corporation meeting

On 19 April 1916, five days before the start of the Easter Rising, Alderman Tom Kelly read a document at a meeting of Dublin Corporation. It was alleged that the document had been leaked from Dublin Castle – hence it became known as the 'Castle Document' – and contained information about 'precautionary measures sanctioned by the Irish Office on the recommendation of the General Officer Commanding the

Forces in Ireland'. These measures included the arrest of all members of the Sinn Féin National Council, the Executive Committee of National Volunteers and the Coiste Gnótha (Business Committee) of the Gaelic League. Also, inhabitants of Dublin would be ordered to 'remain in their houses until such time as the Competent Military Authority may otherwise direct or permit'.

Today it is generally thought that the Castle Document was a forgery, though this has been disputed. Historian Desmond Ryan, who fought in the GPO during the Easter Rising, later wrote that 'Forgery is a strong word, but that in its final form the document was a forgery no doubt can exist whatever.' Joseph Plunkett, one of the signatories of the Proclamation, is said to have printed it in his home in Kimmage on 13 April. However, Plunkett's bride, Grace Gifford, swore that she was with Plunkett when he decoded the message, and that it had been smuggled out of Dublin Castle by telegrapher Eugene Smith (or Smyth).

In any case, Eoin MacNeill, Chief of Staff of the Irish Volunteers, believed it to be genuine. He sent a message to all brigade commanders that began: 'A plan on the part of the government for the suppression and disarming of the Irish Volunteers has become known … Should you be satisfied that such action is imminent you will be prepared with defensive measures. Your object will be to preserve the arms and the organisation of the Irish Volunteers.'

20 April 1954

Last execution in the Irish state

On 20 April 1954, the last execution in the Irish state took place. Michael Manning, a 25-year-old carter from Limerick, was hanged by Albert Pierrepoint, an Englishman who had travelled to Ireland to carry out the punishment for a fee of £5 plus expenses. Pierrepoint's uncle, Tom, had been an active executioner in Ireland, and Albert had inherited the role from him, first assisting him in an execution in Mountjoy Prison in December 1932.

Manning's crime was heinous – he had beaten, sexually assaulted and finally suffocated a nurse, Catherine Cooper, who was 40 years his senior. Manning never denied the crime, but said that he had been drinking heavily in the Black Swan pub in Anacotty, Limerick. Returning home on foot, he spotted Cooper and, in his own words, 'suddenly lost my head and jumped on the woman', remembering 'no more until the lights of a car shone on me'. He was convicted of murder, which carried a mandatory death sentence. Members of Cooper's family signed a petition for clemency on Manning's behalf, but it had no effect on the outcome.

Manning's 22-year-old wife was pregnant at the time of his hanging. She applied for a death certificate shortly afterwards so that she could receive a widow's pension.

It has been argued that Brendan Behan's first play, *The Quare Fellow* – which, coincidentally, premiered in 1954 – went some way towards instilling in the public a sense of revulsion at capital punishment, which was reserved in 1964 by the Criminal Justice Act for those who had killed Gardaí, prison officers or diplomats, though no further executions took place. It was finally abolished in 1990, and a referendum in 2001 saw over 62 per cent of voters endorse a constitutional ban.

21 April 1916

Roger Casement is arrested

On 21 April 1916, Roger Casement was arrested after landing at Banna Strand, Co. Kerry aboard a U-boat with two other men, Robert Monteith and Daniel Bailey. The three had come from Germany, where Casement secured 20,000 rifles, plus ammunition, to be used in what would become known as the Easter Rising.

The rifles were sent over on the *Libau*, a German vessel disguised as a Norwegian ship, the *Aud*. When approaching Tralee Bay, the *Libau* was trapped by a blockade and escorted to Cork Harbour by HMS *Bluebell*. Upon approaching the harbour, its captain, Karl Spindler, scuttled the boat to prevent the rifles falling into the hands of the armed forces.

While Monteith and Bailey continued to Tralee, an exhausted Casement stayed in an ancient fort, where he was subsequently taken into custody by a Royal Irish Constabulary sergeant and constable. Ironically, Casement had known that the plan was doomed from the outset, writing of its 'stupendous idiocy, its fundamental falsity, its foredoomed failure', and had 'urged the dire importance of first sending messengers from here [Germany] to let the "Supreme Council" in Ireland know exactly what was going to be done'. This was refused by his comrades.

Casement was subsequently hanged for treason in Pentonville Prison. He was stripped of his knighthood, which he had received in 1911 for investigating human rights abuses in Peru. His 1904 report on the rubber plantations in the Congo Free State under Leopold II of Belgium documented shocking human rights abuses and earned him a reputation as a humanitarian.

In 1965 his remains were reinterred in Glasnevin Cemetery after a state funeral with full military honours, attended by 30,000 people.

22 April 1969

Bernadette Devlin gives maiden speech

On 22 April 1969, Bernadette Devlin gave her maiden speech in the House of Commons. At 21 years of age, she had just become the youngest ever female MP, elected in Mid-Ulster five days earlier. She stood on a Unity ticket against Anna Forrest of the Ulster Unionist Party, whose husband, George, had just died, vacating the seat. A gifted orator, Devlin held a prominent role in People's Democracy, a student organisation formed in Queen's University Belfast that sought to improve the civil rights of Catholics in Northern Ireland.

For someone like Devlin, who was not part of the unionist tradition, taking seats in Westminster and de facto recognising its legitimacy in Northern Ireland was a controversial step. Though Sinn Féin was not the political powerhouse it would become, its members refused to travel to Westminster, because, as future Deputy First Minister Martin McGuinness explained, they 'would not take an oath of allegiance to the English Queen'. It was a tradition dating back to the 1918 general election, which Devlin invoked: 'I stand here as the youngest woman in Parliament, in the same tradition as the first woman ever to be elected to this Parliament, Constance Markievicz, who was elected on behalf of the Irish people.' Markievicz, unlike Devlin, had refused to take her seat.

Devlin's speech did not play only to the Catholic or nationalist minority.

Responding to Robin Chichester-Clark, MP and brother of future Northern Ireland Prime Minister James Chichester-Clark, Devlin said he had 'no understanding of my people, because Catholics and Protestants are the ordinary people, the oppressed people from whom I come and whom I represent ... There is no place in society for us, the ordinary "peasants" of Northern Ireland.' She was steadfast in her condemnation of what she called the 'bigoted and sectarian Unionist Party, which uses a deliberate policy of dividing the people in order to keep the ruling minority in power and to keep the oppressed people of Ulster oppressed.'

23 April 1014

The Battle of Clontarf

The first Viking longships reached Ireland in AD 795, so Vikings had had a presence there for more than two centuries when the Battle of Clontarf was fought on 23 April (Good Friday) 1014. For longer than that, Ireland had been dominated by the Uí Néill dynasty, though there were also provincial rulers vying for control of the whole island.

One of these was Brian Boru – Brian of Béal Bóraimhe, near Killaloe in Co. Clare – who had ousted Máel Sechnaill mac Domnaill (a member of the Uí Néill dynasty)

as High King of Ireland in 1002. Brian ruled Ireland unchallenged for several years after that, until Máel Mórda mac Murchada, the King of Leinster, took umbrage with him. Brian had married Máel Mórda's sister, Gormflaith, only to discard her. As Máel Mórda was no longer willing to recognise Brian's authority, the stage was set for a battle.

Sitric Silkenbeard, the Viking King of Dublin, shared Máel Mórda's antipathy towards Brian. He sailed towards the Hebrides with a fleet of longships, and returned with men from as far away as Norway and France, led by King Brodar of the Isle of Man and Earl Sigurd of the Orkneys. Though Sitric's side included many Vikings, Brian was also aided by Vikings and foreign mercenaries. Brian himself did not fight on the day of the battle, as it was Good Friday, a Christian day of fasting and prayer. His son, Murchad, led the forces that locked horns with Sitric and Máel Mórda's men.

Many lost their lives, including Máel Mórda, Murchad and Earl Sigurd, and Brian's forces eventually won the battle, with almost all of his Viking enemies killed. However, King Brodar made his way to Brian's tent and killed him with a single blow of a battleaxe.

The victory of Brian's forces marked the beginning of the decline of Viking power in Ireland, though his death led to a power vacuum, meaning that the island was particularly vulnerable during the Norman invasion of 1169.

24 April 1916
Easter Rising begins

On 24 April 1916, the Easter Rising began. This rebellion would light the fuse that led to Sinn Féin winning a majority of Irish seats in the 1918 election on a platform of 'standing by the Proclamation of the Provisional Government', the first Dáil, the War of Independence, partition, and finally, an Irish state independent of the United Kingdom: followed, of course, by the Civil War.

The seven-man Military Council of the Irish Republican Brotherhood decided to proceed with the Rising on Easter Monday, instead of Sunday as originally scheduled, even though Eoin MacNeill, Chief of Staff of the Irish Volunteers, ordered that 'no movement whatsoever' be made upon learning that a ship carrying 20,000

German rifles had been intercepted and scuttled. After Volunteers were stationed throughout Dublin city, Patrick Pearse, who had been elected Commandant-General of the Army of the Irish Republic, read the Proclamation outside the GPO (General Post Office). It began: 'Irishmen and Irishwomen, In the name of God and of the dead generations from which she receives her old tradition of nationhood, Ireland, through us, summons her children to her flag and strikes for her freedom.'

Pearse said that 'the Irish Republic' was 'entitled to, and hereby claims, the allegiance of every Irishman and Irishwoman'. He went on to dismiss 'differences carefully fostered by an alien Government', a reference to Irish unionists, whom he and other IRB members believed had been hoodwinked into loyalty to Britain against their own interests. It ended with the names of the seven signatories: Thomas J. Clarke, Seán Mac Diarmada, Thomas MacDonagh, P. H. Pearse, Éamonn Ceannt, James Connolly and Joseph Plunkett. Shortly after, two flags were flown above the GPO. Eamon Bulfin raised a green flag with the words 'Irish Republic' painted on it in white and gold, and Gearóid O'Sullivan raised the Irish tricolour.

25 April 1938

Anglo-Irish Trade Agreement is signed

The Economic War between the Irish Free State and the United Kingdom began in 1933 when Éamon de Valera began withholding land annuity payments – repayments on loans given by the British to Irish tenant farmers to enable them to buy their land. De Valera had become the Irish head of government (later renamed 'Taoiseach') in 1932, and saw the payments – worth £5 million a year – as a drain on an already weak economy. His party, Fianna Fáil, became the largest in the state partly on a mantra of 'We Owe England Nothing.'

In retaliation, the British slapped a 20 per cent tariff on Irish imports, as well as quotas for Irish livestock. Ireland, in turn, put quotas on goods from the UK, including coal, cement, electrical goods, machinery, iron and steel. The Economic War ended up costing Ireland £48 million. Cattle exports were reduced by 35 per cent, and, according to writer Tim Pat Coogan, unemployment went from 28,934 in 1931 to 138,000 in 1935. There was a shortage of coal, and emigration – which Fianna Fáil had blamed on the British in its 1932 election material – increased.

In 1938, the two governments agreed to put the Economic War to an end, and an agreement was signed on 25 April. Under the terms of the Anglo-Irish Treaty of 1921, three ports in the Irish Free State – at Cobh (then Queenstown), Berehaven and Lough Swilly – were to remain under permanent British jurisdiction. Sensing that a world war was coming, de Valera secured control of the ports as part of the 1938 agreement. This would prove to be vital in retaining Ireland's neutrality during the Second World War. In exchange, Ireland made a one-off payment of £10 million in lieu of continuing the land annuity payments.

26 April 1916
Killing of Francis Sheehy-Skeffington

On 26 April 1916, Francis Sheehy-Skeffington was executed without trial on the orders of Captain John Bowen-Colthurst, in the midst of the Easter Rising. A committed pacifist – as well as a suffragist, atheist and vegetarian – he had expressed worries about the growing militancy of the Irish Volunteers in a letter to Thomas MacDonagh, printed in the *Irish Citizen* newspaper in 1915: 'I was on the point of joining you … I am glad now I did not. For, as your infant movement grows towards the stature of a full-grown militarism, its essence – preparation to kill – grows more repellent to me.'

The day before his killing, Sheehy-Skeffington was arrested on Portobello Bridge. He tried to prevent ransacking in the city, going as far as putting up posters that called upon citizens 'to prevent such spasmodic looting as has been taking place in a few streets'.

Returning from a meeting that evening, he was met by soldiers of the 11th East Surrey Regiment, who took him into custody. Bowen-Colthurst ordered his execution the following day, along with those of two journalists, Thomas Dickson and Patrick McIntyre, neither of whom had republican connections. Upon learning of his death months later, Constance Markievicz reportedly asked, 'Why on earth did they shoot Skeffy? After all he wasn't in it. He didn't even believe in fighting.'

Bowen-Colthurst was later found guilty of murder, but insane. He emigrated to Canada, where he lived until his death in 1965. Meanwhile, Hanna Sheehy-Skeffington, suffragist and wife of Francis, became even more militant later in life.

Arrested for crossing the border to Co. Armagh in 1933, she said during her trial: 'I recognise it as no crime to be in my own country. I would be ashamed of my own name and my murdered husband's name if I did.'

27 April 1916
Hulluch gas attacks

While the Easter Rising was taking place in Dublin, a greater number of Irishmen lost their lives in Hulluch, France than would die in the entire week of the rebellion. Beginning on 27 April 1916 and ending two days later, 538 men of the 16th (Irish) Division were killed when the German army released chlorine gas into their lines. Many of the men had been in the National Volunteers, who had sided with John Redmond when the Irish Volunteers split over whether to fight in the First World War.

At around 4:45 a.m. on 27 April, the Germans released a mixture of chlorine and phosgene gas from 3,800 cylinders, which blew into the trenches held by British troops. According to Lieut. Col. Edward Bellingham from Co. Louth, the commanding officer of the 8th Royal Dublin Fusiliers, 'Nearly all the men were killed or wounded.' Another gas attack came on 29 April.

The casualties in Hulluch compounded John Redmond's reaction to the Easter Rising, which he saw as a betrayal of the peaceful pursuit of Home Rule: 'Is it not an additional horror that on the very day when we hear that the men of the Dublin Fusiliers have been killed by Irishmen on the streets of Dublin, we receive the news of how the men of the 16th Division – our own Irish Brigade, and of the same Dublin Fusiliers – had dashed forward and by their unconquerable bravery retaken the trenches that the Germans had won at Hulluch?'

The Germans tried to capitalise on what was happening in Dublin. On 1 May, they hung placards from their trenches that read 'Irishmen! Heavy uproar in Ireland. English guns are firing on your wives and children.'

28 April 1916
The Battle of Ashbourne

On 28 April 1916, the Battle of Ashbourne took place. It was the only large-scale engagement outside Dublin during the week of the Easter Rising. Thomas Ashe was commandant of the Fingal Battalion (fifth battalion) of the Irish Volunteers, who successfully raided a Royal Irish Constabulary barracks in Ashbourne, Co. Meath. The battalion had already sent 20 of its men to aid James Connolly in the GPO, and so its numbers were depleted. Nevertheless, on 28 April, with vice-commandant Richard Mulcahy, Ashe led the attack.

Ten RIC men were stationed in the barracks: fewer than usual, as some had been sent to help quell the rising in Dublin. Two were stationed at the front, setting up a barricade, when they were disarmed and captured by the rebels. The eight inside refused to surrender, and a gun battle ensued.

This was only the beginning, however. Having caught wind of the rebels' presence in Ashbourne, armed RIC men in a convoy of 24 cars arrived at the scene. There were about 80 in total, to the Volunteers' 40 or so. Despite being outnumbered, the rebels surrounded the policemen and inflicted heavy casualties. Six officers were killed, as well as two travelling salesmen and a chauffeur for the police. Seventy RIC men surrendered.

Two days after the victorious engagement, Ashe would receive word from Patrick Pearse that the Rising was over, and for his men to surrender. Ashe was sentenced to death, though this was commuted to penal servitude. He would die after being force-fed while on hunger strike in Mountjoy Prison, Dublin in 1917. Before that, while in Lewes Jail in England, he wrote a poem, 'Let me carry your Cross for Ireland, Lord!' It would inspire a plaque unveiled in Ashbourne by President Seán T. O'Kelly on Easter Sunday, 26 April 1959.

29 April 1916

Easter Rising ends

On 29 April, Patrick Pearse, accompanied by nurse Elizabeth O'Farrell, surrendered to Brigadier-General William Lowe, thus bringing the Easter Rising to an end. Pearse had been the last man to evacuate the GPO the previous day, and he and the other remaining leaders were holed up in Plunkett's poultry shop at 16 Moore Street.

O'Farrell was the first to deliver the news to the British, meeting General Lowe on Parnell Street, who told her that he expected an unconditional surrender in 30 minutes. After returning with O'Farrell, Pearse delivered a note to Lowe: 'In order to prevent the further slaughter of Dublin citizens, and in the hope of saving the lives of our followers now surrounded and hopelessly outnumbered, the members of the Provisional Government present at headquarters have agreed to an unconditional surrender, and the commandants of the various districts in the City and County will order their commands to lay down arms.'

'Slaughter' was an appropriate word. The Rising had claimed the lives of 485 people, more than half of whom were civilians caught in the crossfire. Forty of those were children (under 17 years of age). Less than a third of those killed were British soldiers or police, and less than a fifth were the rebels themselves. All the leaders would be executed, starting with Pearse, Thomas Clarke and Thomas MacDonagh.

In total, 14 men met with firing squads (in addition to the hanging of Roger Casement). The *Irish Times* published an editorial after the Rising, calling for as much: 'The State has struck but its work is not yet finished ... The rapine and bloodshed of the past week must be finished with a severity which will make any repetition of them impossible for generations to come.' Ironically, it had the opposite effect – turning Pearse, Connolly and the others into martyrs.

30 April 1994
Riverdance debuts at Eurovision

On 30 April 1994, Riverdance was performed for the first time during the interval of the Eurovision Song Contest in the Point Theatre, Dublin, and broadcast to an estimated 300 million television viewers. Though not part of the competition that year, it arguably stole the show from the eventual winners, Paul Harrington and Charlie McGettigan, whose song 'Rock 'n' Roll Kids' was written by Brendan Graham. It was Ireland's third consecutive victory in the competition, a winning streak yet to be bettered.

Riverdance was the brainchild of Bill Whelan, who composed the music and lyrics, and featured the talents of Jean Butler and Michael Flatley, two American-born Irish dancers who choreographed the number. The performance started with a two-minute segment entitled 'Cloudsong', sung by choral ensemble Anúna, leading into Butler and Flatley, and ending with 24 other dancers accompanying them on stage. When it was over, it was greeted with a standing ovation from the audience of 4,000. Gerry Ryan, who co-presented the show with Cynthia Ní Mhurchú, asked the audience, 'Was that, or was that not, the most spectacular performance you have ever seen?' – hyperbole, perhaps, but it captured the mood of the evening.

Moya Doherty, who had commissioned the show for RTÉ, spoke of the impact Riverdance had: 'Just as my life changed with Eurovision 1994, so the cultural image of Ireland was also transformed. Irish culture, expressed in this case through dance and music, and as part of a wider, cultural awakening, took its place with confidence on the world stage.' She and her husband, John McColgan, expanded it into a stage show that had its premiere nine months later, and has since been performed over 11,000 times in 467 venues, in 46 countries, across six continents, to an estimated 25 million people.

1 May 1169
Norman invasion of Wexford

On 1 May 1169, Diarmait Mac Murchada (known also as Dermot MacMurrough) landed at Bannow Bay, Co. Wexford, with a force led by Robert FitzStephen, a Cambro-Norman soldier. In all, three ships, 30 knights, 60 men-at-arms and 300 foot-archers arrived, with the purpose of helping Mac Murchada reclaim his position as King of Leinster. Gerald de Barri of Wales, in his work *Topographia Hibernica*, referred to this as *adventus Anglorum* or 'the arrival of the English', though many academics see such a description as simplistic, given the various origins of those who arrived and subsequently settled in Ireland.

Mac Murchada had been expelled from Ireland in 1166 by Tigernán Ua Ruairc, King of Bréifne, whose hatred of Mac Murchada stemmed partly from the latter's abduction of Ua Ruairc's wife Derbforgaill in 1152. Mac Murchada had an ally in Muirchertach Mac Lochlainn, King of Tír Eoghain and High King of Ireland, until Mac Lochlainn's death in 1166.

Arriving in Bristol, Mac Murchada sought help from Robert Fitzharding, a nobleman and confidant of Henry II. According to the Anglo-Norman poem 'The Song of Dermot and the Earl', Mac Murchada offered to become the 'liege-man' of Henry II in exchange for his assistance. The town of Wexford was offered to Robert

FitzStephen and his half-brother Maurice FitzGerald, who accepted it.

FitzStephen later said to his followers, of Mac Murchada: 'This man loves our race, he is encouraging our race to come here, and has decided to settle them in this island and give them permanent roots here. Perhaps the outcome of this present action will be that the five divisions of the island will be reduced to one, and sovereignty over the whole kingdom will devolve upon our race for the future.'

2 May 1945

De Valera offers condolences to German minister

On 2 May 1945, two days after Adolf Hitler committed suicide, Éamon de Valera visited the Monkstown home of Dr Eduard Hempel, the German minister to Ireland, to offer his condolences. Though ostensibly the act of a neutral head of government, de Valera's decision is seen by many as an enormous diplomatic blunder that sullied the reputation of the Irish state – which had worked closely with the British in the war, albeit behind the scenes – and did a disservice to the tens of thousands of Irish citizens who fought with the Allies.

Defending his actions in a letter to Robert Brennan, the Irish envoy to Washington, de Valera wrote, 'So long as we retained our diplomatic relations with Germany, to have failed to call upon the German representative would have been an act of unpardonable discourtesy to the German nation and to Dr Hempel himself. During the whole of the war, Dr Hempel's conduct was irreproachable … I certainly was not going to add to his humiliation in the hour of defeat.'

Sir John Maffey, the British Representative to Ireland, would write, 'In the public mind, Mr de Valera's condolences gradually took on a smear of turpitude, and for the first time, and at a critical time, a sense of disgust slowly manifested itself.' Years later, Liv Hempel, daughter to the German envoy of the time, said, 'In hindsight, I believe that the reason De Valera called to the house was out of friendship. He and my father were personal friends: it wasn't simply a case of prime minister and diplomat. There was more than that. He visited because he knew my father, and the condolences were to my father because his position was finished … Hitler's death didn't mean a damn thing to my father; he was happy about it – like we are happy about Osama bin Laden.'

3 May 1921
Partition of Ireland

On 3 May 1921, the Government of Ireland Act came into effect and the island was partitioned into two states – Northern Ireland and Southern Ireland. In addition, a Council of Ireland was created, with 'a view to the eventual establishment of a Parliament for the whole of Ireland, and to bringing about harmonious action between the parliaments and governments of Southern Ireland and Northern Ireland'.

Superficially, little had changed. Both jurisdictions were still part of the United Kingdom, and so it would remain until 6 December 1922, when the Irish Free State was established. Immediately after that, on 8 December 1922, Northern Ireland opted out of the newly created dominion, remaining in the United Kingdom.

The Government of Ireland Act is often referred to as the Fourth Home Rule Bill. The First Home Rule Bill had been introduced in 1886, more than three decades earlier, but was scuppered because of opposition from Protestant unionists, predominantly in Ulster, who feared being subsumed in a Roman Catholic-dominated Dublin parliament. The solution reached, albeit with resistance both sides of the eventual border, was for six of the nine counties of Ulster to have their own assembly, and the rest of the island a parliament in Dublin.

Though Éamon de Valera would spend much of his life trying to bring about a united Ireland, he was opposed to forcing Protestant-majority counties in Ulster into an Irish Republic against the will of the people who lived there. Speaking in the Dáil in August 1921, he said that, were the Irish government to use force with Ulster, 'They would be making the same mistake with that section as England had made with Ireland … For his part, if the Republic were recognised, he would be in favour of giving each county power to vote itself out of the Republic if it so wished' (as recorded in *Dáil Debates*).

4 May 1925
Oonah Keogh becomes world's first woman stockbroker

On 4 May 1925, Oonah Mary Irene Keogh, aged 22, became the first woman stockbroker in the world when she was admitted to the Dublin Stock Exchange. In contrast, the first women were admitted to the New York and London Stock Exchanges in 1967 and 1973 respectively.

Keogh remained an active broker until her retirement in 1939. Before that, she had lived in Bayonne, France, to gain fluency in the language, and briefly lived in London. She was the daughter of a stockbroker, Joseph Keogh, who had once been the youngest ever bank manager in Ireland.

After Keogh submitted her application, there was some debate over whether a woman could become a full member of the Dublin Stock Exchange. The application fee was £500, and candidates had to hold securities of more than £2,000. They also had to provide references: her father gave one, as did Patrick Hogan, the Minister for Agriculture.

The approval of new members was the responsibility of the Minister for Finance of the fledging Irish Free State, and so the Committee of the Exchange could not reject Keogh's application on the basis of her sex. Within three weeks, she was approved. Initially an apprentice, she began trading on her father's behalf after he fell ill six months later. However, after his return, the two frequently quarrelled; though Keogh stayed with Joseph Keogh and Co. until 1933, she had become estranged from her father.

In an interview in 1971, Keogh discussed the segregation of men and women at the time: 'One of the disadvantages in those days was that women did not socialise with men in lounges of pubs. When the men retired to Jury's to relax after transacting business, I could not accompany them.'

Keogh later married a Russian exile named Bayan Giltsoff, settling in Kilquade, Co. Wicklow. She also spent some of her later life in Spain before passing away in 1988.

5 May 1981

Death of Bobby Sands

On 5 May 1981, Bobby Sands died after 66 days on hunger strike, the first of 10 hunger strikers to lose their lives between then and 21 August. Before his death, Sands had been elected to the British parliament in a by-election held in Fermanagh and South Tyrone, defeating Ulster Unionist candidate Harry West and receiving

51.2 per cent of votes. Sands stood on the Anti H-Block political label as an abstentionist candidate, with future Sinn Féin MP Owen Carron his election agent.

The day before his death, Sands' mother appeared outside the prison, pleading for calm. She told reporters, 'My son is dying. I want to appeal to the people to remain calm and have no fighting or deaths. My son has offered his life to improve prison conditions and not for death and destruction.'

The following morning, news of Sands' demise sent shockwaves throughout Northern Ireland. Riots broke out in cities, and in the largely nationalist New Lodge area of north Belfast, a milkman, Eric Guiney, and his 14-year-old son Desmond were hit with stones while travelling on his milk float. They lost control and crashed. Guiney died the following day, his son a week later.

Reacting to his death, Margaret Thatcher said, 'Mr Sands was a convicted criminal. He chose to take his own life. It was a choice his organisation did not allow many of his victims.' The Irish Republican prisoners in the Maze soon after released a statement: 'You have got your pound of flesh, now give us our rights. Do not for one minute think that we are going to allow you to rob us of our principles. There are more Bobby Sands in these Blocks and we will continue to die if need be to safeguard these principles.'

6 May 1882

Phoenix Park murders

On 6 May 1882, Lord Frederick Cavendish and Thomas Henry Burke were fatally stabbed in Phoenix Park, Dublin, by members of the Irish National Invincibles, a splinter group from the Irish Republican Brotherhood. Cavendish had arrived in Ireland that very day to take up his post as Chief Secretary, accompanied by Burke, the Head of the Civil Service.

Walking through the park at 5:30 p.m. on their way to Viceregal Lodge, the two were surrounded by nine members of the Invincibles, who attacked them with surgical knives. Burke, despite being a Roman Catholic who supported Home Rule, was the intended target, seen as a traitor by the Invincibles for working with the British administration in Ireland.

The investigation into the killings was headed by Superintendent John Mallon of the Dublin Metropolitan Police, another Catholic whose support for Home Rule did not extend to sympathy for militant nationalism. Several suspects were arrested, including James Carey, leader of the Invincibles, getaway driver Michael Kavanagh, and Joe Hanlon. All three were charged with murder, though Carey decided to testify against his co-conspirators in exchange for a pardon and safe passage to South Africa. As a result of his testimony and that of five other informers, five men – Joe Brady, Dan Curley, Michael Fagan, Thomas Caffrey and Timothy Kelly – were hanged between 14 May and 9 June 1883. Nine other men were sentenced to penal servitude.

Carey was smuggled out of Ireland by the authorities with his family, and boarded a ship bound for the Cape of Good Hope. Travelling under the name James Powers, he befriended another passenger, Patrick O'Donnell. Though there has been speculation that O'Donnell was an agent sent by the Invincibles, the prevailing wisdom is that upon learning of Carey's true identity, he shot him dead. O'Donnell himself was later executed.

7 May 1915
Sinking of the *Lusitania*

On 7 May 1915, the ocean liner *Lusitania* was travelling at 18 knots en route from New York to Liverpool when it was struck by a torpedo from a German U-boat about 11 miles off the Old Head of Kinsale, and sank in 18 minutes. As a result, 1,198 people died – among them 94 children, 34 of whom were infants.

The attack happened shortly after 2:00 p.m., and a message for assistance was received at Queenstown (Cobh) Harbour at approximately 2:15 p.m. Of the people who survived the attack, 761 were ferried to Queenstown, where they were put up in private homes and lodging houses or taken to hospitals.

A couple of days later, 193 of the dead were buried in the Old Church Cemetery in the town. Of these, 45 were unidentified, their coffins marked only by a number. Cork-born art collector Sir Hugh Lane and American businessmen Alfred Vanderbilt were among the more high-profile causalities.

Shortly before the *Lusitania* left New York, the German government had taken out advertisements in American newspapers. One said, 'Notice! Travellers intending to embark on the Atlantic voyage are reminded that a state of war exists between

Germany and her allies and Great Britain and her allies, that the zone of war includes the waters adjacent to the British Isles … travellers sailing in the war zone on the ships of Great Britain or her allies do so at their own risk.'

Given the number of Americans who lost their lives – 128 in total – the sinking of the *Lusitania* is seen as instrumental in changing US public opinion and thereby bringing about American entry to the First World War on 6 April 1917, two months after the US severed diplomatic ties with Germany.

8 May 2007

Ian Paisley and Martin McGuinness are sworn in

On 8 May 2007, Ian Paisley and Martin McGuinness were sworn in as First Minister and Deputy First Minister of Northern Ireland respectively. An image of the two men laughing together became ubiquitous; they were soon dubbed 'the Chuckle Brothers'. Few in Great Britain or on the island of Ireland could have foreseen a day in which Paisley and McGuinness shared a press conference together, let alone a position as leaders of the devolved assembly at Stormont.

For years, Paisley and the DUP had been a bulwark against any power being shared with Irish nationalism. At a press conference in 1998, DUP deputy leader Peter Robinson sneered at the idea of Sinn Féin being allowed into Stormont,

saying, 'The only cabinet the Provos should be in is made of wood and has brass handles.' Likewise, McGuinness, a prominent figure in Sinn Féin for decades, and an admitted member of the Provisional IRA at one time, repeatedly told supporters that his party would not take seats in the Northern Ireland Assembly. In 1988, a statement was issued that said, 'Sinn Féin is totally opposed to a power-sharing Stormont assembly … Stormont is not a stepping stone to Irish unity.'

Now, both would be in a power-sharing executive. Paisley reflected: 'If anyone had told me that I would be standing here today to take this office, I would have been totally unbelieving.' McGuinness, meanwhile, carefully avoided any reference to pledges he once gave not to take a seat in Stormont: 'I am proud to stand here today as an Irish Republican who believes absolutely in a united Ireland … As joint heads of the Executive, the First Minister and I pledge to do all in our power to ensure it makes a real difference to the lives of all our people.'

9 May 1671

Thomas Blood steals the Crown Jewels of England

On 9 May 1671, Thomas Blood attempted to steal the Crown Jewels of England from the Tower of London. This was the most infamous episode in a lifetime of similar adventures for Blood, who was born in Co. Clare, the son of a wealthy blacksmith who owned lands in Co. Meath and Co. Wicklow. Blood had fought in the Irish Confederate Wars, switching sides from the Royalist forces of Charles I to Cromwell's Parliamentarians. He had tried to capture James Butler, the Lord Lieutenant of Ireland, in 1663, but failed and fled to Holland.

His scheme in 1671 was his most elaborate yet. Disguised as a parson, he gained the confidence of Talbot Edwards, the 77-year-old assistant keeper in charge of the Crown Jewels. Blood promised Edwards that he had a nephew who would take Edwards' daughter's hand in marriage. No such nephew existed. On the night in question, Edwards and his family expected to meet this young suitor, who had 'two or three hundred a year in land'. Instead, he was assaulted by Blood and his accomplices after they gained entry to the tower, and tied up.

The men left with the crown and orb, but were stopped by Edwards' son, who had just returned from Flanders, and one Captain Beckham. Blood was overpowered and taken into custody. Amazingly, he managed to charm his way out of what would have been a severe punishment. After appealing to Charles II, Blood not only was pardoned, but received lands worth £500 a year.

English diarist John Evelyn, who met Blood once, said of the attempted Crown Jewels theft: 'How he came to be pardoned, and even received into favour, not only after this, but several other exploits almost as daring both in Ireland and here, I could never come to understand.'

10 May 1318

The Battle of Dysert O'Dea

While the Bruce campaign in Ireland was being conducted by Edward Bruce between 1315 and 1318, other battles occurred that did not directly involve the Scottish nobleman. One of the most decisive of these was the Battle of Dysert O'Dea, which took place in what was once Brian Boru's Kingdom of Thomond on 10 May 1318.

For generations, two factions of the O'Briens had been vying for control of Thomond. In 1318, the king was Murtough, and his challenger Mahon, who was allied with the Anglo-Norman Richard de Clare. The forces of de Clare met with those of Conor O'Dea, an ally of Murtough, in the village of Dysert O'Dea, near the present town of Ennis in Co. Clare.

De Clare divided his army into three columns, one of which he led to the home of Conor O'Dea, believing his opponent to be outnumbered. His forces were promptly ambushed, and de Clare himself was hacked to pieces. The remaining two columns sought immediate revenge, and O'Dea's troops were forced to take refuge in a nearby wood, until they were reinforced by the arrival of chieftain Felim O'Connor, who killed de Clare's son. There were still more Normans than Irish, and it looked as though de Clare's men could be victorious even having lost their leader.

Finally, Murtough and his men saw the burning houses from the battle, and rushed to meet their allies. O'Dea and O'Connor were not sure at first if those approaching were coming to help them, but victory was now assured. After the battle, de Clare's widow fled to England, never to set foot in Ireland again. Thomond remained free of foreign influence for another two centuries as a result of the battle.

11 May 1745
The Battle of Fontenoy

On 11 May 1745, at the Battle of Fontenoy, the Irish Brigade helped secure a victory for the French Army against the forces of the Pragmatic Allies – Austria, Britain, Hanover and the Dutch Republic. Indeed, it has been claimed that officers of the Irish Brigade charged towards the enemy, chanting 'Remember Limerick and Saxon perfidy', a reference to the Treaty of Limerick of 1691, which had ended the Williamite War in Ireland, and allowed around 11,000 of the defeated Jacobite troops to escape to France. However, this is probably apocryphal.

The battle took place during the War of Austrian Succession. French commander Maurice de Saxe placed the city of Tournai, located in the Austrian Netherlands (today Belgium), under siege. The Pragmatic Allies arrived to relieve the city, and Saxe, in turn, formed a defensive line in the village of Fontenoy, positioned at the top of a slope. The British, under the command of the Duke of Cumberland – George II's son – attacked a section of the French line between Fontenoy and the Bois de Barry. Though the British were able to drive the French line back, Saxe succeeded in forming counterattacks, including a ferocious one by the Irish Brigade. Cumberland's troops were forced to retreat.

James Joyce referenced the battle in his magnum opus *Ulysses* when minor character John Wyse Nolan bitterly remarked, 'We gave our best blood to France and Spain, the wild geese. Fontenoy, eh?' In fact, Joyce lived for a while on Fontenoy Street in Dublin, named for the battle.

On the 250th anniversary, Irish Defence Forces personnel, accompanied by representatives from France, England and Belgium, took part in a wreath-laying ceremony at a memorial in Fontenoy. An Post (the Irish postal service) and the Belgian postal service issued joint commemorative stamps.

12 May 1957
The *Rose Tattoo* scandal

On 12 May 1957, Tennessee Williams' *The Rose Tattoo* was staged in the Pike Theatre in Dublin, the opening play of the first Dublin Theatre Festival. Though the festival would grow in stature over the years, becoming the oldest of its kind in Europe, it was at the centre of a major controversy when director Alan Simpson was arrested for 'producing for gain an indecent and profane performance'. Williams' play included a scene in which a condom is dropped onto the floor. As condoms were not available legally in the Irish state at the time, there was uproar, although no condom was used – Anna Manahan, the actress alleged to have dropped the prophylactic onstage, used a paper envelope instead.

Word of the play's content had spread prior to the performance. Festival director Brendan Smith received a letter from a group calling itself the Irish League of Decency, which complained that it promoted the use of 'artificial birth control'. Simpson managed to convince them that it contained nothing of the sort.

His arrest did not happen until almost two weeks after the premiere. Initially, he and his wife, Carolyn Swift – co-founders of the Pike – were, in their own words, 'suddenly sort of celebrities, really, because the play had wonderful reviews'. This was short-lived, however.

On 23 May, a police inspector showed up to tell the couple that the production must be stopped, because its content was 'objectionable'. Two days later, Simpson was arrested. The subsequent court case dragged on for a year – during which Simpson was imprisoned for a short time – before being thrown out by the judge. By that time, legal costs had caused the permanent closure of the Pike.

13 May 1937

Statue of George II is blown up

On 13 May 1937, a bronze statue of George II in St Stephen's Green, Dublin was blown up, the day after the coronation of George VI in Westminster Abbey. It had been the first statue erected in the green, commissioned by Dublin Corporation and sculpted by John van Nost the younger. On a high pedestal, it could be seen from Nassau Street to the north and Aungier Street to the west. It was unveiled in 1758, and had been defaced before. This was more than mere vandalism, however: pieces of the statue's granite pedestal landed 30 yards away.

The *Irish Times* carried news of the incident: 'Shortly after eight o'clock … a deafening explosion shattered the quiet of St Stephen's Green, wrecking many windows in the surrounding houses, and causing a good deal of alarm among residents and passers-by.' Gardaí were on high alert that week, given that a new monarch was being crowned in England. Internal Garda reports later showed that the 'probabilities of attacks on premises and objects having British associations during this period were anticipated by the police, and … all necessary precautionary methods were taken … The advisability of placing an armed plain-clothes Garda to protect the equestrian statue of George II in Stephen's Green was discussed among other things.'

One person who was deeply upset by the bombing was W. B. Yeats, who wrote: 'I would go into mourning, but the suit I kept for funerals is worn out. Our tomfools have blown up the equestrian statue of George II in St. Stephen's Green, the only Dublin statue that has delighted me by beauty and eloquence. Had they blown up any other statue in St. Stephen's Green I would have rejoiced.'

14 May 1974

Ulster Workers' Council strike announced

On 14 May 1974, a debate was held in the Northern Ireland Assembly on a motion condemning the Sunningdale Agreement, which was signed by the British and Irish governments the previous December. The motion was defeated by 44 votes to 28, but Harry Murray, chairman of the Ulster Workers' Council (UWC), announced that a strike would begin, and not finish until a new Assembly election took place.

Though Sunningdale had the support of Brian Faulkner of the Ulster Unionist Party, most unionists were opposed to it. Earlier that year, 11 of the 12 Northern Ireland seats in the House of Commons were won by unionists under the umbrella title of the United Ulster Unionist Council, an organisation intent on bringing Sunningdale down. The following day, the UWC released a press statement: 'The Ulster Workers Council are determined that the Government shall not ignore the will of the majority of the people … A general industrial stoppage has been called.'

The UWC strike saw intimidation and threats of violence – on the second day, loyalist paramilitaries told workers at the Harland & Wolff shipyard that their vehicles would be burned if left in the car park after lunchtime.

Faulkner was outraged. He replied: 'Today's action by a group of people who have taken on to themselves greater importance than the democratically elected representatives of the people amounts to total abuse of the freedom of the press

… Who elected them? What is their authority?' British Prime Minister Harold Wilson made a television broadcast about the strike on 25 May, which struck a nerve with unionists, who he said were choosing to 'viciously defy Westminster, purporting to act as though they were an elected government; people who spend their lives sponging on Westminster and British democracy and then systematically assault democratic methods. Who do these people think they are?'

The strike dragged on until 28 May, when Faulkner stood down and the executive collapsed.

15 May 2007
Bertie Ahern addresses British parliament

On 15 May 2007, Bertie Ahern became the first Taoiseach to address a joint sitting of the House of Commons and the House of Lords at Westminster. Ahern, who was in his tenth year as Irish head of government, was introduced by Prime Minister Tony Blair as 'a personal friend, a true friend of the British people, a man who is changing the history of his own country and of these islands, a great Irishman'.

Ahern's speech lasted more than 20 minutes and touched on several subjects. He mentioned Daniel O'Connell and Charles Stewart Parnell, who 'came to Westminster to be a voice for the voiceless of Ireland and at times a conscience for Britain too'. He also mentioned that 'it was Ireland that first elected a woman, Constance Markiewicz, to the House of Commons – although she chose instead to take her seat in the first Dáil as elected by the Irish people.'

The peace process and the Good Friday Agreement – to which Ahern and Blair had been signatories – loomed large over the occasion, and Ahern was careful to acknowledge the 'thriving community of unionist people, proud of who they are, where they came from, and what they hope for', whom he described as 'a living bridge between us'. He also said that the two countries' 'partnership in the world is expressed most especially in the European Union. Our joint membership has served as a vital catalyst for the building of a deeper relationship between our two islands.'

Ahern concluded: 'Ireland's hour has come: a time of peace, of prosperity, of old values and new beginnings. This is the great lesson and the great gift of Irish history. This is what Ireland can give to the world.'

16 May 1945
De Valera responds to Winston Churchill

On 16 May 1945, Éamon de Valera gave a speech that was broadcast on Radio Éireann, three days after Winston Churchill had attacked Irish neutrality, and de Valera in particular, for being 'at variance with the temper and instinct of thousands of southern Irishmen, who hastened to the battlefront to prove their ancient valour'. De Valera's reply was, all things considered, rather measured. He began by saying: 'Certain newspapers have been very persistent in looking for my answer to Mr Churchill's recent broadcast. I know the kind of answer I am expected to make.'

De Valera went on to acknowledge that Churchill was 'in the first flush of his victory' and so his sense of excitement would be excused, in contrast to the 'quieter atmosphere' in which de Valera found himself. The Taoiseach then defended Irish neutrality by drawing parallels between England's war with Germany and what de Valera saw as Ireland's centuries-long war with England: 'Suppose Germany had won the war, had invaded and occupied England, and that after a long lapse of time and many bitter struggles, she was finally brought to acquiesce in admitting England's right to freedom, and let England go, but not the whole of England, all but, let us say, the six southern counties ... Would he think the people of partitioned England an object of shame if they stood neutral in such circumstances? I do not think Mr. Churchill would.'

'Mr. Churchill is proud of Britain's stand alone, after France had fallen and before America entered the War. Could he not find in his heart the generosity to acknowledge that there is a small nation that stood alone not for one year or two, but for several hundred years against aggression ... a small nation that could never be got to accept defeat and has never surrendered her soul?'

17 May 1974
Dublin and Monaghan bombings

On 17 May 1974, more lives were lost on the island of Ireland than on any other day in the three-decade-long Troubles. The Ulster Volunteer Force (UVF), the largest loyalist paramilitary group in Northern Ireland, planted two car bombs in Dublin

and another in Monaghan. They exploded without warning, killing 33 people and an unborn child and injuring 300 more. The victims ranged in age from 80 years to five months old. One of them was nine months pregnant at the time.

That this happened only a few months after Taoiseach Liam Cosgrave had signed the Sunningdale Agreement showed how hostile some unionists were to any involvement of the Irish government in Northern Ireland. Cosgrave took to RTÉ to address the nation: 'The government and I wish to express our profound sympathy to the relatives of the victims of today's outrages and to those who have been injured and maimed … What has happened today will help to underline the criminal folly and utter futility of violent action as a means for furthering political aims. It also helps to bring home to us here, in this part of our island, what the people in Northern Ireland have been suffering for five long years.'

Brian Faulkner, the sixth and last Prime Minister of Northern Ireland, sent a message to Cosgrave: 'Whatever the differences of opinion which may exist in other matters, I believe the responsible people in Northern Ireland and the Republic alike want to see this island rid forever of the evil forces which are guilty of such acts.'

No one took responsibility until 1993, when Yorkshire Television broadcast a documentary alleging that the UVF had carried out the bombings with the assistance of British security forces. The UVF then released a statement dismissing the second part of this claim: 'The minimum of scrutiny should have revealed that the structure of the bombs placed in Dublin and Monaghan were similar if not identical to those being placed in Northern Ireland on an almost daily basis ... To suggest that the UVF were not, or are not, capable of operating in the manner outlined in the programme is tempting fate to a dangerous degree.'

18 May 2011

Queen Elizabeth speaks in Dublin Castle

On 18 May 2011, a state banquet was held in Dublin Castle for Elizabeth II on her first visit to the Irish state. The last time a British monarch had been in Dublin was 1911, when Elizabeth's grandfather, George V, toured the city with Queen Mary.

After the dinner, Elizabeth rose from her seat to address those assembled with a speech written by her and her deputy private secretary. The first words she spoke would receive more press coverage than the entirety of the rest of her eight-minute oration:

'A Uachtaráin, agus a chairde' ('President and friends'). President Mary McAleese was visibly impressed by the Queen's efforts to use the official language of the state, leading a round of applause.

McAleese, a native of Ardoyne in north Belfast, was only too aware of how contentious the Irish language could be – Rhonda Paisley, daughter of Ian Paisley, had once said it 'drips with … bloodthirsty saliva'. Now Peter Robinson, the leader of the Democratic Unionist Party and First Minister of Northern Ireland, was hearing the British head of state using that same language.

The Queen continued, acknowledging the often fraught relationship between Britain and Ireland: 'It is a sad and regrettable reality that through history our islands have experienced more than their fair share of heartache, turbulence and loss … With the benefit of historical hindsight, we can all see things which we would wish had been done differently or not at all.' She also praised the Belfast Agreement, another issue that divided unionists: 'It is almost exactly 13 years since the overwhelming majority of people in Ireland and Northern Ireland voted in favour of the agreement signed on Good Friday 1998, paving the way for Northern Ireland to become the exciting and inspirational place that it is today.'

19 May 1998

John Hume and David Trimble share stage with Bono

On 19 May 1998, John Hume and David Trimble, respective leaders of the SDLP and Ulster Unionist Party, shared a platform for the first time in the most unusual of circumstances – on stage in Belfast's Waterfront Hall, during a U2 concert. Both urged a 'Yes' vote in the Good Friday Agreement referendum, which was to be held three days later. U2 frontman Bono, never one to spare hyperbole, began: 'I would like to introduce you to two men who are making history, two men who have taken a leap of faith out of the past and into the future.' Hume and Trimble entered from opposite sides of the stage and shook hands, to rapturous applause. Bono then grabbed each by the wrist, and lifted their arms aloft.

Neither Hume nor Trimble addressed the crowd: a wise decision, perhaps. Trimble was a controversial figure – he had held hands with Ian Paisley when an Orange Order parade was allowed to proceed down the Garvaghy Road in 1995, an image seen by many as triumphalist. Though Hume's public persona was gentler, unionists had viewed him with suspicion for a long time – Eileen Paisley, wife of Ian, once referred to him as a 'political Jesuit twister'.

Titled Concert for Yes, this was a free event for schoolchildren across Northern Ireland. Two thousand people attended. Also performing were the band Ash, from Downpatrick, Co. Down.

Hours before, an opinion poll published in the *Belfast Telegraph* showed that 52 per cent of respondents intended to vote 'Yes' in the referendum, with only 34 per cent of Protestant voters supporting it. Precarious though it may have looked, 71.1 per cent of voters in Northern Ireland would endorse the agreement three days later.

20 May 2009

Ryan Report is published

On 20 May 2009, the report of the Commission to Inquire into Child Abuse, better known as the Ryan Report, was published. The 2,600-page document examined child abuse in institutions run by the Catholic Church, and was described by Colm O'Gorman, Executive Director of Amnesty International Ireland, as 'a catalogue of the greatest human rights abuses in the history of the State'. The commission, chaired by Mr Justice Seán Ryan, interviewed more than 500 witnesses, finding that

'Children lived with the daily terror of not knowing where the next beating was coming from' and that 'Sexual abuse was endemic in boys' institutions.'

The report took nine years to compile and was spurred by the documentary television series *States of Fear*, produced by Mary Raftery and broadcast on RTÉ in 1999. This led to questions about abuse being raised in the Dáil, and Taoiseach Bertie Ahern apologised on 11 May 1999, saying, 'On behalf of the State and of all citizens of the State, the Government wishes to make a sincere and long overdue apology to the victims of childhood abuse for our collective failure to intervene, to detect their pain, to come to their rescue.' A national counselling service was set up for the victims, at an estimated cost of €4 million per annum, and it was announced that a commission would investigate the abuses.

The report in 2009 was greeted with horror. President of Ireland Mary McAleese said, 'It was an atrocious betrayal of love … My heart goes out to the victims of this terrible injustice, an injustice compounded by the fact that they had to suffer in silence for so long.' Mary Raftery reflected on the impact that the revelations would have: 'With this knowledge, it's going to be impossible for people to establish the same relationship of trust with the Catholic Church. I think it has vanished.'

21 May 1932

Amelia Earhart lands in Co. Derry

On 21 May 1932, Amelia Earhart landed in Ballyarnett, near Culmore, Co. Derry, becoming the first woman in the world to fly solo across the Atlantic Ocean. Earhart had taken off from Harbour Grace, Newfoundland the day before, and had intended to reach Paris, just as Charles Lindbergh did in 1927. However, bad weather and technical problems forced her to cut short her journey and arrive in the field of the Gallagher family. She had been in the air for 14 hours and 55 minutes.

Two local men, James McGeady and Dan McCallion, were fixing fences at the time and saw Earhart exit her plane, thinking she was a man at first. McGeady asked Earhart if she had travelled far, to which she famously replied, 'Only from America.' Recalling the event three years later in a BBC interview, Mrs Isobel Gallagher said that Earhart 'didn't seem at all excited … I suspected she'd be very hungry, so I got a meal ready for her.'

Earhart was driven to Derry city, five miles away, to phone her husband, and spent the night in the Gallagher home. United States President Herbert Hoover sent a message from Washington, DC: 'I voice the pride of the Nation in congratulating you most heartily upon achieving the splendid pioneer solo flight by a woman across the Atlantic Ocean. You have demonstrated not only your own dauntless courage but also the capacity of women to match the skill of men in carrying through the most difficult feats of high adventure.'

In 2010, seven members of the Gallagher family travelled to the National Air and Space Museum in Washington, DC to present curator Dorothy Cochrane with a framed photograph of Earhart and the Gallagher family together. Back in Derry, the field where Earhart landed is part of the Foyle Golf Centre, and the 14th hole is named 'Amelia's Landing'.

22 May 2015

Same-sex marriage referendum

On 22 May 2015, Ireland became the first country in the world to endorse same-sex marriage by popular vote. In a referendum held that day, 62.07 per cent of voters supported inserting an amendment to the Constitution allowing marriage between 'two persons without distinction as to their sex'. Outside Dublin Castle, a crowd of 2,000 people gathered to hear the results. It is thought that tens of thousands of Irish citizens living outside the state had returned home to vote, Ireland being one of the few countries in Europe not to allow expatriates a franchise.

The same-sex marriage referendum had its origins in the Irish Constitutional Convention, which met from December 2012 to March 2014. This group had 100 members – a chairman, 66 randomly selected citizens, and 33 politicians from across the island – and was tasked with considering eight issues affecting the Constitution of Ireland. The Convention issued its report on same-sex marriage to the Irish government in 2013, with 79 per cent supporting an amendment to the Constitution. Thus, the ground was laid for a referendum.

All major Irish parties supported a 'Yes' vote, but, given more than a third of voters rejected the proposal, it is unsurprising that there were some prominent figures on the 'No' side as well, such as newspaper columnist David Quinn, director of the Dublin-based think-tank the Iona Institute.

The debate was sometimes fraught, but when the results were announced, the crowd outside Dublin Castle was ecstatic. David Norris, a long-time campaigner who had taken Ireland to the European Court of Human Rights over its criminalisation of sexual acts between adult males, spoke: 'I have quite a powerful, carrying voice, but the message from this small, independent republic to the entire world is one of dignity, freedom and tolerance.'

23 May 2002

The Saipan incident

On 23 May 2002, an argument between Mick McCarthy, the Republic of Ireland football manager, and Roy Keane, the team's captain, resulted in Keane's being sent home from the Pacific island of Saipan, where he and the other players were training in preparation for the World Cup. When word got back to Ireland about the dispute, it dominated news coverage for weeks.

Keane was furious about the training conditions in Saipan. In an interview with Tom Humphries of the *Irish Times*, the captain said, 'You wonder why players get injured? Well, playing on a surface like that … It's rock hard. One or two of the lads have picked up injuries ... But you know, we're the Irish team, it's a laugh and a joke.'

When McCarthy raised the interview in a team meeting, Keane exploded. He is said to have responded, 'I didn't rate you as a player, I don't rate you as a manager, and I don't rate you as a person.' The following day, at a press conference, McCarthy told reporters, 'I can't, will not tolerate the level of abuse that was thrown at me, so I have sent him home.'

Irish football fans were distraught. Even Taoiseach Bertie Ahern was dragged into proceedings, telling reporters there was an 'enormous amount of pressure' for him to intervene, and that 'Quite frankly, I will be far happier next Saturday morning if Roy Keane was playing ... I just think that's all very sad and if it can be resolved it would be great.'

Ireland were eventually knocked out of the competition in a penalty shoot-out against Spain in the Round of 16, but the legacy of Saipan, and whether McCarthy or Keane was in the right, led to it being referred to informally as 'Ireland's Second Civil War'.

24 May 1923
The Civil War ends

On 24 May 1923, the Irish Civil War came to an end. It had begun the previous June, when 200 or so IRA members opposed to the Anglo-Irish Treaty had occupied the Four Courts in Dublin, which was then shelled by the National Army of the Irish Free State. For more than 10 months, the Civil War raged. Arthur Griffith and Michael Collins, the two leading Irish signatories of the Treaty, died during this time – the former from a cerebral haemorrhage, the latter in an ambush at Béal na mBláth, Co. Cork.

Anti-Treaty men set fire to the home of Dublin TD Seán McGarry, killing his seven-year-old son, Emmet. Seán Hales, a pro-Treaty TD for Cork, was shot dead. In retaliation, four anti-Treaty captives – Rory O'Connor, Liam Mellows, Richard Barrett and Joe McKelvey – were killed by firing squad. Only the previous year, O'Connor had been best man at the wedding of Kevin O'Higgins, the last cabinet member to give his consent to the men's executions. At least 77 anti-Treaty men were executed by the Free State government; a figure as high as 84 is sometimes cited.

Éamon de Valera is often seen as the face of the anti-Treaty IRA during the Civil War, but it was Liam Lynch who was Chief of Staff of the Irregulars. When Lynch was mortally wounded in April 1923, it made defeat of the anti-Treaty IRA all but inevitable.

On 24 May, de Valera issued a statement to Volunteers: 'Soldiers of the Republic, Legion of the Rearguard: The Republic can no longer be defended successfully by your arms. Further sacrifice of life would now be vain and continuance of the struggle in arms unwise in the national interest and prejudicial to the future of our cause. Military victory must be allowed to rest for the moment with those who have destroyed the Republic.'

25 May 2018

Referendum on repeal of the Eighth Amendment

On 25 May 2018, Ireland held a referendum on whether to lift the constitutional ban on abortion that had been signed into law more than three decades earlier. The Eighth Amendment, which recognised 'the equal right to life of the mother and the unborn', had been added to the constitution in 1983 following a referendum in which 66.9 per cent of voters supported its insertion. In 2018, a similar margin resulted in a reversal of that decision – 66.4 per cent of voters wanted the Eighth Amendment removed.

Fianna Fáil leader Micheál Martin shocked many when he came out in favour of what was called Repeal, though most of his party's TDs were opposed. Fine Gael leader and Taoiseach Leo Varadkar, also supporting 'Yes', said that he had changed his views on abortion over time: 'Things that may seem black and white when you're a young man in your twenties don't seem so black and white as you get on with life and understand more about the different experiences that people have.'

From 1983 to 2017, at least 170,000 Irish women had given Irish addresses when arriving in British clinics and hospitals to have abortions. The 1967 Abortion Act had made terminations legal in Great Britain – but not Northern Ireland – up to 28 weeks. The Irish law being proposed was more restrictive – abortion would be freely available up to 12 weeks, after a three-day waiting period. Some campaigners thought what was being proposed did not go far enough, but in the end, the result was a decisive victory for the pro-choice side.

Varadkar gave his reaction: '100 years since women gained the right to vote, today we as a people have spoken, and we say we trust women and respect women to make their own decisions, and their own choices.'

26 May 1315

Edward Bruce arrives in Ireland

On 26 May 1315, Edward Bruce landed at Larne in Ulster, having been sent to Ireland with an expeditionary force of 6,000 men by his brother Robert Bruce, the King of Scotland. Robert knew that Edward I of England relied heavily on settlers in Ireland to wage his war against the Scottish, and so wanted to form an alliance with the native Irish. According to the Annals of Connacht, Edward arrived with 'the men of three hundred ships, and his warlike slaughtering army caused the whole of Ireland to tremble, both Gael and Gall [foreigner]'.

In June, Edward met with Donall Ó Néill, King of Tír Eóghain, who had previously asked Robert for assistance in combating Normans. Robert agreed, on condition that Edward be recognised as King of Ireland. Edward's forces marched towards Carrickfergus and took the town. It was here that 12 Irish kings came to Edward, who 'took the hostages and lordship of the whole province of Ulster without opposition and they consented to his being proclaimed King of Ireland, and all the Gaels of Ireland agreed to grant him lordship and they called him King of Ireland'.

The Anglo-Irish were unprepared for Edward's arrival. Edmund Butler, the Chief Governor, was in Munster at the time, and the Earl of Ulster, Richard de Burgh, was in Connacht. De Burgh and Bruce met at the Battle of Connor, in which the Earl was defeated and reduced to 'a wanderer up and down Ireland … with no power or lordship'.

Edward would be inaugurated as the last High King of Ireland the following year, but his reign did not last long. In October 1318, he was killed at the Battle of Faughart, fought by the Hiberno-Norman forces of John de Bermingham and Edmund Butler on one side and Edward's Scots–Irish army on the other.

27 May 1936
First Aer Lingus flight

On 27 May 1936, the first Aer Lingus flight took place. A five-seater D. H. Dragon named *Iolar* – Irish for *Eagle* – flew from Baldonnel Aerodrome to Bristol, England, witnessed by Minister for Industry and Commerce Seán Lemass. These were humble beginnings for Ireland's national airline, which had been incorporated just five days earlier. The five on board were pilot Captain Oliver Armstrong; W. A. Morton, the director of Aer Lingus; Mrs Seán Ó hUadhaidh, the wife of the airline's chairman; T. J. O'Driscoll from the Department of Industry and Commerce; and a Mr and Mrs Fitzherbert, presumably the only people to have paid a fare, and therefore the airline's first commercial passengers.

When Lemass arrived at Baldonnel, Army Corps chaplain Father William O'Riordan was blessing the aircraft. Lemass said he thought there was 'a considerable future for aviation in this country', and shortly after 9:00 a.m. they left. *Iolar* passed the Irish coast between Dalkey and Bray, and travelled 4,000 feet above the Welsh Mountains. The flight lasted 90 minutes. After those on board had lunch, it returned to Dublin without Mr and Mrs Fitzherbert. The only freight that had been on board were some copies of the *Irish Times* bound for London.

Ironically, the event was not given any coverage in that newspaper the following day, and was mentioned only briefly two days later. As a result of the lack of publicity, interest in flights was initially slow – only 49 paying customers used the service between 27 May and 4 July. The cost of a one-way ticket was £10.

Captain Armstrong had once been a pilot with the Royal Air Force (RAF), and, coincidentally, *Iolar* was later sold to the RAF. It was shot down by the Luftwaffe over the English Channel in 1941. In 2011, the 75th anniversary of Aer Lingus's inaugural journey was commemorated with a flight to Rush, Co. Dublin and back, with Taoiseach Enda Kenny on board.

28 May 1970

Charles Haughey and Neil Blaney are arrested

On 28 May 1970, two Fianna Fáil TDs – Charles Haughey and Neil Blaney – were arrested and charged with conspiring to import arms and ammunition. Both had held senior positions in government until a few weeks earlier – Haughey was Minister for Finance, Blaney Minister for Agriculture and Fisheries – when they were dismissed by Taoiseach Jack Lynch. Lynch's official statement said he was 'satisfied that they do not subscribe fully to Government policy in relation to the present situation in the Six Counties'.

The previous August, Lynch had called for a United Nations peacekeeping force to be deployed in Northern Ireland to deal with the ever-rising tensions between Protestants and Catholics there. However, he had publicly ruled out sending the Irish Army over the border, telling RTÉ in December 1969, 'If one of our soldiers had appeared across the border in a belligerent or militant fashion, that would open a carnage.'

Haughey denied any involvement, saying, 'I now categorically state that at no time have I taken part in any illegal importation or attempted importation of arms into this country.' Blaney was far more scathing: 'Ireland has always had its British lackeys; you can pick them out in every generation, those hypocrites, those who for their own ends are always ready to play Britain's game in this country.' Another TD, Kevin Boland, resigned in protest, accusing Lynch of 'the greatest treachery of which an Irishman could be guilty'.

On the day he was arrested at home, Haughey was in the company of a judge of the supreme court, Brian Walsh, who had warned him of what might lie ahead. The charges against Blaney were dropped in July, but for Haughey, as well as Captain James Kelly of the Irish Army, Belfast republican and future Sinn Féin MLA John Kelly, and Belgian businessmen Albert Luykx, trial was set for 22 September.

29 May 1972

Official IRA ceasefire

On 29 May 1972, the Official IRA announced a ceasefire. Though some of its members would continue to engage in sporadic acts of violence over the following years, the ceasefire largely brought the group's armed campaign to an end. This came in the wake of the abduction, interrogation and execution of William Best, a 19-year-old Catholic member of the Royal Irish Rangers from the Creggan area of Derry.

The Officials were initially unapologetic. They released a statement referencing the Bloody Sunday shootings of January that year: 'The ruthlessness shown by British forces against the people of Free Derry could only be answered in similar terms. Regardless of calls for peace from slobbering moderates, while the British gunmen remain on the streets in the Six Counties the [Official] IRA will take action against them – in particular a British soldier from the Derry area who could remain in such a force after a massacre of 13 Derrymen by the British Army.'

The day after Best's killing, 500 women marched on the Republican Club offices in protest. The public outcry over this, and the Aldershot barracks bombings in which seven people – mostly female cleaners – were killed, accelerated the Officials' desire to focus entirely on political means. A statement was read out in Dublin: 'The overwhelming desire of the great majority of all the people of the north is for an end to military actions by all sides.' The Northern Ireland Secretary, William Whitelaw, described the statement as a 'step in the right direction'.

The Provisional IRA – the Official IRA's main rivals – were unmoved: 'So far as we are concerned the fight goes on ... We look upon this surrender as a gigantic confidence trick aimed at giving firmer control to the Official wing of their undisciplined members.'

30 May 1986

Knock Airport is opened

On 30 May 1986, Ireland West Airport – popularly referred to as Knock Airport – was officially opened. Roughly 3.5 miles from Charlestown, Co. Mayo, it was largely the brainchild of Monsignor James Horan, the parish priest of Knock, who had famously invited Pope John Paul II to visit Knock Shrine on his visit to Ireland in 1979.

Getting the airport built was far from easy, as Charles Haughey, who flew in for the ribbon-cutting ceremony, noted when he addressed the 4,000-strong crowd: 'From Barnacuig today we send forth a message which is of significance to the entire nation. It is a message of triumph over adversity, of difficulties overcome, of critics confounded.'

The 'critics' in question were the Fine Gael–Labour government of the day. Jim Mitchell, Minister for Communications, had said the idea to build an airport in that part of the country was 'ill-advised in the extreme', as the site was 'far distant from any sizeable town, high on a foggy, boggy hill'. The government had supplied a grant of £9.8 million, but this fell short of the estimated £13 million needed, and so Horan worked tirelessly to raise funds to finish the project. He invoked the charity concert Live Aid when explaining to reporters how it was done: 'There's Life [*sic*] Aid and Sport Aid and Self Aid: the people of Mayo have been practising self-aid for generations, otherwise they would have disappeared.' He described the opening of the airport as 'the greatest thing that has happened in Connacht in the last 100 years and … the greatest day of my life'.

Horan would die peacefully in his sleep just over two months after the official opening, but his legacy had a lasting effect. In 2016, Knock welcomed its 10 millionth passenger – one Lorna Conway from Athlone.

31 May 1941

The North Strand bombing

On 31 May 1941, the Luftwaffe dropped four bombs on Dublin, killing 28 people, injuring 90 and destroying 300 homes. This was not the first time that the Irish state had been hit by German bombs during the course of war – three women had died in a daylight attack on the village of Campile, Co. Wexford in August 1940, and three in Carlow in January 1941. The bombing of the North Strand, however, did by far the most damage. Several German aircraft had been spotted off the coast of Dublin and circled the city, apparently lost. At 12:30 a.m., anti-aircraft guns opened fire but failed to hit any of their targets.

At 1:30 a.m., the first three bombs fell in Ballybough, Summerhill and Phoenix Park, doing some damage to Áras an Uachtaráin, the residence of the President of Ireland, Douglas Hyde, though no one was killed. The fourth claimed the lives of 28 people in the North Strand. The following day, the *Irish Times* reported 'people trapped in the debris crying for assistance ... little children shouting for their mothers, and ... mothers who did not know the fate of their families ... On the footpaths people in their night clothes, covered in blood, lay moaning, and stretchers with the injured or dead passed to and fro from the scene of destruction.'

The German Minister to Ireland, Eduard Hempel, said, 'My very first immediate reaction was one of suspicion and I wondered if the bombing had been done by the British ... to upset Irish neutrality and to get Ireland into the war.' The Germans eventually admitted responsibility, and paid the Irish government £327,000 in compensation. In 1999, a German living in Canada claimed to have been one of the pilots that night, and said their intended target was Belfast, but they had ended up in Dublin by mistake.

1 June 1997

Tony Blair issues statement on the Famine

On 1 June 1997, a statement from Tony Blair was read at an event in Co. Cork commemorating the 150th anniversary of the Famine. Blair had become British Prime Minister less than a month beforehand, and, on the subject of Northern Ireland, the Labour Party manifesto promised voters a commitment to 'reconciliation between the two traditions and to a new political settlement which can command the support of both'. Part of that reconciliation was his being the first British leader to acknowledge that the government at the time of the Famine had not done all it could have to minimise deaths after the potato crop, on which most Irish people depended, was struck by blight.

Though Blair did not go as far as to apologise for the Famine, his message – which was read out to an audience of 15,000 people by the actor Gabriel Byrne – came closer than any previous one by a British head of government. It began: 'The Famine was a defining event in the history of Ireland and of Britain. It has left deep scars. That one million people should have died in what was then part of the richest and most powerful nation in the world is something that still causes pain as we reflect on it today. Those who governed in London at the time failed their people through standing by while a crop failure turned into a massive human tragedy. We must not forget such a dreadful event.'

Not all have seen the statement as appropriate – in 2012, BBC broadcaster Jeremy Paxman accused Blair of 'moral vacuousness' – but the Taoiseach at the time, John Bruton, welcomed it: 'While the statement confronts the past honestly, it does so in a way that heals for the future. The prime minister is to be complimented for the thought and care shown in this statement.'

2 June 1866

The Battle of Ridgeway

On 2 June 1866, the Battle of Ridgeway was fought in Ontario when approximately 600–800 members of the Fenian Brotherhood – all veterans of the American Civil War – crossed the Niagara River from Buffalo, and clashed with hundreds of Canadian soldiers. The plan was described by Irish Republican Brotherhood founder James Stephens as a 'scheme of wreaking revenge upon England through her Canadian possessions', and devised by Cork-born millionaire William Randall Roberts.

Roberts' plan split the Fenian Brotherhood. Founding member John O'Mahony disapproved, as did James Stephens. Nonetheless, on 1 June, they crossed the border into Canadian territory, occupying the town of Fort Erie, and issued a proclamation signed by Thomas William Sweeney:

'To the people of British America: We come among you as foes of British rule in Ireland … looking about us for an enemy, we find him here … To Irishmen throughout these Provinces we appeal in the name of seven centuries of British inequity and Irish misery and suffering, in the names of our murdered sires, our desolate homes, our desecrated altars, our millions of famine graves, our insulted name and race – to stretch forth the hand of brotherhood in the holy cause of fatherland.'

Two Canadian militia units were deployed to the area, led by Lieutenant-Colonel Alfred Booker. Though they at first appeared to get the better of the Fenians, they were eventually routed in a bayonet charge ordered by John O'Neill, a former US Cavalry officer. Nine Canadian soldiers were killed in the battle.

Victory for the Fenians was short-lived. Knowing that 3,000 imperial troops were advancing on the area, O'Neill evacuated his men the following day. Many were arrested by US authorities on their way back, and eventually released on the condition that they would return to their home states.

3 June 1844

Hypodermic needle is used for first time

On 3 June 1844, the hypodermic needle, invented by Irish doctor Francis Rynd, was used for the first time. Rynd fashioned a syringe to inject morphine into the face of a woman with neuralgia in Dublin's Meath Hospital, located on Heytesbury Street, which has since been incorporated into Tallaght Hospital. The patient, Margaret Cox, had tried drinking a solution of morphine to dull her severe pain, but with no success. Rynd sought to help her by injecting medicine directly under her skin, near a facial nerve. He built an improvised syringe, using a small tube (cannula) and a cutting device (trocar), puncturing a hole in the woman's skin and allowing the morphine to flow freely through it.

In March 1845, an article by Rynd was published in the *Dublin Medical Press*, detailing the procedure: 'In the space of a minute all pain (except that caused by the operation, which was very slight) had ceased, and she slept better that night than she had for months. After the interval of a week, she had slight return of pain in the gums of both upper and under jaw. The fluid was again introduced by two punctures made in the gum of each jaw, and the pain disappeared. She left the hospital on the 1st of August in high spirits, and promised to return if she ever felt the slightest pain again.'

The hypodermic needle has since been used billions of times throughout the world. Florence Nightingale wrote of using one to take opium in 1866, after returning from the Crimean War: 'Nothing did me any good, but a curious little new-fangled operation of putting opium under the skin, which relieves one for 24 hours.'

The phlebotomy service in Tallaght University Hospital is called the Rynd Unit in honour of the surgeon.

4 June 1984
Ronald Reagan addresses the Oireachtas

On 4 June 1984, Ronald Reagan became the second US President to address a joint session of the Oireachtas. John F. Kennedy had given a speech to members of the Dáil and the Seanad 21 years earlier, in 1963.

The address was not without disruptions. Three sitting TDs – Proinsias De Rossa and Tomás Mac Giolla of the Workers Party, and Tony Gregory, an independent – noisily exited the chamber shortly after Reagan was introduced by the Ceann Comhairle, Tom Fitzpatrick.

Reagan looked unfazed as he waited for the commotion to die down. He then began: 'I am fully cognisant of the great honour that has been done me by your invitation to speak here.' Before Reagan could continue, the chamber broke into spontaneous applause. 'When I stepped off Air Force One at Shannon a few days ago, and saw Ireland, beautiful and green, and felt again the warmth of her people, something deep inside began to stir.'

Reagan spoke of his roots in Ireland – 'I am the great-grandson of a Tipperary man' – of the relationship between the US and Ireland – 'I am the President of a country with the closest possible ties to Ireland', and the propensity for Irish-Americans to 'get carried away with our ancestral past and want very much to impress our relatives here with how well we have done in the New World'.

He also commented on the killing of Irish soldier Private Patrick Kelly and Garda recruit Gary Sheehan by the Provisional IRA the previous December, comparing it with the bombing of Harrods in London the same week: 'These two events, occurring 350 miles apart – one in Ireland, one in Britain – demonstrated the pitiless, indiscriminate nature of terrorist violence.' Given the support for the Provisional IRA among Irish-Americans, Reagan's words were particularly potent.

5 June 1798

The Battle of New Ross

On 5 June 1798, the bloodiest battle of the United Irishmen rebellion was fought in New Ross, Co. Wexford. The rebels aimed to take control of the town and cross the River Barrow, spreading their movement out of Wexford and into Kilkenny and Munster. However, their opponents in the British Army were well prepared for their advance. Their garrison, numbering 1,500 soldiers, was led by General Henry Johnston, while the rebels were led by Bagenal Harvey. Harvey sent forward his aide-de-camp, Matt Furlong, to negotiate a surrender of Johnston's troops. When Furlong, who was carrying a flag of truce, approached a British outpost, he was shot dead.

John Kelly, the rebel commander of an advance party of 500 men, immediately led a charge in reaction, driving a herd of cattle through the gate of the town. They succeeded in taking two-thirds of New Ross, but suffered heavy causalities and ammunition shortages. British reinforcements arrived at noon, forcing the rebels to retreat. Many of the wounded left behind in the town were killed. The exact number of rebel dead is unknown, but estimated to be over 2,000. In addition, 200 British soldiers lost their lives.

On the same day, in Scullabogue, near Newbawn, 200 prisoners who were loyal to the British Crown were burned alive in a barn, in what some believe to have been retaliation for the execution of wounded rebels in New Ross. The majority of Scullabogue victims were Protestant, though up to 20 Catholics were also killed there.

One person remembered by United Irishmen supporters as a hero at the Battle of New Ross is Mary Doyle of Castleboro, whom some have described as Ireland's Joan of Arc. Doyle is said to have cut the cartridge belts off dead soldiers and passed them to the rebels during the battle.

6 June 1944

Redmond Cunningham earns Military Cross on D-Day

On 6 June 1944, Allied troops landed on the beaches of Normandy in France, after Operation Overlord was launched by US Army General Dwight D. Eisenhower. This had been scheduled to begin one day earlier, but was postponed when weather reports from the lighthouse at Blacksod Bay, Co. Mayo advised against it. Along 50 miles of the French coast, 130,000 men were set to land on five beaches, travelling across the English Channel on 3,400 ships. Though Ireland was officially neutral in the war, that did not stop 66,083 men from the Irish state enlisting with the British Armed Forces, in addition to 64,157 from Northern Ireland.

Only one man from the Irish state received the Military Cross that day, for 'acts of exemplary gallantry'. This was Major Redmond Cunningham, from Co. Waterford. Cunningham landed on Sword beach, in a specialist tank designed to clear obstacles for Allied soldiers. He was forced to abandon his tank under heavy fire, and ended up clearing mines by hand. He would go on to receive the Croix de Guerre from the Belgian government for his help in rescuing civilians in Antwerp following a German attack on the city.

One of the more remarkable examples of Irishmen fighting in the Second World War was that of the five Halloran brothers from Ennistymon, Co. Clare: John, William and Michael served with the British Army, while Jeremiah and Martin – who had been living in New York – served in the US Army. Jeremiah and Martin, like Redmond Cunningham, were among the 130,000 soldiers who landed at Normandy. All returned from the war highly decorated veterans.

7 June 1996

Detective Garda Jerry McCabe is shot dead

On 7 June 1996, Detective Garda Jerry McCabe was shot dead by members of the Provisional IRA during an attempted robbery. He and colleague Ben O'Sullivan were in an unmarked Ford Mondeo in the village of Adare, Co. Limerick, guarding a post office van, when a Pajero jeep rammed into them from behind. Three men wearing balaclavas and holding Kalashnikov automatic rifles emerged, and fired at least 14 shots at O'Sullivan and McCabe. McCabe was hit three times, and died almost instantly. O'Sullivan was seriously injured.

Approximately 50,000 people lined the streets of Limerick for McCabe's funeral. Sinn Féin's leader, Gerry Adams, condemned the killing, saying it was 'completely and utterly wrong'. However, he denied any involvement, saying that 'sections of the media, especially the Dublin Sunday print media, were quite scurrilous in their efforts to link Sinn Féin to this killing.' Garda Commissioner Patrick Culligan was unambiguous in his assessment: 'I and members of the Garda Siochana have no doubt whatsoever that it was carried out by members of the IRA.'

Four men were convicted of the killing in February 1999. Pearse McAuley and Kevin Walsh were sentenced to 14 years each, Jeremiah Sheehy to 12 years, and John Quinn to six years. However, under the terms of the Good Friday Agreement, all qualified for early release: something that the Irish government, led by Bertie Ahern, fought against.

When Walsh and McAuley were released in 2009, they were met by Sinn Féin TD Martin Ferris. The McCabe family issued a statement: 'The life of Anne McCabe is now and will continue to be focused on her five children and six grandchildren who have been denied a loving and gentle father and grandfather because of a treacherous deed for which there is yet no healing word of apology or expression of sorrow.'

8 June 1917
Butte mining disaster

Just before midnight on 8 June 1917, an explosion in a copper mine in Butte, Montana resulted in the death of 166 people. It happened after a three-ton electric cable plummeted 2,500 feet down a granite mine; while a foreman was inspecting the damage, he accidentally set fire to the oil-soaked cable. The resulting explosion trapped scores of men; most of the deaths were from asphyxiation. Rescue attempts also ended in casualties. A foreman, Manus Duggan, helped save 28 others but died himself.

At the time, Butte had the highest proportion of Irish-born residents of any US city, and 19 of those who died were from Ireland, by far the largest group of foreign-born workers. In 1900, some 12,000 people in Butte were of Irish descent out of a population of 47,635. Of the 1,700 people who emigrated from Co. Cork between 1870 and 1915, 1,138 arrived in Butte, and the 'Copper King' of Butte, Marcus Daly, was a native of Ballyjamesduff, Co. Cavan.

Butte was also known as 'the Richest Hill on Earth' thanks to the amount of ore produced there. What kept it rich was the 102 vertical-shaft mines where many of the city's residents worked. Surrounding these mines were Irish neighbourhoods like Dublin Gulch and Corktown. Butte also had three newspapers, 42 churches and approximately 240 bars.

Though the men who worked in the mines were well compensated, it was a highly dangerous job: 2,000 miners lost their lives in various disasters through the years. Butte never recovered from the explosion, and in later years the shafts were abandoned in favour of open-cast mining.

One hundred years on, Mass was held for the memory of Michael Conroy – a 36-year-old father who died in the tragedy – in Barnacarroll Church, Co. Mayo.

9 June 597
Death of St Colmcille

On 9 June 597, Colmcille, also known as St Columba, died on Iona, the small Scottish island from which he helped spread Christianity throughout Great Britain and continental Europe. Consequently, 9 June is celebrated as the Feast of St Columba. He arrived on Iona in 563, aged 42, having left Ireland in the wake of the Battle of Cúl Dreimhne. This clash began when Colmcille was accused of plagiarising a book of psalms belonging to St Finnian, abbot of a monastery at Dromin in Co. Louth.

Colmcille was born in Gartan, Co. Donegal in AD 521. Christened Criomhthann, meaning 'fox', he was ordained a deacon and later a priest, and decided to found a monastery in AD 546 on a hill donated by the High King of Ireland, Aodh Mac Ainmhireach. Known as Doire Columcille, the area eventually gave its name to the city of Derry. For the next 15 years, he founded monasteries throughout Ireland, including one in Co. Meath where the Book of Kells would be produced two centuries later.

The origin of the Battle of Cúl Dreimhne lay in Columba's decision to translate and transcribe a book of psalms belonging to Finnian surreptitiously. Finnian was outraged, and brought the case to the High King, Diarmaid Mac Cearrbheoil, who declared 'to every cow its calf, to every book its copy', forcing Colmcille to return the text. He did not accept this judgement, and tried to rally the men of Donegal to ally themselves with the forces of the King of Connacht, whose son had been executed by Diarmaid.

Three thousand men perished in the subsequent battle, fought on the slopes of

Ben Bulben in Co. Sligo. Remorseful at having been responsible for so much carnage, Colmcille set off for Scotland, promising to convert as many people as had died in the battle. By the time of his death, he had established 60 monasteries in Scotland alone.

10 June 1904

James Joyce meets Nora Barnacle

On 10 June 1904, James Joyce met Nora Barnacle for the first time while walking down Nassau Street in Dublin. Barnacle, a 22-year-old chambermaid from Galway, would become Joyce's wife and muse, inspiring the character of Molly Bloom in his celebrated novel *Ulysses*. She worked in Finn's Hotel, having moved to the capital from the west of Ireland six months earlier.

Joyce was scheduled to sing at a garden fête that day, and had asked his friend Oliver St John Gogarty if he had 'a decent suit to spare or a cricket shirt'. When Joyce spotted Barnacle, he was immediately taken. She, too, was interested enough to engage in conversation with him, believing him to be a sailor because of the yachting cap he was wearing.

They arranged to meet again on 14 June at 8:30 p.m., outside No. 1 Merrion Square, the childhood home of Oscar Wilde. Joyce was left disappointed when Nora failed to turn up. He sent her a note expressing his dismay: 'I may be blind. I looked for a long time at a head of reddish-brown hair and decided it was not yours.' They agreed to schedule a new date for 16 June. Joyce would set his most famous work – *Ulysses* – on this day. They took an evening stroll to Ringsend, where Barnacle is said to have masturbated Joyce. He would later say to her, of that night, 'You made me a man.'

Four months after first meeting, Joyce and Barnacle eloped, travelling to Pula in what is now Croatia. Joyce taught English at the Berlitz School, mostly to Austro-Hungarian naval officers. In March of the following year, the couple moved to Trieste.

Joyce and Nora eventually married in 1931, and remained together until his death in 1941. They had two children, Lucia and Giorgio.

11 June 1925

W. B. Yeats: 'We are no petty people'

On 11 June 1925, William Butler Yeats, then a Senator of the recently established Irish Free State, criticised the government's decision not to allow divorce. A resolution had been passed in the Dáil that standing orders should be changed to prevent the introduction of divorce bills. Yeats first aired his thoughts on this issue in his 'Undelivered Speech', published in the *Irish Statesman* in March 1925. Now he was speaking on the floor of the Seanad about the issue.

Yeats warned Senators, and the reporters present, that the relatively recent partition of Ireland could not be ended without accommodating traditions on the island outside the Roman Catholic majority: 'It is perhaps the deepest political passion with this nation that North and South be united into one nation ... If you show that this country, Southern Ireland, is going to be governed by Catholic ideas and by Catholic ideas alone, you will never get the North.'

Yeats then reminded his fellow Senators that discriminatory laws, as well as putting Northern Protestants off the idea of a united Ireland, would put off Protestants like him, within the Irish state: 'I think it is tragic that within three years of this country gaining its independence we should be discussing a measure which a minority of this nation considers to be grossly oppressive. I am proud to consider myself a typical man of that minority. We against whom you have done this thing, are no petty people. We are one of the great stocks of Europe. We are the people of Burke; we are the people of Grattan; we are the people of Swift, the people of Emmet, the

people of Parnell. We have created the most of the modern literature of this country. We have created the best of its political intelligence.'

12 June 1988

Ireland beat England in Stuttgart

On 12 June 1988, the Republic of Ireland beat England 1–0 in the Neckarstadion, Stuttgart. This was the first time the football team had reached a major international tournament: the UEFA European Championship. The winning goal was scored by Ray Houghton in the sixth minute, and marked the beginning of the golden age of the Jack Charlton era. Charlton had become the manager of the Irish team two years earlier, and had been part of the England team that won the World Cup in 1966.

Looking back on the match, Houghton (pictured below (left) with teammate Ronnie Whelan) said, 'Nobody gave us a prayer … We were certainly the underdogs by a long way, but it was a case of making sure you went out there and did your job.' Houghton qualified to play for Ireland under what was known informally as 'the granny rule', Article 18 of the FIFA Statutes, passed in 1976: 'Any player who is a naturalised citizen of a country in virtue of that country's laws shall be eligible to play

for a national or representative team of that country.' Houghton was born in Glasgow, but his father hailed from Buncrana, Co. Donegal. The 'granny rule' benefited the Republic of Ireland time greatly in 1988 – a majority of the players on the team were born outside the country.

After Houghton's goal, the Irish team managed to keep England at bay for the remainder of the game. Back in Ireland, people were ecstatic. The front page of the *Irish Independent* proclaimed: 'Wild delight as the nation toasts historic victory. A 'green army' of more than 13,000 Irish fans took over this city last night in a wild celebration of their side's greatest ever win.'

Ireland didn't quite make it to the semi-finals, losing to a late goal in their final group match against the Netherlands, but to have got as far as they did was a momentous achievement.

13 June 1912

Members of Irish Women's Franchise League are arrested

On 13 June 1912, Hanna Sheehy-Skeffington and seven other members of the Irish Women's Franchise League were arrested after smashing the windows of Dublin Castle. This was in protest at the recent Home Rule Bill, which did not include the right of women to vote. A Conciliation Bill had come before the House of Commons in March of that year, which would have expanded the franchise but was defeated by 222 votes to 208. All 71 Irish Parliamentary Party (IPP) MPs voted against the bill. This was because the Liberal Prime Minister, H. H. Asquith, was opposed to women's suffrage, and John Redmond, leader of the IPP, wanted to ensure his party stayed on good terms with Asquith long enough for a Home Rule Bill to be passed.

However, Redmond's move was seen as a betrayal by the Irish Women's Franchise League, whose newspaper the *Irish Citizen* declared that 'the Irish Party killed the Conciliation Bill.' Interesting, three Irish MPs did vote for the Conciliation Bill, all members of the All-for-Ireland League – William O'Brien, James Gilhooly and Tim Healy.

At 5:30 a.m. on Thursday 13 June 1912, Sheehy-Skeffington used a wooden stick to break the windowpanes at the back of Dublin Castle. She was arrested, along with Margaret Murphy, Jane Murphy, Marguerite Palmer, Marjorie Hasler, Kathleen Houston, Maud Lloyd and Hilda Webb. A week later, Sheehy-Skeffington, Palmer and the Murphy sisters were sentenced to one month imprisonment. The rest received more severe six-month sentences.

While they were in prison, Francis Sheehy-Skeffington, husband of Hanna, would excoriate Redmond: 'There is stronger and purer Nationalism in Mountjoy prison at this moment than any Mr Redmond's followers can boast … Mountjoy prison where women, Nationalist and Unionist are sacrificing their Liberty for the liberation of the human spirit and the enfranchisement of the entire Irish Nation.'

14 June 1690

William of Orange lands at Carrickfergus

On 14 June 1690, William of Orange landed at Carrickfergus, Co. Antrim. This was his first time to set foot on Irish soil, in the lead-up to what would be one of the most significant clashes in the history of Ireland and Great Britain, the Battle of the Boyne. William and his wife Mary II had been declared joint sovereigns of England, Scotland and Ireland in February 1689, after the deposition of Mary's father, James II. James's Roman Catholic second wife, Mary of Modena, had given birth to a son; this, along with the king's prosecution of seven Anglican bishops for 'seditious libel', was perceived as a threat to the Protestant succession.

However, after fleeing to France, James decided to use Ireland as a base for an attempt to regain control of the Crown, with Louis XIV as an ally. Louis provided James with a French expeditionary brigade, led by the Duke of Lauzun, Antonin Nompar de Caumont, who escorted the deposed king to Kinsale, Co. Cork in March 1689. From there, he moved to Cork city and then Dublin, where he was given a rapturous welcome. However, two cities in Ireland held out against him – Enniskillen in Co. Fermanagh, and Derry–Londonderry. As it was surrounded by a wall, Derry was able to withstand James's demands that it surrender for 105 days, an event that became known as the Siege of Derry.

The stage was set for a confrontation between James and William. William arrived with an army of 36,000 men, including English, Dutch, Danish, French Huguenot and German soldiers. One eyewitness said 'The great numbers of coaches, waggons, baggage horses and the like is almost incredible to be supplied from England, or any of the biggest nations in Europe … I cannot think that any army of Christendom hath the like.'

15 June 1919

Alcock and Brown land in Galway

On 15 June 1919, Captain John Alcock and Lieutenant Arthur Whitten Brown landed in Derrigimlagh Bog, outside Clifden, Co. Galway, completing the world's first non-stop transatlantic flight. They had left Newfoundland 16 hours and 12 minutes earlier, in a Vickers Vimby biplane from the First World War, powered by two Rolls-Royce Eagle engines. Expecting to land on solid ground, they were annoyed when their plane wound up sinking nose first into the bog. Nevertheless, they exited, in the presence of the staff of the Marconi Wireless Station nearby. 'That is the way to fly the Atlantic', Brown proclaimed. 'Now if we only had a shave and a bath we'd be all right', added Alcock.

The flight had not gone as smoothly as they might have hoped. Despite climbing 11,000 feet after take-off, they were unable to rise above the clouds. The plane's heating engine broke, making the freezing cold of the high altitude ever harder to bear. In order to keep the motor running, Brown even had to scrape ice off key components halfway across the Atlantic. However, their journey was now complete.

Irish Times journalist Tom 'Cork' Kenny landed the scoop of a lifetime when he interviewed the men, noting that Alcock 'looked as spruce, attired in a navy lounge suit, and cheerfully smoking a cigarette as any city man enjoying an hour's content'.

For their effort, the men won a £10,000 prize from the *Daily Mail*, presented by Secretary of State for Air Winston Churchill. Alfred Harmsworth, the editor of the paper – himself born in Chapelizod, Co. Dublin – came up with the prize in 1913, though the First World War had prevented anyone from attempting to claim it.

Thirteen years later, another event linking Newfoundland with Ireland would occur when Amelia Earhart became the first woman to fly solo across the Atlantic Ocean.

16 June 1954

The first Bloomsday

James Joyce's most celebrated work, *Ulysses*, is set on 16 June 1904, the date on which Joyce and future wife Nora Barnacle spent their first evening together in Ringsend. On the 50th anniversary of that event, and 13 years after Joyce's death in Switzerland, six men decided to retrace the steps of Leopold Bloom, the central character in *Ulysses*, around the city of Dublin. This was the first of what would become an annual celebration, known as Bloomsday.

The six were Brian O'Nolan, John Ryan, Patrick Kavanagh, Anthony Cronin, Con Leventhal and Tom Joyce. O'Nolan and Ryan were the principal organisers. The former, perhaps better known under his pen names Flann O'Brien and Myles na gCopaleen, was a playwright and novelist; the latter was the founder of literary magazine *Envoy* and had also established the Joyce Society. They had co-edited a book of tributes to Joyce from the likes of Samuel Beckett. The others all had literary credentials: Kavanagh was a poet and novelist, Cronin a poet and arts activist, and Leventhal a lecturer in French at Trinity College. The sixth man, Tom Joyce, was a dentist and a cousin of Joyce.

The first Bloomsday was a relatively quiet affair. Hiring two horse-drawn carriages, the men aimed to visit most of the places mentioned in *Ulysses* – Sandymount Strand, Glasnevin Cemetery, the National Library, Holles Street Maternity Hospital, Barney Kiernan's pub and Nighttown (Dublin's red-light district in Joyce's time, known also as 'Monto').

However, the group failed to complete their journey, ending up in The Bailey, a pub in the city centre, inebriated. 'We hadn't stuck to our master plan but we had enjoyed a very good day, which I recorded for posterity on a colour film', Ryan noted.

Since that day, Bloomsday has been celebrated in over 60 countries around the world.

17 June 1959
Irish voters reject first-past-the-post

On 17 June 1959, Irish voters narrowly rejected a proposal to switch from proportional representation under the single transferable vote (PR-STV) to the British-style first-past-the-post (FPTP) system, by 51.79 per cent of votes cast. This was the first time that they were given the opportunity to endorse such a change – another referendum would be held in 1968, only to be rejected by a bigger margin (60.76 per cent to 39.24 per cent). Both votes were taken while Fianna Fáil were in government.

Ironically, proportional representation had been introduced to Ireland by the British. In 1918, Sinn Féin won 73 seats out of a possible 105 under FPTP, despite receiving 46.9 per cent of the vote. Twenty-five of the seats were uncontested; had they not been, it is likely that Sinn Féin would have received a higher percentage. The British were alarmed that a relatively new party could take so many seats – particularly one pledged to 'withdrawing the Irish Representation from the British Parliament and ... denying the right and opposing the will of the British Government or any other foreign Government to legislate for Ireland'. They therefore brought in the Local Government (Ireland) Act in 1919. The 1920 urban local elections saw Sinn Féin's percentage drop to 27 per cent, with 27 per cent going to unionists, 18 per cent to the Labour Party, 15 per cent to other nationalists and 14 per cent to independents.

The proportional representation system was retained in the Irish Free State after 1922, and in Northern Ireland until 1929, when the Unionist government abolished it (it would not be reinstated until 1973). Though de Valera may have been disappointed with the defeat of his party's proposal in 1959, it was also a moment of personal success for the Fianna Fáil leader – he was elected President of Ireland on the same day, with 56.3 per cent of the vote.

18 June 1264

Earliest recorded meeting of an Irish parliament

On 18 June 1264, the earliest recorded meeting of an Irish parliament took place in Castledermot, Co. Kildare, on the first Wednesday after the Feast of the Holy Trinity. This was not a parliament in the modern sense, being closer to a tribunal or committee hearing. The purpose was to discuss whether Archbishop of Dublin Fulk Bassett de Sandeford had the right to hold courts and exercise justice.

The 750th anniversary of the parliament's sitting was marked in the Seanad. However, not all Senators felt it an occasion worthy of commemoration. Sinn Féin's Trevor Ó Clochartaigh described the 1264 meeting as 'an obscure event that happened 750 years ago which, I believe, is wrongly described as the first Irish parliament … a century after the Anglo-Norman invasion of Ireland'.

Responding to Ó Clochartaigh, independent Senator Fidelma Healy Eames said 'The Normans, who began settling Ireland in 1169, were the first to give it a centralised administration. Our legal system is, in large measure, inherited from them. So, too, is our Legislature, which is directly descended from the Parliament that developed in medieval Ireland. The Minister stated that the first Parliament was not representative of the people of Ireland, but it developed incrementally and covered citizens of the lordship of Ireland based on Norman laws and English practices.'

Senator Ivana Bacik, who was responsible for organising the discussion, drew parallels between the parliament in 1264 and contemporary politics: 'It appeared that the archbishop had been taking it on himself to deal with matters that should have been matters of state. This brings us to a very contemporary theme of church–state relations … Reading the record of 750 years ago reminds one that *plus ça change, plus c'est la même chose.*'

19 June 1920

The Listowel Mutiny

On 16 June 1920, RIC police officers in Listowel, Co. Tipperary, were informed that the British military were to assume control of their barracks, on the orders of Major-General Sir Henry Tudor. Led by Constable Jeremiah Mee, they refused to relinquish control. Three days later, the situation escalated. General Tudor arrived to address those who had refused to comply, accompanied by the District Commissioner for Munster, Lieutenant Colonel Gerard Bryce Ferguson Smyth.

Smyth supposedly told the men that suspects were to be 'thrown out into the gutter' if barracks could not be used, that civilians who did not immediately obey an order to raise their hands should be shot 'with effect', and, though mistakes might be made and innocent persons shot, 'you are bound to get the right persons sometimes. The more you shoot, the better I will like you, and I assure you that no policeman will get into trouble for shooting a man.'

This version of the speech appeared in the Sinn Féin newspaper *Irish Bulletin*, in an account given by Mee, which some have suggested was exaggerated or downright untrue. Smyth himself claimed that he condemned reprisals by the RIC against civilians in the wake of IRA attacks, telling the men: 'I wish to make it perfectly clear to all ranks that I will not tolerate any "reprisals". They bring discredit to the police. I will deal most severely with any officer or man concerned in them.'

After Smyth's speech, Mee allegedly responded: 'By your accent I take it you are an Englishman. You forget you are addressing Irishmen.' Removing his cap, belt and bayonet, Mee continued 'These too are English. Take them as a present from me, and to hell with you, you murderer.' Smyth demanded Mee's arrest, but none of Mee's RIC colleagues would oblige. Fourteen of them stood down, and the incident became known as the Listowel Mutiny.

20 June 1631
The Sack of Baltimore

On 20 June 1631, the village of Baltimore, Co. Cork was attacked by Barbary pirates led by Dutchman Murad Reis: the worst such incident in either Ireland or Great Britain.

The attack was carried out by Janissaries, an elite infantry unit of the Ottoman Empire. Reis, known also as Jan Janszoon, was a convert to Islam, and had learned of the location of the village from John Hackett. Hackett, from Dungarvan, Co. Waterford, was the captain of one of two fishing boats captured off the Old Head of Kinsale before the attack. At around 2:00 a.m. on 20 June, approximately 230 men armed with muskets landed. They proceeded to capture inhabitants until Reis heard a drum being sounded to rouse the rest of the village, and decided to retreat.

In all, 107 people were kidnapped and taken to Algiers, North Africa. Eight members of the same family were among them – William Gunter's wife and their seven sons. Most of those taken were women and children; very few ever saw Ireland again.

Gunter was one of the better-off residents of the village, and was of English descent. Indeed, a look of some of the names of those taken from Baltimore – Arnold, Broddebrooke, Amble – shows that the village was an English settlement. Sir Fineen O'Driscoll, owner of the land, leased it to Sir Thomas Crook, from Cornwall, in 1605; others then started to arrive.

Hackett was subsequently hanged for his role in directing the pirates to the village, and the event inspired a poem by Young Irelander Thomas Davis, titled 'The Sack of Baltimore': 'The yell of "Allah" breaks above the prayer and shriek and roar – O blessed God! the Algerine is lord of Baltimore!'

21 June 1877
Molly Maguires are executed

On 21 June 1877, 10 alleged members of the Molly Maguires, a secret society of Irish coal miners, were hanged in Pennsylvania, accused of killing several supervisors and foremen. Six were hanged in Schuylkill County prison yard in what was, according to a plaque dedicated there in 1980, 'the largest mass execution in Pennsylvania'. Another four were hanged the same day at Mauch Chunk in Carbon County. The day become known in the anthracite region as 'Black Thursday'.

Between 1877 and 1879, 20 men connected to the organisation would hang, including John Kehoe, the so-called 'King of the Mollies'. In September 1978, Governor of Pennsylvania Milton J. Shapp posthumously pardoned Kehoe, telling those present: 'It is impossible for us to imagine the plight of the nineteenth century coal miners in the anthracite region of Pennsylvania, and it was Kehoe's popularity among the miners that led Gowen

to fear, despise, and ultimately destroy him.'

'Gowen' was Franklin B. Gowen, President of the Philadelphia and Reading Railroad, himself the son of an Irish Protestant immigrant. Gowen hired James McParland, a Pinkerton agent and Irish Catholic from Co. Armagh, to infiltrate the Molly Maguires, using the name James McKenna. It was largely on the basis of McKenna's evidence that 51 men – the majority from Donegal or north-central Ireland – faced trial.

Though the Molly Maguires may have been involved in violence in the region – at least 16 men were murdered there between 1862 and 1876 – the evidence against many of those convicted, including Kehoe, was circumstantial. Governor Shapp said in 1978: 'We can be proud of the men known as the Molly Maguires, because they defiantly faced allegations which attempted to make trade unionism a criminal conspiracy.'

22 June 1921

George V opens Northern Ireland parliament

On 22 June 1921, George V visited Belfast for the opening of the new Northern Ireland Parliament. The first meeting of a parliament in Belfast City Hall drove home the reality that, following the Government of Ireland Act, a new political dispensation had come into existence. By and large, Catholics boycotted the event. Cardinal Logue, the Archbishop of Armagh and Primate of All Ireland, turned down an invitation to attend. The atmosphere in the city was as febrile as it had ever been – between July 1920 and June 1922, 455 people were killed, 267 of them Catholics.

The Government of Ireland Act may not have been popular among the Catholic population, but it had included a provision for the 'eventual establishment of a Parliament for the whole of Ireland, and to bringing about harmonious action between the parliaments and governments of Southern Ireland and Northern Ireland'. Of course, any such parliament would still have been within the United Kingdom, and not the independent republic envisaged by Sinn Féin. Nevertheless, it was in that spirit of reconciliation that George V addressed members of the Senate and the House of Commons:

'For all who love Ireland, as I do with all my heart, this is a profoundly moving occasion in Irish history. My memories of the Irish people date back to the time when I spent many happy days in Ireland as a midshipman. My affection for the Irish people has been deepened by the successive visits since that time … May this historic gathering be the prelude of a day in which the Irish people, North and South, under one Parliament or two, as those Parliaments may themselves decide, shall work together in common love for Ireland upon the sure foundations of mutual justice and respect.'

23 June 1985

Air India Flight 182 bombing

On 23 June 1985, Air India Flight 182 disappeared from Shannon Airport radar screens at 31,000 feet, 90 miles from the coast of Ireland. It was travelling from Montreal to New Delhi and Bombay, and was 45 minutes away from a refuelling stop at Heathrow Airport when an improvised explosive device (IED) detonated. All 329 people on board were killed, the majority Canadian citizens of Indian descent. The following day, 131 bodies were recovered in an international search-and-rescue operation by Irish, British and American seacraft. Taoiseach Garret FitzGerald travelled to Cork with the Indian Ambassador, and told reporters that Indian authorities would lead the investigation into the incident.

Though no group ever claimed responsibility, it is widely believed that Sikh extremists linked to Babbar Khalsa (BK), a group seeking to establish an independent state called Khalistan, were behind the attack.

Many Irish people offered to accommodate the relatives of the victims who were arriving in the area. A permanent memorial was erected in Ahakista, near Bantry, the following year, and was visited several times by Dr Bal Gupta, co-ordinator of the Air India Victims' Families Association (AIVFA). Dr Gupta lost his wife of 20 years in the bombing, and said, 'We always feel grateful for the compassion and understanding' of local people.

In 2005, Canadian Prime Minister Paul Martin, Irish President Mary McAleese and around 180 family members attended a ceremony to commemorate the victims. Martin issued a statement: 'On the morning of June 23rd, 20 years ago, innocent Canadians – sons and daughters, fathers and mothers, relatives and friends – were killed in a callous act of hatred ... On this day of remembrance, I join with all Canadians in expressing our sorrow and indignation at this cruel and premeditated act.'

24 June 1993

Homosexuality is decriminalised

On 24 June 1993, homosexuality was decriminalised in Ireland, specifically the practice of homosexual acts between consenting adults. The decision came with the passage of the second phase of the Criminal Law Bill (Sexual Offences) Ireland, introduced by Minister for Justice Máire Geoghegan-Quinn of Fianna Fáil. The road to 1993 was a long one, but a turning point was when Trinity College lecturer David Norris took Ireland to the European Court of Human Rights in 1988, which found that the country's laws were contrary to the European Convention on Human Rights.

Ireland's laws actually predated the birth of the state, and were enshrined in the Offences Against the Person Act of 1861 and the Criminal Law Amendment Act of 1885, under both of which Oscar Wilde had been prosecuted in 1895. Great Britain had repealed those laws with the passing of the Sexual Offences Act in 1967, though homosexuality was decriminalised in Northern Ireland only in 1982, after gay activist Jeffrey Dudgeon took his case to the European Court of Human Rights, seven years before Norris.

The Republic was slower to respond, and debate was often heated. Gay activist Kieran Rose discussed the issue on RTÉ's *Late Late Show* in 1989, when Paddy Monaghan of Christians Concerned for Ireland told him it wasn't 'normal for a man to be preoccupied with another man's back passage'. Now, the laws under which approximately 150 men had been arrested between 1944 and 1993 were being repealed.

Introducing the bill, Geoghegan-Quinn said, it would 'leave those of homosexual orientation free to come to terms with their lives and express themselves in personal relationships without the fear of being branded and being punished as criminals'. It was not universally welcomed: five Dáil deputies spoke against it, including a member of Geoghegan-Quinn's own party, Noel Ahern.

25 June 1938

Douglas Hyde becomes first President of Ireland

On 25 June 1938, Douglas Hyde was inaugurated as the first President of Ireland. Though Hyde was appointed unopposed, subsequent Presidents – or Uachtaráin na hÉireann – would be directly elected by voters.

Installing a president was another major step in the dismantling of symbols connecting the Irish state with Britain. Previously, the monarch of the United Kingdom had been the head of the Irish Free State, but when Edward VIII abdicated in December 1936, Éamon de Valera, then President of the Executive Council, took the opportunity to remove any references to the king in the Irish Free State Constitution, and to abolish the role of Governor-General.

The two frontrunners for the position were Seán T. O'Kelly of Fianna Fáil (who would serve as the second president) and Alfie Byrne, Lord Mayor of Dublin. However, the main political parties agreed that a partisan figure such as O'Kelly could damage the new office, and so Hyde, the founder and first President of Conradh na Gaeilge, the Gaelic League, was chosen. The *Irish Times* saw the choice as the correct one, writing, 'Dr Hyde is a man to whom Ireland owes a great deal.' Hyde was a member of the Church of Ireland, in a state where Roman Catholics made up over 90 per cent of the population. *Time* magazine reported that his being a Protestant might entice the 'inhabitants of stubbornly independent, strongly Protestant Northern Ireland'.

The ceremony on 25 June 1938 lasted just 15 minutes, in which Hyde was administered the oath of office by the Chief Justice and de Valera gave a speech: 'Mr President, on behalf of the Irish nation, on behalf of the living, those who dwell at home as well as our kin beyond the sea, on behalf also of the dead generations who longed to see this day but have not seen it, I salute you.'

26 June 1996

Veronica Guerin is shot dead

On 26 June 1996, journalist Veronica Guerin was shot dead when two men ambushed her car at traffic lights at Newlands Cross in Dublin. She was 36 years old and married, with a six-year-old son.

Guerin was an investigative reporter for the *Sunday Independent*, and had been subject to attacks before. She was scheduled to speak in London two days later, in a discussion titled 'Dying to Tell a Story: Journalists at Risk'. Taoiseach John Bruton made a statement in the Dáil that day: 'We are shocked when we hear of the death of any young person. We are even more shocked when we hear that her death was a result of murder, in cold blood, in broad daylight, on a roadside in Dublin ... That a journalist should be callously murdered in the line of duty is an attack on democracy, because it is an attack on one of the pillars of our democracy.'

Having begun her career with the *Sunday Business Post* and *Sunday Tribune*, Guerin focused exclusively on the Irish underworld from 1994 onwards, specifically drug traffickers. This earned her the ire of crime kingpin John Gilligan, who assaulted her in September 1995 when she confronted him on his lavish lifestyle. He also called her home and threatened her six-year-old son. Nevertheless, she continued her work, receiving an International Press Freedom Award from the Committee to Protect Journalists in New York in December 1995.

Soon after her killing, the Irish government passed the Proceeds of Crime Act and established the Criminal Assets Bureau. John Gilligan fled to Amsterdam the day after Guerin's death, and was later arrested in England with £500,000 in cash. Though acquitted of ordering her killing, he was sentenced to 28 years for smuggling 20 tonnes of cannabis. He served 17 years and was released in 2013.

27 June 1963

John F. Kennedy visits Dunganstown, Co. Wexford

On 27 June 1963, US President John F. Kennedy visited the cottage in Dunganstown, Co. Wexford where his great-grandfather Patrick Kennedy had lived before emigrating to the United States. It was located on a small farm then owned by Mary Ryan, a distant cousin of Kennedy's.

Kennedy had landed in Ireland the day before, becoming the first US President to visit the country while in office. Part of his four-day trip was a wreath-laying ceremony at the John Barry Memorial, a tribute to the Wexford-born captain dubbed 'the father of the American Navy'; it also involved addressing locals in New Ross

Quay, five miles from his family homestead: 'I am proud to be here and I appreciate the warm welcome you have given to all of us.' Referencing his great-grandfather, Kennedy said, 'If he hadn't left, I would be working over at the Albatross Company, or perhaps for John V. Kelly.'

It was a line he would slightly repurpose the following day, when he addressed a joint session of the Dáil and Seanad, referencing the birthplace of Irish President Éamon de Valera: 'If this nation had achieved its present political and economic stature a century or so ago, my great grandfather might never have left New Ross, and I might, if fortunate, be sitting down there with you. Of course, if your own President had never left Brooklyn, he might be standing up here instead of me.'

Kennedy presented the Dáil with the banner flown by the Irish Brigade under Thomas Francis Meagher at the Battle of Fredericksburg, 'in recognition of what these gallant Irishmen and what millions of other Irish have done for my country, and through the generosity of the Fighting 69th'. Meagher had unveiled the Irish tricolour to a crowd in Dublin in 1848.

28 June 1922
The Civil War begins

In March 1922, anti-Treaty IRA men held an army convention in the Mansion House in Dublin, in which they repudiated the authority of Dáil Eireann and elected a 16-man Executive, led by Rory O'Connor and Liam Mellows. On 14 April, O'Connor and 200 anti-Treaty IRA men, also known as 'Irregulars', occupied the Four Courts in Dublin. Michael Collins, Chairman of the Provisional Government, managed to convince a number of anti-Treaty men, including Dan Breen and Seán O'Hegarty, to meet him, Richard Mulcahy and others on the pro-Treaty side. They issued a joint statement on 1 May: 'We, the undersigned officers of the IRA, realising the gravity of the present situation in Ireland, and appreciating the fact that if the present drift is maintained a conflict of comrades is inevitable, declare that this would be the greatest calamity in Irish history, and would leave Ireland broken for generations.'

The statement called for the 'acceptance of the fact, admitted by all sides, that the majority of the people of Ireland are willing to accept the Treaty'. However, the IRA Executive in the Four Courts denounced it. A Dáil peace committee was then established, with five members on either side, but talks broke down within three weeks.

A Joint Army Committee was set up, this time including IRA men from the Executive in the Four Courts, such as Mellows and O'Connor. Eventually, the Executive rejected the calls for peace and declared the June 1922 election illegitimate. In that election, anti-Treaty Sinn Féin had won 36 seats, to the 92 won by pro-Treaty candidates. When anti-Treaty man Leo Henderson was arrested, Irregulars retaliated by kidnapping pro-Treaty J. J. 'Ginger' O'Connell on 26 June, demanding Henderson's release.

Under pressure from the British to deal with the insurgents, Collins bombarded the Four Courts at 4:10 a.m. on 28 June 1922. The Irish Civil War had begun.

29 June 1948

Mike Flanagan steals tanks for Haganah

Born in Foxford, Co. Mayo, Mike Flanagan joined the British Army at age 16, took part in the Normandy beach landings and witnessed the liberation of the Bergen-Belsen concentration camp, where up to 50,000 Jews and other prisoners had died, including Anne Frank. On 29 June 1948, Flanagan was stationed in Haifa; most British troops had withdrawn from Palestine on 14 May that year. Thousands of miles from his country of birth, he was about to become a deserter, stealing two Cromwell tanks from the British and delivering them to the Haganah – the main Jewish paramilitary force in Palestine. Flanagan drove one of the tanks from Haifa to Kibbutz Yagur; fellow soldier Harry McDonald drove the other. The vehicles were hidden for a week, eventually becoming part of the first tank battalion of the Israel Defense Forces (IDF). Flanagan would fight on the side of the IDF throughout the 1948 Arab–Israeli War, being wounded during Operation Yoav in October of that year when a piece of shrapnel passed through the viewing slot of the tank he was driving. After the war, he converted to Judaism upon marrying a woman named Ruth Levy, and changed his name to Michael Peleg.

His grandson, Lior Hertz, later described Flanagan's motives for remaining in Israel: 'Grandfather said he wanted to stay in Israel and help the weak, the Jewish Yishuv … He had sympathy for the Jews.' According to Dan Kurzman in his book *Genesis 1948: The First Arab–Israeli War*, Flanagan 'saw the Jews as displaced Irishmen fighting the same Englishmen his people had fought so bitterly in their own underground'.

In 2015, Ireland's Ambassador to Israel, Eamonn McKee, and Zvi Gabay, the first Israeli Ambassador to Ireland, took part in a ceremony in memory of Flanagan at the IDF Armored Corps Museum in Latrun. Malcolm Gafson, chairman of the Ireland–Israel Friendship League, said, 'We owe a great debt to Mike Flanagan.'

30 June 1922

Public Record Office is destroyed

On 30 June 1922, centuries' worth of Irish documentation was lost when the Public Record Office in the Four Courts was blown up in a battle between anti-Treaty and pro-Treaty forces in Dublin. Since occupying the building in April, the anti-Treaty IRA had used the basement of the Public Record Office to store mines and ammunition. After the building was shelled by pro-Treaty forces demanding the surrender of its inhabitants and the release of J. J. 'Ginger' O'Connell, an explosion occurred.

Countless priceless records were destroyed: military records, transportation records, censuses predating 1861, Church of Ireland parish records dating back to the seventeenth century, wills that dated back to 1500, court records from the thirteenth century, deeds as far back as 1174. The *Irish Times* lamented the loss: 'Those precious records, which would have been so useful to the future historian, have been devoured by the flames or scattered in fragments by the four winds of heaven.' Reflecting on the destruction, Winston Churchill is said to have remarked: 'Better a state without archives than archives without a state.'

It is unclear whether the explosion was deliberately set off. In his memoir *The Singing Flame*, anti-Treaty IRA man Ernie O'Malley noted that officer Paddy O'Brien had said, 'I'll blow up or burn the Four Courts rather than hand them over.' The Provisional Government certainly blamed the anti-Treaty forces: 'By their treacherous explosion of a mine shortly before their unconditional surrender … [they destroyed] one of the most beautiful buildings in Dublin, the invaluable historical records it held and inflicted serious and unnecessary injuries on National Forces.' However, an anti-Treaty IRA statement countered this claim: 'There was a munitions dump at the HQ Block including material for mines which caught fire in the bombardment … The responsibility for the destruction of the Four Courts lies with the "government" that has usurped the Republic.'

1 July 1690

The Battle of the Boyne

On 1 July 1690, the Battle of the Boyne was fought. William of Orange, with an army of 36,000 men, faced the deposed James II, whose Jacobite forces numbered 25,000.

Having landed in Carrickfergus in June, William marched his troops towards the Boyne, deploying them to the north of the river. On the other side were James's troops, the majority of whom where Irish Catholics, in addition to 6,000 French troops raised by Louis XIV. Though the battle is often remembered as being fought along Catholic and Protestant lines, William had the support of Pope Innocent XI, who was opposed to Louis XIV.

The Jacobites were poorly equipped with mostly outdated matchlock muskets, and even scythes and other farming implements. William's army – comprising English, Dutch, Danish, French Huguenot and German soldiers – had flintlock muskets and superior artillery.

William was wounded when a Jacobite soldier fired on him the day before the battle, hitting him in the shoulder. Nevertheless, he proceeded. He sent 9,000 troops

across the river at Roughgrange, to which James responded by sending half his army, though not a single shot was fired, as a deep ravine prevented them from meeting. The Dutch Blue Guards forced back the Jacobite infantry at Oldguard, but were met by a cavalry counterattack under the command of the Earl of Tyrconnell, Richard Talbot. The Williamite cavalry then crossed the river and forced James's troops to retreat.

James fled the scene, learning of William's victory at two in the afternoon, near Slane. Though the casualties for the day were not as high as they might have been – 1,000 Jacobites and 500 Williamites died – the success of William of Orange helped secure the Protestant succession to the throne.

2 July 1990

Nelson Mandela addresses Dáil Éireann

On 2 July 1990, less than five months after his release from prison, where he had spent 27 years, Nelson Mandela addressed Dáil Éireann. He arrived in Ireland the day before, after a 10-hour flight from the United States.

Mandela thanked those assembled, saying, 'We know that your desire that the disenfranchised of our country should be heard in this house and throughout Ireland derives from your determination, born of your experience, that our people should, like yourselves, be free to govern themselves and to determine their destiny.' He drew parallels between the Irish quest for independence and the struggle of Black Africans against the apartheid regime in South Africa: 'The very fact there is today an independent Irish state, however long it took to realise the noble goals of the Irish people by bringing it into being, confirms the fact that we too shall become a free people; we too shall have a country which will, as the great Irish patriots said in The Proclamation of 1916, "Cherish all the children of the nation equally".'

Mandela also referenced the industrial action of Dunnes Stores workers in 1984–1987, who had gone on strike rather than handle goods from South Africa: 'For more than a quarter of a century, your country has had one of the most energetic and effective anti-apartheid movements in the world … We therefore salute your sports people, especially the rugby players, your writers and artists and the Dunnes and other workers.'

After the address, Mandela held a joint press conference with Taoiseach Charles

Haughey, where he was asked if he had any thoughts on how peace in Northern Ireland could be achieved: 'What we would like to see is that the British government and the IRA should adopt precisely the line that we have taken … There is nothing better than opponents sitting down to resolve their problems in a peaceful manner.'

3 July 1863

The 69th Pennsylvania repels Pickett's charge

On 3 July 1863, the 69th Pennsylvania Infantry, a regiment in the Union army mainly comprising Irish immigrants, repelled Pickett's charge at the Battle of Gettysburg. This was the most famous attack of the American Civil War, by 13,000 Confederates under the command of George Pickett, James Pettigrew and Isaac Trimble. That morning, the men of the 69th were positioned behind a low stone wall on Cemetery Ridge, in the middle of the Union line. At 1:00 p.m., an attack from the Confederates saw 150 guns fire at Union positions. This lasted over an hour. Then Pickett's charge began.

The 69th at Gettysburg was commanded by Col. Dennis O'Kane, who had emigrated to the US from Ireland in the 1840s. O'Kane told the men to hold their fire until the Confederates were close enough for their eyes to be seen, and said, 'Let your work this day be for victory or for death.' When the enemy were 30 paces away, the 69th opened fire. Nonetheless, Confederates breached the wall, and fought with Union soldiers hand-to-hand. It looked as though the rebels had the upper hand. The other Union regiments withdrew, but the 69th remained.

Finally, the Confederate soldiers were forced to retreat. There had been huge loss of life for the 69th – of the 248 men in its ranks, 143 were killed in the battle. O'Kane was mortally wounded, and died later that day.

Their importance in preventing a victory for Robert E. Lee was undeniable. Historian Dr Earl J. Hess noted: 'In what proved to be the turning point in repulsing Armistead's penetration of the angle, the 69th refused to give way any further … This regiment put up a magnificent fight that … killed any chance that Pickett's divisions might push the Federals off Cemetery Ridge.'

4 July 1957

De Valera condemns Fethard boycott

In 1957, a boycott of Protestant businesses was called by Fr William Stafford, a priest in Fethard-on-Sea, Co. Wexford. Fethard was a village where about 25 of the 107 residents were Protestant. The boycott arose when Sheila Cloney, a member of the Church of Ireland who was married to Catholic Seán Cloney, fled Wexford with their two daughters, Eileen and Hazel, rather than be forced to raise them in the religion of their father: a stipulation of the *Ne Temere* decree issued by the Catholic Church in 1907. She first went to Northern Ireland, then to the Orkney Islands. Seán Cloney followed her there, and they were reunited.

On 4 July 1957, the Fethard-on-Sea boycott was raised in Dáil Éireann by Dr Noël Browne, who asked the Taoiseach, Éamon de Valera, if he had any statement to make on the matter. De Valera responded by saying that he thought the boycott was 'ill-conceived, ill-considered and futile'. He repudiated 'any suggestion that this boycott is typical of the attitude or conduct of our people', and begged all involved to 'use their influence to bring this deplorable affair to a speedy end'. For years, many had thought that de Valera was in cahoots with the Catholic hierarchy in Ireland, to the point of allowing John Charles McQuaid, who would later become the Archbishop of Dublin, significant input into the drafting of the 1937 Irish Constitution.

Though de Valera condemned the boycott, he also urged Sheila Cloney to 'respect her troth and her promise and to return with her children to her husband and her home' – in other words, to raise her children Catholic. The boycott informally came to an end when Fr Allen, another Catholic priest, bought a packet of cigarettes in Gardiner's, one of two Protestant-owned shops in the village.

5 July 1828

Daniel O'Connell is elected in Clare

On 5 July 1828, Daniel O'Connell was elected a Member of Parliament for Clare, the first Roman Catholic representative since the Test Act was introduced in 1673. He stood against William Vesey-FitzGerald, who had been appointed to the British cabinet by the Duke of Wellington, a move that required him to stand for office.

There was some ambiguity as to whether a Catholic like O'Connell could stand: in order to sit in parliament, MPs had to declare that 'the sacrifice of the Mass and the invocation of the Blessed Virgin Mary and the other saints, as now practised in the Church of Rome, are impious and idolatrous.' However, it was clear that Catholic candidates could be elected without taking their seats, thus forcing the British Government to remove the oath from parliament and pave the way for Catholic Emancipation.

O'Connell told his supporters, 'as a Catholic, I cannot, and of course never will, take the oaths prescribed to members of parliament.' When the election results were announced, O'Connell had received 2,057 votes to Vesey-FitzGerald's 982. In his victory speech, he said: 'Wellington and Peel ... all shall be forgotten, pardoned and forgiven upon giving us Emancipation, unconditional, unqualified, free, and unshackled.'

The following year, on 13 April 1829, the Roman Catholic Relief Act received Royal Assent, applying not only to Ireland but to Great Britain as well. It did receive some criticism – the property qualification to vote in Ireland went from 40 shillings (£2) to £10, significantly reducing the electorate. However, O'Connell confided in a friend, 'It is a comfort to have struggled for this glorious object and to have assisted in achieving a bloodless revolution.'

O'Connell had to stand again, as the act was not retroactive, and was returned unopposed in July 1829.

6 July 1907

Theft of the Irish Crown Jewels

On 6 July 1907, it was discovered that the 'Irish Crown Jewels' (as they were commonly referred to) had been stolen from a safe in Dublin Castle. They were worth much less than their English counterparts – about £40,000 at the time. Officially, they were called the Insignia of the Most Illustrious Order of St Patrick – closer to the English Order of the Garter or the Scottish Order of the Thistle – and had been made in London in 1830 by the firm of Rundell and Bridge for ceremonial use by the Lord Lieutenant of Ireland.

Nevertheless, their theft was a source of great embarrassment to Sir Arthur

Vicars, the Ulster King of Arms, who was entrusted with their safekeeping. Only two keys could open the safe containing the jewels, both of which Vicars had in his possession. They were last seen on 11 June when he showed them to John Hodgson, a librarian to the Duke of Northumberland. Suspicion fell on Francis Shackleton, brother of famed explorer Ernest Shackleton. Shackleton had lived with Vicars for two years and was homosexual; authorities at the time felt that this made him susceptible to blackmail.

The timing of the theft was unfortunate – a royal visit from Edward VIII was scheduled for four days later. Signs went up around Dublin offering £1,000 as a reward for information relating to the jewels' whereabouts. In 1908, the *Freeman's Journal* wrote: 'His majesty is more angry about the incidents connected with the lost Irish Crown Jewels than about anything since his accession, seven years ago.'

No culprit was ever found, and though Shackleton was acquitted – he was not in the country at the time of the theft – he was charged with defrauding the Scottish nobleman Lord Ronald Gower of his fortune in 1913.

7 July 1903

Mother Jones leads the March of the Mill Children

On 7 July 1903, Mary Harris Jones, the Cork-born union organiser better known as Mother Jones, began leading the March of the Mill Children: a walk from Kensington, Pennsylvania to the home of President Theodore Roosevelt in Oyster Bay, New York. On it were nearly 300 men, women and children who worked in the mines of Pennsylvania, demanding a 55-hour work week.

Harris was 66 years old at time. Born in 1837, she had emigrated with her family from Ireland to Toronto, where she worked briefly as a teacher before moving to Memphis, Tennessee and marrying ironworker and union activist George Jones. During the yellow fever epidemic of 1867, she lost her husband and their four children. After that, she dedicated her life to workers' rights and improved employment conditions.

The March of the Mill Children was spurred by a visit to Kensington in the spring of 1903, where 75,000 textile workers were on strike, at least 10,000 of whom were children. There was a state law prohibiting children under the age of 12 from working but, according to Jones, it was poorly enforced. She saw children 'with their hands off, some with the thumb missing, some with their fingers off at the knuckles'. When told that these child labour breaches had not been reported because mill owners had stocks in the newspapers, she replied, 'Well, I've got stock in these little children, and I'll arrange a little publicity.'

When the marchers arrived at Roosevelt's home, Sagamore Hill, they were denied entry by his secretary. Nevertheless, the following year the National Child Labor Committee was formed. Sadly, Jones would not live to see the Fair Labor Standards Act of 1938, part of the New Deal brought in by Franklin D. Roosevelt, which outlawed 'oppressive child labor in commerce or in the production of goods for commerce'.

8 July 1985
Ryanair begins operations

On 8 July 1985, Ryanair began operations with an inaugural flight between Waterford and London Gatwick of a 15-seater turboprop plane. It was a modest beginning for what would become the largest airline in Europe and the fifth largest globally, carrying 138.9 million passengers in 2018.

A small contingent of people – including the Mayor of Waterford – boarded the aircraft, which was scheduled to travel from Waterford to Gatwick once a day from Monday to Friday. Originally, Ryanair catered to business people, offering the flight for £190 return: less than the £210 that was standard for return Dublin–London tickets at the time. In its first year, Ryanair carried 15,000 passengers on this route.

Ryanair was started by Tony Ryan, a businessman from Thurles, Co. Tipperary who had previously worked for Aer Lingus. In its first three years of operation, the airline accumulated losses of £20 million. However, in 1987 Ryan hired Michael O'Leary as his personal financier and tax adviser, a step that revolutionised the company. O'Leary drew inspiration from Southwest, an American low-fare operator established in 1971. He would later tell the *Financial Times*, 'We went to look at Southwest. It was like the road to Damascus. This was the way to make Ryanair work.'

Fast-forward to 2009, and its market capitalisation at the end of the financial year was €7.5 billion, twice that of British Airways. It achieved this by relentlessly driving down fares across Europe.

Ryanair hasn't been short of controversy, with O'Leary referring to EU commissioners as 'communist morons' and officials at the British Airport Authority as 'overcharging rapists'. He has made some bizarre suggestions over the years, such as slapping heavier passengers with a 'fat tax' and forcing people to pay to use the toilet on flights. In his own words, 'We specialize in cheap publicity stunts.'

9 July 1921

Truce in War of Independence

On 9 July 1921, a truce was announced between the IRA and the British forces in Ireland, in a statement issued by Richard Mulcahy, IRA Chief of Staff: 'In view of the conversations now being entered into by our Government with the Government of Great Britain, and in pursuance of mutual conversations, active operations by our forces will be suspended as from noon, Monday, 11 July.'

The truce was signed by two members of the Dáil, Eamonn Duggan and Robert Barton. On the British side were General Sir Nevil Macready, Commander-in-Chief of the British forces in Ireland, Colonel J. Brind, and A. W. Cope. The British agreed that there would be no incoming troops, no 'provocative displays of force', no pursuit of Irish officers, men, war material or military stores, and no 'interference with the movements of Irish persons, military or civil'. In return, the Irish agreed to cease 'attacks on Crown forces and civilians', that there would be no interference with government or private property, and no action 'likely to cause disturbance of the peace'.

The truce divided IRA men, foreshadowing the split that led to the Civil War. Liam Deasy, from Cork, would reflect on the moment he learned of it: 'I well remember that my personal feeling was one of disappointment and I must admit I foresaw defeat and trouble ahead.'

Some last-minute assaults were carried out against British forces: nine people were killed in Castleisland, Co. Kerry on 10 July, including five IRA men and four British soldiers. Still, sporadic attacks aside, the truce brought peace to Ireland for the remainder of the year. De Valera left for London shortly afterwards, accompanied by Barton, Austin Stack and Arthur Griffin, to meet British Prime Minister David Lloyd George.

10 July 1927

Kevin O'Higgins is shot dead

On 10 July 1927, Kevin O'Higgins, the Minister for Justice and Vice-President of the Executive Council of the Irish Free State, was shot and fatally wounded on his way to Sunday Mass in Booterstown, Co. Dublin. The identity of the three men who carried out the attack would not come to light until almost 60 years later, when Harry White, a former Chief of Staff of the IRA, named them in a 1985 interview with Brian Looney of the *Irish Press*: 'Bill Gannon told me that he and Archie Doyle were two of the assassins ... By naming them at this stage, I'm finishing a chapter of Irish history.' The third man was Tim Coughlan. White explained the motives behind O'Higgins's killing: 'As minister for justice, he ordered the murder of his former friends ... That's why he was killed.'

O'Higgins had, indeed, signed the execution order of four anti-Treaty IRA men in 1922, in retaliation for the shooting dead of TD Seán Hales and wounding of another TD, Pádraic Ó Máille. However, O'Higgins had been the last cabinet member to give his consent, and when questioned on it in the Dáil, he said: 'We have no higher aim than to place the people of Ireland in the saddle in Ireland, and let them do their will, but we will not acquiesce in gun-bullying ... One of these men was a friend of mine.' The friend was Rory O'Connor, who had been best man at his wedding.

O'Higgins's death rocked the country and led to changes that would have a lasting effect. W. T. Cosgrave introduced the Electoral Amendment Act, which meant that politicians contesting seats in the Dáil would have to take them or forfeit them. This made abstentionism all but impossible for Fianna Fáil, and so, on 12 August 1927, Fianna Fáil took its seats in Dáil Éireann for the first time.

11 July 1792

Meeting of the Harpers in Belfast

On 11 July 1792, the Meeting of the Harpers was held in Belfast. The principal organisers of this four-day event, which has come to be referred to as the Belfast Harp Festival, were Thomas Russell, Henry Joy and Dr James MacDonnell, the last of whom had been taught to play the instrument by the blind harper Arthur O'Neill.

Robert Simms and Robert Bradshaw assisted with the planning.

There were several links to the Society of United Irishmen, founded in Belfast one year earlier. Thomas Russell and Robert Simms were members of the society, and Henry Joy was uncle to Henry Joy McCracken, who would be executed for his part in the 1798 rebellion. Indeed, just as the Society of United Irishmen was influenced by the French Revolution, the Belfast meeting was timed to coincide with the celebrations in the city to mark three years since the Storming of the Bastille.

An advertisement in the *Belfast News-Letter* in April 1792, having announced that a 'respectable body of the inhabitants of Belfast [have] published a plan for reviving the ancient music of this country', requested that 'Performers of the Irish Harp' assemble in the town in July. It was circulated in newspapers throughout Ireland, but only 11 harpers attended the event, including Arthur O'Neill, MacDonnell's tutor.

Also in attendance was 19-year-old Edward Bunting, from Armagh, who was hired to transcribe the music. So enraptured was Bunting by what he heard that he made it a lifelong goal to collect and record as much traditional Irish music as he could: he published three volumes of *The Ancient Music of Ireland*, beginning in 1796. As Dr Colette Moloney later noted, 'Bunting was the first individual that we explicitly know of who collected and published Irish music obtained from traditional musicians at first hand, in the field, as it were.'

12 July 1691
The Battle of Aughrim

On 12 July 1691, the Battle of Aughrim was fought just outside the Galway village, between Ballinasloe and Loughrea. It was the bloodiest battle ever fought on Irish soil, claiming the lives of between 6,000 and 9,000 men – more than the combined total who died in the battles of Clontarf, Kinsale and Vinegar Hill, and the Easter Rising. It also brought a decisive end to the Williamite War in Ireland, and was followed by the signing of the Treaty of Limerick and the Flight of the Wild Geese – the departure of defeated Irish soldiers to France.

The previous year, at the Battle of the Boyne, the forces of William of Orange had faced those of the deposed James II, who was aided by troops raised by the King of France, Louis XIV. The Jacobite forces lost then, with James fleeing the scene, but the war continued for another year. Jacobite forces controlled Munster and Connacht, while William held Dublin and most of the east. William had tried to capture Limerick but was held off by Patrick Sarsfield, the Earl of Lucan.

At Aughrim, Sarsfield led the Jacobite forces, along with the Marquis de Saint-Ruth, a French general sent by Louis. The Williamite forces were led by the Dutch General Godbert de Ginkel, William having returned to the Netherlands. Though each side had a roughly equal number of troops – around 20,000 – the Williamites had more cavalry and superior artillery. Saint-Ruth was killed in the battle, decapitated by a cannon ball. One eyewitness, surveying the carnage, said, 'Seen from the top of the hill, the unburied dead covered four miles, like a great flock of sheep.'

Sarsfield survived, but the loss of thousands of troops left the Jacobites with only Limerick under their control. After another siege, the Treaty of Limerick was signed on 3 October 1691.

13 July 1985
Live Aid

On 13 July 1985, the Live Aid benefit concert was held simultaneously in Wembley Stadium, London and John F. Kennedy Stadium, Philadelphia. Organised by Bob Geldof and Midge Ure, Live Aid was one of events of the decade. It raised approximately £50 million for famine relief in Ethiopia, and was broadcast to more than a billion viewers in 110 countries. Geldof's country of birth – Ireland – was the largest contributor per capita, donating £7 million.

Geldof had first seen footage of famine in Ethiopia in October 1984. Moved by the sight of tens of thousands of people in dire need, he penned a song with Ure titled 'Do They Know It's Christmas?', released under the name Band Aid. It featured guest vocals from singers such as Sting, George Michael and Bono, and raised millions, reaching number one in 13 countries.

Spurred by the success of the single, and having

seen first-hand the effect of the famine when he visited Ethiopia in early 1985, Geldof decided to stage the concert. In London, Queen, the Who, Elton John, Spandau Ballet and Geldof's own band, the Boomtown Rats, took the stage, among many others. In Philadelphia, audiences were treated to Duran Duran, Eric Clapton, Neil Young, Tina Turner and even the surviving members of Led Zeppelin, who reunited for the one-off gig.

Afterwards, Geldof spoke to the RTÉ radio show *Morning Ireland* to express his gratitude for the generosity of the Irish people: 'I feel extremely privileged to be an Irishman at this point because Ireland more than any country in the entire world … on this day, they have shown the rest of the world what it is possible to do. And Ireland, giving the amount of money they gave, is the equivalent of the Americans giving £250 million or the British giving £60 million.'

14 July 1789

James F. X. Whyte is 'liberated' from the Bastille

On 14 July 1789, the Bastille was stormed. French peasants took over the ancient fortress, which symbolised Louis XVI and the nobility of Paris, as it had been used to house political prisoners for centuries. Between 1417 (the year it was declared a state prison) and 1789, a total of 5,279 prisoners passed through its gates.

However, on the day that it was attacked, the Bastille had only seven inmates. One of them was Dubliner James F. X. Whyte. Born in 1730, Whyte moved to France to become a captain in Lally's Regiment of the Irish Brigade. He married in 1767 in Paris, but in 1781 suffered a mental breakdown, claiming to be either St Louis or Julius Caesar.

After his 'liberation', Whyte was paraded through the streets of Paris. One eyewitness described him as 'a little feeble old man who exhibited an appearance of childishness and fatuity, tottering as he walked and his countenance exhibiting little more than the smile of an idiot'. His beard was said to be almost a yard long.

Whyte's post-Bastille freedom was to be short-lived. The next day, he was transferred to the Charenton Asylum, where the Marquis de Sade was being held.

Whyte was not the only Irish connection at the Storming of the Bastille. One of the two chaplains at the prison, Thomas MacMahon from Co. Galway, celebrated one of the last masses in the building. There are also claims that Joseph Kavanagh, a cobbler from Co. Wexford, led the mob through the streets crying 'To the Bastille!' Another story goes that James Bartholemew Blackwell, from Ennis, Co. Clare led the first contingent to storm the Bastille. Evidence for these, however, is scanty.

15 July 1942

'Paddy' Finucane is shot down over the English Channel

On 15 July 1942, Brendan 'Paddy' Finucane, the youngest wing commander in the history of the Royal Air Force (RAF), was shot down on his way back from a mission in France. He was 21 years of age. Though Winston Churchill and Éamon de Valera had clashed on more than one occasion over the neutrality of the Irish state, Churchill himself would say, 'If ever I feel a bitter feeling rising in my heart about the Irish, the hands of heroes like Finucane seem to stretch out and soothe it away.'

Finucane's father, Andy, was a veteran of a different kind. He had served as second lieutenant under Ned Daly in the Four Courts garrison during the Easter Rising. Brendan was born in Rathmines, Dublin, and had his first experience of flying at Baldonnel Aerodrome in 1932, when he and his brother Raymond went on a 10-minute flight during an air show. In November 1936, the Finucanes moved to Richmond, Surrey, and the future wing commander took a clerical job in London. In 1938 he applied to join the RAF, and was accepted. In June 1940, Finucane was sent for training as a Spitfire pilot.

By 1942 he had moved up the RAF ranks to become wing commander. He led his wing on an attack on a German army camp in northern France on 15 July 1942, but his Spitfire was hit by a burst of machine-gun fire on the way back, and he ditched it into the sea about 10 miles out from Le Touquet.

Finucane's nephew, also Brendan, became a Queen's Counsel and attended a ceremony to commemorate the Easter Rising in 2016. While visiting, he said, 'I'm delighted this is happening at a time of mutual understanding when the Queen's visit to Ireland was welcomed by a very large percentage of the population of Ireland.'

16 July 1936

Assassination attempt on Edward VIII

On 16 July 1936, Irish would-be assassin George Andrew McMahon, also known as Jerome Bannigan, made an attempt on the life of Edward VIII as the monarch was on horseback at Constitution Hill, near Buckingham Palace. McMahon pointed a loaded revolver at the king, but was spotted and subdued by police. The following day, Edward would write to a friend thanking 'the Almighty' for two things: 'Firstly, that it did not rain, and secondly that the man in the brown suit's gun did not go off!' One of the officers who arrested McMahon is alleged to have said, 'These bloody foreigners coming over here to kill our king'.

The story didn't end there. On 31 July, at Bow Street Police Court, McMahon told the magistrate, 'I am a natural born British subject and so were my ancestors so far as I can trace.' At his full trial at the Old Bailey in September, when asked if he was Irish, McMahon replied, 'Irish by birth.' He had been born Jerome Brannigan in Cookstown, Co. Tyrone, the son of Patrick and Eileen Brannigan (or Bannigan). When he was a child, the family moved to Govan in Glasgow. In 1927 he was jailed for embezzlement; on his release he adopted the name George McMahon.

After moving to Dublin, then Liverpool, he eventually settled in London, where he became an informer to the Special Branch in 1935, claiming to have information about gun-running into Ireland by the IRA. Why, if he was working for the British state, did he pull a gun on King Edward in 1936? The answer is still unknown. Some believe there was an Italian plot to assassinate the king, which McMahon deliberately botched. In any case, he was sentenced to 12 months' hard labour for the crime.

17 July 1904

Camogie is first played in public

On 17 July 1904, camogie was played in public for the first time, at the Royal Meath Agricultural Society Grounds in Navan, which later became the site of the GAA stadium Páirc Tailteann. The game was between two Dublin clubs, Keatings and Cúchulainns, and ended with a victory for Keatings, one score to nothing.

The rules of camogie largely came from university student Máire Ní Chinnéide, who would become the first President of the Camogie Association, founded in 1905. Though the game is similar to hurling, there are some small differences to make it less physical, such as the use of a lighter sliothar (ball), and the fact that shouldering is not allowed.

In 2004, the centenary of the first game was celebrated in Croke Park. Speaking at the event, John O'Donoghue, Minister for Arts, Sports and Tourism, said: 'I am sure that those pioneers who organised the first public game of camogie in Páirc Tailteann between Craobh A'Cheithnnigh and Cuchullains in 1904 would be delighted with the way camogie has grown to become one of the most popular and widely played female sports in Ireland with approximately 84,000 players. I would like to pay tribute to those pioneers for introducing a wonderful sport to the multitudes of Irish women who have graced the fields and stadiums of Ireland throughout the last 100 years.'

President of Cumann Camógaíochta na nGael Miriam O'Callaghan noted that the association predated women's suffrage: 'Reaching a centenary is a significant achievement by any standards but reaching it in such a healthy and vibrant state is more than significant. Since 1904 our game has grown beyond the expectations of its founders.'

18 July 1912

Suffragettes protest Asquith's Dublin visit

On 18 July 1912, the British Prime Minister, Herbert Asquith, visited Dublin. He was scheduled to speak at the Theatre Royal to a crowd of 4,000 people, all supporters of his recent Home Rule Bill. However, his stance on women's voting rights, of which he was not a supporter, earned him the ire of suffragettes. Both the British Women's Social and Political Union (WSPU) and the Irish Women's Franchise League (IWFL) decided to stage protests at his visit.

As Asquith's ship arrived in Dublin from Holyhead that morning, he was greeted by members of the IWFL holding placards and demanding voting rights through a megaphone. Members of the IWFL who were imprisoned at the time wore black rosettes in protest. Members of the WSPU took a more forceful approach. On 16 July, Gladys Evans from London and Jennie Baines (alias Lizzie Baker) from Stockport travelled to Dublin in anticipation of Asquith's visit. Two days later, they were joined by Mary Leigh and Mabel Capper. Their visit had been expected by Chief Secretary for Ireland Augustine Birrell, who described them as 'the advanced section of the militant Suffragists'.

As Asquith and John Redmond, leader of the Irish Parliamentary Party, were travelling across O'Connell Bridge, Leigh threw a small axe into their carriage. Attached to it was a note describing it as a 'symbol of the extinction of the Liberal Party for evermore'. The axe grazed Redmond's ear, causing him to bleed, and Leigh disappeared into the crowd.

That night, the four women entered the Theatre Royal and set fire to chairs and carpets before being apprehended by Sergeant Durban Cooper of the Connaught Rangers. Leigh and Evans were sentenced to five years' penal servitude, Baines and Capper to seven months. Leigh and Evans went on hunger strike and were forcibly fed before their releases due to ill-health in September and October of that year respectively.

19 July 1997

Provisional IRA ceasefire

On 19 July 1997, the Provisional IRA announced a 'complete cessation of military operations', its second ceasefire in three years, which would prove to be its last. The following year, 331 out of 350 Sinn Féin delegates at the party's Ard Fheis in Dublin voted to accept the terms of the Good Friday Agreement, and in 2005 the group said it had 'formally ordered an end to the armed campaign'.

The Provisional IRA's 1994 ceasefire had abruptly come to an end with an explosion in the London Docklands in February 1996, which caused £150 million worth of damage and killed two men in a nearby newsagent's. There was therefore scepticism when the July 1997 statement was issued. Ken Maginnis, security spokesman for the Ulster Unionist Party, said: 'I don't expect anyone to take a ceasefire declaration at face value ... There will have to be a definite commitment to a permanent, complete and universal ceasefire with an indication that disarmament and the disbandment of the terrorist organisation can take place.'

The Provisional IRA had blamed unionists and the British government for the breakdown of the 1994 ceasefire, both of whom were said to have 'blocked any possibility of real or inclusive negotiations'. Now, with a new British Prime Minister in Tony Blair and a new Northern Ireland Secretary of State in Mo Mowlam, it was believed that a more equitable offer could be made to assuage republican demands.

In October, Blair become the first Prime Minister to meet with Sinn Féin since the outbreak of the Troubles, arguing that differences should be settled by 'negotiation, discussion and debate' rather than 'the hatred and despair and the killings' that had gone before. US President Bill Clinton also issued a statement, saying, 'On behalf of the American people, I welcome the cease-fire declared by the IRA on July 19.'

20 July 1974

Women 'invade' Forty Foot

On 20 July 1974, a group of about 10 women, styling themselves the Dublin City Women's Invasion Force, led a protest at the hitherto male-only bathing place of Forty Foot, Sandycve, Co. Dublin. Among them were journalist Nell McCafferty, future politician Nuala Fennell and poet Mary D'Arcy. This was symbolic of a growing confidence among the women of Ireland, increasingly set on asserting their rights. In 1971, the Irish Women's Liberation Movement – co-founded by McCafferty – had travelled from Dublin to Belfast to buy contraceptives, illegal in the Irish state since 1935, and in 1973, a ban on women working in the civil service after marriage had been lifted. The sight of women swimming in an area previously used exclusively by men may have seemed minor by comparison, but it was enough to ruffle the feathers of many at Forty Foot that day.

According to McCafferty, 'There was loads of sexist abuse from the men in language that was acceptable at the time.' In footage shot for RTÉ, one angry patron can be heard telling a reporter, 'Get out! There was a time when no self-respecting women would be in here anyway.' The women carried placards with slogans like 'Out from under and into the swim', 'We'll fight them on the beaches, we'll win between the sheets' and 'The Forty Foot is for women too.'

The Forty Foot holds a distinctive place in the history of Dublin. The first chapter of James Joyce's *Ulysses* ends with Buck Mulligan plunging into the 'scrotumtightening sea' for a swim.

A year on from the women's protest, it had been integrated: a move welcomed by one man whom McCafferty met there in 1975, who told her that 'It humanised it.' It wasn't until 2013, however, that the local Sandycove Bathers Association admitted women.

21 July 1976

Assassination of Christopher Ewart-Biggs

On 21 July 1976, a mere 12 days after he had taken up the role of British Ambassador to Ireland, Christopher Ewart-Biggs was killed when a landmine exploded under his car in Sandyford, Co. Dublin. He was 54 years of age. Also killed was Judith Cooke, a 26-year-old civil servant. According to the Secretary of State for Northern Ireland at the time, Merlyn Rees, Cooke was 'someone we had all marked out for higher things'. The Permanent Under-Secretary of the Northern Ireland Office, Brian Cubbon, was seriously injured, as was Irish chauffeur Brian O'Driscoll. The Provisional IRA claimed responsibility for the attack two months later in an interview with the *Sunday Times*: 'We make no apology for it. He was sent here to co-ordinate British Intelligence activities, and he was assassinated because of that.'

The killings caused outrage in Dublin. Taoiseach Liam Cosgrave called an emergency session of the Dáil, and addressed the nation in a television broadcast: 'This atrocity fills all decent Irish people with a sense of shame. The government are determined that all the resources at their disposal will be used to ensure that the perpetrators are brought to justice.' Cosgrave's sentiments were echoed in London by British Prime Minister James Callaghan: 'These miserable men are the common enemy of both Governments and indeed of all decent people who wish to live in peace and amity in all our islands.'

No one was ever convicted of the killings of Ewart-Biggs and Cooke. The late ambassador's legacy lived on through the Christopher Ewart-Biggs Memorial Prize, created in 1977 by his widow, Jane Ewart-Biggs. Its stated purpose was to recognise literary work 'promoting and encouraging peace and reconciliation in Ireland, a greater understanding between the peoples of Britain and Ireland, or closer co-operation between the partners of the European Community.'

22 July 1822

'Martin's Law' is introduced by Galway MP

On 22 July 1822, the first piece of animal welfare legislation in the world (the Cruel and Improper Treatment of Cattle Act 1822, or 'Martin's Law') was passed. Irish MP Richard 'Humanity Dick' Martin, representing Galway County, was largely responsible for it. The punishment for 'wantonly and cruelly' beating, abusing or ill-treating animals such as horses, cows and sheep could be no more than £5 and no less than 10 shillings, provided the complaint was made to a Justice of the Peace or Magistrate within 10 days of the offence. If the person convicted could not or would not pay the fine, he or she would be committed to the 'House of Correction or some other Prison' for up to three months.

Martin was born in Dangan, Galway. Though his parents were Catholics, he was raised Protestant, ostensibly so that he could enter the Irish Parliament, and later the British Parliament. His interest in animal rights was instilled in him at a young age, when he was sent to Harrow School and studied under Samuel Parr. Parr is famous for having said, 'He that can look with rapture upon the agonies of an unoffending and unresisting animal, will soon learn to view the sufferings of a fellow creature with indifference.'

In 1824, two years after his Act was introduced, Martin co-founded the Society for the Prevention of Cruelty to Animals along with more than 20 other reformers, including Thomas Fowell Buxton and William Wilberforce. It was granted royal status by Queen Victoria, and became the Royal Society for the Prevention of Cruelty to Animals (RSPCA). Eleven years later, the Cruelty to Animals Act 1835 ('Pease's Law') consolidated further protections in law for animals. It and all subsequent acts could be traced to Martin's in 1822.

23 July 1803

Robert Emmet's rebellion

On 23 July 1803, Robert Emmet led a rebellion in Dublin that was crushed shortly after it began, but not before approximately 70 people lay dead in the capital city. Emmet, the son of a Protestant doctor who lived at St Stephen's Green, was stirred by the ideas of the Society of United Irishmen and the failed uprising of 1798. He entered Trinity College at age 15 to study maths and chemistry, the latter of which would serve him well when he was concocting explosives for the 1803 rebellion.

Having failed to secure help from France, Emmet had only about 80 men to join in his attempted takeover of Dublin Castle, the seat of British rule in Ireland. The date for the rebellion was brought forward, too, after an accidental explosion at an arms depot on Patrick Street on 16 July fatally wounded two men and alerted the authorities to Emmet's plans.

On 23 July, a proclamation was issued and read by Emmet to his followers: 'We war not against property – We war against no religious sect – We war not against past opinions or prejudices – We war against English dominion.' However, due to poor communication, as well as drunkenness and ill-discipline among the rank and file, the rebellion could not be properly staged.

Soon after, a British soldier was pulled from his horse and killed. Emmet tried to call off the rebellion there and then, but matters were made much worse when the mob that had gathered spotted Arthur Wolfe, the Lord Chief Justice of Ireland, also known as Lord Kilwarden. Kilwarden and his nephew were pulled from their carriage on Thomas Street and hacked to death. Ironically, Kilwarden had argued that Wolfe Tone's court martial in 1798 was unjust.

Appalled at the carnage, Emmet fled the scene. Further clashes took place throughout the day, resulting in the deaths of about 20 British soldiers and 50 rebels.

24 July 1907

Police strike in Belfast

On 24 July 1907, a meeting was held at Musgrave Street Police Barracks in Belfast at which it was decided that the local police force would go on strike, partly in solidarity with the dock workers in the city but also because of their own grievances. The strike marked the arrival of James 'Big Jim' Larkin into the Irish labour movement.

Larkin, a Liverpool-born union organiser of Irish parentage, arrived in Belfast in January of that year, aiming to recruit men to the National Union of Dock Labourers (NUDL). By April, 2,978 of the 3,100 or so dock workers in the city had joined. That month, the Belfast Shipping Company locked out its workers and brought in strike-breakers to crush the union. The breaking point for police came when Constable William Barrett refused orders from District Inspector Keaveney to escort a strike-breaker on a motor-waggon. Barrett was dismissed and became the leader of the 'More Pay Movement', which issued a flyer to police throughout the city inviting them to the 24 July meeting.

Around 200–300 men attended, despite being instructed not to by Acting Commissioner Morrell. When Morrell attempted to intervene on the night, he was punched by Barrett. About 70 per cent of the police force in the city (800 men) supported the strike, which resulted in approximately 6,000 troops being brought in to restore order. The strike eventually collapsed, and Larkin was expelled from the NUDL in 1908, after which he set up the Irish Transport and General Workers' Union (ITGWU).

Before that, however, Larkin co-authored a handbill aimed at uniting the city's workers in solidarity, regardless of religion: 'Not as Catholics or Protestants, as Nationalists or Unionists but as Belfastmen and workers stand together and don't be misled by the employers' game of dividing Catholic and Protestant.'

25 July 1917
First meeting of the Irish Convention

On 25 July 1917, the Irish Convention met for the first time; it continued to meet until April 1918. This was an effort to bring together leaders of all the major political parties in Ireland so that, in the words of British Prime Minister David Lloyd George, 'Irishmen of all creeds and parties might meet together in a Convention for the purpose of drafting a Constitution for their Country.' However, its final report laid bare the divisions that existed on the island.

Shortly after the United States entered the First World War, Walter Hines Page, the American Ambassador to the United Kingdom, received a telegram: 'The President [Woodrow Wilson] wishes that, when you next meet the Prime Minister, you would explain to him that only one circumstance now appears to stand in the way of perfect cooperation with Great Britain … the failure of Great Britain so far to establish a satisfactory form of self-government in Ireland.'

The Convention was chaired by Sir Horace Plunkett, a one-time Unionist MP for South County Dublin who had been converted to the Home Rule cause in 1911. It met in the Regent House in Trinity College and included members of the Irish Parliamentary Party as well as unionists, but was boycotted by Sinn Féin.

The report the Convention produced in April 1918 recommended that self-government be brought to Ireland, but only 44 of the 89 delegates supported this recommendation. Ulster unionists published a separate document, protesting what they called the 'implication in the main report that a measure of agreement regarding Irish self-government had been attained'. Plunkett responded: 'Perhaps unanimity was too much to expect ... There was ... a portion of Ulster where a majority claimed that if Ireland had the right to separate herself from the rest of the United Kingdom, they had the same right to separation from the rest of Ireland.'

26 July 1914

Bachelors Walk killings

On 26 July 1914, three people were shot dead on Bachelors Walk, Dublin, when members of the King's Own Scottish Borderers, an infantry regiment of the British Army, opened fire. They were Mary Duffy (50), Patrick Quinn (46) and James Brennan (18). A fourth person would later die. This occurred on the same day that the *Asgard*, a yacht belonging to writer and future Sinn Féin TD Erskine Childers, landed in Howth carrying 900 Mauser rifles and 29,000 rounds of ammunition.

As the Volunteers were marching back to Dublin with the weapons, they were stopped in Clontarf by soldiers of the Scottish Borderers, accompanied by Assistant Commissioner William Harrell of the Dublin Metropolitan Police. It was at this point that the Volunteers dispersed with the weapons. A scuffle with the police, who disobeyed Harrell's orders, followed, but there were no fatalities. Of the 900 rifles smuggled in, only 19 were seized.

The soldiers and police returned to their barracks in the city centre. Along Bachelors Walk, they were verbally abused and pelted with stones and rotten fruit. They opened fire, and soon three Dubliners, none with any connection to the Irish Volunteers, lay dead.

The Bachelors Walk killings were a disaster for the British Army and a propaganda victory for the Irish Volunteers. Writing to Joe McGarrity of Clan na Gael a few days after, Patrick Pearse said: 'The stirring events of Sunday will rebound enormously to the advantage of the movement … The brutal murders of the unarmed crowd by the soldiers who an hour previously had run from the Volunteers have given public sentiment just that turn that was desirable. The army is an object of odium and derision and the Volunteers are the heroes of the hour. The whole movement, the whole country, has been re-baptised by blood shed for Ireland.'

27 July 1866

First successful transatlantic telegraph cable

On 27 July 1866, the first successful telegraphic connection was established between the continents of Europe and North America, with a cable stretching almost 2,000 miles between Valentia Island, Co. Kerry and Heart's Content, Newfoundland. Long-distance telegraph lines had first been used in 1844, when one was set up between Baltimore and Washington, DC in the United States. The same year, another connected Paddington Station in London and Slough, 19 miles away. The notion of telegraphs crossing bodies of water was not unprecedented, as the Submarine Telegraph Company had laid a cable between Dover and Calais in 1851.

Nevertheless, laying a cable across the Atlantic Ocean was no small feat. That dream came closer to reality in 1858 with the launch of the SS *Great Eastern*, constructed by Isambard Kingdom Brunel, one of England's most renowned engineers. It was by far the largest ship that had been built up to that time: 692 feet long, with a gross displacement of 18,915 tons. In June 1865, Cyrus Field loaded the *Great Eastern* with 7,000 tons of cable. Field was one of the founders of the Atlantic Telegraph Company, which lost a considerable amount of money when the transatlantic cable he set up in 1858 collapsed three weeks after it was officially opened. The attempt of 1865 was unsuccessful, but Field raised enough money to make another attempt in the summer of 1866.

In July 1866, the *Great Eastern* set out from Valentia Island, Co. Kerry. Halfway across the Atlantic, Field received news of the outbreak of the Austro-Prussian War. After 14 days, the ship arrived in Heart's Content, Newfoundland, and the cable was connected. Field sent the first telegraph to his wife: 'We arrived here at nine o'clock this morning. All well. Thank God, the cable is laid, and is in perfect working order.'

28 July 2005

Provisional IRA announces end of campaign

On 28 July 2005, the Provisional IRA announced a formal end to its armed campaign. In a video distributed to the media on DVD, veteran republican Séanna Walsh said he had been asked to read a statement. Walsh, an ex-prisoner who had spent more than half his life in jail at the time of his 42nd birthday, was the first Provisional IRA member to represent the organisation without a mask since 1972. He said that all units had been 'ordered to dump arms', and all volunteers 'instructed to assist the development of purely political and democratic programmes through exclusively peaceful means'.

Earlier that year, the organisation had said it was 'taking all our proposals off the table', in frustration at what it saw as its initiatives being 'attacked, devalued and dismissed by pro-unionist and anti-republican elements, including the British Government'. However, Walsh now said the Provisional IRA would co-operate with the Independent International Commission on Decommissioning (IICD), a body led by John de Chastelain and set up to supervise the handing over of weapons by both republican and loyalist paramilitary organisations.

The leaders of the Irish and British governments welcomed the move. Tony Blair said, 'This may be the day when finally, after all the false dawns and dashed hope, peace replaced war, politics replaces terror on the island of Ireland.' Taoiseach Bertie Ahern said, 'The war is over, the IRA's armed campaign is over, paramilitarism is over and I believe that we can look to the future of peace and prosperity based on mutual trust and reconciliation and a final end to violence.'

29 July 1848

Young Ireland rebellion

On 29 July 1848, a rebellion was staged by the Young Ireland movement in Ballingarry, Co. Tipperary. Given the year in which it took place, it has sometimes been referred to as 'the Famine rebellion', though its impact was relatively minor at the time. Earlier that year, Thomas Francis Meagher and William Smith O'Brien returned from France, where Louis Philippe I had just been overthrown and replaced by Alphonse de Lamartine. However, attempts to replicate that revolution in Ireland did not succeed.

For about a week before the rebellion began, O'Brien, Meagher and John Blake Dillon travelled through the counties of Wexford and Kilkenny in order to incite public protests. On 29 July, O'Brien was in the village of The Commons, in the Slieveardagh region of east Tipperary, where barricades had been erected to prevent his arrest by members of the Irish Constabulary. Seeing the barricades, 47 policemen from Callan, Co. Kilkenny, led by Captain Trant, turned and fled the scene, with rebels in pursuit.

The policemen took refuge in the home of a local widow, Margaret McCormack, along with her five children, who were effectively taken as hostages. McCormack arranged for a negotiation between O'Brien and Trant, though a policeman fired a shot at the rebels, leading to a gunfight that lasted a few hours. The rebellion came to an ignominious end when police reinforcements arrived and the rebels were forced to scatter. *The Times* of London referred to the event as the 'The Battle of the Widow McCormack's Cabbage Patch'.

Eventually, most of the leaders of the Young Ireland movement were arrested, including Meagher and O'Brien, though Meagher escaped and emigrated to the United States, where he fought on the Union side in the American Civil War. Margaret McCormack's home, which came to be known as the 'Famine Warhouse', was designated as a national heritage monument by the Irish government in 2004.

30 July 1928

Pat O'Callaghan wins gold for Ireland at the Olympics

On 30 July 1928, Dr Pat O'Callaghan, a general practitioner from Kanturk, Co. Cork, became the first athlete to win a medal representing Ireland in the Olympic Games. He won gold in the men's hammer throw in the Summer Olympics, held in Paris.

This was a seminal moment for the Irish Free State, established only a few years earlier: something that O'Callaghan knew only too well. Speaking in Kanturk on returning from the ceremony, he said, 'I am glad of my victory, not of the victory itself, but for the fact that the world has been shown that Ireland has a flag, that Ireland has a national anthem, and in fact that we have a nationality.'

O'Callaghan was not the first Irish athlete to compete in the Olympic Games, of course. Tennis player John Pius Boland won gold in both the men's singles and doubles at the first modern Olympics in Athens in 1886. Given that Ireland was part of the United Kingdom at the time, Boland's victory was recorded as one for Great Britain, although Boland was a member of the nationalist Irish Parliamentary Party and would serve as MP for South Kerry between 1900 and 1918. According to his daughter Bridget, after Boland won, a Union flag was raised alongside the German flag of his partner. Boland said, 'Actually, I'm Irish … It's a gold harp on a green ground.'

Interestingly, O'Callaghan was not the first person from Ireland to be awarded an Olympic medal post-independence. Jack Butler Years, brother of the famed poet William, was awarded a silver medal for his painting *The Liffey Swim* in 1924. Back then, the Olympics had an arts and culture segment that was divided into five categories: painting, architecture, music, literature and sculpture. This segment was dropped from the Olympics after 1948.

31 July 1893

The Gaelic League is founded

On 31 July 1893, the Gaelic League, also known as Conradh na Gaeilge, was established in Dublin, 'solely to keep the Irish Language spoken in Ireland'. Its founders were Douglas Hyde, Eoin MacNeill and Fr Eugene O'Growney.

Hyde was the son of a Protestant clergyman from Co. Roscommon. Growing up, he developed a keen interest in the Irish language, interacting with Irish speakers such as Seamus Hart, who belonged to, in Hyde's words, 'the oldest, most neglected, and poorest of the Irish-speaking population'. The 1891 census showed that there were 680,174 Irish-speakers in Ireland (14.5 per cent), a drop from 1,524,286 (23 per cent) in 1851. The moribund status of the language deeply troubled Hyde, who wrote in 1899: 'If we allow one of the finest and the richest languages in Europe, which, fifty years ago, was spoken by nearly four million Irishmen, to die out without a struggle, it will be an everlasting disgrace.'

Eoin MacNeill, a native of Antrim who had learned Irish in Connemara, shared Hyde's enthusiasm. The Gaelic League soon set up branches across Ireland, including Galway, Cork, Derry and Wexford, and even in London. By 1896, 43 branches had registered, eight of which were outside Ireland. The league only grew from there. By 1903, it had 500 affiliated branches throughout the country.

A major turning point came in 1915, when, at an Ard Fheis in Dundalk, Douglas Hyde resigned as president of the organisation, fearing the increasing influence of militant forces behind the scenes. Hyde wanted the League to remain strictly apolitical, and said: 'I will never attach myself nor allow myself to be attached to any body of men which I might think wish to use the Irish language as a cloak for politics, I don't care what kind of politics.'

1 August 1915

Graveside oration for O'Donovan Rossa

On 1 August 1915, Patrick Pearse gave the graveside oration at the funeral of prominent Irish Republican Brotherhood (IRB) member Jeremiah O'Donovan Rossa in Glasnevin Cemetery, Dublin. Pearse's closing words are among the most iconic in the history of Irish nationalism.

O'Donovan Rossa was a shopkeeper from Skibbereen, Co. Cork who had joined the IRB at a young age, and was arrested as part of a crackdown on the leadership of the Fenian movement in 1865. While in prison, he was elected a Member of Parliament for Tipperary, though his victory was declared invalid. In 1870, an amnesty allowed O'Donovan Rossa his freedom provided he leave Ireland. He spent the rest of his life in Staten Island, New York, though he did direct the 'dynamite campaign' of bombings on British cities in the 1880s.

After O'Donovan Rossa's death at age 83, Thomas Clarke, a future signatory of the 1916 Proclamation, sent a message to another exile, John Devoy: 'Send his body home at once.' In Dublin, a guard of honour numbering an estimated 5,000 people was assembled, comprising members of the Irish Volunteers, the Fenians and Na Fianna Éireann. A further 50,000 were said to have attended his burial in Glasnevin. Pearse's tribute to O'Donovan Rossa, whom he described as an 'unrepentant Fenian', touched on the aspiration of both men for an Ireland 'not free merely, but Gaelic as well; not Gaelic merely, but free as well.'

Pearse turned his ire towards the British establishment: 'They think that they have pacified Ireland. They think that they have purchased half of us and intimidated the other half. They think that they have foreseen everything, think that they have provided against everything; but the fools, the fools, the fools! – they have left us our Fenian dead, and, while Ireland holds these graves, Ireland unfree shall never be at peace.'

2 August 1924
First modern Tailteann Games

On 2 August 1924, the opening ceremony of the first modern Tailteann Games was held in Croke Park. Known in Irish as Aonach Tailteann, this was a revival of an ancient Irish festival that was said to date back to 632 BC. Lore had it that the Tailteann Games had first been staged by Lugh Lamb Fhada to commemorate the death of his foster mother, Queen Tailte, the Spanish wife of Eochaidh, king of the Firbolg.

Dublin newspaper *Sport*, reporting on the opening ceremony, drew parallels between the revival of the Ancient Olympics in Athens and what was being attempted by the Cumann na nGaedheal government in the recently established Irish Free State: 'This afternoon there will be inaugurated in Croke Park the greatest sporting carnival ever organised in Ireland and surpassing in its extent and scope even the modern Olympic Games.'

The Chair of the Distinguished Visitors Committee was W. B. Yeats, who acknowledged the presence of so many of the Irish diaspora at the opening banquet: 'In our long struggle for National Independence our people have been scattered through the world, in the seventeenth century our nobility, and in the nineteenth our poor … It was natural and fitting that we should call you together now that at last we are an independent nation, a victor at last in the struggle of centuries.'

No one was more responsible for the 1924 Games than J. J. Walsh, a former Chairman of the Cork GAA. Walsh was Minister for Posts and Telegraphs (then known as Postmaster General) in the Cumann na nGaedheal government. Indeed, the games were largely seen as a Cumann na nGaedheal project. Though they took place twice more, funding was shelved after Fianna Fáil came to power in 1932, and the Games were never staged again.

3 August 1955
Premiere of *Waiting for Godot*

On 3 August 1955, *Waiting for Godot* had its English-language premiere to an audience of around 300 in the Arts Theatre in London, in a production directed by Peter Hall. Written by Dublin-born Samuel Beckett, *Waiting for Godot* was voted the 'most significant English language play of the twentieth century' by the Royal National Theatre, despite the fact that it was originally written in French.

Alan Simpson and Carolyn Swift, owners of the Pike Theatre, attempted to stage the play in Dublin before the London production. Simpson wrote to Beckett in 1953 seeking permission to present *Waiting for Godot*, and Beckett in turn corresponded with Con Leventhal, a lecturer in French at Trinity College, asking his opinion on the Pike and whether he would supervise a future production.

Beckett had arranged with Donald Albery, an English theatre impresario, to have the premiere in London in 1955, but he divulged in a letter to Albery that Simpson wanted it put on in Dublin first. However, Beckett wrote, 'My feeling is that this would be ill-advised. I am very poorly thought of in this town and even a first-class performance of Godot here is likely to provoke very hostile reactions.'

Ironically, the British premiere was subject to censorship: the Lord Chamberlain's office insisted that 12 pages be removed from the official production. When the Pike staged its own production of *Waiting for Godot* in October 1955, it was in fact the first uncensored version of the play to be performed.

Beckett came to be seen as one of the literary greats of the twentieth century to emerge from Ireland. He briefly taught in Trinity College before moving permanently to France; the Drama Department in Trinity was renamed the Samuel Beckett Centre in 1986 to mark his 80th birthday.

4 August 1918
Gaelic Sunday

On 4 August 1918, a series of matches organised by the Gaelic Athletic Association (GAA) were played across Ireland, protesting a recent ban on 'assemblies in public places'. It became known as Gaelic Sunday, and the organisation would later describe the event as 'a day when the clubs of the GAA stood against the British Empire and triumphed in a peaceful protest'. On 4 July that year, Frederick Shaw, Commander-in-Chief of the British forces in Ireland, announced that 'the holding of or taking part in any meetings, assemblies, or processions in public places within the whole of Ireland' was prohibited, unless authorised in writing.

Though not specifically targeting the GAA, it was interpreted as such by Luke O'Neill, the organisation's full-time secretary. On 20 July, the central council of the GAA in Dublin decided unanimously that 'under no circumstances must a permit be applied for either by provincial councils, county committees, leagues, tournament committees, clubs or by a third party', and that 'any individual or club infringing the foregoing order becomes automatically and indefinitely suspended.' The central council also ordered that a series of matches be played throughout each county on Sunday 4 August, 'to be localised as much as possible'.

Approximately 1,500 hurling, football and camogie matches were scheduled to start at 3:00 p.m., with 50,000 players participating. It is unlikely that every game was played – Cork experienced heavy rain on the day, causing some matches to be cancelled.

Nevertheless, the *Freeman's Journal* in Dublin noted that the day was 'brought off without a hitch', and that the 'prohibition against Gaelic games … by police and military' had been withdrawn, which made the protest more symbolic than defiant. It concluded that the day demonstrated 'the popular hold which the Gaelic games have on the interest and sympathy of the Irish people'.

5 August 1901

Peter O'Connor sets world record for long jump

On 5 August 1901, Peter O'Connor set a new world record for the long jump when he leaped 24 feet 11¾ inches in the Royal Irish Constabulary Sports in Ballsbridge, Dublin. The record remained for 20 years, until American Edward 'Ned' Gourdin jumped 3¼ inches further. Still, O'Connor's jump was the best by an Irish athlete for almost a century, until Carlos O'Connell beat it in 1990.

O'Connor would recall that he had an interest in athleticism from a young age, having 'inherited a natural gift of suppleness and spring, without which no athlete, no matter how he trains can hope to win a world record'. Arguably even more memorable than his 1901 world record was his appearance at the 1906 Intercalated Games in Athens, Greece. Though referred to as the 1906 Olympic Games, they occurred two years after the 1904 Olympics in St Louis and two years before the 1908 Olympics in London. O'Connor was one of three athletes entered on behalf of the Irish Amateur Athletic Association and GAA, along with Con Leahy and John Daly.

As Ireland did not have an Olympic committee, the three were seen to be representing the United Kingdom, and O'Connor was irked to see the British flag raised after his silver medal in the long jump. During the medal ceremony, he broke with convention and scaled the flagpole, unfurling a bright green flag with a golden harp and the words 'Erin Go Bragh' on it. This was in front of 50,000 spectators.

Years later, he would reflect on the incident: 'It caused a great sensation – it received wide publicity in the world's press and turned the spotlight very much on the Irish political situation at a period when very few dared to raise a protest against the British domination of our country.'

6 August 1998

Michelle Smith de Bruin receives swimming ban

On 6 August 1998, Michelle Smith de Bruin received a four-year swimming ban from the International Swimming Federation (FINA) for tampering with a urine sample. This effectively ended her career.

In 1996, competing under the name Michelle Smith, she won three Olympic gold medals for Ireland in Atlanta, Georgia, becoming the first Irish woman to win an Olympic gold medal as well as the first Irish competitor to do so in swimming. However, scepticism immediately followed, not least from some members of the American swimming team. Asked about this, Smith said, 'I have really put my heart and soul and everything into this, and this is the combination of all that hard work and nothing else.'

Further suspicion was cast on Smith when she married Erik de Bruin, a Dutch discus thrower and shot putter who tested positive for steroids in 1993. In January 1998, two drug testers showed up at de Bruin's home unannounced to collect a urine sample. It was given, and transported to Barcelona to be examined. A lab report cited 'unequivocal signs of adulteration' and a concentration of alcohol that was 'in no way compatible with human consumption'. Another test was conducted on a sample given in May, which yielded the same results.

Reacting to the four-year ban, Smith de Bruin read out a lengthy prepared statement: 'I would like to confirm again that I have never taken any banned substance at any time and the FINA Doping Panel found that in relation to the doping offence, of which they have found me guilty, that there was no evidence of there being any banned substances in either the A or the B Sample.'

7 August 1986

Peter Robinson is arrested in Clontibret

On 7 August 1986, Peter Robinson, deputy leader of the Democratic Unionist Party (DUP), was arrested in Clontibret, Co. Monaghan. He had led a group of about 150 men over the border into the tiny village, protesting the Anglo-Irish Agreement, which gave the Irish government a consultative role in Northern Ireland for the first time. The DUP, fronted by noted firebrand the Rev. Ian Paisley, was the second-largest unionist party in Northern Ireland after the Ulster Unionist Party (UUP), and seen as the more extreme voice of unionism. However, unionists were united in their opposition to the agreement.

The men crossed the border in 30 cars or so, arriving at approximately 1:30 a.m. Locals in Clontibret claimed that many of them were wearing masks and holding cudgels; Gardaí would later say there was no evidence that firearms had been used. The unionist posse graffitied slogans on buildings in the area, including the local Garda station. When a Garda car arrived on the scene, two officers were kicked to the ground; they were eventually taken to hospital in Monaghan town. Three detectives arrived firing shots, causing the mob to disperse and cross the border.

Jack Marrinan, General Secretary of the Garda Representative Association, said: 'I am concerned that they should have been so violent and so vicious as to kick and seriously injure one or two of my members. But the fact of the matter is, that if they came here to prove that this particular part of the border was so unattended, they could come, and go away without being accosted by the forces of law and order, they were wrong.'

Robinson pleaded guilty to a charge of unlawful assembly, and was forced to pay a fine of IR£17,500, earning him the nickname 'Peter the Punt' after the Irish currency.

8 August 1914

Arthur Griffith opposes Irish involvement in First World War

On 3 August 1914, the day that Britain declared war on Germany, John Redmond stood up in the House of Commons and pledged the support of Ireland, confidently saying: 'the coast of Ireland will be defended from foreign invasion by her armed sons, and for this purpose armed nationalist Catholics in the South will be only too glad to join arms with the armed Protestant Ulsterman in the North.'

However, Arthur Griffith, the leader of Sinn Féin, was vociferously opposed to any Irish involvement, and wrote a scathing rebuke to Redmond in the newspaper that bore his party's name, published on 8 August: 'England wants our aid and Mr. Redmond, true to his nature, rushes to offer it – for nothing.' Griffith made it clear he felt the war on the continent was no concern of the Irish people. 'Ireland is not at war with Germany ... We are Irish Nationalists and the only duty we have is to stand for Ireland's interests, irrespective of the interests of England or Germany or any foreign country.'

He also used the opportunity to attack the 1914 Home Rule Bill, which he saw as insufficiently radical, telling the British government to 'withdraw the present abortive Home Rule Bill and pass ... a full measure of Home Rule and Irishmen will have some reason to mobilize for the defence of their institutions. In the alternative let a Provisional Government be set up in Dublin by Mr. Redmond and Sir Edward Carson and we shall give it allegiance.'

Irish attitudes to Irishmen who fought for Britain in the First World War were generally negative until around 1998, when the tide began to turn towards a more nuanced assessment of their actions. In that year, President Mary McAleese officially opened the Island of Ireland Peace Park in Messines, Flanders, to commemorate Irish soldiers who lost their lives.

9 August 1971

Internment is introduced in Northern Ireland

On 9 August 1971, Brian Faulkner, the last Prime Minister of Northern Ireland, announced that he would be exercising 'the powers of detention and internment'. Internment – imprisonment without trial – saw 342 men arrested (only two of whom were Protestants) from a list of 450 targets. An estimated 100 were members of either the Provisional IRA or the Official IRA. Of those arrested, 116 were released within 72 hours; the remainder were kept in Crumlin Road Prison or the HMS *Maidstone* prison ship. It was known as Operation Demetrius.

Faulkner insisted that internment was not aimed at Catholics in Northern Ireland as a whole, but at the IRA, whose victims, he said, 'have included Protestant and Roman Catholic alike ... I want to say a word directly to my Catholic fellow-countrymen. I do not for one moment confuse your community with the IRA or imagine that these acts of terror have been committed in your name or with your approval.'

The British Home Secretary at the time, Reginald Maudling, later referred to internment as an 'unmitigated disaster', which 'signalled the opening of the most violent period of the Troubles'. Twenty-three people were killed in the three days that followed its introduction. There was also a massive displacement of population: the Northern Ireland Community Relations Commission reported that 2,100 households moved in the first three weeks after internment, 40 per cent of them Protestant and 60 per cent Catholic.

South of the border, Taoiseach Jack Lynch condemned internment, though he was careful not to endorse the actions of paramilitary groups: 'We have asked the Northern minority to be patient ... We have also asked them to reject the use of violence because not only would violence preclude the achievement of their civil rights but it would perpetuate the divisions among the Irish people.'

10 August 1976

Death of the Maguire children

On 10 August 1976, a tragic event occurred in Northern Ireland that would lead to the creation of the Community of Peace People, whose co-founders, Betty Williams and

Mairead Corrigan (later Maguire), would receive the Nobel Peace Prize the following year. Anne Maguire was out walking with her three children – eight-year-old Joanne, two-year-old John and six-week-old Andrew – on Belfast's Finaghy Road North when all four were hit by a car driven by Provisional IRA member Danny Lennon. Lennon was pursued by British soldiers who opened fire, killing him. Andrew and Joanne died instantly, John the next day. Anne was unconscious for days and would die by suicide in 1980, haunted by the deaths of her children.

Betty Williams, a housewife in Andersonstown, witnessed the event. She began a petition, asking those who wanted to see an end to violence to sign it. Within days she had 6,000 signatures. When Mairead Corrigan, Anne Maguire's sister, learned of what Williams had done, she invited her to the children's funeral. That day, the two women met with Ciaran McKeown, a journalist for the *Irish News*, and Women for Peace, later renamed the Community of Peace People, was born. Its first declaration expressed a desire 'to live and love and build a just and peaceful society', while rejecting 'the use of the bomb and the bullet and all the techniques of violence'.

However, the organisation had plenty of critics, including Bernadette McAliskey, who told American singer Joan Baez she would be 'marching with Authority' when she joined a Peace People demonstration in London. Perhaps most controversially, Williams and Maguire decided to keep the £80,000 awarded to them by the Nobel Committee.

They eventually parted ways, and Williams ended up living in the United States. In 1986, she said, 'I didn't walk away from Ulster, I ran.'

11 August 1927

Éamon de Valera signs the oath of allegiance

On 11 August 1927, Éamon de Valera was one of 44 Fianna Fáil deputies to enter Leinster House for the first time, recognising its legitimacy and agreeing to comply with Article 17 of the Irish Free State constitution, which asked that members of the Oireachtas take an oath to be 'faithful to H. M. King George V, his heirs and successors by law in virtue of the common citizenship of Ireland with Great Britain.' It was a bitter pill for de Valera and Fianna Fáil to swallow: they had fought on the losing side of the Civil War five years earlier over that very issue (more so even than the partition of Ireland).

De Valera was the last to enter the office of the Clerk of the House, Colm Ó Murchadha, where they would gain admittance to the Dáil. He was accompanied by Dr James Ryan and Frank Aiken. Presenting Ó Murchadha with a prepared statement, de Valera then spoke, in Irish: 'I want you to understand that I am not taking any oath nor giving any promise of faithfulness to the King of England or to any power outside the people of Ireland. I am putting my name here merely as a formality to get the permission necessary to enter among the other Teachtai that were elected by the people of Ireland, and I want you to know that no other meaning is to be attached to it.'

When signing his name on the line that Ó Murchadha had indicated, de Valera covered the writing above it with some papers, thus obscuring what he was signing: a way to distance himself further from the event. The claim that de Valera had not, in fact, taken the oath was seen by many as risible.

12 August 1969

The Battle of the Bogside

In August 1969, tensions were high in Derry, with the Apprentice Boys, a Protestant fraternal organisation, preparing for its annual march in the city. Fifteen thousand people were expected to participate. In anticipation of civil unrest, Sean Keenan, a member of the IRA, became chairman of the Derry Citizens Defence Association. Six

other co-founders of the association were members of the James Connolly Republican Club. Keenan told residents to defend themselves, if necessary, with 'sticks, stones and the good old petrol bomb'.

On 12 August, trouble began to brew when some Apprentice Boys tossed coins at Catholics located below the city's historic walls. At 2:30 p.m., members of the Royal Ulster Constabulary (RUC) were hit with a handful of nails, thrown from the other side of one of the barricades that had been erected. This led to an explosion of violence. By 4:00 p.m., the Apprentice Boys themselves had been hit by missiles and retaliated.

Catholics stormed the police barricades, and when the RUC pursued them they were led straight into the Bogside, an almost exclusively Catholic neighbourhood. Molotov cocktails were thrown at police from the top of Rossville flats. A water cannon was used to hose the rioters. In one unit of 59 police officers brought in from Co. Down, 43 were injured. Eventually, the use of CS gas was authorised, for the first time in the United Kingdom.

The rioting continued until 14 July and was televised throughout the world, showing a total breakdown of law and order. Mitchel McLaughlin, later General Secretary of Sinn Féin, witnessed it: 'There was this sense of impending invasion. Barricades being thrown up … It was a bit like 1916. Everybody claimed to have been there.'

Jack Lynch, Taoiseach and leader of Fianna Fáil, felt the need to make a public announcement on the chaos the following day.

13 August 1969

Jack Lynch reacts to riots in Derry

On 13 August 1969, Taoiseach Jack Lynch gave a public broadcast on RTÉ in reaction to the rioting in Northern Ireland that week. The Northern Ireland Civil Rights Association (NICRA) had issued a statement, written by vice-chairman Vincent MacDowell, calling on the Irish government to 'take immediate action to have a United Nations peacekeeping force sent to Derry'. However, NICRA would repudiate the statement the following day, saying it 'was not authorised by the Executive'.

Lynch began: 'It is with deep sadness that you and I, Irishmen and women of goodwill, have learned of the tragic events which have been taking place in Derry and elsewhere in the North in recent days.' He then said, in the most famous line of his address, 'It is clear, also, that the Irish government can no longer stand by and see innocent people injured and perhaps worse' (often misquoted as 'stand idly by').

Echoing the NICRA statement written by MacDowell, Lynch said: 'The Irish Government have, therefore, requested the British Government to apply immediately to the United Nations for the urgent despatch of a peacekeeping force to the six counties of Northern Ireland ... Recognising, however, that the reunification of the national territory can provide the only permanent solution for the problem, it is our intention to request the British Government to enter into early negotiations with the Irish Government to review the present constitutional position of the six counties of Northern Ireland.'

Many in Northern Ireland felt his words were unwelcome. James Chichester-Clark, the Prime Minister of Northern Ireland, responded by saying, 'I have heard with indignation the remarks of Mr Lynch. This clumsy and intolerable intrusion into our internal affairs will be deeply resented by the majority of the people in Northern Ireland.'

14 August 1903

Wyndham Land Act is passed

On 14 August 1903, the Wyndham Land Act was passed, creating generous incentives for landlords to sell to their tenants. John Redmond, leader of the Irish Parliamentary Party, described it as 'the most substantial victory gained for centuries by the Irish race for the reconquest of the soil of Ireland by the people'. It was named for George Wyndham, who became Chief Secretary for Ireland in 1900. Wyndham had chosen Sir Antony MacDonnell, an Irish Catholic, to be his Under-Secretary for Ireland, a move seen by some as extending the hand of reconciliation.

In December 1902, the Land Conference was held in the Mansion House in Dublin. This negotiation took place over a month, and featured Redmond, William O'Brien and Timothy Harrington representing tenants. Opposite them were Lord Dunraven and others representing landlords in Ireland. In January, a report was published containing 18 recommendations, including the abolition of dual ownership in favour of tenant proprietorship, and inducements to landlords to sell. Dual ownership had been introduced in the 1881 Land Act but, Wyndham recognised, Irish tenants wanted to 'secure absolutely the fruits of their industry and enterprise'.

In August 1903, the Land Purchase (Ireland) Act was written into law. It advanced £100 million, an enormous amount of money at the time, to tenants so that they could buy the land they were holding. They would then repay the money at a rate of 3.25 per cent over 68 years. Landlords would receive a bonus of 12 per cent for selling to tenants. By 1908, seven million acres had been sold.

At the time, Wyndham wrote a letter to Lord Dunraven, saying, 'I feel fairly confident – nay, sanguine – that 1903 will mark an epoch in Irish history.'

15 August 1998

The Omagh bombing

On 15 August 1998, a bomb planted by the Real IRA exploded in Omagh, Co. Tyrone, killing 29 people, one of whom was seven months pregnant with twins. The victims came from both sides of the border, and included two tourists from Spain. They ranged in age from 20 months to 65 years. This was the most devastating single attack in the history of the Troubles in Northern Ireland, and came less than three months after over 71 per cent of voters there had endorsed the Good Friday Agreement.

The Real IRA broke from the Provisional IRA in October 1997. Michael McKevitt, a senior member of the Provisional IRA, and his wife Bernadette Sands-McKevitt (sister of hunger striker Bobby Sands) were dissatisfied with the direction of the republican movement, in particular Sinn Féin's signing up to the so-called Mitchell Principles, laid down by Senator George Mitchell, US Special Envoy for Northern Ireland. When the Good Friday Agreement was signed, Sands-McKevitt dismissed it, saying: 'Peace is not what our people fought for, they fought for independence.'

The Real IRA phoned Ulster Television (UTV) on the day of the bombing to issue a warning. However, it was vague – 'Bomb, Courthouse, Omagh Main Street, 500 pounds explosion, 30 minutes.' Police evacuated the buildings around the courthouse, but dozens of people were caught in the blast.

The Real IRA admitted responsibility three days later, saying, 'Despite media reports, it was not our intention at any time to kill any civilians. It was a commercial target, part of an ongoing war against the Brits. We offer apologies to the civilians.' Taoiseach Bertie Ahern described it as 'the most evil deed in years', Prime Minister Tony Blair called it 'an appalling act of savagery' and US President Bill Clinton said, 'On behalf of every American, I condemn this butchery.'

16 August 1982

Patrick Connolly resigns ('GUBU')

On 16 August 1982, Patrick Connolly, the Attorney General of Ireland, resigned in the midst of a political scandal. He had been appointed by Taoiseach Charles Haughey only five months earlier.

On 13 August, Malcolm MacArthur was arrested at Connolly's home in Dalkey. MacArthur was sought by the police for the killing of a 27-year-old nurse, Bridie Gargan, in Phoenix Park on 22 July. MacArthur bludgeoned Gargan to death with a hammer while she was sunbathing, and then stole her car. This led to a nationwide manhunt. On 25 July, MacArthur responded to a newspaper advertisement: a farmer in Edenderry, Co. Offaly, was hoping to sell his shotgun. MacArthur turned the weapon on its owner, Donal Dunne, killing him too. He then returned to Dublin.

It is unlikely that Connolly knew MacArthur had killed two people. Initially, the Attorney General was not held for questioning by Gardaí, and proceeded with a planned holiday to the United States. Garret FitzGerald, the leader of the opposition, cut short a holiday in France to accuse Haughey of mishandling the situation. Haughey then summoned Connolly to his home, where he accepted his resignation. Connolly was replaced by John L. Murray.

The following day, Charles Haughey addressed the scandal at a news conference, calling it 'a bizarre happening, an unprecedented situation … a grotesque situation … an almost unbelievable mischance'. The first letters of the four adjectives – grotesque, unbelievable, bizarre, unprecedented – were taken by Conor Cruise O'Brien, a former Labour politician and long-standing critic of Haughey, to create the acronym 'GUBU'. O'Brien wrote: 'the more he insists on how GUBU the situation was, in which he none the less permitted his Attorney General to go on holiday, the more starkly Mr Haughey illuminates the folly of that permission.'

'GUBU' came to be a defining shorthand for Haughey's tenure as Taoiseach.

17 August 1882

The Maamtrasna murders

On 17 August 1882, five members of the Joyce family were murdered in Maamtrasna, on the Galway–Mayo border: a grandmother (aged 80), father, mother, son and daughter. Eight men were arrested for the killings, all from the Gaeltacht, the Irish-speaking region of Connacht. Three would eventually be hanged, while five avoided execution by pleading guilty. One of those sentenced to death was most likely the victim of a miscarriage of justice.

The murders shocked not only Ireland but also Britain. *The Spectator* in London wrote that the event should remind English readers of 'the existence in particular districts of Ireland of a class of peasants who are scarcely civilised beings, and approach far nearer to savages than any other white men … in knowledge, in habits, and in the discipline of life no higher than Maories or other Polynesians'. The most high-profile of those arrested was Maolra Seoighe, or, as his wife would refer to him in a letter pleading for his release, Myles Joyce. Seoighe is said to have spoken only Irish, though the trial was conducted entirely in English. 'Níl mé ciontach' ('I am not guilty') he repeated after being sentenced.

On the eve of their execution, two of the sentenced men admitted their guilt but claimed Seoighe was not involved. However, the Lord Lieutenant of Ireland, Earl Spencer, insisted that 'The law must take its course.' Years after, James Joyce would reference Seoighe in his essay 'Ireland at the Bar': 'The figure of this bewildered old man, left over from a culture which is not ours, a deaf-mute before his judge, is a symbol of the Irish nation at the bar of public opinion.'

In 2018, Seoighe was granted a posthumous pardon by President Michael D. Higgins, who said his hanging was a 'shameful episode in Ireland and Britain's history'.

18 August 1994

Martin Cahill is shot dead

On 18 August 1994, Martin Cahill, the career criminal known as the General, was shot dead in Ranelagh, Dublin. He was driving to a local shop to return a video when a man repeatedly fired a .357 Magnum revolver at him. It was a brutal end for one of the most high-profile figures in Irish organised crime, aged 45. The Provisional IRA, which would announce a ceasefire less than a fortnight later, claimed responsibility: 'It was Cahill's involvement with, and assistance to, pro-British death squads which forced us to act ... The IRA reserves the right to execute those who finance or otherwise assist Loyalist killer gangs.'

For years, Cahill had been known to authorities as a crafty, ruthless operator. In 1986, he and his gang stole 18 paintings worth up to $44 million, including Vermeer's *Lady Writing a Letter with Her Maid*, from Russborough House, Co. Wicklow. Seven of the paintings were found undamaged four miles away the day after.

Cahill was under surveillance by An Garda Síochána, his bêtes noires. In an attempt to humiliate them, he stole 100 files from the Director of Public Prosecutions' office in St Stephen's Green in 1987. On another occasion he dug up the greens of a Garda golf course in Stackstown, Co. Dublin to antagonise the police.

It is alleged that Cahill, feeling the heat over the Russborough House paintings, turned to Billy Wright, an Ulster Volunteer Force (UVF) leader in Portadown, to help sell them. The Provisionals also claimed that Cahill's gang was closely tied to the gang that in May of that year had attempted to bomb the Widow Scallans pub in Dublin, shooting dead Martin Doherty, an IRA volunteer working as a doorman.

In any case, Cahill's death was a startling moment for organised crime in Dublin.

19 August 1504

The Battle of Knockdoe

On 19 August 1504, the Battle of Knockdoe was fought near the village of Lackagh, Co. Galway, between Gerald FitzGerald, the Eighth Earl of Kildare, and Ulick Burke, the Third Earl of Clanrickard. Kildare led his army from the east to face Burke, who had invaded and taken over the territory of Tadhg O'Kelly and was engaged in an affair with O'Kelly's wife. Burke was supported by a number of lords, the most powerful of whom were the O'Briens, who controlled much of the area west of the lower Shannon, and the MacNamaras, who controlled what is now the eastern half of Co. Clare.

Kildare had been made the Lord Deputy of Ireland by Henry VII upon the latter's becoming Lord of Ireland in 1485. However, by 1504, much of what was once under royal control had been lost, controlled by the Burkes (themselves the descendants of

Normans), the O'Briens and other Gaelic or 'Old English' dynasties. Only the 'four obedient shires' of Dublin, Kildare, Louth and Meath – known collectively as the English Pale – were directly loyal to the Tudors. In that sense, the Battle of Knockdoe is seen by some as a reassertion of royal authority over Gaelic Ireland. Kildare's army included Burkes of Mayo, rivals of Clanrickard.

The battle lasted several hours, with Kildare's archers inflicting heavy casualties before it descended into hand-to-hand combat. Burke managed to escape, but his side was soundly defeated. FitzGerald continued west, raiding Burke's castle in Claregalway and occupying the town of Athenry. Once again, those with connections to the English Crown had a foothold outside their comfort zone. For that reason, some historians have referred to Burke's defeat as 'the death of Gaelic Ireland'.

20 August 1775

Tucson, Arizona is founded by Hugh O'Conor

On 20 August 1775, Hugh O'Conor, known also as Hugo Oconór, established a military fort, Presidio San Agustín del Tucsón. This was the founding of what would become the city of Tucson, Arizona. The fort was originally built to defend against attacks from the Apache, and attracted settlers from Spain as well as the Pima, another Native American people. O'Conor, who was born in Dublin in 1734, was Commandant Inspector of the Frontier Provinces of New Spain. He came from a long line of military men who had served in armies outside of Ireland. His great-grandfather, Daniel O'Conor, joined the Spanish Army in the seventeenth century, and his uncle, Thomas O'Conor, was an officer in the French Army. Hugh had signed up as a cadet at age 16.

Perhaps the person who was most influential in O'Conor's life was his Meath-born cousin, Alexander O'Reilly, a brigadier general in the Spanish Army. O'Reilly recommended O'Conor to the viceroy of New Spain, after which he became an interim governor of Texas. In 1775, he was tasked with locating a site for the northernmost presidio of the Spanish Empire. On 20 August 1775, he wrote: 'I, Hugo Oconor, knight of the order of Calatrava, colonel of infantry in His Majesty's armies and commandant inspector of the frontier posts of New Spain ... selected and marked out in the presence of Father Francisco Garces and Lieutenant Juan de Carmona a place known as San Agustin del Tucson as the new site of the Presidio. It is situated at a distance of eighteen leagues from Tubac, fulfils the requirements of water, pasture, and wood and effectively closes the Apache frontier.'

Later in life O'Conor took on the role of Governor of Yucatán, in Mexico, but died two years afterwards, in 1779.

21 August 1879
Apparition in Knock

On 21 August 1879, an apparition allegedly appeared in Knock, Co. Mayo, consisting of Mary, St Joseph, St John the Evangelist and a lamb, standing on an altar before a cross. The first people said to have seen the vision were 26-year-old Mary Beirne and Mary McLoughlin, who was the housekeeper of the parish priest, Archdeacon Bartholomew Cavanagh. When Beirne recounted the story to her parents soon afterwards, locals were alerted. They gathered around the apparition, reciting the rosary for two hours.

The event was noteworthy enough to merit an investigation, launched in October of that year by Archbishop of Tuam John McHale. Three parish priests, including Archdeacon Cavanagh, and six curates interviewed the 15 people who claimed to have witnessed the vision, finding their testimony to be 'trustworthy and satisfactory'.

Such apparitions are often associated with cures, and within a year of the inquiry, on 9 October 1880, 637 'cures' had been recorded, including a deaf person who was able to hear again, 12 days after the appearance. Decades later, in 1935, Archbishop of Tuam Thomas Gilmartin set up a second inquiry. He interviewed Beirne (now Mary O'Connell), who was 86, and John Curry, who was five at the time of the apparition. As with the previous report, it found the witnesses were trustworthy, in particularly Mary O'Connell, who left 'a most favourable impression'.

Sceptics have, of course, doubted that any such apparition took place, and felt that it could have been a collective hallucination or even a hoax. Nevertheless, the site became a pilgrimage venue. The foundation stone for the Basilica of Our Lady, Queen of Ireland, Knock was laid in 1974, and Pope John Paul II visited the shrine in 1979 on his trip to Ireland.

22 August 1922

Michael Collins is shot dead

On 22 August 1922, Michael Collins was killed in an ambush at Béal na mBláth, Co. Cork. The Irish Civil War had broken out in June, and tensions were high, but Collins did not expect such an attack. When Joe Sweeney, the National Army Commandant from Donegal, warned against making the trip through Cork to inspect military posts, Collins is said to have responded, 'No one is going to shoot me in my own county.'

At 6:15 a.m., Collins set off on a tour of West Cork, accompanied by an escort of 15 men. He was scheduled to meet anti-Treaty members of the IRA that evening, but his first stop was Macroom, followed by Bandon, Clonakilty, Rosscarbery and Skibbereen. Along the way, the convoy stopped at Long's Pub to ask for directions, where Collins was spotted by Denny 'the Dane' Long, who promptly informed anti-IRA leader Tom Hales. The ambush was then planned for when Collins returned.

About 7:45 p.m., the convoy arrived at the village of Béal na mBláth. The anti-Treaty men – 37 in all – had taken up positions and laid three mines to block the cars moving through. The shootout lasted somewhere between 20 and 40 minutes, and Collins was the only fatality, struck in the head by what was either a direct hit or a ricocheting bullet. He was 31 years old.

The *Freeman's Journal* informed readers the following day: 'The terrible news we announce today will move Ireland as nothing has moved her in living memory. Michael Collins has fallen by the hands of his own countrymen. He had dared death so often in the struggle with England that men felt he could run all risks and emerge unharmed. That he should be killed by an Irish bullet is a tragedy too deep for tears.'

23 August 1170

Strongbow lands in Waterford

On 23 August 1170, Anglo-Norman knight Richard de Clare, known also as Strongbow, landed in Waterford. He had been summoned to Ireland by the deposed King of Leinster, Diarmait Mac Murchada (Dermot MacMurrough), who lost his title to the High King of Ireland, Ruaidri Ua Conchobair (Rory O'Connor) in 1166.

Shortly after, MacMurrough went to England, seeking the permission of Henry II to raise troops to help regain his throne. Henry granted MacMurrough's request, and several Marcher Lords of Wales – nobles guarding the Welsh–English border – joined him in reclaiming Leinster, being offered land as compensation. These men landed in Wexford in May 1169.

MacMurrough was successful in becoming King of Leinster once again, but was not satisfied with a return to the status quo, and sought to become High King of Ireland. Strongbow would prove his best ally. MacMurrough offered Strongbow the hand of his daughter, Aoife, in marriage; in exchange, Strongbow landed in Waterford in 1170 with a thousand archers and 200 knights. Henry II had sent messages forbidding the attack, which were ignored.

Strongbow easily captured Waterford and then moved on to Dublin. He married Aoife, as promised, ensuring that MacMurrough's powers would be passed on to his Anglo-Norman ally after his death.

After MacMurrough died in May 1171, Strongbow declared himself King of Leinster, the first ruler of an Irish province not born in Ireland. He returned to England to make peace with Henry, giving him control of Dublin and other cities. He died of an infection in his foot in 1176, and was buried in the Holy Trinity Church in Dublin.

Meanwhile, Henry and Rory O'Connor signed the Treaty of Windsor in 1175, giving Henry control of Dublin and the southeast, and the rest of Ireland to O'Connor.

24 August 1990

Brian Keenan is released

On 24 August 1990, Brian Keenan was released after being held hostage in Lebanon for almost four and a half years. Keenan, a native of Belfast, was a lecturer in English at the American University of Beirut when he was kidnapped on 11 April 1986 by Islamic Jihad. For much of his time in captivity, he was blindfolded, chained and kept in rat- and cockroach-infested cells, wearing just a pair of shorts. For nine months he was alone in his cell, taken out once a day for 10 minutes to use the toilet, his food slid under the door. Keenan's sisters, Elaine Spence and Brenda Gillham, campaigned for his release for years, regularly holding press conferences to ensure his name was not forgotten.

Keenan held British and Irish passports, and while the British government refused to negotiate with those who had kidnapped him, the Irish government lobbied the Iranians to negotiate with the kidnappers on its behalf. On 24 August 1990, an Arabic message was delivered to a Beirut newspaper, which translated: 'We have decided to release Irish hostage Brian Keenan. This was done at exactly 9 p.m. Beirut time.' Keenan was taken from Lebanon to Damascus, where he met the Irish Ambassador to Syria, Declan Connolly. His sisters flew out with the Irish Foreign Minister, Gerry Collins, and all four returned to Dublin.

After his release, Keenan spent some time in the Mater Hospital in Dublin, visibly exhausted and malnourished. He attended a brief press conference, saying, 'It's an understatement to say I'm delighted to be home ... It's where the heart is ... I would like to thank everyone, but everyone, who helped to secure my release. Above all, my sisters, and my friends. I never, never once doubted them.'

25 August 1803

Robert Emmet is arrested

On 25 August 1803, Robert Emmet was arrested for his part in the rebellion that took place a month earlier, in which the Lord Chief Justice of Ireland, Lord Kilwarden, and his nephew were killed. Emmet had initially fled to the Wicklow Mountains, and might have escaped but for his love for Sarah Curran, daughter of the well-known barrister John Philpot Curran. Emmet moved to the home of a Mrs Palmer, at Harold's Cross, to be near Curran. He wrote her letters at a time when £300 was being offered for his arrest, and £1,000 for information leading to the men who killed Lord Kilwarden. This correspondence ultimately led to the Palmers' home being raided and Emmet being taken into custody.

What secured Emmet's status as a hero among Irish republicans was the speech he gave from the dock on 19 September 1803, after he was found guilty of high treason. Some, such as the Irish journalist Kevin Myers, have questioned its veracity. In the best-known version, Emmet ended by saying to the court: 'Let no man write my epitaph ... When my country takes her place among the nations of the earth, then, and not till then, let my epitaph be written. I have done.'

The next day, Emmet was hanged outside St Catherine's Church in Thomas Street. His executioner, Thomas Galvin, is said to have displayed his head to the crowd. The remains of his body were taken and buried in what is now the Royal Kilmainham Hospital.

Emmet has grown in stature since his death. The Romantic poet Percy Bysshe Shelley penned a tribute to him, 'On Robert Emmet's Grave'. Ethna Carbery and Alice Milligan, writing in the nationalist publication *The Shan Van Vocht*, described him as 'the most beloved of our patriot-martyrs'. Towns and counties have been named after him in the United States, such as Emmetsburg in Iowa, Emmet in Nebraska and Emmet County in Michigan.

26 August 1913

Dublin Lockout begins

On 26 August 1913, the Dublin Lockout began. William Martin Murphy, a former MP for Dublin and chairman of the Dublin United Tramway Company (DUTC), learned that union leader Jim Larkin had been recruiting Murphy's employees to the Irish Transport and General Workers' Union (ITGWU). In July, he summoned workers to the Antient Concert Hall at midnight, warning them that if they stayed with the ITGWU they would lose their jobs. Soon after, Murphy began dismissing those he suspected of ITGWU membership: not just tram workers but employees of Independent Newspapers, another of his businesses.

Larkin initially advised remaining union members at the DUTC against going on strike, but allowed a ballot to be held on 25 August at the ITGWU headquarters in Liberty Hall. The strike began the next day. On Sunday 31 August, Larkin managed to sneak into Murphy's Imperial Hotel on Sackville Street (later O'Connell Street) and address a crowd from a balcony on the first floor, but this led to members of the Dublin Metropolitan Police and Royal Irish Constabulary baton-charging the crowd. Larkin was arrested, and the day become known as Bloody Sunday: one of many in Irish history.

The Lockout continued for five months, and saw many companies agree not to employ ITGWU members, including the Dublin Coal Merchants' Association, the Dublin Building Trades Employers' Federation and the Dublin Carriers' Association (which sacked employees who refused to handle 'tainted' goods). In total, 20,000 workers were involved in the Lockout, though it ended without success for the strikers.

Larkin had toured England hoping to drum up sympathy, but had no such luck. On 18 January 1914, the ITGWU advised workers to return to work. Larkin publicly admitted, 'We are beaten, we will make no bones about it.'

27 August 1979

Killing of Lord Mountbatten

On 27 August 1979, Lord Louis Mountbatten was assassinated in Mullaghmore, Co. Sligo. He was 79 years old when a bomb planted by the Provisional IRA was detonated on his boat, killing him; 83-year-old Anglo-Irish aristocrat Doreen Knatchbull; her grandson, 14-year-old Nicholas Knatchbull; and Paul Maxwell, a 15-year-old boy from Enniskillen, Co. Fermanagh, who worked as a crew member on the boat. Nicholas's twin brother, Timothy, survived but was blinded in one eye. Mountbatten's killing was one of the most high-profile of the Troubles, and, like that of British Ambassador Christopher Ewart-Biggs in 1976, was a source of embarrassment to the Irish government.

Mountbatten had been visiting the west coast of Ireland for years, holidaying at Classiebawn Castle near the village of Cliffoney, Co. Sligo. As he had been a Royal Navy officer and a Supreme Allied Commander in the Second World War, he was deemed a 'legitimate target' by the Provisional IRA, who released a statement soon afterwards: 'The death of Mountbatten and the tributes paid to him will be seen in sharp contrast to the apathy of the British government and the English People to the deaths of over three hundred British soldiers, and the deaths of Irish men, women and children at the hands of their forces.'

Prince Charles, Mountbatten's grand-nephew, was particularly shaken by the killing: 'I fear it will take me a very long time to forgive those people who today achieved something that two World Wars and thousands of Germans and Japanese failed to achieve.'

The IRA man responsible for planting the device, Thomas McMahon, was arrested by Gardaí two hours before the bomb went off, on suspicion of driving a stolen car. He was sentenced to life imprisonment for murder but released under the terms of the Good Friday Agreement in 1998. He later assisted Martin McGuinness of Sinn Féin in his 2011 presidential campaign.

28 August 1676
Irish donation to Massachusetts

On 28 August 1676, a Dublin-based ship called *Katherine* set sail from the Irish capital to Boston, Massachusetts to relieve New England colonists left distressed as a result of King Philip's war. This conflict resulted from the presence of 50,000 or so white European settlers in New England in 1670, living alongside the Native Americans. 'King Philip' was the name given to Metacom, the leader of the Wampanoag, who was hostile to the Europeans and aimed to drive them out of New England. After Josiah Winslow, the governor of Plymouth Colony, learned of this plan, a two-year conflict followed.

Many towns in Connecticut, Massachusetts and Rhode Island were destroyed, and many inhabitants killed. It is alleged that Ireland was the only European country to send relief to the colonists. The consignment was inspected by the Lord Mayor of Dublin, and three Commissioners were sent to Boston with it. The cost of the freight was £475, a significant amount of money for the time. Forty-seven towns and 2,351 people were said to have benefited from the relief.

During the Irish Famine, Boston returned the favour by sending a relief ship, the

USS *Jamestown*, to Ireland. It departed on 28 March 1847 and was captained by one Robert Bennet Forbes. Forbes wrote: 'The amount of the contributions of Irishmen in 1676, if calculated at compound interest, would amount to a sum so large that I dare not say how much we should still be indebted, after all New England has done and is doing, on that account … we have "cast our bread upon the waters" partly for the payment of an old debt and partly to plant in Irish hearts a debt which will, in future days, come back to us bearing fruit crowned with peace and good will.'

29 August 1975
Death of Éamon de Valera

On 29 August 1975, Éamon de Valera died peacefully in Linden Convalescent Home, Blackrock, Co. Dublin, aged 92. As the last surviving commandant of the Easter Rising, his death marked the end of an era. He had transitioned from President of the Executive Council to Taoiseach, and later to President. His wife, Sinéad, had died on 7 January 1975, aged 96, the day before what would have been their 65th wedding anniversary.

Cearbhall Ó Dálaigh, who was elected unopposed as President after de Valera's successor Erskine H. Childers died in office, drove out to Blackrock to pay his respects, saying of the late leader: 'One of the towering figures in Irish history has answered the last call, with a smile upon his lips … Throughout the world, and, in particular, among peoples striving to be free, his name has been a synonym for the struggle for Irish independence.'

Tributes poured in from the United States, where de Valera was born, and the European Economic Community, of which Ireland had become a member in 1973. President Gerald Ford said, 'We are proud that this son of the United States became the father of modern Ireland. Our sense of loss is heightened by the intimate ties of friendship and kinship between our peoples.' François-Xavier Ortoli, President of the European Commission, said, 'The life of Eamon de Valera was part of the history of Ireland and the history of Europe. The nations will remember his eminent role as a teacher, as a soldier, and as a leader.'

On 2 September, de Valera was given a state funeral, said by his grandson, Fr Seán Ó Cuív. A national day of mourning was marked in the Republic. Over 200,000 people paid tribute to de Valera as the cortège moved towards Glasnevin Cemetery, where he was buried.

30 August 1977

Jimmy Carter makes statement on Northern Ireland

On 30 August 1977, US President Jimmy Carter issued a statement on Northern Ireland. This made him, in the words of Irish Ambassador Seán Donlon, 'the first president to commit his administration on the Northern Ireland issue', though Donlon noted that Carter's intervention came about 'exclusively because of pressure from individual members of the House and Senate' and that many of Carter's senior advisers had 'little understanding not just of Ireland but even of Irish America'.

Carter said: 'It is natural that Americans are deeply concerned about the continuing conflict and violence in Northern Ireland. We know the overwhelming majority of the people there reject the bomb and the bullet. The United States wholeheartedly supports peaceful means for finding a just solution that involves both parts of the community of Northern Ireland, and protects human rights and guarantees freedom from discrimination … I place myself firmly on the side of those who seek peace and reject violence in Northern Ireland.' This was a more balanced view than Carter had taken while campaigning for the presidency the previous year, when he told Irish-Americans in Pittsburgh, 'It is a mistake for our country's government to stand quiet on the struggle of the Irish for peace, for the respect of human rights, and for unifying Ireland.'

The US would have little direct involvement in Northern Ireland during Carter's one-term presidency, nor in the presidency of his successor, Ronald Reagan, who viewed the conflict through a religious lens, telling Irish journalist Conor O'Clery, 'It's tragic that so much is being done in the name of God, and it's the same God.' It was not until Bill Clinton appointed George Mitchell as the United States Special Envoy for Northern Ireland in 1995 that the White House could say it had done something truly significant for peace there.

31 August 1910

Lilian Bland pilots her own plane

On 31 August 1910, Lilian Bland became the first woman in the world to design, build and pilot a plane: the *Mayfly*, which took off from Shane's Castle estate in Randalstown, Co. Antrim and flew at a height of 30 feet for approximately a quarter of a mile. Born in Kent, England, Bland had moved with her father to his native Carnmoney, north of Belfast, after the death of her mother. By 1908, her main obsession, spurred by the success of the Wright Brothers five years earlier, was aviation.

She began constructing her own plane in her uncle's workshop, starting with smaller models that could be flown with a kite before embarking on a full-scale attempt, the *Mayfly*, so called because, according to Bland, 'it may fly or it may not.' She wrote a letter to *Flight* magazine, enclosing two photos: 'I made her entirely myself, with the exception of the metal clips, and, of course the sockets, strainers, etc., were bought from English firms. I think she is the first biplane made in Ireland.'

Bland first tested the *Mayfly* by using thermal currents to help it glide down Carnmoney Hill. She then ordered a two-stroke air-cooled engine from Manchester, paying £100 for it; she travelled to England and brought it back herself after a delay.

Several weeks of wind and rain prevented Bland from taking off from Shane's Castle estate, but when she eventually did, she was thrilled with the result: 'I could hardly believe it.' Decades later, aged 88, Bland would look back on the moment with pride, telling the *Western Morning News*, 'I had proved wrong the many people who had said that no woman could build an aeroplane, and that gave me great satisfaction.'

1 September 1870

Inaugural meeting of Home Government Organisation

On 1 September 1870, the inaugural public meeting of the Home Government Organisation was held in the Round Room of the Rotunda, Dublin. Founded by Isaac Butt in the Bilton Hotel in May of that year, this pressure group, later reconstituted as the Home Rule League, would dominate Irish politics for years to come. In 1874 it won 60 of the 101 Irish seats in the United Kingdom general election.

Butt was born in Glenfin, Co. Donegal in 1813, the son of a Protestant clergyman. He opposed Daniel O'Connell's campaign for repeal of the Union; O'Connell correctly predicted, however, that he would switch sides, saying in 1843, 'A man of his genius must have some yearning for his native land ... depend upon it that Alderman Butt is in his inmost soul an Irishman, and that we will have him with us struggling for Ireland yet.'

The purpose of the Home Government Organisation, according to the official record of its inaugural meeting, was 'to take measures for procuring a Domestic Legislature in Ireland'. It was also noted that 'The attendance was very large and influential. The large room was crowded by public men from every part of Ireland, of all religions and politics.'

The Home Rule League would be dissolved in 1882 and succeeded by the Irish Parliamentary Party, led by Charles Stewart Parnell, a man described by Butt in 1874 as 'a splendid recruit, an historic name, my friend, young Parnell of Wicklow'. Though the goal of self-government in Ireland was not achieved in Butt's lifetime or, indeed, Parnell's (Butt died in 1879), the founding of the Home Government Organisation set the wheels in motion as much as anything else in the nineteenth century.

2 September 1939

The Emergency is declared

On Saturday 2 September 1939, the day after Germany invaded Poland, deputies in Dáil Éireann were summoned to a meeting where the Taoiseach, Éamon de Valera, declared that 'a national emergency exists affecting the vital interests of the State.' The Second World War would be referred to as 'the Emergency' in Ireland. Though the Irish state remained officially neutral for the duration of the conflict, it worked closely with the British behind the scenes, which included allowing the Royal Air Force to use Irish airspace: the so-called Donegal Corridor.

De Valera was still bitter over the partition of Ireland and did not miss the opportunity to raise the subject, saying during the Dáil meeting: 'We, of all nations, know what force used by a stronger nation against a weaker one means. We have known what invasion and partition mean; we are not forgetful of our own history and, as long as our own country, or any part of it, is subject to force ... by a stronger nation, it is only natural that our people, whatever sympathies they might have in a conflict like the present, should look at their own country first.'

Not all in the Irish state supported neutrality. James Dillon, the deputy leader of Fine Gael, said in 1941: 'It may be policy of this Government to stand neutral, but I am not neutral. The issue at stake means whether I want to live or die. I pray Germany and its rulers may be smashed by the Anglo-American alliance. I also pray that the day will dawn when a United Irish People will play their part in helping to smash Germany.'

Tens of thousands of Irishmen would join the British armed forces in fighting Nazi Germany: 64,157 from Northern Ireland and 66,083 from the Irish state.

3 September 1939

Sinking of the SS *Athenia*

On Sunday 3 September 1939, at around 7:38 p.m., a U-boat torpedoed the SS *Athenia* about 250 miles off the Irish coast, between Tory Island, Co. Donegal and Rockall. The 525 ft liner had left Glasgow the previous day, stopping at Liverpool and Belfast to pick up the remainder of its 1,103 passengers, 120 of whom would perish. The Norwegian tanker *Knute Nelson* rescued 430 of the survivors, who were taken to Galway, where nurses in the Central Hospital and members of the Army Medical Corps were there to greet them. It took four hours after the rescue for the *Knute* to arrive, and a further two hours for all the survivors to be taken off, including 10 seriously injured people who were lowered on stretchers under the supervision of three local doctors.

One woman later remarked in the hospital: 'We thought that when we left Liverpool on Saturday night we had come away in good time, and then this happened. It was a terrible time. We were nine hours in the water before being picked up.' Germany initially denied involvement, accusing Winston Churchill, then First Lord of the Admiralty, of masterminding the attack to drum up support for the war.

In 2017, shipwreck-hunter David Mearns claimed to have found the remains of the *Athenia* 650 ft below the surface. 'I can't put my hand on a Bible in front of a judge and say 100 per cent this is the *Athenia*, but all of my experience says it's a very, very high probability. I am 98 per cent-plus certain.' Mearns had been searching for the *Athenia* since 2005.

However, Philip Gunyon, one of the survivors of the attack, was unsure whether there was any benefit to locating the ship: 'I have mixed feelings about the *Athenia* being found. It's a monument to Man's folly, trying to settle arguments by fighting rather than talking.'

4 September 1828

Annaghdown boating tragedy

On 4 September 1828, a boat left Annaghdown Pier, Co. Galway, carrying 31 people, 10 sheep and some timber, destined for a market in Fairhill, Galway city, about eight miles away. The boat was known as *Caisleán Nua* and was in a 'poor and leaky condition' when it began the journey across Lough Corrib. At the time, no road connected Annaghdown with Fairhill.

As it approached Bushypark, a sheep put its hoof through the side of the boat, causing it to flood. An effort was made to plug the hole using someone's coat, but this only made matters worse, and soon *Caisleán Nua* was sinking.

Eleven of the people on the boat were rescued but the remaining 20 drowned. Initially, the *Connaught Journal* reported the condition of the boat and said that 18 had died, with one other person missing, but two more bodies were later located. According to the paper, 'these unhappy creatures were taken out of the lake in the course of the day and presented a most heart-rending scene, being surrounded by their friends who came to identify them, and by whom they were removed on a boat to Annaghdown.'

The Annaghdown Angling Club and Friends erected a memorial stone 150 years after the tragedy. The incident also inspired the poem 'Anach Cuain' (sometimes spelled 'Eanach Dhúin') by the blind fiddler and travelling poet Antoine Ó Raifteirí (Anthony Raftery), who died in 1835. An English translation begins: 'If I live to show it, the world shall know it/The awful drowning at Annach Doon/Left father and mother, and wife and brother/In a shudder and smother of tears and gloom.'

5 September 1926

Dromcollogher fire

On 5 September 1926, 48 people died in a fire in Dromcollogher, Co. Limerick, in a loft being used as a temporary cinema. The casualties represented one-tenth of the population of the village at the time, and more than half the victims were under 25. It was a Sunday, when cinemas were usually closed, and a projectionist from Cork had travelled to Dromcollogher with reels of Cecil B. DeMille's 1926 film *The Ten Commandments*.

Though a generator powered the projector and the lights in the loft, a small candle was kept next to the screen to illuminate the room. When a piece of its wax broke, one of the exposed film reels caught fire, and within minutes, the room was engulfed in flames. Several people tried to leave through windows in the back. However, one woman got stuck, preventing others from being able to escape.

The tragedy had an enormous effect on Dromcollogher. Many lost relatives, and in at least one case, an entire family – mother, father and two children – were killed. Local schoolteacher Jeremiah Buckley died, along with his wife, Ellen, their daughter, Bridget, his brother, Thomas, and their maid, Nora Kirwin. Forty-seven of the victims were buried together in the grounds of the church of Dromcollogher, their names inscribed on the gravestone.

The funeral mass was held on Tuesday 7 September, presided over by Canon John Begley while the celebrant was Fr Daniel O'Callaghan, whose mother, Mary Ann O'Callaghan, was one of the victims. Messages of condolence were sent from far and wide: Canon Begley noted that 'King George and men in exalted positions, both in Great Britain and Ireland have human hearts that throb with sympathy for the poor distressed people of Drumcollogher.'

6 September 1593

Grace O'Malley meets Elizabeth I

On 6 September 1593, Grace O'Malley, known also as Gráinne Ní Mháille, met Elizabeth I at Greenwich Palace, asking for the release of members of her family who had been taken captive by Richard Bingham, the Governor of Connacht. It is said that

this made O'Malley the only Irish woman ever to appear in a British royal court. The two conversed in Latin, though not, as is commonly claimed, because O'Malley spoke no English; she was almost certainly proficient in the language.

Born *c.*1530, Grace was the daughter of Irish chieftain Owen O'Malley (Eoghan Dubhdara Ó Mháille), who owned a large cattle herd and fishing fleet and regularly traded sea salt with France and Spain. She married Donal O'Flaherty (Dónal Ó Flaithbheartaigh) at age 16, bore three children and became mistress of his castles in Bunowen and Ballinahinch. In 1565, Donal was killed by the rival Joyce clan while they attempted to take over Castlekirk in Lough Corrib. Two hundred of his men pledged loyalty to Grace, and she established her home base in Clew Bay.

In 1566, Grace married Richard 'the Iron' Bourke, gaining control of Rockfleet Castle in Newport, Co. Mayo. She divorced him a year later with the words 'I dismiss you', though they remained legally married. Bourke was heir to the MacWilliams and Bourke clans, and in 1584 Richard Bingham, having become Governor of Connacht, attempted to strip the Bourke clan of its wealth. He even had his men kill Grace's eldest son, Eoghan.

That year, Bingham described Grace as 'a notable traitoress and nurse to all rebellions in the province for 40 years'. In this context, Grace travelled to London to meet with Elizabeth I. Not only was her son Tibbot ne Long released, but so too was her fleet in Clew Bay, which had been impounded.

7 September 1948

Repeal of External Relations Act is announced

On 7 September 1948, John A. Costello, on an official visit to Canada as Taoiseach, held a press conference in the Railway Committee Room of the Parliament Buildings in Ottawa. He announced that Ireland intended to repeal the External Relations Act, effectively severing the Irish state's last links with the British Commonwealth.

The announcement was spurred by Costello's feeling that he had been slighted on the trip. Before attending a banquet, he checked with John Hearne, the Irish High Commissioner to Canada, that a toast would be given to honour both George VI and Seán T. O'Kelly, the President of Ireland. However, according to Costello, 'When the dinner took place the only toast given was that of "the King" and this upset me.'

Costello later told O'Kelly, 'There seemed to me to be no proper appreciation of our status ... I made the decision to cut through all this and I made the statement which brought on the repeal of the External Relations Act.' On the official trip, in a speech to the Canadian Bar Association, Costello had referred to the External Relations Act as being 'full of inaccuracies and infirmities'. News of this speech filtered back to Ireland, where it was picked up by Seán MacBride, leader of Clann na Poblachta, which shared power in government with Costello's Fine Gael. It made the front page of the *Sunday Independent* on 5 September under the headline 'External Relations Act to Go'.

Two days later, in the Railway Committee Room, Costello was asked whether this was true, and he replied that it was. He later wrote to William Norton, leader of the Irish Labour Party, telling him, 'I will explain when I return why I decided to state publicly that we intended to repeal the External Relations Act. It was really the article in the *Sunday Independent* that decided me.'

8 September 1798

The Battle of Ballinamuck

On 8 September 1798, the Battle of Ballinamuck was fought in north Co. Longford. A small French force, led by General Joseph Humbert, had landed at Killala, Co. Mayo on 22 August, following a request for assistance from the United Irishmen's representative in Paris. They were joined by thousands of Irish peasants and began the march eastwards, where they would be met by Lord Cornwallis, the Lord Lieutenant of Ireland. He was known for surrendering to Benjamin Lincoln at the Battle of Yorktown in 1781, effectively losing the American colonies for Great Britain. His defeat in the United States was not to be replicated in Ireland, however.

Humbert's men spent the night of 7 September in Cloone, Co. Leitrim, though Cornwallis was aware of their presence, and would later note: 'I felt pretty confident that one more march would bring this disagreeable warfare to a conclusion; and having obtained satisfactory information that the enemy had halted for the night at Cloone, I moved with the troops at Carrick at 10 o'clock on the night of the 7th to Mohill.'

Prior to meeting Cornwallis' men, morale was low among the French. A captain, Jobit, noted that his soldiers were 'extremely fatigued and much depressed by the news of enormous enemy forces dogging and surrounding them'. The next day, Humbert's men clashed with Cornwallis in Ballinamuck. The rebels made their defensive stand on the hill of Shanmullagh, but were outnumbered. General Lake, who accompanied Cornwallis, wrote that the French rearguard were summoned to surrender: when they refused, they were attacked, after which 'upwards of 200 French infantry threw down their arms.'

Humbert rode forward with the flag of parlay, and many of the Irish fled. It is said that up to 500 were executed on the orders of Lord Roden. Thus ended the last battle involving a continental European army on Irish soil.

9 September 1982

Killing of Declan Flynn

On 9 September 1982, 31-year-old Declan Flynn left a pub in Donnycarney in Dublin and made his way towards Fairview Park. The park was a popular gathering place for gay men, at a time when male homosexual acts were still illegal in Ireland. After sitting on a bench, Flynn was ambushed and chased by five youths, who beat him unconscious, robbed him and left him for dead. He was found and brought to Blanchardstown Hospital, where he died within an hour of admission.

None of the youths involved served any jail time for the crime. Justice Seán Gannon gave them suspended sentences for manslaughter, noting that 'this could never be regarded as murder', and complimented the youths on their 'good homes'. (One of them, Robert Alan Armstrong, would be sentenced to 10 years for raping a pregnant woman in Ballymun in 1992.)

There was outrage among the gay and lesbian community in Dublin. Activist Tonie Walsh would later note, 'Pride grew directly out of the gay-bashing killing of Declan Flynn. There was such a sense of anger at the killing and disbelief that the thugs who killed him would get off scot-free that gay people started to mobilise in a concerted way.' After the sentencing of Flynn's killers, 700 people marched from Liberty Hall to Fairview in an event organised by Dublin Gay Collective, demanding an end to violence against gays and women.

In June 1983, Dublin's first Gay Pride parade was held, with 200 people marching from St Stephen's Green to the GPO. It would grow with every passing year. LGBT activist Izzy Kamikaze reflected on the event years later: 'We were the people who organised the Fairview Park march after the killing, which is the thing that people say was "the Irish Stonewall". And perhaps it was.'

10 September 1966

Donogh O'Malley announces free secondary education

On 10 September 1966, Donogh O'Malley, Minister for Education in the Fianna Fáil government, made an announcement that would have a profound impact on the Irish state. Speaking at a dinner of the National Union of Journalists, O'Malley declared that, beginning the following year, 'the opportunity for free post-primary education will be available to all families.'

At the time, education in Ireland was in dire straits. As O'Malley noted, about a third of children who finished primary school – 17,000 – were not proceeding to higher education. Less than 50 per cent of those aged 15 were still in full-time education, and at age 16, only 36 per cent were still at school. This was, in the minister's words, 'a dark stain on the national conscience. For it means that some one-third of our people have been condemned – the great majority through no fault of their own – to be part-educated unskilled labour, always the weaker who go to the wall of unemployment or emigration.'

Within a decade of O'Malley's announcement, the participation rate at second level had doubled. By 2016, half a century on, more than 90 per cent of the population were completing the Leaving Certificate, the final exam of the secondary school system in Ireland.

It is widely acknowledged that the economic boom of the mid-1990s – the 'Celtic Tiger' – stemmed at least partly from O'Malley's decision. Future Taoiseach John Bruton acknowledged as much in 1999. Forgoing a 'partisan approach', Bruton said: 'The foundation of our economic success can probably be attributed to a decision taken by the late Deputy Donogh O'Malley to introduce free secondary education. That, with the decisions to join the European Union and to guarantee a corporate tax rate of 10 per cent ... are among the foundation stones of our current success.'

11 September 1649

Siege of Drogheda ends

On 11 September 1649, the Siege of Drogheda came to an end after eight days. Having been appointed Lord Lieutenant of Ireland, Oliver Cromwell arrived in Dublin in August of that year with 12,000 men and a large artillery train. His path had been cleared by Colonel Michael Jones's victory at the Battle of Rathmines on 2 August, after which James Butler, the Marquess of Ormond, fled north. Butler was loyal to Charles I, and sent his men to key garrison cities such as Drogheda in the hope of slowing down the advance of Cromwell and his forces.

Drogheda was under the command of Sir Arthur Aston, an English soldier from a prominent Roman Catholic family. His garrison numbered around 2,300 men, and the town's medieval curtain walls provided the inhabitants with significant defence. When, on 10 September, Cromwell demanded the surrender of Drogheda, Aston refused. Cromwell then began shelling the town. The next day, two assault attempts by Cromwell's forces ended in failure, but a third was successful. Cromwell showed little mercy to his prisoners. In his own words, 'in the heat of the action, I forbade them to spare any that were in arms in the town and I think that night they put to the sword about two thousand men.'

Aston and about 200 Royalists locked themselves in Millmount Fort. Colonel Daniel Axtell offered to spare their lives if they surrendered, which they did, only to be taken to a nearby windmill and killed an hour later. Eighty other Royalists sought refuge in St Peter's Church, until it was set on fire on the orders of Colonel John Hewson. Thirty people burned to death inside; the rest died fleeing.

Around 3,500 people were killed by Cromwell's forces, 2,700 of whom were Royalist soldiers. The remainder were civilians, prisoners and Catholic clergy. The Parliamentarians recorded losses of around 150.

12 September 1969

Cameron Report is published

After riots broke out in Derry on 5 October 1968, when police blocked a protest march organised by the Derry Housing Action Committee (DHAC), the British government announced that it would hold an inquiry, under the chairmanship of Lord Cameron, a distinguished judge from Scotland. The Disturbances in Northern Ireland Report (or Cameron Report, as it came to be known) was published on 12 September 1969.

It found that 'the police broke ranks and used their batons indiscriminately on people in Duke Street', and that 'the District Inspector in charge used his blackthorn with needless violence.' However, it also reported that 'the conduct of the police and the handling of the situation by the officers in charge on that day deserve commendation apart from a few isolated incidents of indiscipline and misconduct.'

Reaction in Northern Ireland was mixed. Ulster Unionist Brian Faulkner, Minister for Development and later Northern Ireland's last Prime Minister, said, 'I think that it's a very sober and reasonable report of what went on in Northern Ireland prior to the disturbances which currently affect us.'

William Craig, former Minister for Home Affairs, was more dismissive, saying, 'I've only read it once, and read it very quickly, but I did pay particular attention to the portions that criticised me, and I consider that those criticisms have very little meat in them.' However, John Hume, then an Independent Nationalist MP for Foyle, said: 'I think that it's a devastating indictment of the Unionist government, and in any normal society that government would have to resign at once. Unfortunately, we don't have a normal society in the North of Ireland.' Bernadette Devlin described the report as 'inept and incompetent'.

13 September 1961

The Siege of Jadotville

On 13 September 1961, Irish peacekeeping soldiers at Jadotville (now Likasi) in the southeast region of the Democratic Republic of Congo came under attack from mercenaries loyal to Katangese President Moise Tshome. There were about 157 soldiers in 'A' Company, 35th Battalion of the Irish Army, versus 3,000 of the enemy. Congo had declared its independence from Belgium in 1960, but then Katanga, a province that contained most of the country's mineral wealth, attempted to secede. With civil war looming, 'A' Company was sent to Jadotville, to protect the mostly Belgian settlers there.

Commandant Pat Quinlan, sensing the tension in the area, ordered his men to dig a trench 1.5 metres deep around their base, stockpile water and carry their guns at all times. Unbeknown to Quinlan, UN forces in Elisabethville, 80 miles from Jadotville, had seized Katangan positions there. It was after this that mercenaries attacked 'A' Company.

The Irish forces were lightly armed. Noel Carey, a 24-year-old lieutenant at the time, said, 'We had antiquated equipment, armoured cars that you could probably shoot arrows through.' In contrast, the mercenaries were equipped with a Fouga Magister jet fighter, which bombed the base at night.

'A' Company resisted the attacks for five days but eventually were forced to surrender, having run out of water and ammunition. They had killed 300 mercenaries and suffered no fatalities, though five Irish soldiers were wounded. They were held for five weeks, until the UN negotiated their release; they returned to Ireland in December of that year.

For decades, the incident was swept under the carpet, until 2016, when the survivors were honoured with a Presidential Unit Citation by Minister for Defence Paul Kehoe, who said, 'I strongly felt that this was a grievous wrong by successive governments that needed to be put right.'

14 September 1607

The Flight of the Earls

On 14 September 1607, Hugh O'Neill, 2nd Earl of Tyrone, and Rory O'Donnell, 1st Earl of Tyrconnell, set sail from Rathmullan on the Fanad Peninsula in Co. Donegal with approximately 90 of their followers. Their destination was Quillebeuf in France, where they landed 21 days later before moving on to Leuven, and finally Rome on 29 April 1608. This event became known as the Flight of the Earls.

O'Neill had formed an alliance with Hugh Roe O'Donnell, brother of Rory, in the Nine Years' War fought against English rule in Ireland, and had scored some victories. However, after his defeat at the Battle of Kinsale in 1602, and with the signing of the Treaty of Mellifont the following year, O'Neill swore allegiance to Elizabeth I. He retained much of his land, but had to accept the English title of 'Earl'.

Elizabeth died shortly after and was succeeded by James I, under whose rule English and Scottish planters began moving to Ulster. Unable to adapt to the new political settlement, and fearing charges of treason from James, O'Neill and O'Donnell fled. This meant that their lands were forfeited, and James sent even more planters to Ulster: many of them Presbyterians from Ayrshire and Galloway in Scotland. Not only did the earls' departure have an impact on Ireland, but it also affected continental Europe. It is estimated that 10,000 people moved from Ireland to Spain in the first decade of the seventeenth century.

In 2007, to mark the 400th anniversary of the Flight of the Earls, President Mary McAleese unveiled a commemorative sculpture designed by John Behan, and said: 'Even today we struggle to fully comprehend the downstream consequences of the loss, the driving out of our great native leaders … but now we gather the memories of all those who left our shores whether through military force or economic deprivation.'

15 September 1916

Walter Gordon Wilson's tanks are first used

On 15 September 1916, a new weapon of war was deployed for the first time. At the Battle of Flers–Courcelette in France, 49 British tanks were assigned to reach

German lines over a mile away, though only nine succeeded in doing so. Nevertheless, Field Marshal Douglas Haig was so taken with these armoured vehicles that he ordered 1,000 more.

An Irish engineer, Walter Gordon Wilson, had designed the prototype for these tanks. Born in Blackrock, Co. Dublin, Wilson was a Royal Naval Volunteer Reserve officer and, according to military historian Richard Pullen, 'a genius with things like gearboxes'.

In February 1915, Winston Churchill established the Admiralty Landships Committee, whose purpose was to create a mechanical solution to the stalemate on the Western Front. William Tritton, managing director of agricultural machinery company William Foster and Co. in Lincoln, began working on an experimental tracked armoured machine that became known as 'Little Willie', but it was Wilson who solved one of the main problems – its inability to cross wide trenches – by designing a vehicle whose tracks looped around its entire body. This became known as 'Mother', and its prototype was built in 99 days. Wilson then went to the Metropolitan Carriage and Wagon Company, near Birmingham, to supervise the manufacture of Mark I tanks, 125 of which were ordered from Metropolitan and 25 from Lincoln.

The first use of tanks is not widely seen as a success – it allowed the Allies to gain only five miles on the Germans. However, as David Willey, curator of the Bovington Tank Museum, noted, 'The direct military impact of the tank can be debated but its effect on the Germans was immense, it caused bewilderment, terror and concern in equal measure.'

16 September 1937

Kirkintilloch disaster

In the 17th century, Brian Rua U'Cearbhain, a native of Erris, Co. Mayo, is said to have prophesised that 'Carriages on wheels with smoke and fire will come to Achill and the first and last carriages will carry dead bodies.' If so, it could be argued that his vision was fulfilled in 1937 when the bodies of 10 men and boys were transported from North Wall in Dublin to Achill Sound by train, after a tragic fire on 16 September that year. The victims, aged between 13 and 23, were seasonal workers in Kirkintilloch, about eight miles from Glasgow. They had come from Mayo in June to work as 'tattie-hokers' (potato pickers), a common source of income for families in the west and northwest of Ireland.

They were housed in a bothy, or small hut – 26 in total, including 14 girls. It is unclear how the fire started, but at around one o'clock in the morning the son of the foreman discovered the blaze and the alarm was raised. Though the 14 girls managed to escape, all but two of the 12 men and boys perished. Tragically, three of those who died were brothers, aged 13, 15 and 17, members of the Mangan family. The Kilbane family also lost two sons, as did the McLaughlin family.

Eerily, in 1893, 30 harvesters who drowned in Clew Bay were transported to Achill by train, the first time a train journey had been made there, adding credence to Brian Rua U'Cearbhain's prediction. The *Irish Times* reported on the devastating event: 'By this appalling disaster an entire parish has been plunged into the depths of sorrow … In this country we shall wish to know why it is necessary for boys of 13 to 16, who ought to be at school, to go abroad for farming work.'

17 September 1948

W. B. Yeats is reinterred in Sligo

W. B. Yeats died in Menton, France in 1939, and was buried in Roquebrune-Cap-Martin shortly after. However, it had been the poet's wish to be buried in Co. Sligo, where he spent much of his childhood. According to his wife, Georgie Hyde-Lees, Yeats asked that he initially be interred in France, but then, 'in a year's time when the newspapers have forgotten me, dig me up and plant me in Sligo.'

Nine years after – on a bleak and wet Friday, 17 September 1948 – a coffin draped in the Irish tricolour was transported to Galway by a naval corvette. It then made its way to the village of Drumcliff, Co. Sligo, on the orders of Seán MacBride, recently appointed Minister for External Affairs.

Among those present at the reinterment were the Taoiseach, Éamon de Valera, playwright Lennox Robinson and Lord Longford. The Mayor of Sligo, Michael Rooney, paid tribute to Yeats, 'whose genius was inspired by the lakes and mountains of our countryside. And, whose poetry has given the name of Sligo a place in the literature of the world … Today, we have fulfilled the express desires of W. B. Yeats.' Indeed, Yeats's headstone was inscribed with a line from a poem he wrote a year prior to his death, 'Under Ben Bulben'.

A rumour has persisted that the body buried in Drumcliff was not that of Yeats but of an Englishman named Alfred Hollis who died in Roquebrune the same week as the poet. This was strenuously denied by Yeats's family. Hollis' remains had gone missing, though he was known to wear a leather and metal corset similar to that identified by the doctor who had certified Yeats's remains. The truth may never be known for sure.

18 September 1914

Government of Ireland Act is signed into law

On 18 September 1914, the Government of Ireland Act, commonly referred to as the Third Home Rule Bill, was signed into law by George V. The two previous Home Rule Bills had failed: the first, in 1886, was defeated in the House of Commons; the second, in 1893, was passed in the Commons but then defeated in the House of Lords, which had a veto. Knowing that the veto meant it was impossible for Home Rule to be granted, the Irish Parliamentary Party, led by John Redmond, refused to support Herbert Asquith's Liberals in government unless the House of Lords was reformed. In 1911 a Parliament Act was passed that meant the Lords could not veto a bill for more than two years.

The Lords rejected the Government of Ireland Act in 1912 and 1913, but in 1914 they could no longer do so. However, history saw to it that it that the 1914 Act was never fully implemented. A month earlier the United Kingdom had declared war on Germany, and the same day that the Government of Ireland Act was signed into law, so too was the Suspensory Act, which said that the former Act would not be put into operation until 'the present War has ended'.

This was a relief to Asquith, who wrote on 31 August 1914: 'The Irish on both sides are giving me a lot of trouble at a difficult moment. I sometimes wish we could submerge the whole lot of them and their island for, say, ten years, under the waves of the Atlantic.' The 1914 Act would never have extended to the whole of Ireland; to placate Ulster unionists, at least four counties in Ulster would have been excluded.

19 September 1880

Parnell introduces 'boycotting'

On 19 September 1880, Charles Stewart Parnell, the leader of the Irish Parliamentary Party and president of the National Land League, gave a speech to 12,000 people in Ennis, Co. Clare. Parnell set his sights on those who took possession of lands previously occupied by tenant farmers unable to pay their rents: 'When a man takes a farm from which another has been evicted, you must show him on the roadside when you meet him … by isolating him from the rest of his kind as if he were the leper of old … your detestation of the crime he has committed.' This approach was soon piloted on a land agent in Co. Mayo named Captain Charles Boycott.

Boycott, originally from Norfolk, England, was an agent for the third Earl of Erne's estates in Co. Mayo and farmed 600 acres of his own at Ballinrobe. He wrote a letter to *The Times*, published on 18 October 1880, describing in detail how his farm labourers were 'ordered off, under threats of ulterior consequences', his blacksmith menaced, and shopkeepers told not to serve him. William Edward Forster, the Chief Secretary for Ireland, arranged to have 50 men from Co. Monaghan and Co. Cavan sent to help farm Boycott's land. They arrived at the railway station in Claremorris on 11 November, each armed with a revolver.

The work was eventually completed on 26 November, but this was a pyrrhic victory. The British government had spent £10,000 to harvest crops worth only about £500. Boycott would leave Ireland for good in December of that year, but his name would enter the lexicon as a byword for refusal to buy, use, or participate in something as a means of protest.

20 September 1920

The Sack of Balbriggan

At around 9:00 p.m. on 20 September 1920, Royal Irish Constabulary (RIC) Head Constable Peter Burke, from Glenamaddy, Co. Galway, was having a drink with his brother, Sergeant Michael Burke, in Smyth's pub, Balbriggan, when they were shot by local IRA men Michael Rock and John Denham. Peter was killed and Michael wounded. In retaliation, three lorryloads of RIC officers, Auxiliaries and Black and

Tans arrived in the town and burned down four pubs, a factory and nine houses. An additional 30 houses were vandalised, and two local men were killed.

After news of the RIC men's shootings filtered back to Gormanston military camp, three miles away in Co. Meath, an estimated 200 men arrived in the town. They burned down Smyth's, the Gladstone Inn and Derham's Pub, the last of which was owned by John Derham, a local Sinn Féin representative. The Deeds and Templar hosiery factory, which employed 200 people in Balbriggan, was burned to the ground. Most of the houses that were shot up were on Clonard Street; residents were forced to flee into the fields behind them.

Two local IRA volunteers – James Lawless and John Gibbons – were taken to the RIC barracks in Balbriggan, where they were beaten before being bayoneted and shot on Quay Street: their bodies were discovered at 6:00 a.m. on 21 September.

According to Alfred Flint, a former member of the Royal Scottish Regiment, 137 men left the Black and Tans in the weeks following the sacking of the town. Flint said: 'I told them when I joined I thought I was going into a police force, and when they asked me "what did you go into?", I said straight: "it looks as if it was into a corps of bandits."'

21 September 1949

Ireland defeat England on English soil

On 21 September 1949, the Ireland football team became the first foreign side to defeat England on its home soil, winning 2–0 in Goodison Park, Liverpool. This came just five months after Ireland had officially become a Republic: from 1953 onwards the team would be known as the Republic of Ireland, to differentiate it from the other team on the island, Northern Ireland. Only 200 or so fans travelled over for the match, although, given the unofficial status of Liverpool as 'the real capital of Ireland', many residents of the city were possibly rooting for the Irish team.

The odds were not in Ireland's favour. Henry Rose of the *Daily Express*, who would tragically die in the Munich air disaster of 1958, wrote, 'Anybody who thinks the Irish have any chance should make an appointment with a Harley Street psychiatrist.'

However, they had more than a chance. The captain of the Irish team was Johnny (or Jackie) Carey, who played for Manchester United and was the football writers'

player of the year. The coach was Billy Lord, and training took place in Haig Avenue in Southport, Merseyside. There were 51,847 spectators in Goodison Park on the day, which was the second time that England and a team representing the independent Irish state had met. The first match, in September 1946 at Dalymount Park, Dublin, saw England win 1–0 with a goal from Tom Finney.

Ireland were given a penalty 32 minutes into the 1949 game when Bert Mozley took down Peter Desmond. Con Martin scored. Five minutes before the end of the match, Peter Farrell scored a second goal, sealing England's fate. Nevertheless, the England supporters were gracious in defeat.

22 September 1970

Beginning of the Arms Trial

On 22 September 1970, the first Arms Trial began in Dublin. Charles Haughey, who had been dismissed from government earlier that year, faced prosecution for conspiring to import arms illegally, as did Captain James Kelly of the Irish Army, Belfast republican John Kelly and Belgian businessman Albert Luykx. Charges against Neil Blaney, who had also been dismissed from government, were dropped in July. The trial collapsed only a week after it had begun, on 29 September, when Judge Aindrias Ó Caoimh withdrew following accusations of bias.

The retrial began on 6 October and lasted until 23 October. The chief prosecution witness was Jim Gibbons, Fianna Fáil Minister for Defence at the time of the ministers' dismissal, who claimed that Haughey had known about a plan to import weapons, to be given to the IRA in Northern Ireland. Haughey denied this.

In the end, all four men were acquitted. Judge Seamus Henchy summed up the verdict by saying, 'There was a flat contradiction between Mr Haughey's version and Mr Gibbons' version, and the difference seemed to be irreconcilable.' Taoiseach Jack Lynch responded to the verdict: 'No one can deny that there was this attempt to import arms illegally.'

The Arms Trial cast a long shadow on Fianna Fáil and on the Irish state. Many involved in the case, including Captain Kelly, claimed they were made scapegoats by the government, and that Gibbons had ordered the importation with Lynch's knowledge. When Kelly passed away in 2003, Taoiseach Bertie Ahern fell short of confirming this, but said, 'Captain Kelly was prosecuted in the Arms Trial in circumstances of great controversy. He was acquitted of all the charges laid against him. As far as the state is concerned, he was innocent of those charges … Historians will make their own judgments about the events of that era.'

23 September 1911

Edward Carson first addresses Belfast supporters

In 1910, Edward Carson became leader of the Irish Unionist Alliance. Born in Harcourt Street, Dublin to a wealthy Protestant family, Carson was passionately opposed to Home Rule, the form of limited self-government desired by John Redmond and the Irish Parliamentary Party (IPP). At the time, the IPP was a force to be reckoned with: it had won 73 of the 103 Irish seats in the House of Commons in the 1910 election.

In 1911, Carson realised that Redmond's alliance with Herbert Asquith, and the removal of the House of Lords' veto on any Government of Ireland Bill, made Home Rule all the more likely, and on 23 September, he addressed supporters in Ulster for the first time. The demonstration was planned by James Craig, MP for East Down and later the first Prime Minister of Northern Ireland. Carson confided in Lady Londonderry, 'I am much overwhelmed at all that lies before us … I am so nervous about it all and how it will come off.' He travelled to Belfast with his wife, Annette – her first and last visit, as she was to die in 1913.

Around 50,000 people took part in the rally, the majority Orangemen from Grand Lodges in Belfast who travelled from Belfast City Hall to Craig's estate, known as Craigavon. Carson told the crowd: 'I know the responsibility you are putting on me today. In your presence I cheerfully accept it, grave as it is, and I now enter into a compact with you, and every one of you … we will yet defeat the most nefarious conspiracy that has ever been hatched against a free people … We must be prepared – and time is precious in these things – the morning Home Rule passes, ourselves to become responsible for the government of the Protestant Province of Ulster.'

24 September 1914

Irish Volunteers split

On 24 September 1914, the Provisional Committee of the Irish Volunteers released a statement repudiating remarks that John Redmond had made four days earlier in Co. Wicklow. Addressing a parade of Volunteers in the village of Woodenbridge, Redmond urged them to join the British Army and fight in the First World War: 'it would be a disgrace forever to our country … if young Ireland confined their efforts to remaining at home to defend the shores of Ireland from an unlikely invasion, and shrinking from the duty of proving on the field of battle the gallantry and courage which have distinguished their race all through its history.'

It was not the first time Redmond had pledged the support of Irish Volunteers to the war effort. In August of that year, in the House of Commons, he said that 'armed Nationalist Catholics in the South will be only too glad to join arms with the armed Protestant Ulstermen in the North. Is it too much to hope that out of this situation there may spring a result which will be good not merely for the Empire, but good for the future welfare and integrity of the Irish nation?'

Redmond's rhetorical question may have been answered in the negative, as 'Protestant Ulstermen' had no desire to be part of the Irish nation and the Provisional Committee of the Irish Volunteers had no interest in sending its members to fight in 'the interests of England or Germany or any foreign country', as Arthur Griffith put it.

The statement of 24 September said that Redmond was 'no longer entitled, through his nominees, to any place in the administration and guidance of the Irish Volunteer organisation'. The Volunteers split. By October, 158,360 had followed Redmond into the National Volunteers. The other 12,306, retaining the name 'the Irish Volunteers', remained under the leadership of Eoin MacNeill.

25 September 1917

Thomas Ashe dies on hunger strike

On 25 September 1917, Thomas Ashe became the first Irish republican prisoner to die on hunger strike, in the Mater Hospital in Dublin, aged 32. A veteran of the Easter Rising, Ashe had successfully led a raid on an RIC Barracks in Ashbourne, Co. Meath. After the rebellion he was sentenced to death, later commuted to penal servitude, and spent time in Dartmoor and Lewes prisons in England.

Under the general amnesty of June 1917, Ashe was released and received a hero's welcome in his native Co. Kerry. He succeeded Denis McCullough as president of the Irish Republican Brotherhood, but his freedom was to be short-lived. On 25 July, he gave what was deemed to be a seditious speech in Ballinalee, Co. Longford. Arrested under the Defence of the Realm Act, he was court-martialled in Dublin Castle with testimony from Constable Thomas Bowers.

Ashe was sentenced to a year's hard labour in Mountjoy Prison in Dublin, along with Fionán Lynch and Austin Stack, but demanded to be treated as a prisoner of war. On 20 September he began refusing food; five days later, the prison authorities took to force-feeding him. He died a few hours later in the Mater Hospital. The playwright Sean O'Casey, a friend of Ashe's, wrote graphically of his final moments: 'The tube is quickly pulled out, and Thomas Ashe's tortured stomach vomits forth some of the food that has been forced into it. The straps are unbound and the tortured prisoner falls limply forward into a state of collapse.'

Ashe's funeral cortège was met by 150,000 people in Dublin. One hundred priests were in attendance, as were 120 Kerry Volunteers. Michael Collins gave the graveside oration in Glasnevin Cemetery. Following a volley of shots over the coffin, Collins' words were: 'Nothing remains to be said. That volley is the only speech that it is proper to make above the grave of a dead Fenian.'

26 September 1791

The *Queen* convict ship arrives in Sydney

On 26 September 1791, the first convict ship to sail directly from Ireland to Australia – the *Queen* – arrived at Sydney Cove. It had left Cork in March of that year, carrying prisoners from all over Ireland: 133 male convicts, 22 female convicts and four children. The *Queen* was one of 11 ships that made up the Third Fleet, the First Fleet and Second Fleet having sailed from England. The receipt for the prisoners was given to Sir Henry Browne Hayes, the sheriff of Cork, equivalent to its mayor. In 1802, Hayes would himself be sent to Sydney after being convicted of kidnapping Quaker heiress Mary Pike.

Up to 1868, nearly a third of all convicts brought to Australia were Irish. Between 1788 and 1921, approximately half a million Irish people moved to Australia, though only 12 per cent of these arrived on convict ships. On board the *Queen*, the prisoners included 11-year-old David Fay and 12-year-old James Blake, both from Dublin, and John Healy from Limerick city, who was 12. The oldest was Patrick Fitzgerald, a 64-year-old farmer from Co. Limerick. Eighty-two of the convicts had been convicted in Dublin, 10 were from Limerick, nine from Armagh and nine from Cork, with counties such as Antrim, Cavan and Down contributing one to three convicts each.

One of the most famous Irish people to arrive in New South Wales in 1791 was George Barrington, a pickpocket. The theft of a gold watch saw him transported to Australia, sentenced to seven years. However, once he arrived, Barrington convinced his captors to give him a job with the police. By 1796 he had received a full pardon and been made High Constable of Parramatta. He died in 1804.

27 September 1913

SS *Hare* relieves Dublin strikers

On 27 September 1913, the SS *Hare* arrived in Dublin. It carried 60,000 food parcels sent by members of the British Trades Union Congress (TUC) in solidarity with members of the Irish Transport and General Workers' Union (ITGWU) during the Dublin Lockout. At the time, 20,000 workers in Dublin were on strike or locked out, and in a dire need of help. ITGWU founder James Larkin had returned to Britain, where he was born, to muster support for the Dublin strikers. The Dublin & Manchester Steamship Company had been established in 1897 by George Lowen of Manchester, owner of the *Hare*, and Dubliner D. J. Stewart. For years, the ship's activity was recorded as 'trading between Dublin & Manchester carrying General Cargo, Livestock and Passengers'.

The *Hare* would return to Dublin along with the SS *Pioneer* and SS *New Fraternity*. By late November, hundreds of thousands of bags of tea, sugar and potatoes, packets of margarine, loaves of bread, pots of jam, tins of fish, boxes of cheese and tons of coal had arrived. The supplies were stored in the Manchester Shed on Sir John Rogerson's Quay.

One witness to the arrival of the *Hare* was Paddy Butner, a child of one of the strikers. Recalling the event, he said, 'a cheer rose from every throat of those watching when someone cried "It's the SS *Hare*!" ... The hair stood up on my head and I shouted with the rest in joy. As the vessel came abreast of the South Point, we all turned about and kept pace with her; the cheering and the waving continued while tears streamed down the faces of women and, indeed, men too.'

Tragically, the SS *Hare* was to sink en route to Manchester in 1918. Eleven lives were lost, six of them with Dublin addresses. One of the victims, Mrs Arland, was a widow who left four young children.

28 September 1912

The Ulster Covenant is signed

On 28 September 1912, almost half a million people in the province of Ulster signed the Ulster Covenant, or, to use its full name, Ulster's Solemn League and Covenant. The document was drafted by Sir Thomas Sinclair, a merchant from Belfast who was leader of the Ulster Liberal Unionist Association, an organisation that split from the Liberal Party after the latter's support for Home Rule in 1886. Its wording deliberately mirrored the Scottish National Covenant of 1638, signed in opposition to reforms to the Church of Scotland proposed by Charles I.

The Covenant began by stating that its signatories were 'convinced in our consciences that Home Rule would be disastrous to the material well-being of Ulster as well as of the whole of Ireland, subversive of our civil and religious freedom, destructive of our citizenship, and perilous to the unity of the Empire'. Signatories pledged to use 'all means which may be found necessary to defeat the present conspiracy to set up a Home Rule Parliament in Ireland', and that, were such a parliament to be set up, they would 'refuse to recognise its authority'.

Sir Edward Carson, leader of the Irish Unionist Party, was the first to sign the Covenant, followed by Lord Londonderry, representatives of the Protestant churches, and Sir James Craig. In Ulster, 218,206 men signed the Covenant and 228,991 women signed the corresponding women's declaration, even though Carson himself was not in favour of women's suffrage. An additional 19,162 men and 5,055 women living outside the province, who could prove they had been born in Ulster, also signed, in cities like Dublin, Edinburgh, Glasgow, York, Liverpool, London, Manchester and Bristol. In total, 471,414 people attached their names.

The *Irish Times* in Dublin, then a pro-unionist paper, wrote that 'Belfast displayed on Saturday such a civic harmony and passion as the world has hardly seen since Athenian or medieval times'.

29 September 1979

Pope John Paul II visits Ireland

On 29 September 1979, Pope John Paul II landed in Dublin Airport for a three-day visit to Ireland. He was greeted by 20,000 people, including Cardinal Tomás Ó Fiaich, the Archbishop of Armagh and Primate of All Ireland.

After disembarking his plane, the Pope dropped to his knees and kissed the tarmac. His first stop was Phoenix Park, where he celebrated a mass with one-and-a-quarter million people in attendance (at this time, fewer than five million lived on the island of Ireland). More than 200 cardinals were present from all over the world, with 2,000 priests on hand to deliver communion.

The Pope seemed fit and in good spirits. There had been talk of his visiting Northern Ireland, home to hundreds of thousands of Catholics, but, given the assassination of Lord Mountbatten by the Provisional IRA in Co. Sligo a month before his visit, it was decided that a visit to Drogheda, in the diocese of Armagh, would serve the trip better. The Pope pleaded with the IRA to 'turn away from the paths of violence and return to the ways of peace'. Acknowledging that many in Northern Ireland – including the Rev. Ian Paisley – had vilified him, John Paul said, 'May not Irish Protestants think that the Pope is an enemy, a danger or threat. My desire is that instead Protestants see me as a friend and brother in Christ.'

The next day, the Pope travelled to Ballybrit Racecourse in Galway, where he was greeted by a crowd of 280,000 and 800 priests, including Bishop Eamon Casey and Fr Michael Cleary, both of whom were later revealed to have fathered children in contravention of the Vatican's teachings on celibacy. It was here that John Paul said to those assembled, 'Young people of Ireland, I love you.'

30 September 1994
Boris Yeltsin incident at Shannon

On 30 September 1994, Boris Yeltsin, the first directly elected president of Russia, was scheduled to meet Taoiseach Albert Reynolds in Dublin after a trip to the United States. Yeltsin's predilection for alcohol was well known, and would lead to an embarrassing moment when Reynolds and his delegation were left standing on the runway at Shannon Airport. At 12:30 p.m., Yeltsin's plane was within Irish airspace, but it continued circling for half an hour. Nikolai Kozyrev, Russia's ambassador to Ireland, began to feel nervous.

When the plane eventually landed, Kozyrev attempted to board so that he could invite Yeltsin to meet Reynolds and the rest of the delegation. He was stopped by Yeltsin's bodyguard, who told the ambassador, 'You can't go in there, the president is very tired.' In his stead, Deputy Prime Minister Oleg Sokovets would meet with Reynolds. The Taoiseach was visibly disappointed: 'Well now, if he is sick, there is nothing we can do about it … but Mr Yeltsin, my guest, is on Irish soil, and I cannot miss this opportunity to go on board the airplane for five minutes, shake the president's hand and wish him a speedy recovery.' However, Reynolds was not allowed to see Yeltsin.

Asked afterwards at a press conference if the president was unwell, Sokovets replied, in Russian, 'He's just tired.' A high-ranking Irish official, years later, would say of the situation: 'We Irish, like you Russians, also like to drink, and all kinds of things happen here. So if your president had come out to see us, we wouldn't have paid any attention to his state and would have forgiven him, but his refusal to come out of the airplane insulted us to the depth of our souls and showed us that a small country like Ireland wasn't worth reckoning with.'

1 October 1843

O'Connell's last 'monster meeting', Mullaghmast

On 1 October 1843, Daniel O'Connell held what would be the last of his 'monster meetings', in Mullaghmast, Co. Kildare. These were enormous rallies held all over Ireland, aimed at solidifying support for repeal of the Union of Great Britain and Ireland. The largest was in Tara, Co. Meath, traditionally the seat of the High Kings of Ireland, on 15 August 1843: also the Feast of the Assumption of the Blessed Virgin, adding an extra layer of significance. Estimates ranged from 750,000 to a million present.

The meeting in Mullaghmast drew about half a million people. The site was that of a historic event that loomed large for the Catholics of Kildare and Ireland as a whole. The *Nation* newspaper wrote: 'Mullaghmast has been selected for this great meeting, as the scene of a massacre atrocious even for the Saxon. The Earl of Sussex, shortly after the "Reformation", having invited four hundred Chieftains of Leinster to a conference on this hill, murdered them in cold blood.'

At the event, O'Connell was presented with a 'Cap of Liberty', of green velvet and gold, created by sculptor John Hogan and historical author Henry MacManus. Addressing the crowd, the charismatic leader said: 'I accept with the greatest alacrity the high honour you have done me in calling me to the chair of this majestic meeting. I feel more honoured than I ever did in my life, with one single exception, and that related to, if possible, an equally majestic meeting at Tara ... I am for leaving England to the English, Scotland to the Scotch; but we must have Ireland for the Irish ... Stand by me – join with me – I will say be obedient to me, and Ireland shall be free.'

2 October 1996
Death of Brigid McCole

On 2 October 1996, Brigid McCole died of liver failure, aged 56. This came the day after she accepted a compensation offer from the government, relating to contaminated blood she was given by the Blood Transfusion Service Board (BTSB) during a pregnancy in the 1970s. In February 1994, the BTSB revealed in a press conference that anti-D immunoglobulin had been given to new mothers whose blood type was rhesus negative to prevent their developing antibodies that could seriously harm or kill a foetus in a future pregnancy. In the 1960s, around 40 foetuses a year were dying from these antibodies.

However, in 1991, the BTSB was alerted to the fact that blood samples used to create anti-D in 1977 might have been contaminated. Later, it transpired that the donor whose blood was used had hepatitis and jaundice. Dr Joan Power, who worked for the BTSB in Cork, managed to link contaminated anti-D to a number of female donors with hepatitis C. It turned out that around 1,200 women had been exposed to the virus.

One of the women involved, journalist Jane O'Brien, co-founded the group Positive Action to lobby on behalf of those affected. It was warned by the Chief State Solicitor that it would face 'uncertainties, delays, stresses, confrontation and cost' if it were to pursue cases in the High Court rather than through the compensation tribunal set up in 1995.

Minister for Health Michael Noonan offered his apologies in Dáil Éireann shortly after McCole's death: 'I certainly did not mean to question in any way the right of Mrs McCole and her legal team to take the course of action which they did. It is a great personal tragedy for the family and Mrs McCole and I apologise again for any hurt I may have caused.'

3 October 1992
Sinéad O'Connor tears up a photo of the Pope

On 3 October 1992, Sinéad O'Connor appeared on the NBC television programme *Saturday Night Live* as a musical guest. Performing an a cappella version of the Bob

Marley song 'War', O'Connor ended by lifting a photograph of Pope John Paul II as she sang the words, 'We have confidence in the victory of good over evil.' She then tore up the picture of the pontiff, and tossed the pieces on the floor, saying, 'Fight the real enemy.'

The studio sat in complete silence, and NBC cut to a commercial. The backlash against O'Connor was almost instantaneous. NBC received thousands of complaints, though the singer had her share of defenders.

Some were confused about what O'Connor, raised a Catholic, had meant by the gesture. In an interview with *Time* magazine shortly afterwards, she explained her motivations: 'In Ireland we see our people are manifesting the highest incidence in Europe of child abuse. This is a direct result of the fact that they're not in contact with their history as Irish people and the fact that in the schools, the priests have been beating the shit out of the children for years and sexually abusing them. This is the example that's been set for the people of Ireland.'

O'Connor was booed off stage less than two weeks later at a Bob Dylan tribute concert at Madison Square Garden. She was introduced by Kris Kristofferson, who said that her name had become 'synonymous with courage and integrity', but O'Connor could not compete with the jeers from the audience. However, she composed herself, with Kristofferson's help, and returned to reprise the version of 'War' she had sung on *Saturday Night Live*.

Given the Catholic Church's diminished standing in society since 1992, O'Connor could be seen to have been far ahead of her time.

4 October 1940

First Brian O'Nolan column in the *Irish Times*

On 4 October 1940, Brian O'Nolan made his debut as a columnist for the *Irish Times*, writing under the pseudonym Myles na gCopaleen. He had first appeared in the letters section of the paper, using another pseudonym, Flann O'Brien. O'Nolan would continue to write this column, under the title 'Cruiskeen Lawn', until his death in 1966, occasionally in Irish but mostly in English.

Born in Strabane, Co. Tyrone in 1911, O'Nolan moved with his family to Dublin in 1922, shortly after the partition of Ireland. Irish was the language spoken in his home, with English used outside – his father, Michael Nolan, and mother, Agnes Gormley, had met at an Irish language class.

He began working as a civil servant in 1935, one reason to mask his identity when writing his first letter to the editor of the *Irish Times* in 1939, which began, 'I do not know whether the petulant bickering which is going on in your columns, between Mr [Seán] O Faoláin and Mr [Frank] O'Connor is a private affair or whether any puling high-brow gentleman of refined tastes may take a part.'

He published the novel *At Swim-Two-Birds* in 1939, which is thought to have been the last book James Joyce ever read: apt, considering that O'Nolan would be one of the six men who retraced the steps of Leopold Bloom, the central character in Joyce's *Ulysses*, on the first Bloomsday in 1954.

He died of a heart attack in 1966, aged 54. Reflecting on O'Nolan's life, novelist Roddy Doyle noted: 'His fate, at least I think so, was to suffer one of the worst things that can happen: to be brilliant at something you don't like doing. He deserved better than the disappointment, and the raucous praise of a small town. He was maybe our unluckiest genius.'

5 October 1968

Duke Street march in Derry

On 5 October 1968, a protest march was organised by the Derry Housing Action Committee (DHAC), with support from the Northern Ireland Civil Rights Association (NICRA). It was planned to begin on Duke Street, in the Waterside area of Derry, and finish at the Diamond in the city centre. However, two days earlier, William Craig, Minister for Home Affairs in the Northern Ireland government, banned the march. NICRA sent a telegram to James Callaghan, the British Home Secretary, expressing its dismay ('Situation inflammatory. People will not continue to suffer the indignity of second-class citizenship').

It was decided that the march should go ahead. According to Eamonn McCann, one of the DHAC organisers, turnout was disappointing. This may have been because Derry City football club was playing a home game on the same day, drawing more of a crowd. The marchers included McCann, Gerry Fitt, Eddie McAteer and John Hume. The Royal Ulster Constabulary brought in 130 police officers to where it was to begin.

The police blocked the route of the march shortly after it had started, and then, according to the Cameron Report, Fitt and McAteer were clubbed with batons, 'at a time when no order to draw batons had been given and in circumstances in which the use of batons on these gentlemen was wholly without justification or excuse'. Soon after, the police were ordered to disperse the crowd, who scattered across Craigavon Bridge.

Gerry Fitt, reflecting on his assault, would later say, 'I uttered a prayer of thanks as the blood spilled over my face and on my shirt ... I knew that at last Northern Ireland as she really was would be seen before the world.'

6 October 1175

Treaty of Windsor is signed

On 6 October 1175, the Treaty of Windsor was signed by the High King of Ireland, Rory O'Connor (Ruaidrí Ua Conchobair), and Henry II of England, and witnessed by the archbishop of Dublin, Laurence O'Toole (Lorcan Ua Tuathail). It gave the Anglo-Normans control of Dublin and the southeast, and the rest of Ireland to O'Connor.

In the treaty, O'Connor is referred to as Roderic, the King's 'liegman', and granted the kingdom of Connacht to hold 'as fully and as peacefully as he held it before the lord king entered Ireland'. Others who held land in O'Connor's territory could retain it provided they 'remain in the fealty of the king of England, and continue to pay him faithfully and fully his tribute and the other rights which they owe him'.

The Treaty went on to say that anyone who became 'rebels to the king of England' would have to be dealt with by O'Connor, or the 'constable of the king of England in that land Ireland shall, when called upon him, aid him to do what is necessary'. Tributes to the king were to be doled out as follows: 'out of every ten animals slaughtered, one hide, acceptable to the merchants both in his land and as in the rest'.

However well-intentioned the Treaty of Windsor may have been, it was ultimately a failure. Neither Henry nor O'Connor could control those on his own side. The following April, Strongbow, the Anglo-Norman knight who had landed in Ireland in 1170, died, and a collapse followed, with more Normans encroaching on the land that had been assigned to O'Connor.

7 October 1843

Daniel O'Connell cancels rally in Clontarf

On 7 October 1843, Daniel O'Connell received word that the 'monster meeting' he was scheduled to hold in Clontarf the next day had been declared illegal by Dublin Castle. That summer, O'Connell had travelled all over Ireland addressing hundreds of thousands of people, notably on the Hill of Tara in Co. Meath. In Clontarf, he hoped to draw on the symbolism of speaking where the forces of Brian Boru had been victorious over those of Máel Mórda in 1014.

The proclamation issued by Earl de Grey, Lord Lieutenant of Ireland, stated that the 'motives and objects of the persons to be assembled thereat are not the fair legal exercise of constitutional rights and privileges, but to bring into hatred and contempt the government and constitution of the United Kingdom … [I] hereby strictly caution and forewarn all persons whatsoever, that they do abstain from attendance at the said meeting … if, in defiance of this our proclamation, the said meeting shall take place, all persons attending the same shall be proceeded against according to law.'

O'Connell was faced with a difficult dilemma. As he knew that there was a risk of violence – which he abhorred – if the meeting were to go ahead, he issued a statement to his followers requesting that 'all well-disposed persons shall immediately, upon receiving this intimation, repair to their own dwellings, and not place themselves in peril of any collision, or of receiving any ill-treatment from any person whatsoever … we deem it prudent and wise, and above all things, humane, to declare that the intended meeting is abandoned, and will not be held.'

This badly affected O'Connell's credibility in the eyes of many of his supporters, who felt he should have proceeded with the meeting regardless, and he never regained the popularity he had once enjoyed.

8 October 1871

Catherine O'Leary is blamed for Great Chicago Fire

On 8 October 1871, flames were seen coming from a barn belonging to Patrick and Catherine O'Leary, Irish immigrants living at 137 DeKoven Street in the city of Chicago, Illinois. The authorities were notified and firefighters arrived on the scene within 20 minutes, but by then the entire block was engulfed in flames. To make matters worse, with winter approaching, fuel was being stored in many of the buildings to which the fire spread. By 10 October, when the inferno had finally been extinguished, 300 people had died, 100,000 had been left homeless, and 10 square kilometres of the city lay in ruins.

Residents were eager to find a culprit, and Catherine O'Leary was soon blamed. She was reported to have been in the barn milking her cow, which kicked over a lantern and ignited the blaze. The reporter largely responsible for spreading this rumour was Michael Ahern, who, 40 years later, admitted to having fabricated it. There was an undercurrent of prejudice to some of the theories postulated: for example, the *Chicago Times* wrote that Catherine had deliberately started the fire in retaliation for her welfare being cut off, although neither she nor her husband was in receipt of any welfare at the time.

In 1997, Catherine was officially exonerated. Chicago City Council alderman Edward M. Burke sponsored the resolution that found her innocent, saying, 'In 1871, journalists, eager to sensationalize the events of the Great Fire, were quick to find in Mrs. Kate O'Leary an easy scapegoat for the calamitous inferno. As a working-class immigrant and a woman, Kate O'Leary was an easy target for those publications who always found it comfortable to vilify Irish Catholics who had not yet assimilated into the dominant American middle-class culture.'

The true cause of the fire has never been definitively established.

9 October 1979

Josie Airey wins free legal aid case

On 9 October 1979, Cork woman Josie Airey won a case she had brought to the European Court of Human Rights concerning the lack of free legal aid in Ireland. She had begun campaigning for a change in the law seven years earlier, when her marriage broke down. She and her husband had four children, whom Airey struggled to raise after the separation, working as a cleaner in a hospital while seeking maintenance orders against her spouse. At the time, divorce was not available for couples living in the Irish state, but Airey had the option of seeking a divorce *a mensa et thoro* (legal separation) from the High Court at a cost of £1,000, which she could not afford.

Airey sent letters to several prominent politicians, but the only TD willing to support her was Eileen Desmond of the Labour Party. In 1973, Airey wrote to the European Commission of Human Rights in Strasbourg about her case, and it provided her with legal aid. Her barrister was Mary Robinson, who would later become the first woman elected President of Ireland, and her solicitor was Brendan Walsh.

In 1977, the case opened before the Commission, with Airey claiming the Irish government was in breach of three articles of the Convention of Human Rights, specifically Article Six, which stated that 'everyone is entitled to a fair and public hearing'. In 1979, the case went on to the European Court of Human Rights, and Niall McCarthy SC, representing the Irish state, announced that free legal aid would be introduced before the end of the year. The court later ruled that the Irish government was in breach of Article Six.

Airey was able to obtain her legal separation, and received £3,140 in damages.

10 October 1918
Sinking of RMS *Leinster*

On 10 October 1918, the RMS *Leinster* was travelling from Kingstown – now Dún Laoghaire – to Holyhead, carrying military personnel either going on or returning from leave. Ships travelling across the Irish Sea were rarely escorted by destroyers, and this made them vulnerable to attack. The ship was struck by two of three torpedoes fired at it by German submarine UB-123, and sank. In all, 564 people died: the largest loss of life ever to occur in the Irish Sea. The dead were from Ireland, Great Britain, the United States, Canada, New Zealand and Australia. The First World War would end a month later, on 11 November 1918.

The Dublin Steam Packet Company had begun operating a mail service between Ireland and Britain in 1850, and since 1894 had used four ships, each named after an Irish province: the RMS *Leinster*, RMS *Connaught*, RMS *Munster* and RMS *Ulster*. RMS stood for Royal Mail Steamer, as the ships carried post across the Irish Sea. Each had a post office on board, staffed by members of the Dublin Post Office. The *Leinster* was not the first to be hit by a German U-boat: in 1917, the *Connaught* was torpedoed in the English Channel, leading to the deaths of three crewmen.

In total, 144 military casualties of the sinking were buried in Grangegorman

Military Cemetery in Dublin. One of the survivors was Michael Joyce, an Irish Parliamentary Party MP for Limerick City.

On the centenary of the *Leinster*'s sinking, the Minister for Culture, Heritage and the Gaeltacht, Josepha Madigan, said: 'As we mark the centenary of this tragedy, we have developed an appreciation of the complex narratives around Ireland's involvement in World War I and a mature understanding of the context of that time.'

11 October 1988

Ian Paisley interrupts Pope John Paul II

On 11 October 1988, the Rev. Ian Paisley, one of three Members of the European Parliament (MEPs) for Northern Ireland, interrupted Pope John Paul II as the pontiff was speaking in the parliament in Strasbourg. Paisley, founder of the Free Presbyterian Church of Ulster, was known for his fiercely anti-Catholic views. In 1963, after the death of Pope John XXIII, Belfast City Hall had lowered its flag to half-mast out of respect. Paisley led a rally of 500 people to the building, declaring, 'This Romish man of sin is now in hell.'

In the subsequent quarter-century, Paisley's views on the head of the Catholic Church had not softened. The day before the Pope's visit, which was part of a four-day tour of France, Paisley warned that he would interrupt him. In response, a dozen or so security people in the European Parliament lined the wall behind where he was sitting before the Pope entered the chamber. The Pope was introduced to the parliament by Lord Plum, President of the European Parliament. John Paul II began 'Ladies and gentlemen, first of all, permit me to say, how much I …'

At that moment Paisley stood up, holding a banner with the words 'Pope John Paul II – Antichrist', and shouting, 'I renounce you as Christ's enemy.' Other MEPs were audibly furious. German MEP Dr Otto von Habsburg snatched the banner from Paisley's hands; after Lord Plum warned him three times that his interruptions would not be tolerated, the DUP leader was ejected from the chamber, to applause.

Paisley explained himself to the press later that day: 'I used exactly the words of Archbishop Cranmer, and Archbishop Cranmer was taken and he was burnt. And if those members in there today could have burned me, they would have done it.'

12 October 1975

Oliver Plunkett is declared a saint

On 12 October 1975, Oliver Plunkett was officially declared a saint by Pope Paul VI, making him the first Irish person to be canonised since Laurence O'Toole in 1225. Taoiseach Liam Cosgrave led an Irish delegation to Rome, where an open-air mass was held in St Peter's Square. Originally, President Cearbhall Ó Dálaigh was to accompany Cosgrave, but it was felt that the presence of both the head of government and the head of state might send the wrong signal about a 'formal commitment to Catholic sympathies' in the Irish state.

Born in Co. Meath, Plunkett was appointed Archbishop of Armagh in 1669. He was implicated in the 'Popish Plot' of 1681, whereby Catholics were alleged to have planned to assassinate Charles II. He was subsequently sentenced to death, and hanged, drawn and quartered.

In 1958, Giovanna Martiriggiano, a pregnant woman from Naples, was thought to be hours from death but remarkably recovered, ultimately living for another 50 years. Sr Cabrini Quigley from Donegal, a nun in the hospital Martiriggiano was in, had prayed to Oliver Plunkett for the woman's health, and so this alleged miracle was attributed to him.

Speaking on the day of his canonisation, the Pope described Plunkett as 'a triumph of Christ's grace, a model of reconciliation for all'. The Pope also touched on the violence that was then a daily occurrence in Northern Ireland: 'Let this then be an occasion on which the message of peace and reconciliation in truth and justice, and above all the message of love for one's neighbour, will be emblazoned in the minds and hearts of all the beloved Irish people.'

On the same day, a ceremony was held in St Peter's Church in Drogheda, where a shrine holds relics of Plunkett.

13 October 1792

James Hoban oversees White House construction

On 13 October 1792, the cornerstone of the White House was laid, using the design of Irish architect James Hoban, a native of Co. Kilkenny. Hoban's vision for the home of the US president was modelled on Leinster House in Dublin, which would be the seat of the Irish parliament from 1922 onwards.

Born in Desart near Callan in 1755, Hoban had established himself as an architect in Philadelphia in 1785. His work on various buildings in Charleston, North Carolina, including the County Courthouse, led to acclaim in the United States, so it was not surprising that he won a contest to design the White House, with a prize of $500.

There was disagreement between George Washington and Thomas Jefferson on the size of the building: the latter wanted a modest residence; the former envisaged something grander. Washington took it on himself to expand on Hoban's design, though compromises were made: two floors instead of three, and a mixture of stone, brick and wood.

The result may have been more modest that Washington originally wanted, but it was still criticised at the time. One newspaper described it as 'big enough for two emperors, one pope and the grand lama in the bargain'. Hoban supervised much of the construction, using skilled and unskilled European labourers as well as slaves. It was completed in November 1800.

Hoban was drafted in to help reconstruct the building after it was badly damaged in a fire during the British invasion of Washington in 1814. He died in 1831.

In 2000, Bill Clinton confessed to Bertie Ahern that he sometimes felt haunted by the ghost of James Hoban.

14 October 1906

Laurence Ginnell launches Ranch War

On 14 October 1906, Laurence Ginnell, an MP for the Irish Parliamentary Party (IPP), launched the Ranch War at a meeting in Downs, Co. Westmeath. Though the Wyndham Land Act of 1903 was seen as an enormous victory for Irish tenant farmers, some felt left behind. The main target of Ginnell's ire was graziers: farmers who reared cattle or sheep and were seen to have benefited from the surrender of large tracts of land over the centuries – particularly during the Famine – that were now underpopulated. The *Irish Times* reported on 6 October that the upcoming meeting was a 'a demonstration of all who wished to smash and finish ranching and land monopoly and to recover the land for the people'.

Ginnell's solution to what he saw as land inequality was cattle-driving, i.e. moving herds of cattle off the land of ranchers and graziers during the night. He explained to those assembled in Downs: 'If the graziers found their ranches empty some fine morning and after six or eight weeks found their cattle not all together, but some in Connacht, some in Munster, and some among the Wicklow mountains, and some in the glens of Antrim; and if this wandering mania became fashionable among ranching cattle all over the country, and if you persisted in it from now until Christmas, the ranchers would lose their taste for the people's land … neither man nor demon would dare to stand another hour between the people and the land that ought to be yours.'

Cattle driving became a regular occurrence in Ireland throughout 1907 and 1908, but petered out in 1909, coinciding with the Birrell Land Act. The same year, Ginnell was expelled from the IPP after asking to inspect the party's accounts. He sat as an independent nationalist before joining Sinn Féin in 1917.

15 October 1842

First issue of *The Nation* is published

On 15 October 1842, the first issue of *The Nation* was published. It was founded by Thomas Davis, John Blake Dillon and Charles Gavan Duffy. Davis was a Trinity-educated Protestant, born in Cork to a Welsh father and an Irish mother; Dillon a Catholic from Ballaghaderreen, on the Mayo–Roscommon border; Duffy, another

Catholic, was born in Monaghan and educated in Belfast. All three were under the age of 30 and members of the Young Ireland movement, which grew out of Daniel O'Connell's Repeal Association, eventually seceding in 1847, the year of O'Connell's death. Young Ireland sought inspiration from France; the title *The Nation* was a homage to French newspaper *Le National*, which itself played a role in the February Revolution of 1848.

From the outset, *The Nation* made no secret of its political leanings. The prospectus in the first issue, written by Davis, stated, 'Nationality is their first great object, a nationality which will not only raise our people from their poverty, by securing to them the blessings of a domestic legislature, but inflame and purify them with a lofty and heroic love of country … a nationality which may embrace Protestant, Catholic and Dissenter, Milesian and Cromwellian, the Irishman of a hundred generations and the stranger who is within our gates.'

The first issue sold out, and soon *The Nation* had a higher circulation than any other newspaper in Ireland. Davis was the main contributor, authoring 200 essays and editorials in the first year alone, and Duffy was the editor. Perhaps its most lasting influence was a song written by Davis and published in 1844, titled 'A Nation Once Again', which soon became synonymous with the growing Irish nationalist movement.

Davis died in 1845, and *The Nation* went through many iterations before merging with the *Irish Weekly Independent* in 1900.

16 October 1843

William Rowan Hamilton discovers quaternions

On 16 October 1843, William Rowan Hamilton was walking with his wife to the Royal Irish Academy in Dublin when he suddenly deciphered the formula for quaternion multiplication. Quaternions are a four-dimensional number system, where the order in which the numbers are multiplied affects their product.

Eager not to forget it, he etched this new formula into Broom (or Brougham) Bridge in Cabra. He explained to his son years later: 'an undercurrent of thought was going on in my mind, which gave at last a result, whereof it is not too much to say that I felt at once an importance … Nor could I resist the impulse – unphilosophical as it may have been – to cut with a knife on a stone of Brougham Bridge as we passed it, the fundamental formula.'

Born in Dublin in 1805, Rowan spent much of his childhood in Trim, Co. Meath. He was inspired to study maths after losing to American prodigy Zerah Colburn in a mental arithmetic contest in 1813. While an undergraduate at Trinity College studying mathematics and classics, he was appointed Andrews Professor of Astronomy and Royal Astronomer of Ireland. For most of his adult life he lived in Dunsink Observatory in Co. Dublin.

A plaque commemorating Rowan's 'flash of genius' was unveiled in 1958 by Éamon de Valera, himself a devotee of mathematics who taught the subject in various Dublin schools. In 1990, Professor Tony O'Farrell began the Hamilton Walk, an attempt to retrace the astronomer's footsteps on the day he made his discovery. The event is sometimes referred to as 'Broomsday', echoing the other tradition of retracing the steps of a Dubliner (albeit a fictitious one), Leopold Bloom.

Quaternions have been used in everything from solving the gimbal lock problem on the Apollo 11 mission to the moon to achieving smoother 3D graphics in the 1996 video game *Tomb Raider*.

17 October 1907

Wireless message is sent from Clifden to Nova Scotia

On 17 October 1907, the first commercial transatlantic message was transmitted, from Guglielmo Marconi's wireless telegraphy station in Clifden, Co. Galway to Glace Bay, Cape Breton in Nova Scotia. Marconi had come to Ireland in 1905. The Italian inventor had Irish roots – his mother, Annie Jameson, was born at Daphne Castle, Co. Wexford, and was the granddaughter of John Jameson, founder of the eponymous whiskey distillery in Dublin.

Construction of the station at Clifden was completed in the summer of 1907, while Marconi was alternating between there and Cape Breton. He and his wife were in Glace Bay on 17 October when William Entwistle, the manager of the station at Clifden, notified Marconi that he was ready to send and receive public transatlantic messages. The first one was from Lord Avebury to the *New York Times*, sent at approximately 11:30 a.m. Marconi then sent a congratulatory message to Clifden.

Messages continued to flow between the two stations all day. The Dublin Stock

Exchange congratulated the New York Stock Exchange. The Governor General of Canada sent greetings to King Edward. By 7:30 p.m., 10,000 words had been exchanged. R. N. Vyvyan, the engineer in charge of the Glace Bay station, would later write: 'Only those who worked with Marconi throughout these four years realize the wonderful courage he showed under frequent disappointments, the extraordinary fertility of his mind in inventing new methods to displace others found faulty, and his willingness to work, often for sixteen hours at a time when any interesting development was being tested.'

On the centenary of the event, Marconi's daughter, Princess Elettra Marconi, and her son, Prince Guglielmo, attended a celebration in Clifden. Princess Elettra said, 'I feel at home here, I have been so many times, and I am so glad my father picked a beautiful fascinating coastline to build his radio station.'

18 October 1791

Inaugural meeting of United Irishmen

On 18 October 1791, the inaugural public meeting of the Society of United Irishmen of Belfast, founded days earlier, was held. It adopted a declaration and resolutions written by Theobald Wolfe Tone, a barrister from Dublin who had published a pamphlet earlier that year titled *An Argument on Behalf of the Catholics of Ireland.* Tone, a Protestant, sought the 'complete emancipation' of Catholics, who he said had been 'now for above a century in slavery'. However, he did not disguise his views on the Roman Catholic Church, and wrote that the emancipated Catholics would not 'attend to the rusty and extinguished thunderbolts of the Vatican'.

In Belfast, many of the members were Presbyterians, such as Henry Joy McCracken and Samuel Neilson. All were inspired by the French Revolution of 1789, and in particular by Thomas Paine's *Rights of Man.* The resolutions passed at the society's first meeting were threefold: first, that the 'weight of English influence' could only be countered by 'a cordial union among all the people of Ireland'; second, a 'complete and radical reform of the representation of the people in Parliament' was required; and third, 'no reform is practicable, efficacious, or just, which shall not include Irishmen of every religious persuasion.'

A sister organisation – the Society of United Irishmen of Dublin – was formed in November of that year. The United Irishmen were constitutionalists initially, but that was to change gradually. In 1794, the government ordered the Dublin society to disband, only for it to be reconstituted in 1795 as a secret oath-based organisation. It formed an alliance with the Defenders, a Catholic organisation set up to resist attacks from the Protestant Peep o' Day Boys. It was this alliance, along with Tone's efforts to recruit military support from France, that led to the defeated United Irishmen Rebellion of 1798.

19 October 1989

Guildford Four are released

On 19 October 1989, Gerard Conlon, Patrick Armstrong and Carole Richardson of the Guildford Four were released, having served 14 years in jail. They had been wrongfully convicted of pub bombings carried out in 1974 by the Provisional IRA, in which seven people had died. Paul Hill, who was convicted of killing a British soldier in Belfast in 1974, was flown back to Belfast and released on bail; his conviction was quashed in 1994. Along with the conviction of the Birmingham Six – Catholics from Northern Ireland who served 16 years after being wrongly convicted of the Birmingham pub bombings – this was considered one of the worst miscarriages of justice in recent British history.

On 5 October 1974, the Provisional IRA detonated two no-warning bombs in Guildford, Surrey. Four off-duty British soldiers were killed – Caroline Slater (18), Ann Hamilton (19), William Forsyth (18) and John Hunter (17). A 22-year-old plasterer, Paul Craig, also lost his life. On 7 November, another off-duty British soldier, Richard Dunne (42), and 20-year-old sales clerk Alan Horsley were killed in a pub bombing in Woolwich. Public revulsion at these attacks led to Conlon, Armstrong, Richardson and Hill being arrested. They signed confessions admitting to the bombings, but maintained during their trial that they had been coerced into doing so by beatings from the police.

In 1989, their case was appealed. Speaking on their behalf, Roy Amlott QC said: 'New evidence of great significance has come to light after a police inquiry ... the Crown is now unable to say that the convictions of any of the four were safe or satisfactory.'

After being released, Conlon told the press, 'I know what happened was a tragedy at Guildford, Woolwich, and Birmingham, but you don't compound the tragedy by making other tragedies.' Conlon also said he hoped the Birmingham Six would be freed; they were, in 1991.

20 October 1881

Land League is proscribed

On 20 October 1881, William Ewart Gladstone, the British Prime Minister, announced that the Irish National Land League was proscribed. This came just over a week after Charles Stewart Parnell was arrested for 'speeches pointing to ... treason or treasonable practices'.

Parnell was the first President of the Land League, an organisation co-founded by Michael Davitt in 1879. In February 1881, Davitt was arrested, leading to protests in the House of Commons that saw 36 Irish Parliamentary Party MPs suspended. However, Gladstone tried to satisfy the desire for land reform in Ireland by introducing the Land Act of 1881. This addressed the so-called Three Fs that the Land League had been pushing for: fair rents, fixity of tenure and free sale.

The Land League was divided on the 1881 Act. Parnell wanted to test it, but his colleague John Dillon felt it did not go far enough. Dillon was arrested shortly after Parnell, along with Thomas Sexton, J.J. O'Kelly, William O'Brien and others. On 18 October, from Kilmainham Gaol, the executive of the Land League issued a 'No Rent' manifesto, advising tenant-farmers to 'pay no rent under any circumstances to their landlords until the Government relinquishes the existing system of terrorism and restores the constitutional rights of the people'.

Gladstone's response was to ban the Land League. Parnell was released from prison in May 1882 as part of the so-called Kilmainham Treaty. For this, Gladstone agreed to alter the 1881 Act to address the issues of tenant farmers in arrears. Parnell, for his part, had to dissuade supporters of the Land Act from participating in any violence.

Later, under Parnell's leadership, the Land League was dissolved; it was succeeded by the Irish National League, founded in October 1882. If the Land League had fought for, and won, land reform, the National League had a different goal in mind – Irish self-government.

21 October 1975

Siege to rescue Tiede Herrema begins

On 21 October 1975, members of the Gardaí and the Irish Defence Forces surrounded a house in Monasterevin, Co. Kildare, where Tiede Herrema was being held by the Provisional IRA. A siege followed, which lasted for 17 days.

Herrema was a native of the Netherlands, and had fought in the Dutch Resistance during the Second World War, being imprisoned by the Nazis in Poland. Later in life he became an industrialist, and in the 1970s the steel cord manufacturing plant of which he was managing director, Ferenka, employed 1,400 people in Limerick.

On 3 October, Herrema was kidnapped by a gang of four led by Eddie Gallagher and Marian Coyle, members of the Provisional IRA. Gallagher was romantically linked to Rose Dugdale, an English heiress imprisoned in Limerick for her part in the 1974 theft of paintings worth £8 million from Russborough House, Co Wicklow. Dugdale gave birth to Gallagher's child in December 1974, and it was his desire to see her that motivated the kidnapping. The Provisional IRA demanded the release of Dugdale as well as Kevin Mallon and J. B. O'Hagan, both imprisoned in Portlaoise at the time.

The Irish government responded by launching a nationwide manhunt, with 9,000 soldiers drafted in to assist. Eventually Brian McGowan, who had participated in the kidnapping, was arrested and interrogated, leading to the location of the house where Herrema was being kept.

Coyle and Gallagher barricaded themselves in an upstairs bedroom. Release of the prisoners was refused, but Garda Commissioner Edmund Garvey offered Gallagher and Coyle reduced sentences – four and two years respectively – if they surrendered. On 7 November they agreed, and were detained. Herrema was in relatively good shape, save for neck pains, and even showed police a .38 bullet from the gun that had been trained on him throughout the kidnapping, given to him by Gallagher as a souvenir.

22 October 1884

Nine Graces are awarded degrees

On 22 October 1884, nine women were awarded degrees from the Royal University of Ireland. They were the first women in either Ireland or Great Britain to receive university degrees, and became known as the Nine Graces, though some may have objected to such a description. Six had studied at Alexandra College in Dublin. Their names were Isabella Mulvany, Alice Oldham, Jessie Twemlow (later Meredith), Marion Kelly, Annie Mary Sands, Eliza Wilkins, Charlotte M. Taylor, Louisa M. McIntosh, and Emily E. Eberle.

Isabella Mulvany is probably the best known of the nine. She was the daughter of Christopher Mulvany, a civil engineer for the Grand Canal Company. Her mother was an English Protestant and her father an Irish Catholic, though he later converted.

She had begun studying in Alexandra College at age 14, after receiving a Governesses' Association scholarship, allowing her two years of free education. Ann Jellicoe, the pioneering Irish woman who founded Alexandra College, was quite taken by her, and made Mulvany her personal secretary in 1875.

In 1880, Mulvany became the Principal of Alexandra College. She was instrumental in getting the school out of debt: when she took over, it owed £600, and had only 67 students. By 1889 this number had increased to 250 and Mulvany had successfully raised thousands of pounds, to be spent on new buildings in Earlsfort Terrace in September of that year.

She remained the principal of Alexandra College for almost 47 years, retiring in July 1926. In 1904, she was the first woman to sign Dublin University's register as a graduate, after being awarded an honorary doctorate of laws. For many years, Mulvany was President of the Irish Women Graduates' Association.

23 October 1986

Disappearance of Philip Cairns

On 23 October 1986, schoolboy Philip Cairns was last seen returning to Coláiste Éanna in Rathfarnham, Dublin, the secondary school that he had begun attending a month earlier. The disappearance of the 13-year-old sparked a nationwide hunt and one of the most high-profile missing persons cases in the history of Ireland.

Cairns lived in Ballyroan Road in Rathfarnham with his parents, four older sisters and a younger brother. On the day he went missing, he was at home on his lunch-break. Shortly after one o'clock he began the 15-minute walk back to school.

His parents began to worry when he did not return home. His mother, Alice, contacted Paddy Cloke, a member of An Garda Síochána and the father of Philip's best friend. Cloke then called Rathfarnham Garda Station, and the investigation into Philip's disappearance began. Gardaí in the neighbouring areas of Terenure and Tallaght were alerted, and hundreds of volunteers joined security forces in searching the nearby Wicklow Mountains.

A week later, on 30 October, two schoolgirls found Philip's schoolbag in a laneway a few hundred yards from his house. It is unclear whether it was left there by a person who abducted Philip, or whether a bystander found it and left it to one side.

Sadly, the case of Philip Cairns remains unsolved. In 2016, a group of 500 people marched from Marian Road to the alleyway where the schoolbag was found to mark 30 years since his disappearance. A former student of Coláiste Éanna said that the event 'stole the innocence of an entire community … People talk about it all the time.'

24 October 1641

Phelim O'Neill issues Proclamation of Dungannon

On 22 October 1641, Irish nobleman Sir Phelim O'Neill entered Charlemont Fort, a garrison in Co. Armagh, with some followers. Charlemont, which was guarded by 150 soldiers, was under the command of Sir Toby Caulfield. O'Neill and his companions managed to overpower the men keeping watch and took control of the garrison. Simultaneously, Dungannon Castle, in the neighbouring county of Tyrone, was taken over by members of the Donnellys, another Irish family.

Over the next two weeks, forts all over Ulster were seized by Irish rebels. The only areas to withstand attack were Derry, Enniskillen, and parts of Antrim and Down. It was decided that a forum be established for the Catholics of Ireland, both native and the descendants of medieval settlers.

On 24 October, O'Neill issued a proclamation from Dungannon outlining the reasons for the rebellion: 'These are to intimate to all in this country that the present meeting and assembly of Irish is in no way intended against the King, or to hurt any of his subjects either of the English or Scottish nation; but only for the defence and liberty of ourselves and the natives of the Irish nation.' It is striking that these rebels supported Charles I, who was seen as being pro-Catholic, in marked contrast to contemporary Irish nationalism, which has little truck with British royalty.

However courteous O'Neill may have intended the rebellion to be, the native Irish soon turned on the settlers. The killing of hundreds of Protestants in Portadown in November 1641 cast a particularly long shadow, referred to by Oliver Cromwell in his 1649 declaration as the 'most barbarous massacre' in history.

The Confederate General Assembly would meet a year later, in October 1642, ushering in the Eleven Years' War.

25 October 1996

Last Magdalene Laundry closes

On 25 October 1996, the last Magdalene Laundry in Ireland closed. It was located on Sean MacDermott Street in Dublin, and belonged to the Convent of the Sisters of Our Lady of Charity. These were institutions established to house 'what were offensively and judgementally called "fallen women"', according to Taoiseach Enda Kenny: in other words, women who had become pregnant outside wedlock or were suspected of being promiscuous. At the time of its closure, 40 women lived in the Gloucester Street laundry, as it was known, and would continue to reside there. At its height, 150 women were working there.

Though the Magdalene Laundries were primarily Roman Catholic institutions, the first was founded by the Church of Ireland in 1765, known as the Magdalen Asylum for Penitent Females. An estimated 30,000 women passed through the institutions, which were often brutal places. One woman, Mary Smith, said she was sent to one after being raped, and that women there 'didn't know when the next beating was going to come'.

A scandal broke in 1993 when land owned by the Sisters of Our Lady of Charity in High Park, Drumcondra was being sold to a property developer to pay off debts. The bodies of 155 women were found buried in a mass grave, though only 133 were named in an exhumation licence granted to the Sisters. Death certificates could be produced for only 75 of the 133.

In 2013, Enda Kenny gave a formal apology in the Dáil to the women who had survived the institutions: 'I, as Taoiseach, on behalf of the State, the Government and our citizens deeply regret and apologise unreservedly to all those women for the hurt that was done to them, and for any stigma they suffered, as a result of the time they spent in a Magdalene laundry.'

26 October 1988

Case of Norris v. Ireland is decided

On 26 October 1988, the case of Norris v. Ireland was decided by the European Court of Human Rights. It found that Ireland's laws criminalising same-sex activities were contrary to the European Convention on Human Rights.

In 1977, David Norris – a lecturer at Trinity College Dublin – began campaigning against two archaic laws in Ireland, the Offences Against the Person Act of 1861 and the Criminal Law Amendment Act of 1885, both of which were held over from when all of Ireland was part of the United Kingdom. They had been used to prosecute Oscar Wilde for 'gross indecency' in 1895.

Norris took his case to the High Court of Ireland, where it was dismissed. He then appealed to the Supreme Court of Ireland, where it was also rejected, in 1983. In that case, Chief Justice Tom O'Higgins ruled that 'the deliberate practice of homosexuality is morally wrong … it is damaging to the health both of individuals and the public and … it is potentially harmful to the institution of marriage.' Undeterred, Norris brought his case to the European Commission of Human Rights, which found in his favour on 12 March 1987. It was then referred to the European Court of Human Rights, where the verdict was reached by eight votes to six.

Speaking after the 1988 verdict, Norris said: 'I hope it will lead to the development of civil rights for gay people, because I think it's all too easy to look for civil rights for other people, when they don't threaten you. It's easy for us in the South to look for an extension of civil rights for Roman Catholics in the North, at the same time ignoring the plight of our own minorities here.'

The case led to the decriminalisation of homosexual acts in Ireland in 1993.

27 October 1904

New York City Subway opens

On 27 October 1904, the New York City Subway opened for the first time. Irish contractor John B. McDonald oversaw its construction, after his bid of $35 million was accepted.

McDonald was born in Fermoy, Co. Cork in 1844, and left for the United States with his family in 1847. As a young man, he began working on Central Park's avenue improvement, and he was made chief inspector in 1872. It was here that he gained the knowledge of tunnel construction that would serve him well when the New York City Subway was being built.

McDonald's bid for the subway saw an influx of immigrants to New York from Italy. Indeed, though the Irish had been involved in construction in America for decades, Fr Michael J. Henry, director of the Mission of Our Lady of the Rosary, warned Irishmen not to emigrate to America because they would 'have to enter into competition with pick-axe and shovel and other nationalities – Italians, Poles, etc. to eke out a bare existence. The Italians are more economic, can live on poor fare and consequently can afford to work for less wages than the ordinary Irishman.'

McDonald hired thousands of Italians to dig the tunnels for the subway; often there was tension with the Irish who worked alongside them. Nevertheless, the project was completed in October 1904, when Mayor George McClellan took control of the subway, which travelled 9.1 miles through 28 stations. Though not the first in America – one had been completed in Boston in 1897 – it would eventually become the largest rapid transit system in the world.

28 October 1927

The Cleggan Bay disaster

On 28 October 1927, several boats capsized during a gale in Cleggan Bay, Co. Galway. Forty-five fishermen drowned, in what became known as the Cleggan Bay disaster.

That evening, a retired medical practitioner, Dr Holberton, heard on his radio at Cleggan farm that a storm was coming. He sent his farmhand, Tommy Mullen, to warn local fisherman not to venture into the waters, but they had already left. When the storm arrived, it was so fierce that it tore the slates off the roof of the Star of the Sea church.

One survivor of the incident, James Cloherty of Inishbofin, recalled being caught up in the storm: 'I heard terrible screams and shouts in the darkness and knew that something had happened to our companions … Later there was further terrible screams, and I thought we were lost ourselves as we made no headway. For 12 hours we continued to row and at last, when we abandoned all hope, a wave threw us up safe on Boffin beach.' Sixteen fishermen from Rossadilisk, Cleggan, died, as did 10 from Inishbofin, 10 from Lacken Bay and nine from Inishkea, Co. Mayo.

The disaster had a devastating impact on the local community. The fishing industry went into decline; the families of many who lost their lives had to emigrate, and in some cases were split up.

In 2017, on the 90th anniversary of the tragic event, Mass was held in Claddaghduff and Inishbofin to mark the occasion, and up to 200 family members of those who died were invited. Also remembered at this event was Michael Heffernan of Gráinne Uáile Sub Aqua Club in Ballina, who drowned in 1997 while rescuing a family in a cave off north Mayo.

29 October 1816

Burning of Wildgoose Lodge

On 29 October 1816, eight people died when their house, Wildgoose Lodge in rural Co. Louth, was set on fire. Located five miles northeast of Roodstown, the house belonged to Edward Lynch, a prosperous farmer in the area.

In April of that year, three Ribbonmen – members of a Catholic secret society – showed up at Lynch's home, demanding guns. This led to a confrontation, after which Lynch informed the authorities of what had happened. Michael Tiernan, Patrick Stanley and Phillip Conlan were found guilty of breaking and entering, and hanged in Ardee, though there were doubts that they were the ones involved in the original attack. In October, men showed up at Lynch's home, swearing revenge.

Approximately 75 Ribbonmen – some of whom had been sworn to secrecy by schoolteacher Patrick Devane – surrounded Wildgoose Lodge and set it on fire. Lynch was killed, as were three members of his family – his daughter, her husband

and the couple's five-month-old baby – and four servants.

The event sent shockwaves through Co. Louth, and 18 men, one of whom was Devane, were found guilty and executed. Before their sentencing, Judge Fletcher said that 'religious bigotry had no part in producing these monstrous crimes. There were not here two conflicting parties arrayed under the colours of orange and green; not Protestant against Catholic, nor Catholic against Protestant – no; it was Catholic against Catholic. Why do not their clergy exert their power over these people? We all know that by means of confession they possess much information of what is transacting in the country.'

Many of the bodies of those executed were displayed in public, and some were seen by the Irish writer William Carleton. Having researched the crimes, he was inspired to pen a story called 'Wildgoose Lodge' about the burning of Edward Lynch's home.

30 October 1997

Mary McAleese is elected President

On 30 October 1997, Mary McAleese was elected the eighth President of Ireland, making Ireland the first country in the world to elect two female heads of state consecutively. Her predecessor, Mary Robinson, had resigned early to accept a role as United Nations High Commissioner for Human Rights.

Hailing from Co. Antrim, McAleese was the first Irish President from Northern Ireland. Her election, in the midst of the peace process that led to the Good Friday Agreement of 1998, was not without controversy. She had grown up in Ardoyne, north Belfast – a predominantly Roman Catholic area – and in 1997, leaked memos from the Department of Foreign Affairs alleged that she was sympathetic to Sinn Féin.

Gerry Adams, the leader of the party, said that he would vote for her if given the opportunity.

She denied these allegations, noting that she had been 'along with Sir Rupert Smith, the officer commanding troops in Northern Ireland … invited to a very private luncheon with Her Majesty the Queen' and adding, 'I was delighted to attend.' This did not stop scepticism from some quarters, including unionism. Ulster Unionist Party MP Ken Maginnis told her: 'I hope you win, Mary … Your election will help unionists to explain why any meaningful relationship with the Republic is, increasingly, becoming impossible.'

In her inauguration speech on 11 November, McAleese said: 'Our dancers, singers, writers, poets, musicians, sportsmen and women, indeed our last President herself, are giants on the world stage. Our technologically skilled young people are in demand everywhere.' Despite the fears of some, relationships between unionists and the Irish state were arguably never better than during her presidency, particularly when she hosted dinner for Elizabeth II in Dublin Castle in 2011: an event attended by Peter Robinson, First Minister of Northern Ireland and leader of the DUP.

31 October 1981

The 'Armalite and ballot box' strategy

On 31 October 1981, Danny Morrison, Director of Publicity for Sinn Féin, introduced a phrase that would come to be associated with the party for years. Touching on the recent electoral victories of Bobby Sands, Owen Carron and James McCreesh, standing as 'Anti H-Block' candidates, Morrison asked a rhetorical question at the Sinn Féin Ard Fheis in Dublin: 'Who here really believes we can win the war through the ballot box? But will anyone here object if, with a ballot paper in this hand, and an Armalite in this hand, we take power in Ireland?'

And so, the phrase 'Armalite and ballot box' was born. Morrison was clear to point out that he was not advocating that the Provisional IRA cease their attacks in Northern Ireland.

Martin McGuinness expressed similar sentiments in 1986. He said that Sinn Féin members elected to Dáil Éireann should take their seats, while maintaining, 'Our position is clear and it will never, never, never change – the war against British rule must continue until freedom is achieved.'

The phrase was often used against Sinn Féin before the Provisional IRA announced a permanent end to its campaign. After a soldier was killed in a bombing in Lisburn in 1996, Taoiseach John Bruton said, 'The strategy of the ballot box in one hand and a gun in the other was first originated by the Nazis.'

The expression also became a source of parody, as in 1983, when a constitutional ban on abortion – strongly supported by the Catholic Hierarchy – was endorsed by over two-thirds of Irish voters. One campaigner against the amendment in Dublin was seen carrying a sign that said, 'This referendum has been won with a Carmelite in one hand and a ballot box in the other.'

1 November 1884

Gaelic Athletic Association is founded

On 1 November 1884, seven men met in Hayes's Hotel, Thurles, Co. Tipperary, with the intention of founding an organisation 'for the preservation and cultivation of our national pastimes'. It became known as the Gaelic Athletic Association (GAA).

Those present were Michael Cusack, Maurice Davin, John Wyse Power, John McKay, J. K. Bracken, Thomas St George McCarthy and Joseph O'Ryan. Cusack was the driving force behind the organisation in its infancy, having written an anonymous letter, 'A Word about Irish Athletics', in *United Ireland*, the weekly newspaper of the Irish National Land League. However, it was Davin who was inaugurated as president of the GAA, the only person to serve two terms in the role. Cusack, Power and McKay would serve as joint secretaries.

At the meeting, little time was spent on the rules of hurling or Gaelic football. These would be published in the *United Irishman* the following January. The men decided that they would ask Charles Stewart Parnell, Michael Davitt and Thomas Croke, Archbishop of Cashel, three major political and religious figures in nationalist Ireland, if they would be patrons of the organisation. A second, much larger meeting was held in the Victoria Hotel in Cork on 27 December.

In 1908, Frank Dineen purchased a ground in Dublin for £3,250; it was sold to the GAA five years later and the iconic Croke Park stadium was established, named for Archbishop Croke. It is one of the largest stadiums in Europe, with a capacity of

82,300. Hill 16, the terrace at the railway end of Croke Park, is named for the 1916 Easter Rising, and the Hogan Stand for Michael Hogan, the Gaelic footballer who was shot dead by RIC Auxiliaries on Bloody Sunday in 1920.

2 November 1847

Killing of Denis Mahon

On 2 November 1847, Major Denis Mahon, a landlord with a 6,000-acre estate in Strokestown, Co. Roscommon, was ambushed and shot dead. His killing occurred in the worst year of the Famine, when 6,000 families were evicted from their homes, as compared to 3,500 evicted in 1846.

Mahon sought to improve the property he had inherited, and offered to pay the passage to Canada for his tenants, a proposal accepted by 810 of them. The majority, however, refused to move. Mahon, in response, evicted over 3,000 of them, including, it is alleged, 84 widows. Most of those evicted died within a year, either on the roads or in the workhouses. Those who opted for emigration fared little better – 268 died at sea.

Mahon's violent death caused a sensation in Britain. The issue was raised in the House of Lords, where a local priest, Michael McDermott, was accused by Lord Clarendon of inciting violence against McMahon. Clarendon warned Prime Minister John Russell that 'servile war against all landlords and English rule' was imminent, and urged greater action to protect landowners in Ireland.

Russell, however, did not mince words when condemning Mahon's eviction of his tenants: 'It is quite true that landlords in England would not be shot like hares and partridges. But neither does any landlord in England turn out fifty persons at once, and burn their houses over their heads, giving them no provision for the future. The murders are atrocious, so are the ejectments.' McDermott denied any involvement in the killing. By February 1848, all the inhabitants of the village of Doorty, where Mahon was killed, had been evicted.

Three murder suspects were arrested, one of whom, James Hasty, was hanged. His last words denounced 'that accursed system of Molly Maguireism' (Molly Maguires being the secret society blamed for the assassination).

3 November 1324

Petronilla de Meath is burned at the stake

On 3 November 1324, Petronilla de Meath, a maidservant to Dame Alice Kyteler, was flogged and burned at the stake in Kilkenny, after the first trial to link witchcraft and heresy in either Ireland or Great Britain. Petronilla was accused of helping Kyteler to plot the murder of her husband, John le Poer.

Kyteler had been married three times before she met le Poer, and in each case assumed the wealth of her late spouse upon his death. After le Poer fell ill, and later died, his children went to the Bishop of Ossory in Kilkenny, Richard de Ledrede, accusing Kyteler of having poisoned him. Ledrede did not look favourably on Kyteler as it was – she was prosperous, unusual for a woman at that time.

Before she could be brought to trial, having been accused of witchcraft and heresy, Kyteler fled to England. Many others were also named, including Petronilla's daughter, Sarah, who left with Kyteler, and William Outlaw, Kyteler's son. Kyteler was said to have renounced Christ and concocted potions in the skull of a convicted criminal, made from unbaptised babies and dead men's fingernails. Though she was no longer in Ireland, her property was confiscated and she was excommunicated. Petronilla was less fortunate: she was flogged six times before her execution by burning.

Kyteler lived under the protection of Edward III in England. In 1329, in retaliation for Ledrede's accusations, she had the Bishop's revenues seized and he too was accused of heresy, by the Archbishop of Dublin, forcing him into exile. He sought protection from the Pope and did not return to Ireland until the late 1340s.

4 November 1908

Irish Women's Franchise League is formed

On 4 November 1908, the Irish Women's Franchise League (IWFL) was formed in the home of Hanna and Francis Sheehy-Skeffington by them and another couple, Margaret and James Cousins. Hanna had previously been on the executive committee of the Irish Women's Suffrage and Local Government Association (IWSLGA), which was established by Anna and Thomas Haslam in 1874.

Anna Haslam differed from Sheehy-Skeffington in one regard: she was a unionist who did not support the goal of Home Rule, let alone an independent Ireland, whereas Sheehy-Skeffington was a nationalist. Ostensibly, the IWFL was formed as a reaction to events in England, in particular Women's Sunday on 21 June 1908, when over a quarter of a million people were said to have demonstrated in Hyde Park, London.

Reflecting on rallies such as this, Margaret Cousins wrote: 'These exciting and enthusiastic doings had at last roused some of the Dublin women; and on November 4, 1908, at the house of Frank and Hannah [*sic*] Skeffington ... the idea was mooted that such a movement and organisation was needed as much in Ireland as in England.'

As the women said they had 'no desire to work under English women leaders: we could lead ourselves', they approached Haslam on 6 November to tell her they were forming a group 'along more militant lines'. Haslam regretted what she saw as a duplication of effort, but wished the IWFL well. Indeed, the IWSLGA noted in its annual report in 1909: 'Another proof of the freshly-awakened interest has been the formation of the Irish Women's Franchise League, intended to extend our movement in directions which our resources have not enabled us to reach; and we wish them every success in their efforts.'

5 November 1913

William Mulholland turns on Los Angeles Aqueduct

On 5 November 1913, William Mulholland declared, 'There it is. Take it', as water emerged from the Los Angeles Aqueduct for the first time. Mulholland had supervised the building of the aqueduct, a project that took eight years and more than 2,000 workers to complete, spanning 233 miles from the Owens River to the San Fernando Valley.

Born in Belfast and educated in Dublin by the Christian Brothers, Mulholland left home at age 15 and joined the British Merchant Navy. At age 19, he disembarked in New York and made his way towards Michigan.

In 1877, Mulholland settled in Los Angeles, which would become his permanent home. At the time, the population of the city was only 9,000. He worked as a ditch-digger for the Los Angeles Water Company, supervised by future Mayor of Los

Angeles Fred Eaton. Eaton and Mulholland shared a belief that the growth of the city depended on its access to water, which was in short supply in the San Fernando Valley, so they planned to build an aqueduct connecting the region to the Owens River. Construction began in 1905. When Mulholland turned on the aqueduct in 1913, the population of Los Angeles stood at 500,000.

Though it was undeniably a feat of engineering, the Los Angeles Aqueduct attracted controversy for diverting water from Inyo County to Los Angeles County, destroying much of the economy in Owens Valley. In 1924, dynamite planted on the aqueduct destroyed it at a critical point. Mulholland later said that 'there were no longer enough trees to hang all the troublemakers who live in Owens Valley'. Nonetheless, he is an important figure in the history of Los Angeles, as anyone who has driven on Mulholland Drive, named for him in 1924, can attest.

6 November 1887

Celtic football club is founded

On 6 November 1887, a meeting was held in St Mary's Church Hall in Calton, Glasgow, at which Brother Walfrid (Andrew Kerins), a native of Ballymote, Co. Sligo, founded a football club to help alleviate poverty – the Celtic Football and Athletic Club. A circular issued in January 1888 announced that its main aim was to raise funds for needy children in the city: 'Many cases of sheer poverty are left unaided through lack of means. It is therefore with this object that we have set afloat the "Celtic".'

Born in May 1840, Walfrid left Ireland for Scotland at age 15 to work on the railways. He joined the Marist Brothers, a Catholic religious order, in 1864, training in France before returning to Glasgow four years later. Glasgow, the destination of a third of Irish emigrants to Scotland, was one of the poorest cities in the United Kingdom at the time – of its 11,675 deaths in 1888, 4,750 were children under the age of five.

Celtic was not the first Scottish football club to be started by an Irish clergyman – in 1875, Canon Edward Joseph Hannan founded Edinburgh Hibernian. It was after seeing the celebrations of that team's victory in the Scottish Cup in 1887 that Walfrid was inspired to create a similar club in Glasgow. Celtic went on to become the first club in the United Kingdom to win the European Cup, beating Inter Milan in the 1967 final.

In 2005, the *Sligo Champion* newspaper described the unveiling of a monument to Brother Walfrid in his native Ballymote: 'Brother Walfrid provided the Irish in Glasgow with a source of pride and a beacon of hope. He provided the exiled with a place they could call "home" and a victimised people with an opportunity to raise their spirits every weekend, and proudly wear their colours, fly their flag and sing their songs.'

7 November 1990

Mary Robinson becomes first female President of Ireland

On 7 November 1990, the tenth Irish presidential election was held. It was won by Mary Robinson, the candidate nominated by the Labour Party, who received 51.9% of the final vote, making her the first female President of Ireland.

Robinson defeated Brian Lenihan of Fianna Fáil, who was the frontrunner until a recorded interview he had given earlier that year surfaced. On 25 October, less than two weeks before voters were to go to polls, a tape of the interview, conducted by postgraduate student Jim Duffy, was played at a press conference in Dublin. Lenihan was heard admitting that he had phoned President Patrick Hillery in 1982 asking him not a grant a dissolution of the Dáil. Had Hillery granted his request, Fianna Fáil, led by Charles Haughey, could have formed a new government without the need for a general election.

Lenihan denied what he said in the interview with Duffy, declaring on television, 'I am absolutely certain, on mature recollection at this stage, that I did not ring President Hillery.' He faced calls to resign as Tánaiste, and was dismissed by Taoiseach Charles

Haughey minutes before a motion of no confidence against the Fianna Fáil–Progressive Democrats coalition government was defeated. Robinson had been 17 points behind Lenihan in a poll published in the *Irish Times* on 10 October. After the Duffy tape, Lenihan trailed Robinson by 21 points in a poll, conducted by the *Irish Independent*.

On the night she was elected, Robinson addressed her supporters with a rousing speech: 'I was elected by men and women of all parties and none, by many with great moral courage who stepped out from the faded flag of the civil war and voted for a new Ireland, and above all by the women of Ireland, mná na hÉireann, who instead of rocking the cradle rocked the system, and who came out massively to make their mark on the ballot paper and on a new Ireland.'

8 November 1960

Niemba ambush

On 8 November 1960, nine Irish soldiers were killed in an ambush by Baluba tribesmen in Niemba, northern Katanga: the first time that the Irish Army had been embroiled in a battle since the end of the Civil War in 1923. They had been deployed to the region as United Nations peacekeepers after Katangan rebels tried to break away from the newly formed Republic of the Congo.

On the morning of the attack, Lieutenant Kevin Gleeson of the 33rd Infantry Battalion led his platoon of 11 men on patrol in Niemba. After they arrived at a bridge, the tribesmen – who mistook the Irish soldiers for the white-led Katangan rebel army – ambushed them using bows and arrows, clubs and other weapons.

Gleeson was killed, as were Sergeant Hugh Gaynor, Corporal Peter Kelly, Corporal Liam Dougan, Private Matthew Farrell, Trooper Thomas Fennell, Private Michael McGuinn and Private Gerard Killeen. Some 25 Baluba tribesmen were also killed. All but two of the men were from Co. Dublin: Gleeson and McGuinn were from Co. Carlow. Trooper Anthony Browne was missing, presumed dead, until his body was found in November 1962. He was posthumously awarded the first ever An Bonn Míleata Calmachta (Military Medal for Gallantry), the highest military honour of the Irish Defence Forces. There were two survivors – Private Joe Fitzpatrick and Trooper Thomas Kenny.

The men involved in the incident were not given awards until 1998, as part of a general award to all Irish soldiers who died overseas serving as UN peacekeepers. Between 1960 and 1964, 12 Irish Defence Force units, comprising 6,200 troops, served with the Organisation des Nations Unies au Congo (ONUC), and 26 lost their lives. Of the 33 countries that contributed soldiers, the only ones to suffer higher causalities than Ireland were Ghana (49 deaths), India (39) and Ethiopia (28).

9 November 1888

Last Jack the Ripper victim is killed

On 9 November 1888, Mary Jane Kelly, a native of Co. Limerick, became the last known victim of Jack the Ripper, the serial killer who ran amok in London in the late nineteenth century. Mary was the youngest of the Ripper's victims, aged 25.

Known under various names, such as Marie Jeanette, Fair Emma, Ginger and Black Emma, Mary was one of nine children. Her father, John Kelly, was an iron worker who moved the family to Wales when Mary was a child. According to Joseph Barnett, a fishmonger with whom she was cohabiting in London, Mary was from a 'fairly well off' family. This was corroborated by her former landlady, one Mrs Carthy, who said that Mary was 'an excellent scholar and an artist of no mean degree'.

At age 16, Mary married a coal miner with the surname Davis, who was killed in a pit explosion a couple of years later. In 1884, she moved to London. By 1886, she was living in Cooley's lodging house on Thrawl Street, where she met Barnett, himself of Irish descent, though London-born. One of the last people to see Mary alive was a friend, 20-year-old Lizzie, who claimed that Mary told her she was 'heartily sick of the life she was leading and wished she had money enough to go back to Ireland where she said her people lived'.

Jack the Ripper had already killed four women before Mary's body was discovered by her landlord at the time, John McCarthy, and a rent collector, Thomas Bowyer. McCarthy would later describe the moment: 'The sight we saw I cannot drive away from my mind … It looked more like the work of a devil than of a man.'

10 November 1798

Wolfe Tone's speech from the dock

In October 1798, Theobald Wolfe Tone was captured on board the French flagship *Hoche*, having travelled from France to participate in the United Irishmen rebellion of that year. After the vessel was towed into Lough Swilly, Tone and other prisoners were brought on shore at Buncrana, Co. Donegal. This marked the end of the United Irishmen rebellion that year, in which it is estimated that 50,000 rebels fought against 76,000 soldiers of the Crown, resulting in the deaths of 30,000 people. Tone was brought to Dublin and tried by court martial, where he was found guilty of treason.

In his speech from the dock on 10 November, Tone admitted to having planned to establish an Irish Republic, completely separate from Great Britain: 'From my earliest youth I have regarded the connection between Great Britain and Ireland as the curse of the Irish nation, and felt convinced that, while it lasted, this country could never be free nor happy.'

Tone distanced himself from 'atrocities' that had been 'committed on both sides' during the rebellion, 'But I hear it is said that this unfortunate country has been a prey to all sorts of horrors ... I designed, by fair and open war, to procure a separation of two countries. For open war I was prepared, but, instead of that, a system of private assassination has taken place.'

Tone accepted his fate: 'As to the connection between this country and Great Britain, I repeat it – all that has been imputed to me (words, writings, and actions), I here deliberately avow ... Whatever be the sentence of the court, I am prepared for it.' He was sentenced to death by hanging despite having requested that he be shot ('the death of a soldier'), but died from a self-inflicted wound to the throat on 19 November 1798. His grave in Bodenstown, Co. Kildare is the site of annual commemorations by those who see him as the father of Irish republicanism.

11 November 1919

First Armistice Day in Ireland

On 11 November 1919, the first Armistice Day in Ireland was observed, on the one-year anniversary of the ending of the First World War. At the time, Ireland was still part of the United Kingdom, though the First Dáil had convened on 21 January that year.

Just as the outbreak of the war had divided the Irish Volunteers, Ireland was divided over how to mark the occasion. George V said, on 6 November, that it was his 'desire and hope that at the hour when the Armistice came into force – the eleventh hour of the eleventh day of the eleventh month – there may be for the brief space of two minutes a complete suspension of all our normal activities.'

In Dublin, at 11:00 a.m., work was suspended in government offices, railways, banks and several factories, and flags were flown from Protestant churches, several shops and Trinity College. Along O'Connell Street, trams stopped, cars halted and many pedestrians paused to take off their hats.

However, the day was not without tension. One newspaper reported, under the headline 'Sinn Feiners clash with Dublin students', that a group from Trinity College, singing 'God Save the King' met with Sinn Féin supporters at St Stephen's Green. This was followed by 'a free-fight lasting an hour' in which 'sticks and stones were frequently used before the combatants separated.'

In Clonmel, Co. Tipperary, a requiem mass was held in SS Peter and Paul's for 300 local soldiers who had died in the War. Indeed, the death toll of Irish people in the Great War was quite extraordinary – Ireland's Memorial Records, compiled by the Committee of the Irish National War Memorial and published in 1923, show that at least 30,986 Irish-born soldiers died in the war. Some estimate the figure is as high as 40,000. Over 210,000 Irish-born soldiers fought, the majority in the British Army; 4,731 fought with Australia and 19,327 with Canada.

12 November 1216

Magna Carta Hiberniae

On 12 November 1216, the Magna Carta Hiberniae, or Great Charter of Ireland, was issued in the name of Henry III. The day before it was introduced, a meeting in Bristol was attended by William Marshal, lord of Leinster, and Walter de Lacy, lord of Meath. It was on Marshal's instructions that the Magna Carta Hiberniae was issued to Ireland.

The original Magna Carta was drafted as a bill of rights in 1215, to broker peace between King John and his rebellious barons. The version sent to Ireland, where it was transmitted in February 1217, changed many of the references of the original document to reflect geography. The 'Thames, the Medway' was replaced with 'the Anna Liffey', 'the whole of England' with 'the whole of Ireland', and 'London' with 'Dublin'.

The original edition of the Magna Carta Hiberniae did not survive, though a copy was reproduced in the Red Book of the Exchequer of Ireland, published in the 14th century. Sadly, the copy was destroyed in the Four Courts explosion of 1922. Nevertheless, the Magna Carta Hiberniae is retained in Ireland under the Statute Law Revision Act 2007. When President Michael D. Higgins visited the United Kingdom on an official state visit in 2014, he referenced the document in his address to the British parliament:

'At the very foundation of British democracy is, of course, the Magna Carta which includes the powerful statement: "To no one will we sell, to no one will we deny or delay, right or justice." Those beautiful and striking words have echoed down the centuries and remain the beating heart of the democratic tradition. Their resonance was felt almost immediately in Ireland through the Magna Carta Hiberniae – a version of the original charter reissued by the guardians of the young Henry III in November 1216.'

13 November 1887

Bloody Sunday (London)

On 13 November 1887, the Irish National League and the Social Democratic Federation (SDF) organised a march towards Trafalgar Square, London, to demand the release of William O'Brien MP. After police attacked the march, the day became known as 'Bloody Sunday'. O'Brien, a member of the Irish Parliamentary Party, had organised a rent strike in Mitchelstown, Co. Cork with John Mandeville, and had been arrested under the Criminal Law and Procedure Act (Ireland).

Those marching on 13 November were not just protesting O'Brien's imprisonment, but were reacting to the hanging of four anarchists in Chicago two days earlier for their part in the Haymarket labour riots of 1886. Two prominent faces on the march were Robert Cunninghame Graham, a Liberal MP for North West Lanarkshire, and John Burns, a trade unionist, who joined 10,000 protestors making their way towards Trafalgar Square. Also present was Irish playwright George Bernard Shaw. Sir Charles Warren, the head of the London Metropolitan Police, forbade the 'organised procession', as he had been doing in that part of the city since 1884. He had 2,000 policemen and 500 soldiers on hand to deal with protestors in the event of their arrival.

When the forces of law and order met with the marchers, they proceeded to bludgeon them with batons, resulting in the deaths of three people. According to activist Annie Besant, an eyewitness to the scene, Cunninghame Graham and Burns 'tried to pass through the police, and were savagely cut about the head and arrested. Then ensued a scene to be remembered; the horse police charged in squadrons at a hand-gallop, rolling men and women over like ninepins, while the foot police struck recklessly with their truncheons, cutting a road through the crowd that closed immediately behind them.'

14 November 1926

IRA raids Garda stations

On 14 November 1926, the anti-Treaty IRA launched co-ordinated raids on 12 Garda stations throughout the country. Two gardaí were shot dead in these attacks: Sergeant James Fitzsimons, aged 23, and Hugh Ward, aged 29. Their killings caused considerable controversy and led to the arrest of 110 men, including two TDs: Michael Kilroy, an abstentionist member of Dáil Éireann who would be one of 44 Fianna Fáil members elected in 1927, and Dr John Madden, a member of Sinn Féin.

In 1924, overall membership of the IRA was 14,541. By 1926 it had dropped to 5,042, a sign that the organisation's strength was waning. The aim of the raids was to seize important documents and hinder investigations into republicans throughout the country.

Both victims of the attacks were veterans of the War of Independence. Fitzsimons was born in Strangford Lower, Co. Down, into a nationalist family. He had served in the Irish Volunteers in the 3rd Northern Division, and, like many nationalists, decided to move south after the partition of Ireland. Ward had been quartermaster of the Nobber Division of the IRA in Co. Meath, and was once 'almost kicked to death' for refusing to give information to the Black and Tans.

The attacks occurred between 6:00 p.m. and 7:30 p.m., targeting mostly rural stations, in areas such as Kilmessan, Co. Meath, Castleisland, Co. Kerry and Rathgormack, Co. Waterford. Tallaght Military Camp in Co. Dublin was also raided. It was in Cork city that Fitzsimons was shot, immediately after three men forcibly entered St Luke's Garda Station. Sixty miles away, in Hollyford, Co. Tipperary, Garda Hugh Ward was killed.

Fitzsimons was given a state funeral, where W. T. Cosgrave described him and Ward as 'the guardians of all, ready to protect the rights of their slayers as of every other citizen of the State'.

15 November 1985

Anglo-Irish Agreement is signed

On 15 November 1985, the Anglo-Irish Agreement was signed by Margaret Thatcher and Dr Garret FitzGerald at Hillsborough Castle, Co. Down. It was the first time that the respective heads of the British and Irish governments had reached a consensus on Northern Ireland in the form of a legal document since the Sunningdale Agreement of 1973, which had failed largely as a result of unionist opposition.

The Agreement offered the Irish government a consultative role in Northern Ireland, saying that the British government now accepted that 'the Irish Government will put forward views and proposals on matters relating to Northern Ireland.' However, it reaffirmed that 'any change in the status of Northern Ireland would only come about with the consent of a majority of the people of Northern Ireland.'

This was included to assuage unionist fears, but it did little good. The only parties in Northern Ireland who supported the agreement were the SDLP and Alliance. The UUP and DUP were furious at what they saw as interference in their affairs by a foreign government. Ian Paisley bellowed, to 100,000 or so protestors outside Belfast City Hall, that he and other unionists would 'never, never, never' accept that the Republic 'must have some say in our province'.

Unionists were not the only people opposed. Charles Haughey, leader of Fianna Fáil and FitzGerald's bête noire, lamented that the agreement represented 'an abandonment of Irish unity and a copper-fastening of the partition of our country'. Gerry Adams, leader of Sinn Féin, was also scathing: 'Garret FitzGerald insults the long-suffering nationalist people of the Six Counties when he tells us in Gaelic that we can now raise our heads.'

16 November 1688

Ann Glover is hanged in Boston

On 16 November 1688, Ann Glover became the last person to be hanged in Boston, Massachusetts as a witch. Glover was born in Ireland and brought to Barbados to work as an indentured servant. From there she went to Boston, where she was employed as a housekeeper by John Goodwin, along with her daughter, Mary. She worked in the Goodwin household for several years, until the summer of 1688, when four of the five children in the family became ill.

Dr Thomas Oakes, a well-known physician, concluded that 'nothing but a hellish witchcraft could be the origin of these maladies.' Ann was subsequently arrested and tried for witchcraft. During the trial, she refused to renounce her Roman Catholicism. The fact that she could only recite the Lord's Prayer in Irish, and in broken Latin, did not bode well for her.

Cotton Mathers, a New England Puritan, described Glover as 'a scandalous old Irishwoman, very poor, a Roman Catholic and obstinate in idolatry'. She was found guilty and executed. Robert Calef, a Boston merchant who knew Glover, did not mince words in describing what had happened: 'Goody Glover was a despised, crazy, poor old woman, an Irish Catholic, who was tried for afflicting the Goodwin children ... The proof against her was wholly deficient.'

As time went on, Glover was vindicated. In 1988, 300 years after her hanging, Boston City Council formally recognised that she had been the victim of an injustice; it proclaimed 'Goody Glover Day', condemning her arrest, trial and execution. A placard in Boston's North End District remembers Glover as 'an elderly Irish widow ... hanged as a witch because she had refused to renounce her Catholic faith ... she was unjustly condemned to death. This memorial is erected to commemorate Goody Glover as the first Catholic martyr in Massachusetts.'

17 November 1890

Parnell is named in O'Shea divorce case

On 17 November 1890, Captain William O'Shea was granted a decree for divorce from his wife, Katharine, who had for 10 years been in a relationship with Charles Stewart Parnell, leader of the Irish National League. O'Shea was estranged from Katharine at the time, but the fact that the two were still legally married led to a political scandal not just in Ireland but in Great Britain. Former Prime Minister W. E. Gladstone did not want his reputation to be tarnished by association with Parnell, seen by many as an adulterer.

Gladstone, though initially declining to be 'a judge of faith and morals', urged Parnell to step down as head of the Irish National League. In a letter to John Morley, Chief Secretary for Ireland, he said that Parnell's continuance as leader 'would not only place many hearty and effective friends of the Irish cause in a position of great embarrassment, but would render my retention of the leadership of the Liberal party, based as it has been mainly upon the prosecution of the Irish cause, almost a nullity'. Parnell refused to step down, and though he was re-elected leader, a split soon followed: 44 MPs supported Justin McCarthy, who formed the anti-Parnellite Irish National Federation; the remaining 26, including John Redmond, supported Parnell in the Irish National League.

In July 1891, a letter was signed by all but three of the Catholic archbishops and bishops in Ireland. It stated that Parnell, who was a Protestant, had 'by his public misconduct ... utterly disqualified himself to be the political leader'.

Parnell married Katharine O'Shea in June 1891, but died a few months later, in October 1891. The pro- and anti-Parnellite factions would not reunite until 1900, under the leadership of John Redmond.

18 November 1916

The Battle of the Somme ends

On 18 November 1916, one of the longest and bloodiest battles of the First World War came to an end, after four-and-a-half gruelling months and a loss of 146,000 lives on the British side and 164,000 on the German. On 1 July, Field Marshal

Douglas Haig had given orders for 13 divisions of the British Fourth Army to emerge from their trenches and advance towards the German front lines. Among those who went over the top was the 36th (Ulster) Division.

On the first day alone, this division lost close to 2,000 men. More than 3,000 more were injured. Captain Wilfred Spender, a native of Plymouth, England, served as a general staff officer to the 36th (Ulster) Division, and was famously quoted the following day: 'I am not an Ulsterman but yesterday, the 1st July, as I followed their amazing attack, I felt that I would rather be an Ulsterman than anything else in the world.'

The 16th (Irish) Division, a division mainly recruited from John Redmond's National Volunteers, joined the battle in September of that year. Like the 36th, the 16th suffered heavy casualties. Between 3 and 9 September, it lost more than half its officers. On 9 September, it captured the German-held village of Ginchy, but 534 men were killed.

One of these was Tom Kettle, a poet and Irish nationalist who had been an Irish Parliamentary Party MP for East Tyrone. Kettle had famously said to friends in Bettystown before he left for France that the executed 1916 leaders 'will go down to history as heroes and martyrs and I will go down – if I go down at all – as a bloody British soldier'. Days before his death, Kettle penned a poem for his only child, titled 'To My Daughter Betty, the Gift of God'.

19 November 1984

Margaret Thatcher dismisses New Ireland Forum findings

In 1983, the New Ireland Forum was established by Taoiseach Dr Garret FitzGerald to discuss possible solutions to the conflict in Northern Ireland, and included representatives from Fianna Fáil, Fine Gael, Labour and the SDLP. Unionist parties were conspicuous by their absence. A report of the forum's findings was published on 2 May 1984, acknowledging 'the desire of nationalists for a united Ireland in the form of a sovereign, independent Irish state to be achieved peacefully and by consent … In addition to the unitary state, two structural arrangements were examined in some detail – a federal/confederal state and joint authority.'

FitzGerald was careful to stress the need for consent from unionists, stating at a press conference after the publication of the report: 'We have emphasised that any movement towards Irish unity must be by agreement and consent.' Charles Haughey, leader of Fianna Fáil, insisted that a 'unitary state – not any other type of state' was what the report called for. Deputy DUP leader Peter Robinson would later dismiss the New Ireland Forum as 'absolute nonsense'.

Six months after the publication of the forum's findings, FitzGerald met British Prime Minister Margaret Thatcher at the second summit of the Anglo-Irish Inter-governmental Conference at Chequers. The day after this meeting, Thatcher aired her thoughts on the forum in a rather blunt manner: 'I have made it quite clear … that a unified Ireland was one solution. That is out. A second solution was confederation of two states. That is out. A third solution was joint authority. That is out.'

FitzGerald said that the language Thatcher used was 'gratuitously offensive', while Haughey accused him of leading the country into 'the greatest humiliation in recent history'. Nevertheless, both FitzGerald and Thatcher would sign the Anglo-Irish Agreement a year later, to the consternation of unionists.

20 November 1807

Sinking of *Rochdale* and *Prince of Wales*

On 20 November 1807, two ships found themselves caught in a violent storm, having left Dublin Bay the previous day. They were the *Prince of Wales*, commanded by Captain Robert Jones, and the *Rochdale*, both of which were carrying soldiers and their families en route to Liverpool. Jones, who survived, said that the sea began to swell when he was opposite Bray Head. The ship's anchors were thrown down, but did little to prevent the vessel being pulled towards Dunleary Point, where it was dashed against the rocks at around six or seven o'clock in the evening.

Jones made it back to Blackrock on a longboat with nine seamen, two soldiers and two women with children. However, 120 seamen and soldiers from the 18th Regiment of Foot on board the *Prince of Wales* drowned. Over the weekend, bodies were taken to be buried in Monkstown and Merrion cemeteries. Jones was subsequently arrested and tried for murder, but the case was dismissed for lack of evidence.

The *Rochdale* was commanded by Captain Hodgson, and wrecked on the rocks near the Martello tower at Seapoint. It carried staff of the 97th regiment, and there were no survivors: 265 people were killed. A memorial at St Begnet's graveyard in Dalkey reads: 'Sacred to the memory of the soldiers belonging to His Majesty's 18th regiment of foot and a few belonging to other corps ... who were unfortunately shipwrecked on this coast in the Prince of Wales packet and perished.'

At the time, no harbour existed at Dunleary; the events of that day precipitated the building of one. This was under construction in 1821 when George IV visited Dunleary, officially renamed Kingstown in his honour. It was renamed Dún Laoghaire in 1920.

21 November 1920

Bloody Sunday (Dublin)

On the morning of 21 November 1920, 14 men were shot dead on the orders of Michael Collins; another died later from his wounds. In the afternoon, members of the Royal Irish Constabulary (RIC) Auxiliary Division opened fire at a Gaelic football match in Croke Park in retaliation, killing 14 people. The day became known as Bloody Sunday.

Collins's aim was to wipe out the so-called Cairo Gang, a group of British intelligence agents living in Dublin at the time. Lieutenant Peter Ames and Lieutenant

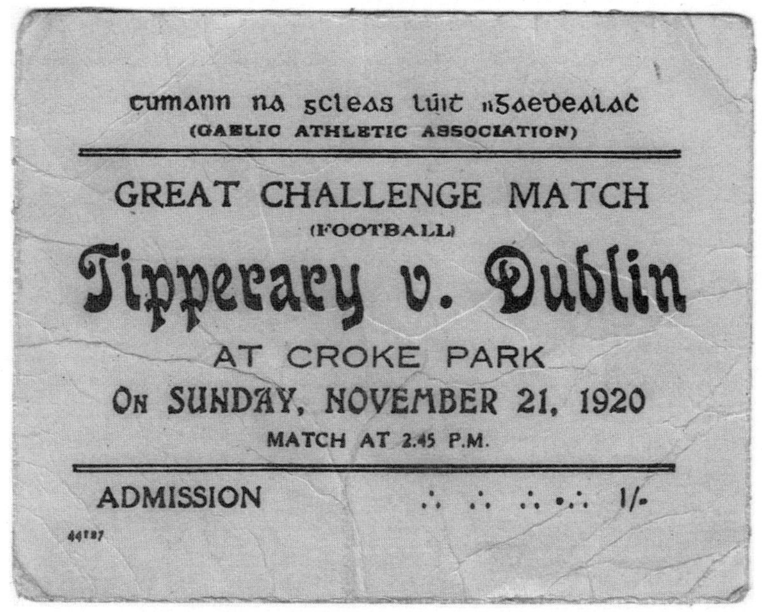

George Bennett, said to be the leaders of the gang, were shot dead by Vinny Byrne of Collins's assassination unit, 'the Squad'. Most of the others killed also worked for British intelligence or as RIC Auxiliaries, though at least one – Castlebar-born Captain Patrick Francis McCormack – was killed in what appears to have been a case of mistaken identity, and another, landlord Thomas Smith of 117 Morehampton Road, had no connection to British intelligence except that Lieutenant Donald MacLean was staying at his lodgings with his wife and six-year-old son.

The response to the assassinations was brutal. Army trucks drove to Croke Park, where a Gaelic football match was being played being played between Tipperary and Dublin. When the trucks reached the bridge overlooking the stadium, men got out and began firing.

The first person to be shot was 11-year-old William Robinson, who died two days later, though he was not the youngest victim – 10-year-old Jerome O'Leary was hit by a bullet while sitting on a wall at the back of the Canal End. Michael Hogan (24), captain of the Tipperary team and a member of the IRA, was shot dead. The only woman to die was Jane Boyle (26), who was to be married a week later. She was buried in her wedding gown. In total, 14 of the people shot in Croke Park died.

22 November 1963

Assassination of John F. Kennedy

On 22 November 1963, US President John F. Kennedy was shot dead in Dallas, Texas. Kennedy had visited Ireland only five months earlier, telling the crowd at Green Park Race Course in Limerick, 'This is not the land of my birth, but it is the land for which I hold the greatest affection and I certainly will come back in the springtime.' Sadly, he never got a chance to fulfil that promise.

Irish sports journalist Michael O'Hehir happened to be in New York at the time of Kennedy's assassination, and it was he who relayed the news to RTÉ listeners in Ireland: 'Here in New York everybody seems to be stunned and shocked by the terrible news ... First, the news that an assassination attempt had been made on President Kennedy on that motorcade that we got to know so well in Ireland during the summer ... And then, 35 minutes after he had been removed from the scene of the shooting to the hospital the news came through – President John Fitzgerald Kennedy was dead … Before he died, he received the last rites of the Church.'

That evening, President Éamon de Valera spoke on RTÉ, telling viewers: 'We sympathize with all the people of the United States, but in particular with his grief-stricken wife and other members of his family. During his recent visit here, we came to regard the President as one of ourselves, though always aware that he was head of the greatest nation in the world today. We were proud of him as being one of our race, and we were convinced that through his fearless leadership the United States could continue to increase its stature amongst the nations of the world and its power to maintain world peace.'

A national day of mourning was announced for Tuesday 26 November and a requiem mass held at the Pro-Cathedral in Dublin, attended by Taoiseach Seán Lemass and members of the government, the Oireachtas, the clergy and the diplomatic corps.

23 November 1867

Manchester Martyrs are hanged

On 23 November 1867, three members of the Irish Republican Brotherhood – William Allen, Michael Larkin and Michael O'Brien – were hanged in Salford. The trio, who became known as the Manchester Martyrs, had been arrested after Police Sergeant Charles Brett was shot dead two months before, during the rescue of two other IRB members, Thomas Kelly and Timothy Deasy. Kelly and Deasy were smuggled out of England to New York, although a reward of £300 was offered for information leading to their capture.

Irish people made up about one-fifth of the population of Manchester in 1861, and 62 were rounded up in the aftermath of Brett's killing, of whom 23 faced trial. After only 16 days, five men were found guilty under the 1848 Treason Felony Act. As well as Allen (aged 19), Larkin (32) and O'Brien (31), Thomas Maguire and Edward O'Meagher Condon were convicted.

Though Condon was spared execution by virtue of his US citizenship, his words on being sentenced inspired a song by Timothy Daniel Sullivan that became the unofficial Irish national anthem for several decades: 'I have nothing to regret, or to retract, or take back. I can only say, God Save Ireland!' Maguire did not face the death penalty as a campaign on his behalf demonstrated that witnesses had perjured themselves. The US Secretary of State, William Seward, lobbied for O'Brien, also a US citizen, to be released, but to no avail.

When the three men were executed on 23 November, thousands gathered outside New Bailey Prison in Salford. Mass protests were held in Dublin, Cork and Limerick, and even in New York and New Zealand. Friedrich Engels, in a letter to Karl Marx, wrote that the executions 'accomplished the final act of separation between England and Ireland. The only thing the Fenians had lacked were martyrs. They have been provided with these.'

24 November 1995

Divorce referendum

When the Constitution of Ireland (Bunreacht na hÉireann) was introduced in 1937, it included an article stating that 'No law shall be enacted providing for the grant of a dissolution of marriage.' On 24 November 1995, Irish voters approved by referendum an amendment to the constitution that lifted the ban on divorce. It was the narrowest margin in the history of the state, with 50.28 per cent opting for 'Yes'. The difference was a mere 9,114 votes.

In 1986 a proposed amendment introduced by the Fine Gael–Labour government led by Dr Garret FitzGerald was defeated by 63.48 per cent of voters to 36.52 per cent, largely due to a statement from the Catholic hierarchy: 'While it would alleviate the pain of some it would, we believe, release in society a force which would bring pain to a much greater number.' Fianna Fáil, led by Charles Haughey, also opposed the proposed amendment.

In 1995 the Fifteenth Amendment, which stated that a 'Court designated by law may grant a dissolution of marriage', was introduced by Labour TD and Minister for Equality and Law Reform Mervyn Taylor. Again the Catholic hierarchy opposed it. Michael Farrell, chairman of the Irish Council for Civil Liberties, framed the amendment in the context of the island of Ireland as a whole, saying, 'Many Northern Protestants harbour a deep-seated fear of the Republic as a predatory, Catholic-dominated society. Ending the ban could make a real contribution to easing tension between the communities on this island.'

Though polls tightened in the days prior to the referendum, the amendment was approved: the highest turnout of 'Yes' voters (68.2 per cent) was in Dún Laoghaire. One of the most infamous moments of the campaign came as the votes were being counted, when anti-divorce campaigner Úna Bean Nic Mhathúna sneered at the victorious side, 'G'way, ye wife-swapping sodomites.'

25 November 1892

'The Necessity for De-Anglicising Ireland'

On 25 November 1892, Douglas Hyde gave a lecture before the Irish National Literary Society titled 'The Necessity for De-Anglicising Ireland'. He decried what he saw as the 'constant running to England for our books, literature, music, games, fashions, and ideas'.

The son of a Protestant clergyman from Co. Roscommon, Hyde developed a keen interest in the Irish language while growing up, keeping a diary *as Gaeilge* from the age of 14. His 1892 lecture was a pivotal moment in the Gaelic revival. The following year, with Eoin MacNeill and Fr Eugene O'Growney, he would found the Gaelic League.

Hyde began by making it clear that his was not a vision outlined solely for the benefit of Irish nationalism: 'This is a question which most Irishmen will naturally look at from a National point of view, but it is one which ought also to claim the sympathies of every intelligent Unionist – and which, as I know, does claim the sympathy of many.' He went on to point out the paradoxical nature of those 'who read English books, and know nothing about Gaelic literature', but nevertheless profess to 'hate the country which at every hand's turn they rush to imitate'.

He also said, referencing the politics of the day, that, should Home Rule be granted, 'the Irish language, which so many foreign scholars of the first calibre find so worthy of study, shall be placed on a par with – or even above – Greek, Latin, and modern languages, in all examinations held under the Irish Government.' Only by doing so, and by restoring Irish as the first language of Ireland, Hyde said, 'can the Irish race once more become what it was of yore – one of the most original, artistic, literary, and charming peoples of Europe'.

26 November 1998

Tony Blair addresses the Oireachtas

On 26 November 1998, Tony Blair became the first British Prime Minister to address a joint session of Dáil Éireann and Seanad Éireann. Blair was greeted by Taoiseach Bertie Ahern on arriving at Leinster House, and led into the national parliament, where he met the leaders of the major political parties in the Irish state. Ceann Comhairle Seamus Pattison welcomed the premier and reminded him of Britain's influence on the Irish political system: 'Ireland has a strong tradition of parliamentary democracy, which owes so much not only to the founding fathers of this State, but also to the basic bedrock of the British parliamentary tradition.'

Blair began: 'Standing here as the first British prime minister ever to address the joint Houses of the Oireachtas, I feel profoundly both the history in this event, and I feel profoundly the enormity of the honour that you are bestowing upon me. From the bottom of my heart, *go raibh mile maith agaibh.*' He said that his mother was born in Donegal, 'in the flat above her grandmother's hardware shop on the main street of Ballyshannon'.

Blair explored the ways in which Britain and Ireland were 'irredeemably linked', saying, 'it has always been simplistic to portray our differences as simply Irish versus English – or British ... No one should ignore the injustices of the past, or the lessons of history. But too often between us, one person's history has been another person's myth. We need not be prisoners of our history.'

The peace process, which was at that point at an impasse, unsurprisingly formed a large part of Blair's address: 'The Good Friday Agreement, overwhelmingly endorsed by the people on both sides of the border, holds out the prospect of a peaceful long-term future for Northern Ireland, and the whole island of Ireland.'

27 November 1985

Anglo-Irish Agreement is passed in House of Commons

On 27 November 1985, the Anglo-Irish Agreement, signed earlier that month by Margaret Thatcher and Dr Garret FitzGerald, went before the House of Commons in London. It was passed by 473 votes to 47, giving Thatcher the biggest majority of her premiership. However, it was not without detractors. Ian Gow, the Minister of State for the Treasury, resigned from government in protest. The Provisional IRA later killed him with a car bomb planted outside his home in East Sussex.

In Northern Ireland, all 15 unionist MPs would resign their seats and run for re-election on a policy of opposition to the Agreement. This backfired on Jim Nicholson of the UUP, who failed to be re-elected as MP for Newry and Armagh, that seat going to Seamus Mallon of the SDLP. Northern Ireland unionist influence in the House of Commons was not as potent as it once had been.

Randolph Churchill, father of Winston, had famously said that 'the Orange card would be in the one to play' in 1886, siding with Ulster unionists in their opposition to Home Rule, and bringing down the Liberal government in the process. However, in 1985, Merlyn Rees, former Secretary of State for Northern Ireland, said, 'the Orange card will no longer be a trump card.'

One person who lent his support to Thatcher and the agreement was former Prime Minister Edward Heath, who had co-signed the Sunningdale Agreement of 1973 with Taoiseach Liam Cosgrave. Heath recalled being the 'odd man out' in meetings with Cosgrave and Brian Faulkner, the last Prime Minister of Northern Ireland, and said, 'I confess that I have always found the Irish, all of them, extremely difficult to understand ... It is because we want to work closely together that I so strongly support this agreement.'

28 November 1920
Kilmichael Ambush

On 28 November 1920, the Kilmichael Ambush took place. It was led by Tom Barry, commander of the 3rd West Cork Brigade flying column of the IRA. Barry was a former British soldier who had served in the First World War, an experience that served him well in staging the ambush.

On the day of the attack, an IRA unit of 36 men lay in wait for the two Crossley Tender trucks carrying the Auxiliaries to their base in Macroom. Around 1½ miles south of Kilmichael, Barry waited, wearing a tunic and a Sam Browne belt to give the impression that he himself was an Auxiliary. He flagged down the trucks at around 4:20 p.m., and a hand grenade was thrown at the first vehicle, mortally wounding the patrol commander, Francis Crake, and its driver. Barry blew his whistle, his cue for the hidden riflemen to start shooting.

What happened with the second Crossley Tender truck is disputed. Some believe the Auxiliaries pretended to surrender, only to then open fire, mortally wounding three IRA men – Michael McCarthy, Jim O'Sullivan and Pat Deasy. Others believe that the Auxiliaries fired only when they believed they were about to be executed. Either way, by the finish, 16 Auxiliaries were dead. Another, Cecil Guthrie, was badly wounded and went to a local house for help, where he was met by three IRA men. He was then executed.

The Kilmichael Ambush marked an escalation in the War of Independence. Reflecting on the incident shortly afterwards, British Prime Minister David Lloyd George said it was of 'a different character from the preceding operations. The others were assassinations. This last was a military operation and there was a good deal to be said for declaring a state of siege or promulgating martial law in that corner of Ireland.' Martial law was introduced in Cork, Tipperary, Limerick and Kerry on 10 December 1920, and in Clare, Waterford, Kilkenny and Wexford the following month.

29 November 1996

Michael Lowry revelations

On 29 November 1996, a news story by investigative journalist Sam Smyth in the *Irish Independent* alleged that TD Michael Lowry had received £207,820 from businessman Ben Dunne in 1993, and used it to refurbish his Georgian home in Co. Tipperary. Dunne had been ousted as executive director of Dunnes Stores in 1993, after which his sister, Margaret Heffernan, discovered irregularities in payments he made not only to Lowry but to former Taoiseach Charles Haughey.

Lowry resigned almost immediately and gave a personal statement in the Dáil on 19 December, saying, 'I now accept that some of my tax obligations are still outstanding. I apologise to the Taoiseach, the House and the public for failing in that regard.' However, Lowry maintained that the money he received was 'an entirely proper and legitimate payment' to his company Streamline Enterprises, a refrigeration business that provided services to Dunnes Stores.

Shortly afterwards, Fine Gael leader John Bruton informed Lowry that he would not be re-selected as a Fine Gael candidate in the 1997 general election. Lowry stood as an independent, and managed to top the poll in Tipperary North in that and subsequent elections.

In February 1997, Bruton set up the McCracken Tribunal, chaired by High Court judge Brian McCracken. It produced a 100-page report that August, which found that Lowry had an 'unhealthy business relationship' with Ben Dunne. McCracken concluded: 'Notwithstanding the fact that there appears to have been no political impropriety involved, the Tribunal considers it quite unacceptable that Mr Charles Haughey, or indeed any member of the Oireachtas, should receive personal gifts of this nature, particularly from prominent businessmen within the State.'

30 November 1909

'People's budget' sparks Constitutional crisis

On 30 November 1909, the 'people's budget' that H. H. Asquith's Liberal government had introduced earlier that year was rejected by the House of Lords. This led to a constitutional crisis, in which John Redmond and the Irish Parliamentary Party (IPP) would gain a foothold in British politics and see significant progress on the issue of Home Rule.

With his budget, Chancellor of the Exchequer David Lloyd George sought to raise taxes, including on land, in order to fund social programmes. This was anathema to many in the House of Lords; they voted it down by 350 votes to 75. A general election was then called for January.

John Redmond had already written to John Morley MP: 'The political conditions in Ireland are such that, unless an official declaration on the question of Home Rule be made, not only will it be impossible for us to support Liberal candidates in England, but we will most unquestionably have to ask our friends to vote against them.' Asquith responded in a speech in December in which he promised to 'set up in Ireland a system of full self-government in regard to purely Irish affairs'.

In the January 1910 election the Liberals fell short of a majority, and relied on IPP votes to form a government. Two previous Home Rule Bills had been brought down. In order to have a third one pass, the House of Lords' veto would have to be removed: this was done in 1911 as part of the Parliament Act. The Lords could therefore only delay rather than prevent the implementation of Home Rule. The Third Home Rule Bill was introduced in 1912 and rejected by the House of Lords that year and in 1913, but allowed to pass in 1914.

1 December 1494
Poynings' parliament is summoned

Sir Edward Poynings, the son of a Kentish squire, was appointed Lord Deputy of Ireland by Henry VII. On 1 December 1494, he assembled a parliament in Drogheda where the Statute of Drogheda, better known as Poynings' Law, was passed. The full title was 'An Act that no Parliament be holden in this land until the Acts be certified into England'. In other words, no Irish parliament could assemble without the permission of the Lord Deputy of Ireland and its Privy Council, as well as the Privy Council of England and its monarch. In addition, any laws that an Irish parliament wrote could not be enacted without being approved by the English monarch and his privy council.

The aim of this act was to reduce the threat of Yorkist pretenders to the throne. In 1487, England had been invaded by an army of Irish troops provided by Garret Mór FitzGerald, Earl of Kildare, to accompany Lambert Simnel, a 10-year-old boy claiming to be the Earl of Warwick. Simnel tried and failed to dethrone Henry VII. Four years later, Perkin Warbeck tried to muster support in Ireland for a similar attempted takeover in England. When Poynings assumed the role of Lord Deputy, he had the Earl of Kildare imprisoned.

Poynings' Law also revived the Statutes of Kilkenny of 1366, which aimed to prevent marriages between the English and Irish in Ireland, though this failed to take hold at either time.

Poynings' Law remained in place until 1782, when it was lifted to allow for the creation of what became known as Grattan's Parliament, after Henry Grattan. The 1800 Act of Union rendered it moot.

2 December 1999

Articles 2 and 3 are changed

On 2 December 1999, Articles 2 and 3 of the Constitution of Ireland were officially changed in line with the Good Friday Agreement. When two referendums were held concurrently on 22 May 1998, voters in the Republic were asked whether to approve the agreement and change their constitution.

Since the ratification of Bunreacht na hÉireann (Constitution of Ireland) in 1937, Articles 2 and 3 had been among the most controversial. They claimed that the 'national territory consists of the whole island of Ireland' and affirmed the 'right of the parliament and government established by this constitution to exercise jurisdiction over the whole territory'. In other words, Northern Ireland rightfully belonged in a united Ireland, not in the United Kingdom.

Articles 2 and 3 may have been aspirational, but unionists in Northern Ireland were hostile to them. In 1991 the Rev. Ian Paisley said, 'If we could get rid of Articles 2 and 3 … the Berlin Wall which the Constitution built between North and South would be removed.' David Trimble had referred to President Mary Robinson as 'the physical embodiment of the aggressive territorial claim in the Irish Constitution'.

A staggering 94.39 per cent of voters in the Irish state approved the proposed changes. Now Articles 2 and 3 would state the 'entitlement and birthright of every person born in the island of Ireland … to be part of the Irish Nation', and that 'a united Ireland shall be brought about only by peaceful means with the consent of a majority of the people, democratically expressed, in both jurisdictions in the island.'

After signing in the changes, Bertie Ahern said, 'Every Irish person is entitled to feel a great sense of pride today in what we have been able to achieve together in bringing about peace throughout Ireland.'

3 December 1925

Boundary Commission agreement

On 3 December 1925, W. T. Cosgrave, James Craig and Stanley Baldwin signed an agreement. It sought to resolve the issue of the border on the island of Ireland, referenced in Article 12 of the 1921 Anglo-Irish Treaty, which said that 'a Commission

… shall determine in accordance with the wishes of the inhabitants, so far as may be compatible with economic and geographic conditions, the boundaries between Northern Ireland and the rest of Ireland.'

The Boundary Commission met for the first time on 11 December 1924, and many expected to see a transfer of territory from Northern Ireland to the newly independent Irish Free State, not least in Counties Tyrone and Fermanagh, which had Catholic majorities. However, on 7 November 1925, the *Morning Post* carried a leak of the Commission's findings, which said that there would be very little change to the border. Cosgrave now faced embarrassment at home, but a solution of sorts was found.

Article 5 of the Anglo-Irish Treaty stated that the 'Irish Free State shall assume liability for the service of the Public Debt of the United Kingdom.' This was to be waived in exchange for the Irish Free State not contesting where the border lay. It ultimately passed in the Dáil by 71 votes to 20, but many nationalists in Northern Ireland were unhappy.

Cahir Healy, MP for Fermanagh and South Tyrone, said, 'John Redmond was driven from public life for even suggesting Partition for a period of five years. The new leaders agree to a Partition forever.' Éamon de Valera said: 'The worst of this bargain is the complexion that will be put upon it, for it will be said that we have sold our countrymen for the meanest of all considerations – a money consideration.'

4 December 1971

McGurk's Bar bombing

On 4 December 1971, a bomb planted by the Ulster Volunteer Force exploded in the Tramore Bar, commonly known as McGurk's, north of the city centre, in Belfast's New Lodge area. Fifteen people were killed, all Catholics. Patrick McGurk, owner of the pub, lost his 46-year-old wife, Philomena, and 14-year-old daughter, Maria. It was the biggest loss of life in a single incident in Belfast during the Troubles.

Brian Faulkner, the Prime Minister of Northern Ireland, said, 'Only insane fanatics could place or even handle a gelignite bomb in premises crowded with ordinary citizens.' Gerry Fitt, MP for West Belfast and Second World War veteran, said it was 'worse than the horror of the last war'.

The next day, a group identifying itself as the Empire Loyalists issued a statement that was printed in the *Belfast Telegraph*, accepting responsibility for the bombing and saying it had 'proved beyond doubt that meetings of IRA Provisionals and Officials were held there'. In 1977, UVF member Robert James Campbell was charged with the bombing and given 16 life sentences. He had driven the car that carried the explosive to the pub, but the person who planted the bomb was never found. Campbell served 15 years in prison, being released in 1993.

In February 2011, a public statement from Police Ombudsman Al Hutchinson on the bombing found that 'inconsistent police briefings, some of which inferred that victims of the bombing were culpable in the atrocity, caused the bereaved families great distress, which has continued for many years.' The report also stated, 'There is no evidence or intelligence that the RUC had any information, which if acted upon, could have prevented the bombing of McGurk's Bar.'

5 December 1640

John Atherton is hanged

On 5 December 1640, John Atherton, Anglican Bishop of Waterford and Lismore, was publicly hanged in Dublin for the crime of sodomy. He and his steward, John Childe, were accused of being lovers, and Childe would be hanged the following year in Cork.

What is notable about Atherton's execution is that he himself had campaigned to have stricter laws against male homosexual acts introduced in Ireland. On 11 November 1634, An Act for the Punishment for the Vice of Buggery was passed in the Irish House of Commons, largely on the back of Atherton's campaigning. He became the first man to be hanged under the act.

Born in Somerset, Atherton became prebendary of St John's in Dublin in 1630 and Lord Bishop of Waterford and Lismore in 1636. Later, an anonymous pamphlet was produced, titled *The Life and Death of John Atherton*, with illustrations of Atheron and Childe hanging from the gallows.

This was only the second case where men were executed for homosexuality in either Ireland or Great Britain. The first involved Lord Audley, who was convicted in 1631 along with two of his manservants.

According to Irish gay rights campaigner and academic David Norris, it was after Lord Audley's execution that Atherton noticed a 'gap in the sodomy laws which meant that for technical reasons this vicious apparatus of persecution had not yet been extended to Ireland'. Norris even drew parallels between Atherton and the Rev. Ian Paisley, who mounted the unsuccessful Save Ulster from Sodomy campaign in the late 1970s and early 1980s in an effort to prevent the decriminalisation of homosexual acts, as part of the 1967 Sexual Offences Act, applying to Northern Ireland.

6 December 1922

Irish Free State is established

On 6 December 1922 the Irish Free State, independent of the United Kingdom, was formally established, a year to the day after the Anglo-Irish Treaty was signed by, among others, Michael Collins, Arthur Griffith, David Lloyd George and Winston Churchill. Though the Treaty came after the partition of Ireland, it included, in Article 12, a clause that said the rules of the Irish Free State would 'no longer extend' to Northern Ireland if an address were presented by both Houses of the Parliament of Northern Ireland to the King within a month. It was a foregone conclusion that this would happen, and it did, almost immediately.

The evening that the state was established, about 80 of 88 deputies took their seats in Leinster House. W. T. Cosgrave was elected President of the Executive Council. He expressed 'pardonable pride in being the first man called upon to preside over the first Government set up under the Treaty'. Kevin O'Higgins was made Vice President and Minister of Home Affairs, and General Richard Mulcahy was appointed Minister of Defence. Senators named included William Butler Yeats; Sir Horace Plunkett; the Earls of Mayo, Kerry and Dunraven; Lord Monteagle; Lord Powerscourt; and Lord Glenavy.

The *Irish Times*, traditionally a unionist paper, marked the occasion with an editorial stressing its significance: 'It is an almost bewildering moment of transition ... Today all things are made new. The Irish people, by their own deliberate choice, are left to their own resources. They will make their own laws, shape their own progress, establish their own traditions of government. Their future will be what they choose to make it and the honour of success or the shame of failure will fall upon themselves alone.'

7 December 1995

Seamus Heaney accepts the Nobel Prize

On 7 December 1995, Seamus Heaney accepted the Nobel Prize for Literature at a ceremony in Stockholm.

Born to Catholic parents near the village of Casteldawson in Co. Derry, Heaney was the first of nine children. Growing up, the gifted young poet was acutely aware of the contentious nature of identity in Northern Ireland.

At the time of the award, Heaney lived in Dublin, where he had resided since 1976, between teaching appointments at the likes of Harvard, Berkeley and Oxford. Taoiseach John Bruton extolled the virtues of Heaney's work when he was announced as the winner: 'His poetry, which has enriched and illuminated Irish life, from simple everyday events to his reflection on the divisions which have afflicted the island of Ireland, truly deserves this international recognition and acclaim.'

In his public lecture upon accepting the award, Heaney referenced the first Irish Nobel laureate, William Butler Yeats. Yeats was awarded the prize in 1923, at a time when Ireland was emerging from the throes of a traumatic civil war. Recalling his own childhood, Heaney described being 'impelled to deplore the atrocious nature of the IRA's campaign of bombings and killing' as well as being 'appalled by the ruthlessness of the British Army on occasions like Bloody Sunday in Derry in 1972'.

However, there was an optimism to his speech: 'In spite of devastating and repeated acts of massacre, assassination and extirpation, the huge acts of faith which have marked the new relations between Palestinians and Israelis, Africans and Afrikaners, and the way in which walls have come down in Europe and iron curtains have opened, all this inspires a hope that new possibility can still open up in Ireland as well.'

8 December 1980

First Anglo-Irish summit in Dublin Castle

On 8 December 1980, the first major Anglo-Irish summit was held in Dublin Castle. Though it was not the first time that a British Prime Minister visited the Irish state – Edward Heath flew into Baldonnel Aerodrome for a meeting with Liam Cosgrave in 1973, and Harold Wilson attended the Dublin European Council in 1975 – the meeting of Margaret Thatcher with Fianna Fáil leader Charles Haughey on Irish soil was significant. It saw the two heads of government release a joint communiqué detailing the purpose and outcome of the meeting.

Northern Ireland was not the sole topic of the meeting – the 'future development of the European Community, including the budget, the Common Agricultural Policy, EMS and fisheries' was mentioned – but the conflict loomed large. The communiqué stated: 'The Taoiseach and the Prime Minister agreed that the economic, social and political interests of the peoples of the United Kingdom of Great Britain and Northern Ireland and the Republic are inextricably linked; but that the full development of these links has been put under strain by division and dissent in Northern Ireland.'

Speaking afterwards, Haughey said the talks were of 'very great significance indeed. They are something entirely new. Something very important, and directed towards a political development in the situation.' Nevertheless, he was slightly vague on details. Asked if he saw it as an acceptance by Thatcher of his 'long-standing feeling that Northern Ireland is no longer a proper political entity', Haughey said, 'I think the communiqué clearly acknowledges that it's at the level of government to government – sovereign government to sovereign government – that the possibility of a solution can be found.'

9 December 1973

Sunningdale Agreement is signed

On 9 December 1973, the Sunningdale Agreement was signed by the heads of the British and Irish governments as well the leaders of the Ulster Unionist Party, the SDLP and Alliance. This ambitious bilateral treaty set out to establish a power-sharing executive in Northern Ireland, as well as a Council of Ireland with a consultative assembly of 60 members: 30 from the Dáil and 30 from the Northern Ireland Assembly.

However, Sunningdale was scuppered by unionist opposition and by that of hardline republican groups, specifically Sinn Féin and the Provisional IRA. The assembly that it established, with Brian Faulkner as Chief Executive and Gerry Fitt Deputy Chief Executive, lasted only five months, collapsing in the wake of the Ulster Workers' Council Strike in May 1974.

As part of the agreement, the Irish government 'fully accepted' that Northern Ireland would remain part of the United Kingdom until a majority of its people desired a change, and the British government 'solemnly accepted' that it would respect the wishes of the people of Northern Ireland if they sought to do that. Speaking after it was signed, Liam Cosgrave said, 'There are no winners, and no losers here at Sunningdale today. We reached accommodation with one another on many practical issues.'

Ferocious unionist opposition to Sunningdale is well documented. Less so is republican opposition. *Republican News*, published by Sinn Féin, accused Gerry Fitt of having 'sold out the people of Ireland'. John Hume was also criticised, described as 'the fish-selling school teacher from Derry' who had 'bartered his birthright for the position of commerce'. Indeed, in 1997, when Sinn Féin came round to accepting that the constitutional status of Northern Ireland could not change without the consent of a majority of its population, Seamus Mallon famously remarked: 'When you strip away the verbiage from the Sinn Féin position, all we are talking about is Sunningdale for slow learners.'

10 December 1998

John Hume and David Trimble receive Nobel Peace Prize

On 10 December 1998, John Hume and David Trimble – the respective leaders of the largest nationalist and unionist parties in Northern Ireland, the SDLP and the Ulster Unionist Party – received the Nobel Peace Prize. The ceremony took place in Oslo, in the presence of the King Harald and Queen Sonja of Norway. Earlier in the day, Hume and Trimble lit a flame representing peace before entering the town hall, where thousands of Norwegian schoolchildren were in attendance.

James Galway, the virtuoso flute player from Belfast, provided music before Hume and Trimble spoke. Though the two largest nationalist parties in Northern Ireland – the SDLP and Sinn Féin – had supported the Good Friday Agreement, unionists had been more divided. The DUP, led by the Rev. Ian Paisley, urged its supporters to vote against it, and even some members of the UUP, such as Jeffrey Donaldson and David Burnside, were at odds with Trimble over it.

Trimble's speech was cautious and far from triumphalist: 'Ulster Unionists, fearful of being isolated on the island, built a solid house, but it was a cold house for Catholics. And Northern nationalists, although they had a roof over their heads, seemed to us as if they meant to burn the house down. None of us are entirely innocent.'

Hume drew parallels between the peace process in Northern Ireland and the reconciliation between nation states in Europe after the Second World War: 'It is now clear that European Union is the best example in the history of the world of conflict resolution and it is the duty of everyone, particularly those who live in areas of conflict to study how it was done and to apply its principles to their own conflict resolution.'

11 December 1920

The Burning of Cork

On 11 December 1920, two Crossley Tender lorries carrying RIC Auxiliaries were leaving their barracks near Dillon's Cross in Cork. It was known that the Auxiliaries usually left Victoria Barracks – later renamed Collins Barracks – at around 8:00 p.m., and an ambush was planned by Seán Ó Donoghue of the Cork No. 1 Brigade of the IRA. Twelve Auxiliaries were injured; one – Spencer Chapman – died the next day. The IRA men managed to escape. Soon after, a second group of Auxiliaries arrived at the scene and began emptying houses nearby, looking for the culprits. When they got no answers from the locals, the Auxiliaries began setting their homes on fire.

Another group of Auxiliaries gathered on St Patrick's Bridge before marching down St Patrick's Street, breaking shop windows and firing their weapons. Grant's Drapery Store and Cash's Department Store were set on fire. Alfred Hudson, the superintendent of Cork Fire Brigade, had few men on duty and was unable to deal with the many blazes spreading throughout the city. Later, roaming gangs of Auxiliaries also set the City Hall and the Carnegie Free Library on fire.

The home of Daniel Delaney on Dublin Hill was raided. His sons Jeremiah and Cornelius were known to be in the IRA, but had not participated in the ambush. Jeremiah was shot dead at the scene and Cornelius mortally wounded, dying six days later.

When the burning of Cork had finished, five acres of property, valued at £20 million, was destroyed and 1,000 people had lost their jobs. The newly formed 'K' Company of RIC Auxiliaries responsible were quickly redeployed to Dunmanway in West Cork, where, only a few days later, they killed Canon Thomas Magner and local man Tadhg Crowley.

12 December 1936

External Relations Act is signed into law

On 11 December 1936, Edward VIII abdicated the throne to marry American socialite Wallis Simpson, less than a year after he had taken over from his father, George V. This led to a crisis in the United Kingdom, but in the Irish Free State, Éamon de Valera, President of the Executive Council, seized the opportunity to push through legislation that would greatly reduce the role of the British monarch.

On the day Edward VIII abdicated, the Irish cabinet agreed to delete all references to the King and the Governor General from the Constitution of the Irish Free State. The King would now factor into Irish affairs only when the Free State was dealing with other dominion nations, such as Australia, Canada, New Zealand and South Africa, as a 'symbol of their co-operation'. Two acts were actually passed by the Dáil: on 11 December, the Constitution (Amendment No. 27) Act and on 12 December, the Executive Authority (External Relations) Act.

Introducing the bills in the Dáil, de Valera explained, 'What is happening, then, is that from the King are being taken away any functions internal, either direct or indirect, in the Administration of the Government and in the internal Executive of the country, and we are retaining the King for those purposes for which he was used hitherto. He is being retained for these purposes because he is recognised as the symbol of this particular co-operation in the States of the Commonwealth. If the Irish people do not wish to continue him for these purposes they can end that by legislation.'

De Valera hoped that retaining the British monarch to some degree would help reconcile Northern Ireland with the Irish state. However, James Craig, Prime Minister of Northern Ireland, had little interest.

13 December 1999

First meeting of North/South Ministerial Council

On 13 December 1999, the North/South Ministerial Council had its inaugural meeting in Armagh. This was the body set up under the Good Friday Agreement to bring together elected representatives in Northern Ireland and the Irish state to 'develop consultation, co-operation and action within the island of Ireland'. First Minister David Trimble and Deputy First Minister Seamus Mallon acted as joint chairmen for the inaugural meeting, and Bertie Ahern led the Irish government delegation.

Before the meeting, members of the Irish government stressed the Council's importance. Liz O'Donnell, Minister of State for Foreign Affairs, said: 'I know that without Seamus Mallon's unswerving commitment to seeing the agreement he worked so hard to bring about fully implemented, we would not be making such progress this week. David Trimble has also proved himself a courageous leader of his people. He has taken considerable personal and political risks, we owe him a great deal.'

A joint communiqué detailed who had attended and what had been discussed: 'Both sides in the Council acknowledged the importance of the occasion as a significant further step in the implementation of the Good Friday Agreement.'

Healing the wounds of the Troubles was also on the agenda: 'Both sides also agreed, recalling the commitment in the Good Friday Agreement to the principles of partnership, equality and mutual respect as the basis of relationships between North and South, that the Council should play a central role in promoting reconciliation within, and in ensuring a better future for all the people on the island.'

14 December 1918

Sinn Féin wins a majority of Irish seats

On 14 December 1918, voting took place in the United Kingdom general election. Of the 707 seats in the House of Commons, 105 went to MPs on the island of Ireland. Sinn Féin won 73 of these seats, almost completely obliterating the Irish Parliamentary Party (IPP). Of the votes cast, 46.9 per cent were for Sinn Féin, though 25 of its members were elected unopposed. The Irish Unionist Party received 25.3 per cent of the vote and 22 seats, and the IPP won a mere six seats on 21.7 per cent of the vote. In East Mayo, IPP leader John Dillon had been returned in every election since 1885. His defeat to Sinn Féin leader Éamon de Valera was catastrophic for the party, which would dissolve in 1922: the year that the Irish Free State seceded from the United Kingdom.

Sinn Féin's manifesto for the 1918 election drew explicit parallels to the Rising of two years earlier, in which de Valera had been a commandant. It promised to stand by 'the Proclamation of the Provisional Government of Easter 1916, reasserting the inalienable right of the Irish nation to sovereign independence', and would do so by 'withdrawing the Irish Representation from the British Parliament' and by 'making use of any and every means available' to combat what it described as the 'subjection by military force' of Ireland by England. It even anticipated the 'contemplated mutilation of our country by partition', which it blamed on the constitutional nationalism of the Irish Party.

The Irish Unionist Party, led by Edward Carson, was unmoved by Sinn Féin promises of 'national self-determination'. Speaking at the Ulster Unionist Council in Belfast weeks before the election, Carson asked, 'Self-determination by whom and of what? Self-determination by the south and west of Ireland of the destinies of Ulster? Never!'

15 December 1993
Downing Street Declaration is issued

On 15 December 1993, British Prime Minister John Major and Taoiseach Albert Reynolds released the Downing Street Declaration, also known as the Joint Declaration on Peace. In it, the two heads of government reaffirmed their commitment to bringing peace to Northern Ireland and normalising relations between the two countries.

Reynolds, who had taken over from Charles Haughey, was less bullish on Northern Ireland and Irish unity than his predecessor. Both the 1985 Anglo-Irish Agreement and the 1973 Sunningdale Agreement were signed by seemingly more conciliatory Fine Gael leaders, Dr Garret FitzGerald and Liam Cosgrave. Reynolds was the first Fianna Fáil leader to make considerable headway on the issue.

The Downing Street Declaration came shortly after the Maastricht Treaty took effect, creating the European Union. Reynolds and Major were Europhiles, and the European Single Market, introduced at the start of 1993, meant that customs posts between Northern Ireland and the rest of the island would soon be a thing of the past. Recognising this, the 12-point document said that 'the development of Europe will, of itself, require new approaches to serve interests common to both parts of the island of Ireland, and to Ireland and the United Kingdom as partners in the European Union.'

The Downing Street Declaration also gave a green light to Sinn Féin to 'participate fully in democratic politics', provided it 'establish a commitment to exclusively peaceful methods'. However, the party was initially sceptical. Mitchel McLaughlin, its Northern Ireland Executive chairman, said, 'Already the general reaction among many nationalists is one of disappointment.' Some unionists were also sceptical, if not downright condemnatory. The Rev. Ian Paisley told Major he had 'sold Ulster to buy off the fiendish republican scum!'

16 December 1983

Rescue of Don Tidey

On 24 November 1983, Don Tidey, chairman and chief executive of Associated British Foods – owner of Ireland's first supermarket chain, Quinnsworth – was abducted by the Provisional IRA while taking his 13-year-old daughter to school in Rathfarnham, Co. Dublin. He was bundled into a van and driven to Derrada Woods, near Ballinamore, Co. Leitrim. His kidnappers demanded £5 million from Associated British Foods for his release; the company and the Irish government refused, fearing that payment would lead to further kidnappings.

A 1,000-man search party of Gardaí and members of the Irish Defence Forces set about locating Tidey, and finally stumbled upon the gang's hideout in Derrada Woods on 16 December. In a panic, the IRA threw a grenade at the approaching security forces and opened fire before escaping. Private Patrick Kelly and Garda recruit Gary Sheehan were shot dead. Kelly, who had served on UN peacekeeping duties in Lebanon and Cyprus, was 35 years old and a father of four. Sheehan, a native of Carrickmacross, Co. Monaghan, was 23.

Tidey was rescued unharmed, but the killing of Kelly and Sheehan sullied what should have been a moment of victory for the Gardaí and the Irish Army. The death of the two men made headlines again in 2011, when Sinn Féin's Martin McGuine ness, while running for President of Ireland, was confronted by Patrick Kelly's son, David, in Westmeath. McGuinness denied knowing who the killers were, though he had condoned their actions in a 1985 interview with *Hot Press*, in which he said that killings of Irish security forces were wrong, 'Except in certain circumstances, like in Ballinamore, where IRA volunteers felt they were going to be shot dead and were defending themselves against armed Gardaí and soldiers.'

17 December 1834

First dedicated commuter railway line opens

On 17 December 1834, the first dedicated commuter railway line in the world began operations. It linked Dublin city to Kingstown (as Dún Laoghaire was then known), 10 kilometres away. In 1831, the Dublin and Kingstown Railway Company had been formed by men who knew that coastal properties in towns like Kingstown, Booterstown, Blackrock and Salthill were of enormous value, and often served as second homes for wealthy residents of Dublin city. At the time, the most common way to reach these areas was by horse-drawn carriage, and the much smoother method of rail travel had potential.

The contract to construct the Dublin–Kingstown railway was given to William Dargan, the son of a tenant farmer from Co. Carlow, who had established a reputation constructing roads and canals. Dargan beat six competitors for the role. The engineer was Charles Blacker Vignoles, a native of Woodbrock, Co. Wexford.

Work began in April 1833. By September of that year, over 1,800 men were involved in the construction on the railway route. Granite sourced from quarries in Dalkey was used to build the bridges along which the train would travel. Some landowners objected, specifically Baron Cloncurry of Maretimo and the Rev. Sir Harcourt Lees of Blackrock House, though both were satisfied when Dargan promised to include bathing houses near their properties as part of the construction.

When the railway line was completed, trains travelled at 20 miles per hour and each was divided into three categories – first class, which was one shilling; second class, eight pence; and third class, sixpence. Dargan would later move to Belfast, where he helped construct Ireland's second railway, from Belfast to Lisburn, completed in 1839.

18 December 1834

Rathcormac massacre

On 18 December 1834, nine people were shot dead in Gortroe, near Rathcormac, Co. Cork, while protesting at having to pay tithes to the local Church of Ireland parish. Three more people would later die from their wounds.

Initially, tithes were to be one-tenth of farm produce, paid twice monthly, but this was later changed to a cash levy of a set amount. From 1830 onwards, many Catholics in Ireland began withholding payments, ushering in the so-called Tithe War. In the case of Gortroe, the levy was to be paid to Archdeacon William Ryder.

On the day in question, Ryder was accompanied by soldiers of the 4th Royal Irish Dragoon Guards as well as foot soldiers of the 29th Regiment, and police. On their way to collect a tithe from a widow, Johanna Ryan, they were met by a group of people, armed with sticks and spades, near Bartlemy Cross. Ryder ordered the soldiers to draw their bayonets, after which the protesters retreated to Ryan's home. The soldiers and police attempted to force their way in, without success.

Captain Bagley announced to his men, 'You must dislodge the peasants from the haggart and the yard. If they do not go quietly, you must try the bayonet. If that is not sufficient you must fire; but do not fire except in the last resort.' Eventually, the soldiers did just that. Ryder entered Ryan's house from the rear, and received his tithes, after which he and the soldiers left.

Commenting on the mood in the area shortly afterwards, Cork newspaper the *Southern Reporter* wrote: 'To describe the state of the country since the tragic occurrence was enacted is not in the power of the writer ... The people are dark and sullen, desperate and reckless.'

19 December 1973

Contraceptive laws are ruled unconstitutional

On 19 December 1973, the Supreme Court of Ireland ruled that a ban on importing or selling contraceptives was unconstitutional. The case had been brought by Mary McGee, a 27-year-old mother of four who was told her life would be in danger if she had another pregnancy. Section 17 of the 1935 Criminal Law Amendment Act stated that it was not lawful 'for any person to sell, or expose, offer, advertise, or keep for sale or to import or attempt to import into Saorstát Eireann for sale, any contraceptive'.

After being diagnosed with toxaemia, which meant that having another child might have been fatal, Mary McGee ordered spermicidal jelly from England, but it was seized by Irish Customs. McGee received a letter informing her of what had happened: 'I couldn't believe it. I just thought "no way, I have to do something about this", not realising the enormity of what I was taking on. I think we were all ready for change though. People wanted children but they also wanted a life.' She initially took her case to the High Court, which dismissed her claim; she then appealed to the Supreme Court. Her attorney was a young activist named Mary Robinson, who would go on to become the first female President of Ireland.

Ireland was still a very conservative country, deeply influenced by Catholic orthodoxy. James McGee, Mary's husband, recalled being asked in the witness box whether he and his wife 'would not consider living as brother and sister'. Nevertheless, a four-to-one verdict found that laws on contraceptives in Ireland were outdated.

It was not until 1979, when Minister for Health Charles Haughey introduced the Health (Family Planning) Act, described as 'an Irish solution to an Irish problem', that contraceptives became available in the Irish state: and even then, in a very limited way.

20 December 1909

James Joyce opens Ireland's first cinema

On 20 December 1909, James Joyce established the Volta Theatre, the first regular cinema in Ireland. The idea for a dedicated cinema in Dublin had come from Joyce's sister Eva and one of his students, Nicolò Vidacovich. Joyce was living in Trieste, and persuaded four Italian entrepreneurs to give financial backing to the picture house. As a result, it was named after the Italian inventor Alessandro Volta, and mainly showed films from Italy.

Joyce returned to Dublin in October 1909 to scout for locations, settling on a building at 45 Mary Street. After being refurbished, the Volta had a capacity of 420 people. Two of the Italian businessmen – Antonio Machnich and Giovanni Rebez – arrived in November and a third, Francesco Novak, shortly before the opening. Novak brought with him Guido Lenardon, who would be the projectionist. The launch was announced in the British film magazine *The Bioscope* on 9 December.

On Monday 20 December, the electrician tasked with overseeing the opening night could not be found, and Joyce had to seek another in the city, delaying the first screening. Finally, it began, with *The First Paris Orphanage*, *La Pouponnière* and *The Tragic Story of Beatrice Cenci*, the last of which, according to the *Freeman's Journal*, was 'hardly as exhilarating a subject as one could desire on the eve of the festive season but it was very much appreciated and applauded'. The newspaper went on to say, 'Mr James Joyce, who is in charge of the exhibition, has worked apparently indefatigably in its production and deserves to be congratulated.'

Sadly, Joyce's involvement with the Volta was short; the investors sold it to the British Provincial Cinema Company the following June at a loss of £1,000.

21 December 1967

Solar alignment is observed at Newgrange

On 21 December 1967, Michael J. O'Kelly entered the inner chamber at Newgrange, a megalithic passage tomb in Co. Meath. Discovered in 1699, Newgrange formed part of the archaeological site Brú na Bóinne, along with Knowth and Dowth. In 1915, Irish archaeologist R. A. S. Macalister said of it: 'There is not, north of the Alps, a relic of antiquity more impressive than this mound … Even Stonehenge, though to the eye more imposing, is second in interest to New Grange.' Locals believed that Newgrange was the burial place of the High Kings of Tara, but Michael O'Kelly dismissed this, claiming the site was built around 3200 BC, predating the Pyramids of Egypt by approximately 500 years.

O'Kelly began excavating the site in 1962, and noticed a small rectangular opening above the tomb's entrance, which he called the roof box. Chunks of crystallised quartz had been used as a shutter for the box, O'Kelly believed, but he could not figure out its purpose.

One theory was that during midsummer, the light of the rising sun shone through the box and illuminated the chamber. This, O'Kelly thought, was impossible, as the entrance was south-facing and the midsummer sun rose in the northeast, but it later occurred to him that the midwinter sun might have shone through the passage. And so, he travelled from his home in Cork to the site in December 1967. At daybreak, around nine o'clock, the inner chamber flooded with light, which travelled 60 feet along a tunnel.

Recalling it, O'Kelly said, 'I was literally astounded. I expected to hear a voice or perhaps feel a cold hand resting on my shoulder, but there was silence.' The chamber was lit up for 17 minutes before returning to darkness.

News of O'Kelly's discovery soon spread, and, as time went on, tens of thousands of people applied for the opportunity to visit Newgrange each midwinter. In 1993, UNESCO designated Brú na Bóinne a World Heritage Site.

22 December 1691

The Flight of the Wild Geese

On 22 December 1691, the Flight of the Wild Geese took place. This was the mass exodus of Irish Jacobite soldiers – around 12,000 – to France after their defeat at the Battle of Aughrim on 12 July that year. On 3 October, Patrick Sarsfield, a leading figure on the side of the deposed James II, signed the Treaty of Limerick, ending the Williamite War in Ireland and giving troops the option of leaving for France to continue to serve under James II. These 'wild geese' were absorbed into all-Irish regiments of the French Army under Louis XIV in 1697.

In 1969, former French President Charles de Gaulle visited Dublin. His ancestor Anthony McCartan had left Ireland in 1691 with Sarsfield and the rest of the wild geese. McCartan, a native of Co. Down, served as a captain in the Irish Brigade in France. The McCartans settled in Lille in northern France, many of them practising medicine. In 1837, de Gaulle's great-great-grandfather Dr Andronicus McCartan travelled to Dublin to research the family's genealogy; in 1887, de Gaulle's paternal grandmother, Joséphine de Gaulle (née Maillot), wrote a biography of Daniel O'Connell.

During his visit in 1969, de Gaulle hosted a reception for members of the McCartan family in Áras an Uachtaráin, the official residence of the President of Ireland. It was the first time since the end of the Second World War that de Gaulle was not in France for the anniversary of his appeal of 18 June 1940, seen by many as the origin of the French Resistance.

Reporting de Gaulle's visit to Ireland, the *Irish Times* wrote: 'The presence of General de Gaulle in Sneem, Co. Kerry, is almost as bizarre, in its first impact, as would be the announcement that Chairman Mao had arrived in Bangor, Co. Down, to enjoy the amenities of Pickie Pool.'

23 December 1920

Government of Ireland Act is given royal assent

On 23 December 1920, the Government of Ireland Act 1920 was given royal assent, having passed through both houses of parliament in London. Under the act, two parliaments would be created on the island of Ireland, to govern six and 26 counties respectively, coming into effect on 3 May 1921. On 11 November 1920 the bill had been approved by 183 votes to 52 in the House of Commons.

Despite the comfortable majority, it was not without detractors. Chief among them was Joseph Devlin, who had taken over from John Dillon as leader of the Irish Parliamentary Party after Dillon's defeat in the 1918 election.

Devlin, a Catholic from the Lower Falls area of Belfast, was appalled at the prospect of partition, which he saw as creating minorities on both sides of the border: 'How has this Government proceeded to deal with this question of minorities? They have placed the Protestant minority in 26 counties in Ireland absolutely at the mercy of the Catholic majority … and my friends and myself, 340,000 Catholics in the six-county Parliament, covering a population of 1,200,000, are to be left permanently and enduringly at the mercy of the Protestant Parliament in the North of Ireland.'

Edward Carson was in favour of the bill, despite his misgivings about the partition of Ireland: 'I hope with all my heart that this Bill will be a success. I hope with all my heart that in the long run it will lead to unity and peace in Ireland, that in the long run it will lead the hon. Gentleman opposite and myself to see Ireland one and undivided, loyal to this country and loyal to the Empire.'

24 December 1895

Kingstown lifeboat disaster

On 24 December 1895, the Civil Service number 7, a lifeboat manned by volunteers in Kingstown (now Dún Laoghaire), Co. Dublin, was sent to rescue the Finnish SS *Palme*, which had set sail from Liverpool for South America but had run aground in Dublin Bay. On board the *Palme* were Captain Robert Wiren, his wife, their five-month-old child and 17 crew members.

The weather was atrocious, and the men on the lifeboat had only 16-foot oars to transport themselves towards the *Palme*. Disaster struck when the lifeboat overturned. Some of the men managed to hold on to the keel, but their limbs were numbed by the cold and they perished one by one. Fifteen men died. The 20 people onboard the *Palme* were rescued the next day by Thomas McCombie, Captain of the SS *Tearaght*, who received a gold medal. The lifeboat volunteers were buried together in Deans Grange Cemetery.

On the centenary of this event, a large crowd gathered in Dún Laoghaire for a memorial to those who had lost their lives. A local woman, Maureen Byrne, a relative of one of the men, told *RTÉ News* that she recalled her mother saying, 'It was very sad for the town. They had lost men at sea here a lot, but that was the worst, because they hadn't got the equipment they have today.'

The names of the men who died in the incident are recorded on a stone memorial opposite the present lifeboat station: John Baker, John Bartley, Edward Crowe, Thomas Dunphy, William Dunphy (brother of Thomas), Francis McDonald, Edward Murphy, Patrick Power, James Ryan, Francis Saunders, George Saunders (brother of Francis), Edward Shannon, Henry Underhill, Alexander Williams and Henry Williams.

25 December 1351

William Buí O'Kelly hosts Christmas feast

On 25 December 1351, William Buí O'Kelly (Uilliam Buidhe Ó Cellaigh) held a Christmas feast for the poets of Ireland in his home in Galey Castle in Co. Roscommon. He invited not only poets but bards, harpers, gamesters and jesters. The event was immortalised by the bardic poet Gofraidh Fionn Ó Dálaigh, who died in 1387. Eleanor Hull, co-founder of the Irish Texts Society, of which Douglas Hyde was President, translated Ó Dálaigh's poem 'Filidh Éireann go haointeach' ('The Poets of Ireland to One House'):

'The grandson of Conchobhar of Glandore is not a mere Irishman; William with his curly, ringleted, spreading locks, is Grecian and Spanish ... The poets of the Irish land are preparing to seek O'Kelly. A mighty company is approaching his house, an avenue of peaked hostels is in readiness for them. Hard by that – pleasant is the aspect – a separate street has been appointed by William for the musicians that they may be ready to perform before him. The chroniclers of comely Ireland, it is a gathering of a mighty host, the company is in the town; where is the street of the chroniclers? The fair, generous-hearted host have another spacious avenue of white houses for the bardic companies and the jugglers.'

The 1351 feast was, according to Katherine Simms' 1978 article 'Guesting and Feasting in Gaelic Ireland' (*Journal of the Royal Society of Antiquaries of Ireland*), 'the earliest recorded instance of an Irish lay-patron providing a feast exclusively for the benefit of the learned classes'.

O'Kelly died in 1381; his obituary in the Annals of the Four Masters describes him as 'a man of the greatest character, worth, and renown, of his own tribe; the man who had given a general invitation of hospitality to the schools of Ireland, and had given them all their own demands.'

26 December 1883

Harbour Grace Affray

On 26 December 1883, a clash between Protestant Orangemen and Roman Catholics, mostly of Irish descent, in the town of Harbour Grace in Newfoundland and Labrador resulted in the deaths of five people. Traditionally, the Loyal Orange Association would have its annual march on 12 July, as in Ulster and elsewhere. However, members in Newfoundland were usually occupied with fishing at that time of year, so it was decided to hold it on the day after Christmas Day (St Stephen's Day, alternatively known as Boxing Day).

Harbour Grace was divided into Protestant and Catholic neighbourhoods, Riverhead being one of the latter. On the day of the march, approximately 400 Orangemen were marching down Harvey Street in the town when they were met by 150 Catholics demanding they venture no further. Constable Edward Doyle, an Ulster Protestant, had told his policemen to be on the lookout for trouble, expecting a confrontation. When it occurred, shots were fired, and five men lay dead – three Orangemen, one Catholic and one bystander.

Doyle was arrested for the killing of the Catholic, Patrick Callahan, though he was later acquitted. So too were five other men, though they never came to trial.

Nineteen Catholics, whose names – Michael Coady, Nicholas Shannahan, Thomas

Morrisey – revealed their roots, were arrested for murder but acquitted, much to the outrage of the Protestant community in Harbour Grace.

Voting in Newfoundland had traditionally taken place along religious lines. In 1885, the Reform Party elected 14 Protestant representatives and the Liberals elected 14 Catholics, with an all-Protestant cabinet then named. In 1886, the cabinet was joined by two Catholic opposition members. As Canadian senator and writer Frederick William Rowe would note, 'The year 1886 must be regarded as a turning point in Newfoundland history … All the bigotry, discrimination and antagonisms did not disappear in 1886. But from that time on, every party and every administration leaned over backwards to see that the major religious groups were adequately represented within the legislature and in the government service.'

27 December 1904

Abbey Theatre opens

In 1897, in the home of Lady Augusta Gregory at Coole Park in Co. Galway, she, W. B. Yeats and Edward Martyn drafted the Manifesto for Irish Literary Theatre, in which they stated, 'We propose to have performed in Dublin in the spring of every year certain Celtic and Irish plays, which whatever be their degree of excellence will be written with a high ambition, and so to build up a Celtic and Irish school of dramatic literature … We will show that Ireland is not the home of buffoonery and of easy sentiment, as it has been represented, but the home of an ancient idealism.'

Seven years later, on 27 December 1904, the Abbey Theatre, which would become the permanent home of the Irish National Theatre Society, opened in its doors in Dublin for the first time with a double bill of Yeats's *On Baile's Strand* and Lady Gregory's *Spreading the News*.

The Irish Literary Theatre's inaugural performance had been on 8 May 1899: a production of Yeats's *The Countess Cathleen* in the Antient Concert Rooms on Great Brunswick Street in Dublin. The following night, Martyn's *The Heather Field* was performed. Plays continued to be staged for the next five years, including the first in the Irish language, *Casadh an tSúgáin* (*The Twisting of the Rope*) by Douglas Hyde, before a permanent theatre for the company was found.

The Irish National Theatre Society was being pulled in three directions. One, centred on George Russell, wanted the theatre to remain semi-amateur. Another, led by Arthur Griffith and Maude Gonne, wanted it to be more politically nationalistic. The third, of which Yeats was the leader, wanted the plays to be of the highest professional standard. In this, Yeats was supported by Lady Gregory and John Millington Synge. It was his vision that ultimately prevailed.

28 December 1969

IRA splits into Official and Provisional factions

On 28 December 1969, the Provisional IRA released its first public statement, acknowledging it had split from what would become known as the Official IRA. One reason given was the decision by the IRA and its political wing, Sinn Féin, to contest seats in the Northern Ireland Parliament at Stormont, the House of Commons at Westminster, and Dáil Éireann in Dublin. Another was the perceived failure of the IRA leadership in Dublin to sufficiently protect what the Provisional IRA described as 'our people in the North': Catholic families who had been burned out of their homes in August 1969, after which British troops were deployed to the streets to restore order.

IRA Chief of Staff Cathal Goulding said on 18 August 1969: 'the Army Council has placed all volunteers on full alert and has already sent a number of fully equipped units to the aid of their comrades in the Six Counties.' Jack Lynch, the Taoiseach, was outraged, saying, 'No group has any authority to speak or act for the Irish people except the lawful Government of Ireland.'

In December, Goulding held an IRA Army Convention in Dublin at which a proposal was made that abstentionism should be dropped. Though a majority of delegates supported this move, the Provisionals (as they became known) did not. They released a statement on 28 December outlining their position: 'In view of a decision by a majority of delegates at an unrepresentative convention of the Irish Republican Army to recognise the British, Six County and Twenty-Six County parliaments, we the minority of delegates at that convention ... do hereby repudiate those compromising decisions and reaffirm the fundamental Republican position. We declare our allegiance to the Thirty-Two County Irish Republic proclaimed at Easter 1916.'

29 December 1937

Constitution of Ireland comes into force

On 29 December 1937, the Constitution of Ireland, also known as Bunreacht na hÉireann, came into force, having been approved by 56.52 per cent of voters at a plebiscite on 1 July that year. Drafted by legal adviser John Hearne with the supervision of Éamon de Valera, the Constitution established that the 'name of the State is Éire, or, in the English language, Ireland.' It also controversially claimed that the 'national territory consists of the whole island of Ireland', which was seen as deliberately provocative by unionists in Northern Ireland.

Much of what has come to define Ireland as an independent country was introduced in the 1937 Constitution. Having removed almost all references to the British monarch with the External Relations Act of 1936, de Valera saw to it that there would be a new head of state, 'elected by direct vote of the people', to be known as the President of Ireland (Uachtarán na hÉireann). The first incumbent was Douglas Hyde, founder of the Gaelic League. The Constitution also introduced the term 'Taoiseach, that is, the head of the Government or Prime Minister'.

Aside from the territorial claim to Northern Ireland, controversial aspects included the recognition of 'the special position of the Holy Catholic Apostolic and Roman Church as the guardian of the Faith professed by the great majority of the citizens'. This jarred with the secular ethos to which most republics aspire, and was removed by referendum in 1972.

On the day that the Constitution was enacted, the tricolour was flown from all public buildings, and the 4th Howitzer Battery fired a 21-gun salute at the Royal Hospital, Kilmainham, which, according to the *Irish Press* (de Valera's newspaper) 'echoed, not only through the streets of its capital, but from shore to shore of this island'.

30 December 999

The Battle of Glenn Máma

On 30 December 999 in the Battle of Glenn Máma or Glenmama, Brian Boru, King of Munster, defeated a revolt by King Máel Mórda of Leinster. Born in 941, Brian was the son of Cennétig, king of the Dál Cais people of Co. Clare. In 982, Brian began to challenge the supremacy of Máel Sechnaill mac Domnaill, the High King of Ireland, who was of the Uí Néill dynasty. In 997, Máel Sechnaill and Brian agreed to a treaty at Bleanphuttoge, near Lough Ree, Co. Westmeath, which granted the lower half of Ireland to Brian. His territory now included Leinster and Munster, within which many Hiberno-Norse cities existed.

In 999, Máel Mórda mac Murchada, King of Leinster, rebelled against Brian's claim to the province. Máel Mórda was aided by Sitric Silkenbeard, the Hiberno-Norse king of Dublin. Details of what happened at the Battle of Glenn Máma are not entirely clear, but according to the Annals of Clonmacnoise, Máel Sechnaill fought on Brian's side. The exact location is also disputed: Newcastle Lyons in Co. Dublin is one of the places it may have taken place, or possibly Dunlavin in Co. Wicklow.

In the words of medieval Irish text Cogad Gáedel re Gallaib (The War of the Irish with the Foreigners), the battle was 'bloody, furious, red, valiant, heroic, manly; rough, cruel, heartless; and men of intelligence and learning say that since the battle of Magh Rath, to that time, there had not taken place a greater slaughter'.

According to medieval historian Ailbhe Mac Shamhráin, Brian's victory at Glenn Máma gave him a 'psychological advantage' that led to his breaking the treaty of 997, and in 1002 he ousted Máel Sechnaill mac Domnaill as High King of Ireland. However, when Brian fell at the Battle of Clontarf in 1014, Máel Sechnaill's position as High King was restored.

31 December 1759

Brewery is leased to Arthur Guinness

On 31 December 1759, the premises of a defunct brewery in the St James's Gate area of Dublin were formally leased to Arthur Guinness for an unprecedented 9,000 years, at an annual rent of £45. Born in 1725, Arthur Guinness was the oldest son of Richard Guinness of Celbridge, Co. Kildare, who worked for Dr Arthur Price, Archbishop of Cashel.

When Price died, he left Richard and Arthur £100 each, and it was with this money that Arthur began his first brewery – established on 29 September 1756 in Leixlip – at the age of 31. When Arthur obtained the lease of the brewery at St

James's Gate, he left his Leixlip brewery to Richard.

The property was spacious but the brewery part was small and poorly equipped. However, Guinness made it a success. In 1763 he was elected Warder of the Dublin Corporation of Brewers, and in 1769 Guinness exported its first batch of beer to London: six-and-a-half barrels, a modest amount considering that Guinness stout would eventually be brewed in 49 countries and sold in over 150. Porter, a dark beer so called because of its popularity with river porters, was becoming increasingly popular in Dublin by the end of the century, and so in 1799, Guinness switched to brewing black beers exclusively.

In 1862, the harp was registered as Guinness's trademark. This led to problems for the newly established Irish Free State government in 1922, which wished to use the musical instrument on its Great Seal. In order not to infringe the Guinness copyright, the image of the harp used on government documents had to face in the opposite direction.

Bibliography

Articles

'100 Defining Moments', *Sunday Independent*, 24 April 2016, p. 22.

Abernethy, Laura, 'Homage to gallantry of Somme replaces mural glorifying loyalist killers', *Belfast Telegraph*, 9 March 2016, p. 15.

'Address by Nelson Mandela to Dáil Éireann', *Irish Times*, 8 June 2013.

Adelman, Juliana, 'The Irish engineer who broke new ground in study of earthquakes', *Irish Times*, 13 September 2018, p. 10.

'Ahern says statement marks the end of war', *Irish Times*, 28 July 2005.

Anderson, Nichola, 'History was in their hands as they heartily shook on', *Belfast Telegraph*, 5 April 2007, p. 1.

Arnold, John, 'The day 12 men were killed in a cold-blooded Cork massacre', *echolive.ie*, 13 December 2019 (www.echolive.ie/nostalgia/arid-40138595.html, accessed 3 May 2021).

'Assembly of Sinn Feiners is Ignored by Govt', *Calgary Daily Herald*, 22 January 1919, p. 7.

'Attitudes may have changed but gay-bashing still happens', *Irish Independent*, 20 June 2013, p. 41.

Black, Fergus, 'At the going down of the sun and in the morning, we will remember them', *Irish Independent*, 12 November 2009, p. 11.

Blair, Tony, 'We have come too far to go back now' (address to the joint Houses of the Oireachtas), *Irish Times*, 27 November 1998, p. 6.

Blakemore, Erin, 'How Ireland turned "fallen women" into slaves', *history.com*, 21 July 2019 (www.history.com/news/magdalene-laundry-ireland-asylum-abuse, accessed 2 May 2021).

Bhreathnach, Edel, 'The Gathering? It's nothing new', *Irish Times*, 26 June 2013, p. 12.

Bielenberg, Kim, 'War in the skies: the Blitz and the Irish fighter pilots who kept Hitler's forces at bay', *Irish Independent*, 5 September 2020, p. 20.

Boland, Rosita. 'Ann Lovett: Death of a "strong kick-ass girl"', *Irish Times*, 24 March 2018, p. 2.

Bouchier-Hayes, Frank, 'An Irishman's Diary', *Irish Times,* 26 August 2008, p. 15.

Bourke, Edward J., 'The sinking of the Rochdale and the Prince of Wales', *Dublin Historical Record*, 61 (2), 2008, 129–135.

Browne, Colette, 'Gay saved my mother's sanity – and he helped to make this country a more liberal, open society', *Irish Independent*, 6 November 2019, p. 27.

Burke, Jason, 'The Craigavon House Demonstration of 1911', *Shankill and East Belfast Extra*, May 2019.

Burke, Ray, 'An Irishman's Diary', *Irish Times*, 22 July 2019, p. 13.

Burke-Kennedy, Eoin, 'Pilot's error blamed for bombs that brought second world war to Dublin', *Irish Times*, 30 May 2011, p. 6.

Burke-Kennedy, Eoin, 'Shedding light on solstice at Newgrange', *Irish Times*, 19 December 2013, p. 14.

Campbell, Patrick, 'Irish saint laid the

foundations of British Christianity', *Irish Times*, 17 June 1997, p. 14.

Carbery, Genevieve, 'Families express relief at findings', *Irish Times*, 24 January 2009, p. 7.

Carroll, Joe, 'This is not the land of my birth, but it is the land for which I hold the greatest affection', *Irish Times*, 21 June 2003, p. 53.

Carroll, Joe, 'De Valera's condolences given out of courtesy', *Irish Times*, 26 January 2005, p. 12.

Carroll, Steven, '"My heart goes out to victims" – President', *Irish Times*, 22 May 2009, p. 11.

Carroll, Steven, 'Philip Cairns: Forever remembered as boy who disappeared on way back to school', *Irish Times*, 11 June 2016, p. 4.

Carson, Edward, 'Ulster's New policy has been outlined by unionist leader', *Vancouver Daily Sun*, 29 December 1918, p. 7.

Cashman, Greer Fay, 'Preserving unity', *Jerusalem Post*, 3 June 2015, p. 16.

'Cigarette machine group "faces darkest day"', *Irish Times*, 18 February 2004.

Cleere, Ray, 'Annaghdown boating tragedy: 190 years ago', *irelandsown.ie* (www.irelandsown.ie/annaghdown-boating-tragedy-190-years-ago/, accessed 6 May 2021).

Cobh Heritage Centre, 'Lusitania exhibition', *cobhheritage.com* (www.cobhheritage.com/lusitania/, accessed 4 May 2015).

'Coghlan shatters indoor mile record', *The Province*, 28 February 1983, p. 19.

'Compassion of the people recognised', *Irish Times*, 11 December 1998, p. 10.

'Cork remembers Air India crash tragedy', *Irish Times*, 19 June 2005.

Corless, Damian, 'Night of the Big Wind: A stormy start for pensions', *Irish Independent*, 5 January 2019, p. 10.

'Cosgrave government blocked Ó Dálaigh trip to Rome', *Irish Times*, 31 December 2005, p. 6.

'Countdown to Gaelic Sunday commemorations', *gaa.ie*, 5 July 2018 (www.gaa.ie/news/countdown-to-gaelic-sunday-commemorations/, accessed 27 April 2021).

'Courageous action led to free legal aid in civil cases', *Irish Times*, 31 August 2002, p. 14.

Crooks, Peter, 'The past as a bucket of ashes? CIRCLE: A Calendar of IRish Chancery LEtters, c.1244–1509', *History Ireland*, 19 (4), 2011, 16–18.

Crooks, Peter, 'Exporting Magna Carta: Exclusionary liberties in Ireland and the world', *History Ireland*, 23 (4), 2015, 14–17.

Cunningham, Peter, 'An Irishman's Diary', *Irish Times*, 27 March 2006.

Curley, Daniel, 'William Buide O'Kelly and the late medieval renaissance of the Uí Maine lordship', *History Ireland*, 27 (6), 2015, 14–17.

Cusack, Jim, 'Government accepts IRA killed garda in Adare', *Irish Times*, 14 June 1996, p. 1.

Daly, Mary, 'A meeting that made global news', *Irish Times*, 21 January 2019, p. 19.

De Bréadún, Deaglán, 'Killing of garda utterly wrong – Adams', *Irish Times*, 14 June 1996, p. 7.

De Bréadún, Deaglán, 'Carter's staff did not take North "seriously"', *Irish Times*, 31 December 2009, p. 10.

De Valera, Éamon, 'A nation with no language is half a nation' (broadcast 17 Marc h1943), *Irish Times*, 17 March 2003, p. 16.

'De Valera says he escaped to do the country's work', *www.rte.ie* (www.rte.ie/centuryireland/index.php/articles/de-valera-says-he-escaped-to-do-the-countrys-work, accessed 19 April 2021).

Dooley, Chris, 'John Redmond's Finest Hour', *Irish Times*, 19 September 2015, p. 4.

Doyle, Martin, 'Breaking the silence on the Manchester Martyrs', *Irish Times*, 23 November 2014.

'Dublin sued after blowing up of royal statue', *Daily Province*, 4 June 1937.

Duffy, Sean, 'Three kings and a queen', *Irish Times*, 10 April 2014, p. 2.

Dungan, Myles, 'An Irishman's Diary', *Irish Times*, 3 July 2006, p. 15.

Dwyer, Ryle, 'Remembering Kevin O'Higgins and his three IRA killers', *Irish Examiner*, 10 July 2017.

'Earnest wish of king that Ireland may cease strife', *Calgary Daily Herald*, 23 June 1921, pp. 1, 20.

Elliot, Christopher, 'Unionists split by scepticism over motives', *The Guardian*, 19 July 1997.

'Excerpts from homilies Pope John Paul II delivered in Drogheda and in Dublin', *New York Times*, 30 September 1979 (www.nytimes.com/1979/09/30/archives/excerpts-from-homilies-pope-john-paul-ii-delivered-in-drogheda-and.html, accessed 10 May 2021).

Fanning, Megan, 'UCD introduces smoking ban', *University Observer*, 1 September 2014 (universityobserver.ie/ucd-introdues-smoking-ban/, accessed 21 April 2021).

Farmer, Ben, 'First ship sunk by Nazis found off Irish coast', *Daily Telegraph*, 6 October 2017, p. 7.

Farrell, Rachel, '"I listened to the women in my life" – Taoiseach on why he changed views on Eighth Amendment', *Irish Independent*, 23 May 2018.

Farrell, Tom, 'An Irishman's Diary', *Irish Times*, 15 September 1997, p. 15.

'First Armistice Day in Ireland marked by silence and scuffles', *rte.ie* (www.rte.ie/centuryireland/index.php/articles/first-armistice-day-in-ireland-marked-by-silence-and-scuffles, accessed 2 May 2021).

FitzGerald, Garret, 'How the myth over VAT on children's footwear still endures', *Irish Times*, 9 September 2000, p. 16.

'Flann O'Brien: Our unluckiest genius', *Irish Times*, 3 September 2011, p. 9.

Freeman, Norman, 'An Irishman's Diary', *Irish Times*, 14 December 2015, p. 15.

GAA Museum, 'The Gaelic Athletic Association through history and documents 1870–1920' (crokepark.ie/BlankSite/media/Images/secondary-schools-resource-pack.pdf, accessed 2 May 2021).

'Garda heroes: Impressive funeral of raid victims', *An t-Óglách*, 20 November

1926. (antoglach.militaryarchives.ie/PDF/1926_11_20_Vol_5_No20_An%20t-Oglac-21.pdf, accessed 2 May 2021).

Gartland, Fiona, 'Fortieth anniversary of women's "invasion" of Forty Foot', *Irish Times*, 19 July 2014, p. 7.

Garvin, Tom, 'Showing Blueshirts in their true colours', *Irish Times*, 12 January 2001, p. 16.

Gibney, Fintan, 'Royal Canal bridge stands as an old unique mathematical shrine', *Irish Times*, 19 July 2001, p. 13.

Gimson, Andrew, 'Cameron carries the day with refusal to defend the indefensible', *Daily Telegraph*, 16 June 2010, p. 6.

Glackin, Neil, 'The man who spoke Irish in the British parliament', *thejournal.ie*, 25 October 2018 (www.thejournal.ie/readme/irish-mp-speaks-irish-in-house-of-commons-4304272-Oct2018/, accessed 19 April 2021).

Gleeson, Colin, 'Endlessly inventive Irishman received 38 patents', *Irish Times*, 12 March 2014, p. 17.

Government of Canada, 'Prime Minister pays Canadians' respects to victims of the Air India disaster', 22 June 2005 (www.canada.ca/en/news/archive/2005/06/prime-minister-pays-canadians-respects-victims-air-india-disaster.html, accessed 10 May 2021).

Graham, Ian, 'Sinn Fein leaders in "run IRA" claim', *Daily Post*, 21 February 2005, p. 17.

Greene, Andy, 'Flashback: Sinead O'Connor booed offstage at Bob Dylan celebration', *rollingstone.com*, 19 November 2013 (www.rollingstone.com/music/music-news/flashback-sinead-oconnor-booed-offstage-at-bob-dylan-celebration-189352/, accessed 1 May 2021).

'Guns salute the Republic in midnight ceremony: Thousands gather in city centre', *Irish Times*, 18 April 1949, p. 1.

Hanlon, Michael, 'Britain's secret army dares to kill', *Toronto Star*, 13 March 1988.

Hannigan, Dave, 'Sports book of the week: *The King of Spring*', *Sunday Times*, 30 May 2004, p. 14.

Harper, Keith, 'With flying colours', *The Guardian*, 15 January 2000.

Hayes, Richard, 'Biographical dictionary of Irishmen in France: Part XXII', *Studies: An Irish Quarterly Review*, 36 (144), 1947, 476–482.

Healy, Alison, 'Ash urges State to sue tobacco industry', *Irish Times*, 29 March 2005, p. 5.

Hennessy, Mark, 'Bruton calls on victims of Troubles to forgive', *Irish Times*, 5 April 2005, p. 7.

Hennessy, Mark, 'Joint visit to Battle of Boyne site', *Irish Times*, 5 April 2007, p. 7.

Hennessy, Mark and Liam Reid, 'Ahern pays tribute to Capt Kelly', *Irish Times*, 17 July 2003, p. 1.

Hennigan, Michael, 'Political and economic reform in conservative Ireland and the promise of an "everlasting boom"', *finfacts.ie*, 18 September 2009 (www.finfacts.ie/irishfinancenews/article_1017922.shtml, accessed 4 May 2021).

Higgins, Michael D., 'Remarks at a reception to celebrate the 20th anniversary of Bord

Scannán na hÉireann', *president.ie*, 25 April 2013 (president.ie/en/media-library/speeches/remarks-at-a-reception-to-celebrate-the-20th-anniversary-of-bord-scannan-na, accessed 21 April 2021).

Hilliard, Mark, 'Survivor recalls Cavan orphanage fire', *Irish Times*, 23 February 2018, p. 6.

Hogan, Vincent, 'Republic of Ireland v England, February 1995: The night shameful English fans left their country's reputation in tatters', *Belfast Telegraph*, 27 May 2013.

Hogan, Vincent, 'Six days in '88 that brought light to our grey country', *Irish Independent*, 21 December 2018, p. 70.

Hoge, Warren, 'Northern Ireland picks up the reins of its government'. *New York Times*, 3 December 1999 (www.nytimes.com/1999/12/03/world/northern-ireland-picks-up-the-reins-of-its-government.html, accessed 3 May 2021).

Holland, Merlin, 'The Real Wilde at Last', *The Independent*, 10 July 2014, p. 38.

Hu, Winnie, 'Failing New York Subway? Not always — once there were chandeliers', *New York Times*, 11 April 2019 (www.nytimes.com/2019/04/11/nyregion/city-hall-station.html, accessed 2 May 2021).

Humphreys, Joe, 'Inquiry sought on Saor Eire link', *Irish Times*, 4 July 2002, p. 5.

'Importance of North/South Ministerial Council stressed', *Irish Times*, 2 December 1999, p. 6.

Ingle, Sean, 'Football: England v Republic of Ireland: Bad memories from England's night of shame', *Observer*, 26 May 2013, p. 8.

'IRA to abandon violence campaign', *Edmonton Journal*, 27 February 1962, p. 5.

'Irish divisions laid bare in Convention report', *rte.ie* (www.rte.ie/centuryireland/index.php/articles/irish-divisions-laid-bare-in-convention-report, accessed 27 April 2021).

Irwin, Liam, '"The Calamitous Burning": The Drumcollogher disaster of 1926', *North Munster Antiquarian Journal*, LIII (2013), 241–265.

Jeter, Jon, 'Letter from Chicago: Putting a myth out to pasture', *Washington Post*, 29 October 29 (www.washingtonpost.com/archive/politics/1997/10/29/letter-from-chicago/1fef1932-2d68-4fd1-a813-71d73055e010/, accessed 2 May 2021).

'John Delaney: FAI stands firmly behind Mick McCarthy', *Irish Examiner*, 28 May 2002.

Johnston, Frank, 'An Irishman's Diary', *Irish Times*, 21 October 2006, p. 17.

'Joint communique issued after Armagh meeting', *Irish Times*, 14 December 1999, p. 8.

Joyce, Joe, 'September 17th, 1937: Harvest trek led to deaths of 10 young Irishmen', *Irish Times*, 17 September 2009, p. 17.

Joyce, Joe, 'WB Yeats laid to rest in Drumcliffe', *Irish Times*, 18 September 2009, p. 15.

Joyce, Joe, 'May 31st 1986', *Irish Times*, 31 May 2011, p. 28.

Keena, Colm, 'Haughey left AIB officials chasing £1m debt', *Irish Times*, 17 February 1999, p. 1.

Keena, Colm, 'Hundreds march to mark 30 years since Dublin schoolboy disappeared', *Irish Times*, 24 October 2016, p. 5.

Kelleher, Olivia, 'Irish and Native Americans "bonded by difficulties endured"', *Irish Times*, 19 June 2017.

Kelly, Laura, 'The 1876 "Enabling Act"', *womensmuseumofireland.ie* (womensmuseumofireland.ie/articles/the-1876-enabling-act, accessed 18 April 2021).

Kennedy, Geraldine, 'Lowry to make statement today', *Irish Times*, 19 December 1996, p. 1.

Kennedy, Lucy, 'Ellis Island's first immigrant honoured', *Irish Times*, 13 October 2008, p. 9.

Keogh, Dermot, 'A new state of pride, euphoria and civil war', *Irish Times*, 6 December 2002, p. 13.

Kilfeather, Sean, 'Golden age now a distant memory', *Irish Times*, 14 June 1997, p. 8.

Kinealy, Christine. 'Private donations to Ireland during An Gorta Mór', *Seanchas Ardmhacha: Journal of the Armagh Diocesan Historical Society*, 17 (2), 1998, 109–120.

King, Steven, 'Many unionists unsettled by the speed of recent events', *Irish Times*, 14 October 1997, p. 16.

Knight, Robert M., 'The pirate queen', *Chicago Tribune*, 12 March 1989.

Kozyrev, Nikolai, 'Yeltsin and the "comedy of errors" at Shannon', *Irish Times*, 28 March 2008, p. 13.

Landers, Brendan, 'An Irishman's Diary', *Irish Times*, 6 August 2009, p. 19.

Lawlor, David, 'The fearless Irish rebels with a cause to help Jews', *Daily Mail*, 8 May 2018, p. 13.

'Lemass–O'Neill talks focused on "purely practical matters"', *Irish Times*, 2 January 1998, p. 11.

Lennon, Colin, 'Dublin's great explosion of 1597', *History Ireland*, 3 (3), 1995.

Lister, Sam, 'Ireland's hour has come: Ahern', *Belfast Telegraph*, 16 May 2007, p. 1.

Long, Siobhán, 'Music maestro', *Irish Times*, 4 February 2002, p. 12.

Lynch, Brendan, 'An Irishman's Diary', *Irish Times*, 15 May 2004, p. 15.

Lysaght, Charles, 'Winston Churchill: "I hope there will be a united Ireland"', *Irish Times*, 24 January 2015, p. 6.

Marks, Kathy, 'Blair issues apology for Irish Potato Famine', *The Independent*, 2 June 1997, p. 2.

Marlowe, Lara, 'The end of Yeats: Work and women in France', *Irish Times*, 28 January 2014, p. 11.

McAdam, Noel, 'Dublin adds to pressure on republican activists', *Belfast Telegraph*, 21 February 2005, p. 1.

McAleer, Phelim, 'Massacre of the innocent in a quiet country town', *Sunday Times*, 16 August 1998, p. 3.

McAleese, Mary, 'We hope and pray, indeed we insist, that we have seen last of the violence' (inaugural address), *Irish Times*, 12 November 1997, p. 7.

'McAleese unveils Flight of Earls statue', *Irish Times*, 14 September 2007.

McCann, Debbie, 'Helping McGuinness,

bomber who killed two children along with Mountbatten', *Mail on Sunday*, 23 October 2011, p. 8.

McCarthy, Michael, 'The Franco-Irish Ambulance Brigade 1870–71', *Old Limerick Journal*, 25, 1989, 132–138.

McGarry, Patsy, 'An apparition or a magic lantern: What happened at Knock 140 years ago?', *Irish Times*, 21 August 2019.

McGee, Harry, 'New Stardust report dismisses 1982 verdict of probable arson', *Irish Times*, 24 January 2009, p. 1.

McGreevy, Ronan, 'New figures show almost 20,000 Irishmen fought for Canada in WW1', *Irish Times*, 1 August 2014.

McGreevy, Ronan, 'Irish soldiers in the first World War: Who, where and how many?', *Irish Times*, 2 August 2014, p. 2.

McGreevy, Ronan, 'Rising families gather from all over the globe', *Irish Times*, 26 March 2016, p. 4.

McGreevy, Ronan, 'Easter Week 1916: the gassing of the Irish', *Irish Times*, 16 April 2016, p. 4.

McGreevy, Ronan, 'Out for the count – An Irishman's Diary on George Plunkett's North Roscommon byelection victory in 1917', *Irish Times*, 31 January 2017.

McGreevy, Ronan, '"IRA kidnapped Shergar" claim', *Irish Times*, 4 June 2018, p. 2.

McGreevy, Ronan, 'Waterford man who escaped from German POW camp finally honoured', *Irish Times*, 17 December 2018, p. 3.

McGreevy, Ronan, 'When de Gaulle came to stay for six weeks', *Irish Times*, 13 June 2019, p. 5.

McGreevy, Ronan, 'How a jealous lover's revenge led to the execution of six young Irish soldiers', *Irish Times*, 11 November 2019.

McGreevy, Ronan, 'Class warfare and shadowy gunmen: How the 2020 election echoes 1932', *Irish Times*, 6 February 2020.

McGreevy, Ronan, 'Bloody Sunday 1920: the 32 Dead', *Irish Times*, 21 November 2020, p. 3.

McKittrick, Martin, 'How Martin McGuinness left behind the grim rhetoric of war', *Irish Times*, 22 March 2017, p. 3.

McLaughlin, Brighid, 'Mary Boyle – a stolen child', *Irish Independent*, 16 May 1999.

McMahon, James, 'Chairman Coghlan of the Boards', *rte.ie*, 25 April 2020 (www.rte.ie/sport/athletics/2020/0422/1134221-chairman-coghlan-of-the-boards/, accessed 19 April 2021).

McNally, Frank, 'An Irishman's Diary', *Irish Times*, 28 January 2008, p. 17.

McNally, Frank, 'An Irishman's Diary', *Irish Times*, 17 April 2010, p. 15.

McNally, Frank, 'An Irishman's Diary', *Irish Times*, 8 May 2015, p. 15.

McNally, Frank, 'An Irishman's Diary', *Irish Times*, 10 June 2017, p. 13.

McNally, Frank, 'An Irishman's Diary', *Irish Times*, 9 May 2019, p. 15.

McNally, Frank, 'An Irishman's Diary', *Irish Times*, 13 May 2020, p. 11.

'Method used in Barcelona on third analysis

of samples not recognised by IOC, says swimmer', *Irish Times*, 8 August 1998, p. 6.

Molony, Senan and Niamh Lyons, 'Frying pan to the *Hot Press* ... McGuinness "forgets" 1985 remarks', *Daily Mail*, 21 October 2011, p. 13.

Moonan, Niall, 'I want to see end of Provos', *Daily Mirror*, 14 March 2005, p. 2.

Montalbano, William D., 'Irish poet 1st million-dollar Nobel Prize', *Los Angeles Times*, 6 October 1995 (www.latimes.com/archives/la-xpm-1995-10-06-mn-53926-story.html, accessed 3 May 2021).

Moran, Seán, 'Camogie's centenary plans revealed', *Irish Times*, 26 November 2003, p. 27.

Moriarty, Gerry, 'Explainer: What happened on Bloody Sunday in 1972?', *Irish Times*, 14 March 2019.

Morris, Allison, 'Peter Robinson: Martin McGuinness's "traitor" comments may have saved lives following Stephen Carroll and Massereene deaths', *irishnews.com*, 7 March 2019 (www.irishnews.com/news/northernirelandnews/2019/03/07/news/peter-robinson-martin-mcguinness-traitor-comments-helped-prevent-escalation-of-violence-following-stephen-carroll-and-mas-1566953, accessed 20 April 2021).

Mullally, Una, 'Ireland in 100 quotes', *Irish Times*, 11 March 2017, p. 11.

Mullin, John, 'Blair back in Ulster to seal peace poll', *The Guardian*, 20 May 1998.

Mulvihill, Mary, 'Our best-kept secrets: the Irish doctor who invented the syringe', *Irish Times*, 5 December 2002, p. 16.

Murphy, Blanaid, 'Apology plaque to survivors', *The Sun*, 19 October 2009, p. 12.

Murray, Theresa D., 'From Baltimore to Barbary: The 1631 Sack of Baltimore', *History Ireland*, 14 (4), 2006.

Myers, Kevin, 'An Irishman's Diary', *Irish Times*, 24 July 2003, p. 15.

Newman, Marisa, 'British deserter who stole tanks for Haganah dies', *Times of Israel*, 2 February 2014 (www.timesofisrael.com/british-deserter-who-stole-tanks-for-haganah-dies/, accessed 16 May 2021).

Nordheimer, Jon, 'Gunmen wound I.R.A. Political Leader', *New York Times*, 15 March 1984 (www.nytimes.com/1984/03/15/world/gunmen-wound-ira-political-leader.html, accessed 20 April 2021).

Norris, David, 'Proposed transfer of Abbey Theatre to GPO', *davidnorris.com* (senatordavidnorris.ie/proposed-transfer-of-abbey-theatre-to-gpo/, accessed 3 May 2021).

Nugent, Ryan, 'Wreckage off west coast believed to be first British ship sunk in WWII', *Irish Independent*, 6 October 2017, p. 22.

O'Brien, Kevin, 'How a GAA broadcasting legend found himself commentating on JFK's funeral', *the42.ie*, 19 July 2020 (www.the42.ie/michael-ohehir-jfk-funeral-commentary-5152945-Jul2020/, accessed 2 May 2021).

Ó Cathaoir, Brendan, 'Tenants beg to be left on their farms', *Irish Times*, 22 November 1997, p. 4.

Ó Cathaoir, Brendan, 'An Irishman›s Diary',

Irish Times, 7 February 2003, p. 17.

Ó Cathaoir, Brendan, 'Sowing the seeds of nationalism', *Irish Times*, 13 August 2005, p. 10.

Ó Cathaoir, Brendan, 'An Irishman›s Diary', *Irish Times*, 1 June 2016, p. 15.

O'Connell, Brian, 'An Irishman's Diary', *Irish Times*, 4 September 2006, p. 15.

O'Connell, Jennifer, 'Witchipedia: Ireland's most famous witches', *Irish Times*, 28 October 2017, p. 17.

O'Doherty, Ian, 'We're far from a perfect society, but don't compare it to the 1980s', *Irish Independent*, 20 January 2018, p. 10.

O'Donnell, Ian, 'Grisly anniversary a timely reminder of death penalty', *Irish Times*, 18 April 2014, p. 16.

'Official IRA wing orders ceasefire', *Vancouver Sun*, 30 May 1972, p. 1.

O'Keefe, Cormac, 'Ceremony marks single biggest loss of life of Irish soldiers abroad', *Irish Examiner*, 7 November 2020

O'Halloran, Marie, 'Public record corrected to state there is no evidence fire deliberate', *Irish Times*, 4 February 2009, p. 10.

O'Loughlin, Joe, 'The Donegal Corridor during the Second World War', *Clogher Record*, 18 (2), 2004, 341–350.

'On the trail of a maths genius', *Irish Times*, 26 September 2002, p. 17.

'On this day … 20 December', *jamesjoyce.ie*, 20 December 2013 (jamesjoyce.ie/on-this-day-20-december/, accessed 4 May 2021).

'One government, one army', *An Phoblacht*, 16 March 1973, p. 1.

O'Neill, Úna, 'Mary Aikenhead: in the service of the poor', *catholicireland.net* (www.catholicireland.net/mary-aikenhead-in-the-service-of-the-poor/, accessed 19 April 2021).

O'Reilly, Ronan, 'From bete noire to one half of the Chuckle Brothers', *Daily Mail*, 13 September 2015, p. 6.

O'Riordan, Dick, 'Handel's bittersweet opera gets an Irish makeover', *Sunday Business Post*, 11 March 2017.

O'Shea, Brendan, 'The burning of Cork', *Irish Times*, 3 June 2020, p. 31.

'Our relationship has moved from doubting eyes of estrangement to the trusting eyes of friendship', *Belfast Telegraph*, 9 April 2014, p. 6.

'Pardon is 140 years too late for hanged man', *The Times*, 5 April 2018, p. 4.

Parsons, Michael, 'Hitler's death didn't mean a damn thing to my father', *Irish Times*, 14 May 2011, p. 4.

Paul VI, Pope, 'Canonization of Oliver Plunkett', *La Santa Sede*, 12 October 1975 (www.vatican.va/content/paul-vi/en/homilies/1975/documents/hf_p-vi_hom_19751012.pdf, accessed 2 May 2021).

Pogatchnik, Shawn, 'IRA dissident killings unite Northern Ireland's leaders', *Telegraph-Journal*, 11 March 2009.

Pollak, Sorcha, 'Irish battalion honoured for Jadotville bravery', *Irish Times*, 17 September 2016.

Pope, Conor, 'Flying into history', *Irish Times*, 8 June 2019, p. 15.

'Principles unchanged for sister of hunger striker', *Irish Times*, 9 May 1998, p. 12.

Quinn, John, 'The air war II', *culturenorthernireland.org*, 26 April 2006. (www.culturenorthernireland.org/features/heritage/air-war-ii, accessed 19 April 2021).

'RIC constables mutiny in Kerry over plans for military take-over', *rte.ie* (www.rte.ie/centuryireland/index.php/articles/ric-constables-mutiny-in-kerry-over-plans-for-military-take-over, accessed 25 April 2021).

Roberts, Ivor, 'Address at Christopher Ewart-Biggs memorial service', *Irish Times*, 25 July 2001.

Roche, Barry, '900 pubs join cig ban revolt', *The Sun*, 17 October 2003, p. 18.

Roche, Barry, 'Victim's son critical of legal failure', *Irish Times*, 9 January 2019, p. 5.

Rota, Kara, 'Butte: Montana's Irish mining town', *irishamerica.com* (irishamerica.com/2010/08/montanas-mining-town/, accessed 25 April 2021).

Ryan, Carol, 'Anniversary of family planning case brings a sense of déjà vu', *Irish Times*, 7 May 2013, p. 13.

Ryan, Órla, '"Devastation on both sides of the Atlantic": 100 years on from Ireland's worst maritime disaster', *thejournal.ie*, 15 April 2018 (www.thejournal.ie/rms-leinster-centenary-3956124-Apr2018/, accessed 2 May 2021).

'Sacred dawn', *Irish Times*, 21 December 2002, p. 57.

'September 6th 1939', *Irish Times*, 6 September 2010, p. 22.

Sheahan, Fionnán, 'Dáil has a duty not to desecrate graves of Private Kelly and Garda Sheehan', *Irish Independent*, 15 December 2020, p. 8.

Sheehy-Skeffington, Francis, 'Open letter to Thomas MacDonagh', *Irish Times*, 21 March 2016, p. 14.

Siggins, Lorna, 'Marconi celebrated in Clifden', *Irish Times*, 13 October 2007, p. 2.

Siggins, Lorna, 'Delphi Lodge on its role in Famine deaths', *Irish Times*, 13 May 2013, p. 8.

Siggins, Lorna, 'A wrongful hanging in Connemara, 1882', *Irish Times*, 20 May 2016, p. 15.

Siggins, Lorna, 'Cleggan Bay disaster of 1927 to be marked this weekend', *Irish Times*, 26 October 2017.

Simms, Katherine, 'Guesting and feasting in Gaelic Ireland', *Journal of the Royal Society of Antiquaries of Ireland*, 108 (1978), 67–100.

Simpson, Janice C., 'People need a short, sharp shock', *Time*, 9 November 1992, p. 78.

'Sinn Feiners clash with Dublin students', *Vancouver Daily Province*, 12 November 1919, p. 16.

Smith, Alan, 'Golden goal: Ray Houghton for Republic of Ireland v England (1988)', *The Guardian*, 10 June 2016.

Smyth, Gerry, 'The Beckett Letters', *Irish Times*, 17 September 2011, p. 7.

'Speech by Donogh O'Malley TD announcing free universal secondary education (10th

Sept 1966)', *fiannafail.ie* (www.fiannafail.ie/speech-by-donogh-omalley-td-announcing-free-universal-secondary-education-10th-sept-1966/, accessed 28 July 2021).

Sweeney, Tanya, 'A trailblazer from good stock', *Daily Mail*, 17 March 2020, p. 13.

'The Harbour Grace Affray' (ngb.chebucto.org/Articles/et1883.shtml, accessed 11 May 2021).

'The SS Hare: a tale of solidarity, hope and stout', *eastwallforall.ie* (eastwallforall.ie/?p=3895, accessed 6 May 2021).

'The tragedy at Maamtrasna', *The Spectator*, 18 November 1882, p. 7.

'Triple tragedy on Inisbofin again highlights the hardships and hazards of life on the islands', *Irish Times*, 10 July 1999, p. 12.

Vousden, Petrina, 'Tuskar missile ruled out – a bird may have caused crash', *The Sun*, 25 January 2002, p. 4.

Watson, Greig, 'World War One: the tank's secret Lincoln origins', *bbc.com*, 24 February 2014 (www.bbc.com/news/uk-england-25109879, accessed 28 April 2021).

Waugh, Paul, 'Armed struggle is over claims the IRA', *Evening Standard*, 28 July 2005, p. 2.

'"We did not come to Ireland for this" – ex-Black and Tan reveals reasons for resignation', *rte.ie* (www.rte.ie/centuryireland/index.php/articles/we-did-not-come-to-ireland-for-this-sort-of-work-ex-black-and-tan-reveals, accessed 29 April 2021).

Weinraub, Bernard, 'Britain's envoy in Dublin killed by mine', *New York Times*, 22 July 1976.

White, Michael, 'Heat is on the gunmen: Sinn Fein offered hope of early talks', *The Guardian*, 16 December 1993.

Whitney, Craig R., 'I.R.A. attacks 10 Downing Street with mortar fire as cabinet meets', *New York Times*, 8 February 1991, p. 1.

Wilson, Simon, 'Riverdance 25 years on', *Nottingham Evening Post*, 7 May 2019, p. 22.

Wright, Oliver, 'How a fruit cake helped Eamon de Valera escape Lincoln Prison', *bbc.com*, 3 February 2019 (www.bbc.com/news/uk-england-lincolnshire-47057379, accessed 19 April 2021).

Books

Adams, Ralph James Q., *Balfour: The Last Grandee* (London: John Murray, 2007).

Aldous, Richard (ed.), *Great Irish Speeches* (London: Quercus, 2007).

Altholz, Joseph L., *Selected Documents in Irish History* (New York: M. E. Sharpe, 2000).

Andrews, Ann, *Newspapers and Newsmakers: The Dublin Nationalist Press in the Mid-Nineteenth Century* (Liverpool: Liverpool University Press, 2014).

Augusteijn, Joost, *Patrick Pearse: The Making of a Revolutionary* (Basingstoke: Palgrave Macmillan, 2010).

Bairner, Alan, *Sport and the Irish: Histories, Identities, Issues* (Dublin: University College Dublin Press, 2005).

Baker, David V., *Women and Capital*

Punishment in the United States: An Analytical History (Jefferson, NC: McFarland, 2015).

Bardon, Jonathan, *A History of Ireland in 250 Episodes* (Dublin: Gill & Macmillan, 2008).

Besant, Annie, *Annie Besant: An Autobiography* (London: Fisher Unwin, 1893).

Bell, J. Bowyer, *The Secret Army: A History of the IRA* (Dublin: Academy Press, 1970).

Bell, J. Bowyer, *In Dubious Battle* (Dublin: Poolbeg, 1999).

Bennett, Richard, *The Black and Tans: The British Special Police in Ireland* (New York: Barnes and Noble, 1959).

Bew, Paul, *Ireland: The Politics of Enmity 1789–2006* (Oxford: Oxford University Press, 2007).

Bew, Paul, *Enigma: A New Life of Charles Stuart Parnell* (Dublin: Gill & Macmillan, 2011).

Bishop, Patrick, *The Man Who Was Saturday: The Extraordinary Life of Airey Neave* (London: William Collins, 2019).

Blake, Debbie, *Daughters of Ireland: Pioneering Irish Women* (Dublin: History Press Ireland, 2015).

Bloomfield, David. *Political Dialogue in Northern Ireland: The Brook Initiative, 1989–92* (Basingstoke: Macmillan, 1998).

Bourke, Angela, *The Burning of Bridget Cleary* (London: Penguin, 1999).

Boylan, Henry, *A Dictionary of Irish Biography*, 3rd ed. (Dublin: Gill & Macmillan, 1998).

Brewer, John and Gareth Higgins, *Anti-Catholicism in Northern Ireland, 1600–1998: The Mote and the Beam* (Basingstoke: Macmillan, 1998).

Broderick, Marian, *Bold, Brilliant and Bad: Irish Women from History* (Dublin: O'Brien Press, 2018).

Browne, Harry, *The Frontman: Bono (In the Name of Power)* (London: Verso, 2013).

Bunbury, Turtle, *Ireland's Forgotten Past: A History of the Overlooked and Disremembered* (London: Thames & Hudson, 2020).

Burns, James MacGregor, *The Vineyard of Liberty* (New York: Vintage, 1982).

Carroll, James Robert, *One of Ourselves: John Fitzgerald Kennedy in Ireland* (Bennington, VT: Images from the Past, 2003).

Carstens, Patrick Richard and Timothy L. Sanford, *The Republic of Canada Almost* (Bloomington, IN: Xlibris Corporation, 2013).

Churchill, Winston S., *The World Crisis, Vol. IV: 1918–1928: The Aftermath* (London: Bloomsbury, 2015, first published 1929).

Cawthorne, Nigel, *Witches: The History of a Persecution* (London: Arcturus Publishing, 2019).

Cobain, Ian, *Cruel Britannia: A Secret History of Torture* (London: Portobello Books, 2012).

Coffey, Donal K., *Constitutionalism in Ireland, 1932–1938: National, Commonwealth, and International Perspectives* (Basingstoke: Palgrave Macmillan, 2018).

Coogan, Tim Pat, *Ireland In The 20th Century* (London: Arrow Books, 2004).

Coogan, Tim Pat, *Michael Collins: A Biography* (London: Head of Zeus, 2015).

Coogan, Tim Pat, *Wherever Green Is Worn: The*

Story of the Irish Diaspora (New York: Head of Zeus, 2015).

Coogan, Tim Pat, *The GAA and the War of Independence* (London: Head of Zeus, 2016).

Corless, Damian, *Looks Like Rain: 9,000 Years of Irish Weather* (Cork: Collins Press, 2013).

Cousins, James H. and Margaret E. Cousins, *We Two Together* (Madras: Ganesh, 1950).

Crawford, Elizabeth, *The Women's Suffrage Movement in Britain and Ireland: A Regional Survey* (Abingdon: Routledge, 2013).

Crowley, Tony (ed.), *The Politics of Language in Ireland 1366–1922: A Sourcebook* (London: Routledge, 2000).

Curtis, Liz, *The Cause of Ireland* (London: Beyond the Pale, 1994).

Depuis, Nicola, *Mná na hÉireann: Women who Shaped Ireland* (Cork: Mercier Press, 2009).

De Rossa, Peter, *Rebels: The Irish Rising of 1916* (New York: Fawcett Columbine, 1990).

Devoy, John, *Recollections of an Irish Rebel* (Shannon: Irish University Press, 1929, reprint 1969).

Doherty, Gabriel and Dermot Keogh, '"Sorrow but no despair – the road is marked": the politics of funerals in post-1916 Ireland', in Gabriel Doherty and Dermot Keogh (eds), *Michael Collins and the Making of the Irish State* (Cork: Mercier Press, 2006).

Doherty, Richard, *In the Ranks of Death: The Irish in the Second World War* (Barnsley: Pen & Sword, 2010).

Dooley, Chris, *Redmond: A Life Undone* (Dublin: Gill & Macmillan, 2015).

Dorney, John, *The Civil War in Dublin: The Fight for the Irish Capital 1922–1924* (Newbridge: Merrion, 2017).

Doyle, Rose and Leo Quinlan, *Heroes of Jadotville* (Dublin: New Island Books, 2006).

Duffy, Patrick J., 'Wiring the countryside: Rural electrification in Ireland', in S. D. Brunn (ed.), *Engineering Earth: The Impacts of Megaengineering Projects* (Dordrecht: Springer, 2011).

Duffy, Sean, *Medieval Ireland: An Encyclopedia* (New York: Routledge, 2005).

Dunlap, Orin Elmer, *Marconi: The Man and His Wireless* (New York: Macmillan, 1937).

Edmonds, Sean, *The Gun, the Law and the Irish People* (Tralee: Anvil Books, 1971).

Ellmann, Richard, *James Joyce* (New York: Oxford University Press, 1982).

English, Richard, *Armed Struggle: A History of the IRA* (Oxford: Oxford University Press, 2008).

English, Richard, *Irish Freedom: The History of Nationalism in Ireland* (London: Macmillan, 2008).

Ferriter, Diarmaid, *The Transformation of Ireland 1900–2000* (London: Profile, 2010).

Ferriter, Diarmaid, *Ambiguous Republic: Ireland in the 1970s* (London: Profile Books, 2012).

Fisk, Robert, *The Point of No Return: The Strike Which Broke the British in Ulster* (London: Times Books/André Deutsch, 1975).

Fisk, Robert, *In Time of War: Ireland, Ulster and the Price of Neutrality 1939-45* (London: André Deutsch Limited, 1983).

Flewelling, Lindsey, *Two Irelands Beyond the Sea: Ulster Unionism and America, 1880–1920*

(Liverpool: Liverpool University Press. 2018).

Forbes, Robert Bennet, *The Voyage of the Jamestown on Her Errand of Mercy* (Boston: Eastburn Press, 1847).

Flynn, Barry, *Pawns in the Game: Irish Hunger Strikes, 1912–1981* (Wilton: Collins Press, 2011).

Foster, R. F., *W. B. Yeats: A Life II: The Arch-Poet 1915–1939* (Oxford: Oxford University Press, 2003).

Galvin, Anthony, *Blood on the Streets: A Murderous History of Limerick* (Edinburgh: Mainstream Publishing, 2013).

Geoghegan, Patrick M., *King Dan: The Rise of Daniel O'Connell 1775–1829* (Dublin: Gill & Macmillan, 2008).

Gordon, R. Michael, *Alias Jack the Ripper: Beyond the Usual Whitechapel Suspects* (Jefferson, NC: McFarland, 2000).

Grayson, Richard, *Dublin's Great Wars: The First World War, the Easter Rising and the Irish Revolution* (Cambridge: Cambridge University Press, 2018).

Gregory, Kenneth (ed.), *The Last Cuckoo: The Very Best Letters to the Times since 1900* (London: Akadine, 1996).

Grehan, John and Martin Mace, *British Battles of the Napoleonic Wars: Despatched from the Front* (Barnsley: Pen & Sword, 2013).

Griffith, Lisa Marie, *Stones of Dublin: A History of Dublin in Ten Buildings* (Cork: Collins Press, 2014).

Grob-Fitzgibbon, Benjamin, *Turning Points of the Irish Revolution: The British Government, Intelligence, and the Cost of Indifference, 1912–1921* (Basingstoke: Palgrave Macmillan, 2007).

Gwynn, Denis, *The Life of John Redmond* (London: George G. Harrap & Co., 1932).

Harris, J. Paul, 'Great Britain', in Richard F. Hamilton and Holger H. Herwig (eds), *The Origins of World War I* (Cambridge: Cambridge University Press, 2003), pp. 266–99.

Hayes, Richard Francis, *The Last Invasion of Ireland: When Connacht Rose* (M. H. Gill and Son, 1937).

Haywood, John, *The Celts: Bronze Age to New Age* (Abingdon: Routledge, 2014).

Henry, Robert Mitchell, *The Evolution of Sinn Fein* (Dublin: Talbot Press, 1920).

Hess, Earl J., *Pickett's Charge: The Last Attack at Gettysburg* (Chapel Hill, NC: University of North Carolina Press, 2001).

Hewitt, James, *Eye-Witnesses to Ireland in Revolt* (Reading: Osprey Publishing, 1974).

Hogan, Robert and Richard Burnham, *The Years of O'Casey, 1921–1926: a Documentary History* (Newark, DE: University of Delaware, 1992).

Home Government Association, *Report of the Inaugural Public Meeting of the Home Government Association* (Dublin, 1870).

Ignatiev, Noel, *How the Irish Became White* (London: Routledge, 1995).

Jobling, Job, *U2: The Definitive Biography* (New York: Thomas Dunne Books, 2014).

Johnson, Keith and Michael Flynn, 'Convicts of the Queen', in Bob Reece (ed.), *Exiles from Erin* (Basingstoke: Macmillan, 1991).

Johnston, Roy, *The Musical Life of Nineteenth-Century Belfast* (Farnham: Ashgate, 2015).

Jones, David S., 'The cleavage between graziers and peasants in the land struggle, 1890–1910', in Samuel Clark and James S. Donnelly Jr (eds), *Irish Peasants: Violence and Political Unrest, 1780–1914* (Madison, WI: University of Wisconsin Press, 1983).

Joyce, Patrick, *The State of Freedom: A Social History of the British State since 1800* (Cambridge: Cambridge University Press, 2013).

Joyce, Patrick Weston, *A Concise History of Ireland from the Earliest Times to 1608* (London: Longmans, Green, 1904).

Kanter, Douglas, *The Making of British Unionism, 1740–1848* (Dublin: Four Courts Press, 2009).

Kearns, Kevin C., *Ireland's Arctic Siege: The Big Freeze of 1947* (Dublin: Gill & Macmillan, 2011).

Kee, Robert, *The Green Flag: A History of Irish Nationalism* (London: Penguin, 2000).

Kelly, James, *Poynings' Law and the Making of Law in Ireland 1660–1800: Monitoring the Constitution* (Dublin: Four Courts Press, 2007).

Kelly, Mary, *Ireland's Great Famine in Irish American History: Enshrining a Fateful Memory* (Lanham, MD: Rowman & Littlefield, 2014).

Kennedy, Liam, *Unhappy the Land: The Most Oppressed People Ever, the Irish?* (Dublin: Irish Academic Press, 2015).

Kennedy, Michael, *Division and Consensus: The Politics of Cross-Border Relations in Ireland, 1925–1969* (Dublin: Institute of Public Administration, 2000).

Kerr, Donal A., *'A Nation of Beggars'? Priests, People and Politics in Famine Ireland, 1846–1852* (Oxford: Clarendon Press, 1994).

Kerr, Gordon and Phil Clarke, *Hostages: Dramatic Accounts of Real-Life Events* (London: Futura, 2009).

Kinealy, Christine, *Daniel O'Connell and the Anti-Slavery Movement: 'The Saddest People the Sun Sees'* (Abingdon: Routledge, 2015).

Kissane, Noel, *Parnell: A Documentary History* (Dublin: National Library of Ireland, 1991).

Klein, Christopher, *When the Irish Invaded Canada: The Incredible True Story of the Civil War Veterans Who Fought for Ireland's Freedom* (New York: Penguin Random House, 2020).

Kurzman, Dan, *Genesis 1948: The First Arab–Israeli War* (New York: World Publishing, 1970).

Laffan, Brigid and Jane O'Mahony, *Ireland and the European Union* (Basingstoke: Palgrave Macmillan, 2008).

Lee, Celia, *HRH The Duke of Kent: A Life of Service* (London: Seymour Books, 2015).

Lee, Joseph, *The Modernisation of Irish Society 1848–1918* (Dublin: Gill & Macmillan, 2008).

Levenson, Leah, and Jerry H. Natterstad, *Hanna Sheehy-Skeffington: Irish Feminist* (Syracuse, NY: Syracuse University Press, 1986).

Lucey, Charles, *Harp and Sword, 1776: The Irish*

in the American Revolution (Washington, DC: Charles Lucey, 1976).

Lunney, Linde, 'Mulvany, Isabella Marion Jane (1854–1934)', *Dictionary of Irish Biography* (Cambridge: Cambridge University Press, 2009).

Lynch, John, *Speeches and Statements on Irish Unity, Northern Ireland, Anglo-Irish relations, August 1969–October 1971* (Dublin: Government Information Bureau, 1972).

Lynch, Patrick and John Vaizey, *Guinness's Brewery in the Irish Economy, 1759–1876* (Cambridge: Cambridge University Press, 1960).

Lydon, James, *The Making of Ireland: From Ancient Times to the Present* (Abingdon: Routledge, 2012).

Mac Giolla Chríost, Diarmait, *The Irish Language in Ireland: From Goídel to Globalisation* (Abingdon: Routledge, 2005).

MacNeill, John Gordon Swift, *How the Union was Carried* (London: Kegan Paul, Trench & Co., 1887).

Macrae, Alasdair D. F., *W. B. Yeats: A Literary Life* (Basingstoke: Macmillan, 1995).

Mac Shamhráin, Ailbhe, 'The Battle of Glenn Máma, Dublin and the High-Kingship of Ireland: A Millennial Commemoration', in Seán Duffy (ed.), *Medieval Dublin II* (Dublin: Four Courts Press, 2001).

Madden, Richard Robert, *The United Irishmen, Their Lives and Times* (London: J. Madden, 1842).

Malloch, Hedley, *The Killing of the Iron Twelve* (Barnsley: Pen & Sword, 2019).

Manganiello, Stephen, *Concise Encyclopedia of the Revolutions and Wars of England, Scotland, and Ireland, 1639–1660* (Lanham, MD: Rowman & Littlefield, 2004).

Martin, F. X., 'Diarmait Mac Murchada and the coming of the Anglo-Normans', in Art Cosgrave (ed.), *A New History of Ireland, Vol. 2: Medieval Ireland, 1169–1534* (Oxford: Oxford University Press, 1987).

Matthew, Colin, *Gladstone 1809–1898* (Oxford: Clarendon Press, 1997).

May, Allyson N., *The Fox Hunting Controversy 1781–2004: Class and Cruelty* (Farnham: Ashgate, 2013).

McCabe, Ian, *A Diplomatic History of Ireland 1948–1949: The Republic, the Commonwealth and NATO* (Dublin: Irish Academic Press, 1991).

McCarthy, M. J. F., *Five Years in Ireland 1895–1900* (Dublin: Hodges, Figgis, 1901).

McCracken, Mr Justice B., *Report of the Tribunal of Inquiry (Dunnes Payments)* (Dublin: Stationery Office, 1997).

McCullagh, David, *John A. Costello, the Reluctant Taoiseach* (Dublin: Mercier Press, 2010).

McDonald, Henry and Jim Cusack, *UVF: The Endgame* (Dublin: Poolbeg, 2008).

McGarry, Fearghal, *Eoin O'Duffy: A Self-Made Hero* (Oxford: Oxford University Press, 2005).

McGarry, Stephen, *Irish Brigades Abroad: From the Wild Geese to the Napoleonic Wars* (Dublin: History Press, 2013).

McGuirk, Brian, *Celtic FC: the Ireland*

Connection (Edinburgh: Black & White Publishing, 2013).

McKerns, Gerald, *The Black Rock that Built America: A Tribute to the Anthracite Coal Miners* (New York: Xlibris, 2007).

McKittrick, David, *Lost Lives: The Stories of the Men, Women, and Children Who Died as a Result of the Northern Ireland Troubles* (Edinburgh: Mainstream, 2001).

McLoone, Martin and John MacMahon, *Television and Irish Society: 21 Years of Irish Television* (Dublin: Raidio Telefís Éireann, 1984).

Meagher, Thomas Francis, *Speeches on the Legislative Independence of Ireland* (New York: Redfield, 1853).

Miller, Ian, *A History of Force Feeding: Hunger Strikes, Prisons and Medical Ethics, 1909–1974* (Basingstoke: Palgrave Macmillan, 2016).

Mitchell, Angus, *One Bold Deed of Open Treason: The Berlin Diary of Roger Casement, 1914–1916* (Sallins: Merrion Press, 2016).

Mitchell, Arthur and Pádraig Ó Snodaigh (eds), *Irish Political Documents: 1916–1945* (Dublin: Irish Academic Press, 1985).

Mooney, Thomas, *A History of Ireland from Its First Settlement to the Present Time* (Boston: Patrick Donahoe, 1845).

Moore, Cormac, *The GAA v Douglas Hyde: The Removal of Ireland's First President as GAA Patron* (Cork: Collins Press, 2012).

Morrison, Robert, *The Regency Years: During Which Jane Austen Writes, Napoleon Fights, Byron Makes Love, and Britain Becomes Modern* (New York: W. W. Norton & Company, 2019).

Moses, Paul, *An Unlikely Union: The Love–Hate Story of New York's Irish and Italians* (New York: New York University Press, 2017).

Moysey, Steve, *The Road to Balcombe Street: The IRA Reign of Terror in London* (Abingdon: Routledge, 2008).

Mullally, Una, *In the Name of Love: The Movement for Marriage Equality in Ireland, an Oral History* (Dublin: History Press Ireland, 2014).

Mulroe, Patrick, *Bombs, Bullets and the Border – Policing Ireland's Frontier: Irish Security Policy, 1969–1978* (Newbridge: Irish Academic Press, 2017).

Murphy, Denis, *Cromwell in Ireland: A History of Cromwell's Irish Campaign* (Dublin: M. H. Gill & Son, 1883).

Naughtie, James (ed.), *Playing the Palace: A Westminster Collection* (Edinburgh: Mainstream, 1984).

Nevin, Donal, *James Larkin: Lion of the Fold* (Dublin: Gill & Macmillan, 2014).

New Ireland Forum Report (Dublin: Stationery Office, 1984).

Norman, Diana, *Terrible Beauty: A Life of Constance Markievicz* (London: Hodder & Stoughton, 1987).

Norton, Rictor, 'Atherton, John', in Robert Aldrich and Garry Wotherspoon (eds), *Who's Who in Gay and Lesbian History: From Antiquity to the Mid-Twentieth Century* (Abingdon: Routledge, 2020).

Northern Ireland Civil Rights Association, *'We*

Shall Overcome' … The History of the Struggle for Civil Rights in Northern Ireland 1968–1978 (Belfast: Northern Ireland Civil Rights Association, 1978).

Oakley, Robin, *Sixty Years of Jump Racing: From Arkle to McCoy* (London: Bloomsbury Sport, 2017).

Oates, Ken, and Tony Topham, *The Making of the Labour Movement. The Formation of the Transport and General Workers' Union 1870–1922* (Nottingham: Spokesman, 1994).

O'Ballance, Edgar, *Terror in Ireland: The Heritage of Hate* (Novato, CA: Presidio Press, 1981).

Ó Beacháin, Donnacha, *Destiny of the Soldiers—Fianna Fáil, Irish Republicanism and the IRA, 1926–1973: The History of Ireland's Largest and Most Successful Political Party* (Dublin: Gill & Macmillan, 2014).

O'Brien, Conor Cruise, *Herod: Reflections on Political Violence* (London: Hutchinson, 1978).

O'Brien, Michael J., *A Hidden Phase of American History: Ireland's Part in America's Struggle for Liberty* (New York: Dodd, Mead, and Company, 1920).

O'Brien, Paul, *Havoc: The Auxiliaries in Ireland's War of Independence* (Cork: Collins Press, 2017).

O'Brien, Richard Barry, *Thomas Drummond Under-Secretary in Ireland 1835–40: Life and Letters* (London: Kegan Paul, 1889).

Ó Cathaoir, Brendan, *John Blake Dillon, Young Irelander* (Dublin: Irish Academic Press, 1990).

O'Clery, Conor, *Ireland in Quotes* (Dublin: O'Brien Press, 1999).

O'Connell, Daniel, *The Life and Speeches*, edited by John O'Connell (Dublin: J. Duffy, 1846).

O'Connor, T. P., *Lord Beaconsfield: A Biography* (London: W. Mullen, 1879).

O'Day, A. and J. Stevenson (eds), *Irish Historical Documents since 1800* (Dublin: Gill & Macmillan, 1992).

O'Day, Alan, *Irish Home Rule, 1867–1921* (Manchester: Manchester University Press, 1998).

O'Donoghue, Florence, *Tomas MacCurtain* (Tralee: Kerryman, 1958).

O'Dowd, Niall, *A New Ireland: How Europe's Most Conservative Country Became Its Most Liberal* (New York: Skyhorse, 2020).

Ó Faoleán, Gearóid, *A Broad Church: The Provisional IRA in the Republic of Ireland 1969–1980* (Newbridge: Irish Academic Print 2019).

O'Ferrall, Fergus, *Daniel O'Connell* (Dublin: Gill & Macmillan, 1981).

Ó Gráda, Cormac, *A Rocky Road. The Irish Economy since the 1920s* (Manchester: Manchester University Press, 1997).

O'Keefe, C. M., *The Life and Times of Daniel O'Connell* (Dublin: John Mullany, 1864).

O'Leary, Brendan, *A Treatise on Northern Ireland, Volume I: Colonialism* (Oxford: Oxford University Press 2019).

O'Malley, Ernie, *The Singing Flame* (Dublin: Anvil Books, 1978).

Ó Ruairc, Pádraig Óg, *Truce: Murder, Myth and the Last Days of the Irish War of Independence*

(Cork: Mercier Press, 2016).

Owen, Arwel Ellis, *The Anglo-Irish Agreement: The First Three Years* (Cardiff: University of Wales Press, 1994).

Parris, James, *The Man in the Brown Suit: MI5, Edward VIII and an Irish Assassin* (Cheltenham: History Press, 2019).

Pearse, Patrick, *The Letters of P. H. Pearse,* edited by Seamas O'Buachalla (Atlantic Highlands, NJ: Humanities Press, 1980).

Perry, Robert, *Revisionist Scholarship and Modern Irish Politics* (Farnham: Ashgate, 2013).

Phillips, Walter Alison, *The Revolution in Ireland* (London: Longmans, Green and Company, 1923).

Rees, Merlyn, *Northern Ireland: A Personal Perspective* (London: Methuen, 1985).

Restorick, Rita, *Death of a Soldier: A Mother's Search for Peace in Northern Ireland* (Belfast: Blackstaff, 2000).

Reynolds, Andrew, *The Children of Harvey Milk* (Oxford: Oxford University Press, 2018).

Richey, Alexander George, *A Short History of the Irish People* (Dublin: Hodges, Figgis and Company, 1887).

Rourke, Richard, *Peace in Ireland: The War of Ideas* (London: Pimlico, 2003).

Rouse, Paul, *Sport and Ireland: A History* (Oxford: Oxford University Press, 2015).

Rowe, Frederick William, *A History of Newfoundland and Labrador* (Toronto: McGraw-Hill Ryerson, 1980).

Rowe, Peter, *The Impact of Human Rights Law on Armed Forces* (Cambridge: Cambridge University Press, 2006).

Ryan, Desmond, *The Rising: The Complete Story of Easter Week* (Dublin: Golden Eagle, 1949).

Ryan, Louise, *Irish Feminism and the Vote: An Anthology of the Irish Citizen Newspaper* (Dublin: Folens, 1996).

Sharrock, David and Mark Devenport, *Man of War, Man of Peace? The Unauthorised Biography of Gerry Adams* (London: Macmillan, 1997).

Sherlock, Thomas and J. S. Mahoney, *The Life and Times of Charles Stewart Parnell* (New York: Murphy and McCarthy, 1881).

Shiels, Damian, *The Irish in the American Civil War* (Dublin: History Press, 2013).

Sigillito, Gina, *Daughters of Maeve* (New York: Citadel, 2007).

Slide, Anthony, *A Special Relationship: Britain Comes to Hollywood and Hollywood Comes to Britain* (Jackson: University Press of Mississippi, 2015).

Taaffe, Carol, *Ireland Through the Looking-Glass: Flann O'Brien, Myles Na GCopaleen and Irish Cultural Debate* (Cork: Cork University Press, 2008).

Taylor, Peter, *Provos: The IRA and Sinn Féin* (London: Bloomsbury, 1998).

Taylor, Peter, *Brits: The War against the IRA* (London: Bloomsbury, 2001).

Trotter, Mary, 'Gregory, Yeats and Ireland's Abbey Theatre', in Mary Luckhurst (ed.), *A Companion to Modern British and Irish Drama, 1880–2005* (Oxford: Blackwell, 2008).

Van Pelt, Lori, *Amelia Earhart: The Sky's No*

Limit (New York: Tom Doherty Associates, 2005).

Valiulis, Maryann Gialanella, *Portrait of a Revolutionary: General Richard Mulcahy and the Founding of the Irish Free State* (Lexington, KY: University Press of Kentucky, 1992).

Verge, Patricia, *Equals and Partners: A Spiritual Journey Toward Reconciliation and Oneness* (Victoria, Canada: FriesenPress, 2018).

Wallace, Martin, *Drums and Guns: Revolution in Ulster* (London: Geoffrey Chapman, 1970).

Walsh, Dick, *Des O'Malley: A Political Profile* (Dingle: Brandon, 1986).

Watt, David, *The Constitution of Northern Ireland: Problems and Prospects* (Farnham: Ashgate, 1981).

Weatherhill, Rob, *The Anti-Oedipus Complex: Lacan, Postmodernism and Philosophy* (New York: Routledge, 2017).

Whelan, Yvonne, *Reinventing Modern Dublin: Streetscape, Iconography and the Politics of Identity* (Dublin: UCD Press, 2003).

White, Robert W., *Out of the Ashes: An Oral History of the Provisional Irish Republican Movement* (Newbridge: Merrion Press, 2017).

Williams, Joseph A., *The Sunken Gold: A Story of World War I Espionage and the Greatest Salvage in History* (Chicago: Chicago Review Press Incorporated, 2017).

Williams, Paul, *Badfellas* (Dublin: Penguin, 2011).

Wills, Clair, *That Neutral Island: A Cultural History of Ireland during the Second World War* (London: Faber, 2007).

Woodham-Smith, Cecil, *The Great Hunger: Ireland 1845–1849* (London: Penguin, 1962).

Woosley, Anne I. and Arizona Historical Society, *Early Tucson* (Charleston, SC: Arcadia Publishing, 2008).

Television/Online media

'Ann Lovett: The story that couldn't remain local', *Scannál*, RTÉ, 23 February 2004.

'Bob Geldof Live Aid and the generous Irish', *Morning Ireland*, 16 July 1985 (www.rte.ie/archives/2015/0713/714508-bob-geldof-on-live-aid/, accessed 5 May 2021).

'Brian Keenan is free from captivity', *This Week*, 26 August 1990 (www.rte.ie/archives/2015/0824/723162-brian-keenan-released/, accessed 6 May 2021).

'Derrynaflan chalice unearthed in County Tipperary', *RTÉ News*, 1 May 1980 (www.rte.ie/archives/2015/0217/680773-discovery-of-derrynaflan-chalice/, accessed 19 April 2021).

'Finding solutions to the Troubles', RTÉ News, 2 May 1984 (www.rte.ie/archives/2014/0502/614662-new-ireland-forum-report-1984/, accessed 10 May 2021).

'First British Prime Minister to address Dáil', *RTÉ News*, 26 November 1998 (www.rte.ie/archives/2018/1122/1012676-tony-blair-addresses-dail/, accessed 2 May 2021).

'Guildford Four Free', *RTÉ News*, 19 October 1989 (www.rte.ie/archives/2014/1017/652817-guildford-four-released-from-prison/, accessed 2 May 2021).

'Lifeboat men perish', *RTÉ News*, 24 December 1995 (www.rte.ie/archives/2015/1221/755386-kingstown-lifeboat-tragedy/?imz_s=n4fq9jad4aa21fjmohaodb7d05, accessed 4 May 2021).

'A new chapter in Anglo-Irish relations', *RTÉ News*, 8 December 1980 (www.rte.ie/archives/2015/1201/750438-haughey-on-thatcher-talks/, accessed 3 May 2021).

'Northern Ireland can work together', *RTÉ News*, 10 December 1973 (www.rte.ie/archives/2018/1203/1014816-sunningdale-agreement-signed/, accessed 3 May 2021).

'Peter Robinson arrested', *RTÉ News*, 7 August 1986 (www.rte.ie/archives/collections/news/21221527-peter-robinson-arrested/, accessed 6 May 2021).

'Reaction to Cameron Report', RTÉ News, 1969 (www.rte.ie/archives/exhibitions/1031-civil-rights-movement-1968-9/1041-cameron-report/, accessed 6 May 2021).

'Scandal of the Rose Tattoo at the Pike Theatre', RTÉ News, 23 October 2002 (www.rte.ie/archives/2017/0522/877010-the-rose-tattoo-scandal/, accessed 5 May 2021).

Oireachtas

Dáil Éireann debate – Saturday, 7 January 1922. Debate on Treaty. www.oireachtas.ie/en/debates/debate/dail/1922-01-07/2/

Dáil Éireann debate – Friday, 8 December 1922. Debate on Mountjoy executions. www.oireachtas.ie/en/debates/debate/dail/1922-12-08/9/

Dáil Éireann debate – Friday, 11 December 1936. Constitution (Amendment No. 27) Bill, 1936—Second Stage. www.oireachtas.ie/en/debates/debate/dail/1936-12-11/12/

Dáil Éireann debate – Saturday, 2 September 1939. First Amendment of the Constitution Bill, 1939—First Stage. www.oireachtas.ie/en/debates/debate/dail/1939-09-02/3/

Dáil Éireann debate – Thursday, 4 July 1957. Fethard-on-Sea boycott. www.oireachtas.ie/en/debates/debate/dail/1957-07-04/18/

Dáil Éireann debate – Thursday, 29 March 1979. Health (Family Planning) Bill, 1978: Second Stage (Resumed). www.oireachtas.ie/en/debates/debate/dail/1979-03-29/4/

Dáil Éireann debate – Friday, 4 June 1984. Address by President Reagan. www.oireachtas.ie/en/debates/debate/dail/1984-06-04/2/

Dáil Éireann debate – Wednesday, 26 June 1996. Killing of Dublin journalist. www.oireachtas.ie/en/debates/debate/dail/1996-06-26/23/

Dáil Éireann debate – Wednesday, 16 October 1996. Hepatitis C infection: Statements. www.oireachtas.ie/en/debates/debate/dail/1996-10-16/16/

Dáil Éireann debate – Thursday, 19 December 1996. Personal statement by member. www.oireachtas.ie/en/debates/debate/dail/1996-12-19/18/

Dáil Éireann debate – Friday, 2 July 1999. Adjournment of Dáil: Motion. www.oireachtas.ie/en/debates/debate/dail/1999-07-02/9/

Seanad Éireann debate – Wednesday, 12 March 2008. Air accident Investigations. debatesarchive.oireachtas.ie/Debates%20 Authoring/debateswebpack.nsf/takes/ seanad2008031200009?opendocument

Dáil Éireann debate – Wednesday, 19 February 2013. Magdalen Laundries Report: Statements. www.oireachtas.ie/en/debates/ debate/dail/2013-02-19/29/

Seanad Éireann debate – Wednesday, 18 June 2014. 750th anniversary of first Irish parliament. www.oireachtas.ie/ga/debates/ debate/seanad/2014-06-18/11/

Miscellaneous

Carter, Jimmy, 'Northern Ireland: Statement on U.S. policy', *The American Presidency Project*, 30 August 1977.

Clinton, Bill, 'Statement on the cease-fire in Northern Ireland', *Public Papers of the Presidents of the United States,* 19 July 1997.

Disturbances in Northern Ireland: Report of the Commission Appointed by the Governor of Northern Ireland, Honourable Lord Cameron, D.S.C., Chairman. Cmd. 523 (Belfast: Her Majesty's Stationery Office, 1969).

House of Commons debate – Tuesday, 13 March 1832. Tithes (Ireland). api.parliament.uk/historic-hansard/ commons/1832/mar/13/tithes-ireland.

House of Commons debate – Thursday, 11 November 1920. Government of Ireland Bill. api.parliament.uk/historic-hansard/ commons/1920/nov/11/government-of-ireland-bill

House of Commons debate – Monday, 18 December 1985. Anglo-Irish Agreement. api.parliament.uk/historic-hansard/ commons/1985/nov/18/anglo-irish-agreement

House of Commons debate – Wednesday, 27 December 1985. Anglo-Irish Agreement. api.parliament.uk/historic-hansard/ commons/1985/nov/27/anglo-irish-agreement

Ireland Today, Issues 856–878 (Dublin: Information Section, Department of Foreign Affairs, 1974).

Public statement by the Police Ombudsman under Section 62 of the Police (Northern Ireland) Act 1998 Relating to the complaint by the relatives of the victims of the bombing of McGurk's Bar, Belfast on 4 December 1971, Police Ombudsman for Northern Ireland (PONI), 21 February 2011.

Chronology

9 June 597	Death of St Colmcille	158
30 December 999	The Battle of Glenn Máma	331
23 April 1014	The Battle of Clontarf	116
1 May 1169	Norman invasion of Wexford	123
23 August 1170	Strongbow lands in Waterford	222
6 October 1175	Treaty of Windsor is signed	260
12 November 1216	Magna Carta Hiberniae	291
1 April 1234	The Battle of the Curragh	97
18 June 1264	Earliest recorded meeting of an Irish parliament	167
26 May 1315	Edward Bruce arrives in Ireland	146
10 May 1318	The Battle of Dysert O'Dea	131
3 November 1324	Petronilla de Meath is burned at the stake	284
25 December 1351	William Buí O'Kelly hosts Christmas feast	327
18 February 1366	The Statutes of Kilkenny	61
1 December 1494	Poynings' parliament is summoned	308
19 August 1504	The Battle of Knockdoe	219
6 September 1593	Grace O'Malley meets Elizabeth I	234
11 March 1597	Explosion destroys Dublin quays	79
3 January 1602	The Battle of Kinsale	21
14 September 1607	The Flight of the Earls	242
20 June 1631	The Sack of Baltimore	168
5 December 1640	John Atherton is hanged	311

24 October 1641	Phelim O'Neill issues Proclamation of Dungannon	275
19 March 1642	Adventurers' Act is passed	86
28 March 1646	The first Ormond Peace	94
11 September 1649	Siege of Drogheda ends	239
27 March 1650	Kilkenny surrenders to Cromwell	93
9 May 1671	Thomas Blood steals the Crown Jewels of England	130
28 August 1676	Irish donation to Massachusetts	227
16 November 1688	Ann Glover is hanged in Boston	295
14 June 1690	William of Orange lands at Carrickfergus	163
1 July 1690	The Battle of the Boyne	178
12 July 1691	The Battle of Aughrim	187
22 December 1691	The Flight of the Wild Geese	325
13 April 1742	Handel's *Messiah* makes world debut in Dublin	108
15 March 1745	First maternity hospital in the British Empire is founded	82
11 May 1745	The Battle of Fontenoy	132
31 December 1759	Brewery is leased to Arthur Guinness	332
20 August 1775	Tucson, Arizona is founded by Hugh O'Conor	220
7 April 1776	John Barry leads capture of HMS *Edward*	102
16 April 1782	Henry Grattan: 'Ireland is now a nation'	110
14 July 1789	James F. X. Whyte is 'liberated' from the Bastille	189
26 September 1791	The *Queen* convict ship arrives in Sydney	252
18 October 1791	Inaugural meeting of United Irishmen	270
11 July 1792	Meeting of the Harpers in Belfast	186
13 October 1792	James Hoban oversees White House construction	266
5 June 1798	The Battle of New Ross	155
8 September 1798	The Battle of Ballinamuck	236
10 November 1798	Wolfe Tone's speech from the dock	290
6 February 1800	Irish parliament approves the Act of Union	51
23 July 1803	Robert Emmet's rebellion	196
25 August 1803	Robert Emmet is arrested	224
4 March 1804	Castle Hill rebellion	74

20 November 1807	Sinking of *Rochdale* and *Prince of Wales*	298
1 February 1815	Daniel O'Connell duels with John Norcott D'Esterre	47
29 October 1816	Burning of Wildgoose Lodge	279
22 July 1822	'Martin's Law' is introduced by Galway MP	196
24 January 1824	Daniel O'Connell introduces Catholic Rent	40
5 July 1828	Daniel O'Connell is elected in Clare	181
4 September 1828	Annaghdown boating tragedy	233
3 March 1831	First clash of Tithe War	73
22 February 1832	First interment in Glasnevin Cemetery	64
23 January 1834	St Vincent's is founded: first hospital staffed by women	39
17 December 1834	First dedicated commuter railway line opens	321
18 December 1834	Rathcormac massacre	321
6 January 1839	The Night of the Big Wind	23
28 January 1842	Address from the People of Ireland is read in Boston	43
15 October 1842	First issue of *The Nation* is published	267
1 October 1843	O'Connell's last 'monster meeting', Mullaghmast	256
7 October 1843	Daniel O'Connell cancels rally in Clontarf	261
16 October 1843	William Rowan Hamilton discovers quaternions	268
3 June 1844	Hypodermic needle is used for first time	153
9 February 1846	Robert Mallet presents paper on earthquakes	54
13 March 1846	Ballinlass evictions	81
13 January 1847	Queen Victoria appeals for famine relief	29
23 March 1847	Choctaw Nation raises money for famine relief	89
2 November 1847	Killing of Denis Mahon	283
14 April 1848	Irish tricolour is unveiled for the first time	108
29 July 1848	Young Ireland rebellion	201
30 March 1849	The Doolough Tragedy	95
3 July 1863	The 69th Pennsylvania repels Pickett's charge	180
2 June 1866	The Battle of Ridgeway	152
27 July 1866	First successful transatlantic telegraph cable	200
5 March 1867	Fenian Rising	74
23 November 1867	Manchester Martyrs are hanged	301
12 January 1870	Pope Pius condemns Fenianism	29

1 September 1870	Inaugural meeting of Home Government Organisation	230
5 January 1871	The Franco-Irish Ambulance Brigade is released from duty	22
8 October 1871	Catherine O'Leary is blamed for Great Chicago Fire	261
17 April 1876	The *Catalpa* rescue	111
10 January 1877	Eliza Walker Dunbar becomes first woman doctor	27
21 June 1877	Molly Maguires are executed	169
21 March 1879	First successful test of Brennan torpedo	87
21 August 1879	Apparition in Knock	221
2 February 1880	Parnell addresses House of Representatives	47
4 February 1880	The 'Black' Donnellys are murdered	49
19 September 1880	Parnell introduces 'boycotting'	246
20 October 1881	Land League is proscribed	272
6 May 1882	Phoenix Park murders	127
17 August 1882	The Maamtrasna murders	218
26 December 1883	Harbour Grace Affray	328
22 October 1884	Nine Graces are awarded degrees	274
1 November 1884	Gaelic Athletic Association is founded	282
8 April 1886	Gladstone introduces First Home Rule Bill	103
6 November 1887	Celtic football club is founded	286
13 November 1887	Bloody Sunday (London)	292
9 November 1888	Last Jack the Ripper victim is killed	289
17 November 1890	Parnell is named in O'Shea divorce case	296
1 January 1892	Annie Moore passes through Ellis Island	19
25 November 1892	'The Necessity for De-Anglicising Ireland'	303
31 July 1893	The Gaelic League is founded	203
22 March 1895	Discovery of Bridget Cleary's body	88
5 April 1895	Oscar Wilde is arrested	100
24 December 1895	Kingstown lifeboat disaster	326
19 February 1901	Irish is spoken in the House of Commons	62
5 August 1901	Peter O'Connor sets world record for long jump	207
7 July 1903	Mother Jones leads the March of the Mill Children	183
14 August 1903	Wyndham Land Act is passed	215

2 January 1904	Arthur Griffith publishes 'The Resurrection of Hungary'	20
10 June 1904	James Joyce meets Nora Barnacle	159
17 July 1904	Camogie is first played in public	191
27 October 1904	New York City Subway opens	278
27 December 1904	Abbey Theatre opens	329
14 October 1906	Laurence Ginnell launches Ranch War	267
6 July 1907	Theft of the Irish Crown Jewels	182
24 July 1907	Police strike in Belfast	197
17 October 1907	Wireless message is sent from Clifden to Nova Scotia	269
4 November 1908	Irish Women's Franchise League is formed	284
4 January 1909	The Irish Transport and General Workers' Union is founded	21
30 November 1909	'People's budget' sparks Constitutional crisis	307
20 December 1909	James Joyce opens Ireland's first cinema	323
31 August 1910	Lilian Bland pilots her own plane	230
23 September 1911	Edward Carson first addresses Belfast supporters	249
31 March 1912	Home Rule monster meeting in Dublin	96
9 April 1912	Balmoral anti-Home Rule demonstration	104
13 June 1912	Members of Irish Women's Franchise League are arrested	162
18 July 1912	Suffragettes protest Asquith's Dublin visit	192
28 September 1912	The Ulster Covenant is signed	253
26 August 1913	Dublin Lockout begins	225
27 September 1913	SS *Hare* relieves Dublin strikers	252
5 November 1913	William Mulholland turns on Los Angeles Aqueduct	285
20 March 1914	The Curragh incident	87
26 July 1914	Bachelors Walk killings	199
8 August 1914	Arthur Griffith opposes Irish involvement in First World War	210
18 September 1914	Government of Ireland Act is signed into law	245
24 September 1914	Irish Volunteers split	250
25 February 1915	Execution of the Iron 12	67
7 May 1915	Sinking of the *Lusitania*	128
1 August 1915	Graveside oration for O'Donovan Rossa	204

19 April 1916	'Castle Document' is read at Dublin Corporation meeting	112
21 April 1916	Roger Casement is arrested	114
24 April 1916	Easter Rising begins	117
26 April 1916	Killing of Francis Sheehy-Skeffington	119
27 April 1916	Hulluch gas attacks	120
28 April 1916	The Battle of Ashbourne	120
29 April 1916	Easter Rising ends	121
15 September 1916	Walter Gordon Wilson's tanks are first used	242
18 November 1916	The Battle of the Somme ends	296
25 January 1917	Sinking of the *Laurentic*	41
5 February 1917	George Plunkett is elected abstentionist MP	50
8 June 1917	Butte mining disaster	157
25 July 1917	First meeting of the Irish Convention	198
25 September 1917	Thomas Ashe dies on hunger strike	251
4 August 1918	Gaelic Sunday	206
10 October 1918	Sinking of RMS *Leinster*	263
14 December 1918	Sinn Féin wins a majority of Irish seats	318
21 January 1919	The first sitting of Dáil Éireann	37
3 February 1919	Éamon de Valera escapes from Lincoln Prison	48
15 June 1919	Alcock and Brown land in Galway	164
11 November 1919	First Armistice Day in Ireland	290
25 March 1920	Black and Tans arrive in Ireland	91
19 June 1920	The Listowel Mutiny	167
20 September 1920	The Sack of Balbriggan	246
21 November 1920	Bloody Sunday (Dublin)	299
28 November 1920	Kilmichael Ambush	305
11 December 1920	The Burning of Cork	316
23 December 1920	Government of Ireland Act is given royal assent	326
3 May 1921	Partition of Ireland	125
22 June 1921	George V opens Northern Ireland parliament	170
9 July 1921	Truce in War of Independence	185
7 January 1922	Dáil Éireann ratifies the Anglo-Irish Treaty	24
16 January 1922	Dublin Castle is handed over to Michael Collins	32

28 June 1922	The Civil War begins	175
30 June 1922	Public Record Office is destroyed	177
22 August 1922	Michael Collins is shot dead	222
6 December 1922	Irish Free State is established	312
24 May 1923	The Civil War ends	144
29 February 1924	Last killing of a Dublin Metropolitan Police officer	70
2 August 1924	First modern Tailteann Games	205
4 May 1925	Oonah Keogh becomes world's first woman stockbroker	125
11 June 1925	W. B. Yeats: 'We are no petty people'	160
3 December 1925	Boundary Commission agreement	309
11 February 1926	W. B. Yeats: 'You have disgraced yourselves again'	55
5 September 1926	Dromcollogher fire	234
14 November 1926	IRA raids Garda stations	293
10 July 1927	Kevin O'Higgins is shot dead	186
11 August 1927	Éamon de Valera signs the oath of allegiance	212
28 October 1927	The Cleggan Bay disaster	278
12 April 1928	First transatlantic flight from east to west	107
30 July 1928	Pat O'Callaghan wins gold for Ireland at the Olympics	202
10 February 1932	Army Comrades Association is formed	54
16 February 1932	Fianna Fáil becomes largest party in Irish state	60
21 May 1932	Amelia Earhart lands in Co. Derry	141
27 May 1936	First Aer Lingus flight	147
16 July 1936	Assassination attempt on Edward VIII	191
12 December 1936	External Relations Act is signed into law	317
13 May 1937	Statue of George II is blown up	133
16 September 1937	Kirkintilloch disaster	243
29 December 1937	Constitution of Ireland comes into force	331
25 April 1938	Anglo-Irish Trade Agreement is signed	118
25 June 1938	Douglas Hyde becomes first President of Ireland	173
2 September 1939	The Emergency is declared	231
3 September 1939	Sinking of the SS *Athenia*	232
4 October 1940	First Brian O'Nolan column in the *Irish Times*	258
21 February 1941	First flight over the Donegal Corridor	64

15 April 1941	The Belfast Blitz	109
31 May 1941	The North Strand bombing	150
26 January 1942	First American troops arrive in Belfast	41
9 March 1942	Tom McGrath escapes German POW camp	78
15 July 1942	'Paddy' Finucane is shot down over the English Channel	190
23 February 1943	Fire in St Joseph's Orphanage	65
17 March 1943	Éamon de Valera's 'happy maidens' St Patrick's Day address	84
6 June 1944	Redmond Cunningham earns Military Cross on D-Day	155
2 May 1945	De Valera offers condolences to German minister	124
16 May 1945	De Valera responds to Winston Churchill	136
15 January 1947	Electricity is introduced to rural Ireland	31
19 January 1947	The Big Freeze begins	35
29 June 1948	Mike Flanagan steals tanks for Haganah	176
7 September 1948	Repeal of External Relations Act is announced	236
17 September 1948	W. B. Yeats is reinterred in Sligo	244
18 April 1949	Republic of Ireland is declared	112
21 September 1949	Ireland defeat England on English soil	247
11 April 1951	Dr Noël Browne resigns over Mother and Child Scheme	106
20 April 1954	Last execution in the Irish state	113
16 June 1954	The first Bloomsday	165
3 August 1955	Premiere of *Waiting for Godot*	206
12 May 1957	The *Rose Tattoo* scandal	132
4 July 1957	De Valera condemns Fethard boycott	181
17 June 1959	Irish voters reject first-past-the-post	166
8 November 1960	Niemba ambush	288
20 January 1961	John F. Kennedy is inaugurated	36
13 September 1961	The Siege of Jadotville	241
26 February 1962	IRA border campaign ends	68
27 June 1963	John F. Kennedy visits Dunganstown, Co. Wexford	174
22 November 1963	Assassination of John F. Kennedy	300
7 March 1964	Arkle wins Cheltenham	76
14 January 1965	Seán Lemass and Terence O'Neill meet	30
13 February 1966	'Bishop and nightie' incident on *The Late Late Show*	57

10 September 1966	Donogh O'Malley announces free secondary education	238
29 January 1967	Northern Ireland Civil Rights Association is formed	44
21 December 1967	Solar alignment is observed at Newgrange	324
24 March 1968	Tuskar Rock air disaster	90
5 October 1968	Duke Street march in Derry	259
22 April 1969	Bernadette Devlin gives maiden speech	115
12 August 1969	The Battle of the Bogside	213
13 August 1969	Jack Lynch reacts to riots in Derry	214
12 September 1969	Cameron Report is published	240
28 December 1969	IRA splits into Official and Provisional factions	330
11 January 1970	Sinn Féin splits over abstentionism	28
3 April 1970	First killing of a Garda in the Troubles	98
28 May 1970	Charles Haughey and Neil Blaney are arrested	148
22 September 1970	Beginning of the Arms Trial	248
9 August 1971	Internment is introduced in Northern Ireland	211
4 December 1971	McGurk's Bar bombing	310
22 January 1972	Ireland signs Treaty of Accession to the European Communities	38
30 January 1972	Bloody Sunday (Derry)	45
29 May 1972	Official IRA ceasefire	149
8 March 1973	Northern Ireland border poll	77
9 December 1973	Sunningdale Agreement is signed	314
19 December 1973	Contraceptive laws are ruled unconstitutional	322
12 March 1974	Senator Billy Fox is shot dead	80
14 May 1974	Ulster Workers' Council strike announced	134
17 May 1974	Dublin and Monaghan bombings	136
20 July 1974	Women 'invade' Forty Foot	194
29 August 1975	Death of Éamon de Valera	228
12 October 1975	Oliver Plunkett is declared a saint	265
21 October 1975	Siege to rescue Tiede Herrema begins	273
21 July 1976	Assassination of Christopher Ewart-Biggs	195
10 August 1976	Death of the Maguire children	211
18 March 1977	Disappearance of Mary Boyle	85

30 August 1977	Jimmy Carter makes statement on Northern Ireland	229
18 January 1978	Judgement is reached in 'Ireland v. the United Kingdom'	34
2 March 1978	U2 make television debut	72
8 January 1979	The Whiddy Island disaster	25
28 February 1979	Charles Haughey: 'An Irish solution to an Irish problem'	70
27 August 1979	Killing of Lord Mountbatten	226
29 September 1979	Pope John Paul II visits Ireland	254
9 October 1979	Josie Airey wins free legal aid case	262
9 January 1980	Charles Haughey: 'living away beyond our means'	26
17 February 1980	Derrynaflan Chalice is found	60
8 December 1980	First Anglo-Irish summit in Dublin Castle	313
14 February 1981	Stardust fire	58
1 March 1981	Bobby Sands begins hunger strike	71
5 May 1981	Death of Bobby Sands	126
31 October 1981	The 'Armalite and ballot box' strategy	281
27 January 1982	Dáil is dissolved over VAT on children's shoes	43
16 August 1982	Patrick Connolly resigns ('GUBU')	217
9 September 1982	Killing of Declan Flynn	237
8 February 1983	Shergar is kidnapped	53
27 February 1983	Eamonn Coghlan sets world record for indoor mile	69
16 December 1983	Rescue of Don Tidey	320
31 January 1984	Death of Ann Lovett	46
14 March 1984	Assassination attempt on Gerry Adams	82
4 June 1984	Ronald Reagan addresses the Oireachtas	154
19 November 1984	Margaret Thatcher dismisses New Ireland Forum findings	297
20 February 1985	Desmond O'Malley abstains on Family Planning bill	63
23 June 1985	Air India Flight 182 bombing	171
8 July 1985	Ryanair begins operations	184
13 July 1985	Live Aid	188
15 November 1985	Anglo-Irish Agreement is signed	294
27 November 1985	Anglo-Irish Agreement is passed in House of Commons	304
30 May 1986	Knock Airport is opened	150
7 August 1986	Peter Robinson is arrested in Clontibret	209

23 October 1986	Disappearance of Philip Cairns	274
6 March 1988	Gibraltar killings	75
16 March 1988	Milltown Cemetery attack	83
12 June 1988	Ireland beat England in Stuttgart	161
11 October 1988	Ian Paisley interrupts Pope John Paul II	264
26 October 1988	Case of Norris v. Ireland is decided	277
19 October 1989	Guildford Four are released	271
26 March 1990	*My Left Foot* wins two Oscars	92
2 July 1990	Nelson Mandela addresses Dáil Éireann	179
24 August 1990	Brian Keenan is released	224
7 November 1990	Mary Robinson becomes first female President of Ireland	287
7 February 1991	Provisional IRA attempts to assassinate John Major	52
17 January 1992	Peter Brooke sings 'Oh My Darling, Clementine'	34
3 October 1992	Sinéad O'Connor tears up a photo of the Pope	257
2 April 1993	Annie Murphy is interviewed on *The Late Late Show*	98
24 June 1993	Homosexuality is decriminalised	172
15 December 1993	Downing Street Declaration is issued	319
30 April 1994	Riverdance debuts at Eurovision	122
18 August 1994	Martin Cahill is shot dead	218
30 September 1994	Boris Yeltsin incident at Shannon	255
15 February 1995	Lansdowne Road football riot	59
24 November 1995	Divorce referendum	302
7 December 1995	Seamus Heaney accepts the Nobel Prize	313
7 June 1996	Detective Garda Jerry McCabe is shot dead	156
26 June 1996	Veronica Guerin is shot dead	173
2 October 1996	Death of Brigid McCole	257
25 October 1996	Last Magdalene Laundry closes	276
29 November 1996	Michael Lowry revelations	306
12 February 1997	Last killing of a British soldier in the Troubles	56
1 June 1997	Tony Blair issues statement on the Famine	151
19 July 1997	Provisional IRA ceasefire	193
30 October 1997	Mary McAleese is elected President	280
10 April 1998	The Good Friday Agreement is signed	105

19 May 1998	John Hume and David Trimble share stage with Bono	139
6 August 1998	Michelle Smith de Bruin receives swimming ban	208
15 August 1998	The Omagh bombing	216
26 November 1998	Tony Blair addresses the Oireachtas	304
10 December 1998	John Hume and David Trimble receive Nobel Peace Prize	315
2 December 1999	Articles 2 and 3 are changed	309
13 December 1999	First meeting of North/South Ministerial Council	317
23 May 2002	The Saipan incident	143
29 March 2004	Smoking ban is introduced	95
6 April 2005	Gerry Adams tells IRA: 'Now there is an alternative'	101
28 July 2005	Provisional IRA announces end of campaign	201
24 February 2007	'God Save the Queen' is sung in Croke Park	66
4 April 2007	Ian Paisley shakes hands with Bertie Ahern	99
8 May 2007	Ian Paisley and Martin McGuinness are sworn in	129
15 May 2007	Bertie Ahern addresses British parliament	135
10 March 2009	Martin McGuinness deems dissident republicans 'traitors'	78
20 May 2009	Ryan Report is published	140
18 May 2011	Queen Elizabeth speaks in Dublin Castle	138
22 May 2015	Same-sex marriage referendum	142
25 May 2018	Referendum on repeal of the Eighth Amendment	145

obrien.ie

obrien.ie